James Johnson Kane

Ilian

Or, the curse of the Old South church of Boston. A psychological tale of the late civil war

James Johnson Kane

Ilian

Or, the curse of the Old South church of Boston. A psychological tale of the late civil war

ISBN/EAN: 9783337000295

Printed in Europe, USA, Canada, Australia, Japan

Cover: Foto ©Lupo / pixelio.de

More available books at **www.hansebooks.com**

ILIAN;

OR, THE

CURSE OF THE OLD SOUTH CHURCH OF BOSTON.

A PSYCHOLOGICAL TALE OF THE LATE CIVIL WAR,

BY

CHAPLAIN JAMES J. KANE,
UNITED STATES NAVY,
AUTHOR OF "ADRIFT ON THE BLACK WILD TIDE."

PHILADELPHIA:
J. B. LIPPINCOTT COMPANY.
LONDON: 10 HENRIETTA STREET, COVENT GARDEN.
1888.

Copyright, 1888, by JAMES J. KANE.

All rights reserved.

THIS BOOK

IS RESPECTFULLY DEDICATED, WITH THE AUTHOR'S BEST WISHES,

TO HIS HIGHLY ESTEEMED FRIEND,

DR. DAVID J. HILL, LL.D.,

PRESIDENT OF THE UNIVERSITY OF ROCHESTER, N. Y.; LATE PRESIDENT OF BUCKNELL UNIVERSITY, LEWISBURG, PA.

INTRODUCTION.

THIS volume is the narration of a great crime and the punishment meted out to the guilty. I do not hold myself in any way bound to explain the problems presented in this work; the deductions are left to the reader. I have reason to believe that very few books can claim to have been written in so many places where these pages were prepared.

I began it on an ocean steamer, after leaving New York; continued it in my hotel in Liverpool, Manchester, London, Paris, Naples; went on with it on board of the U. S. flag-ship "Pensacola," when we visited Messina, Malta, Alexandria, Jaffa, Beyrout, Smyrna, Constantinople, Syra, Athens, Leghorn; and at a number of places visited when away on leave; also, on my return, in Genoa, Nice, and Palermo; again at Malta, on our winter tour, and once more in Alexandria and Cairo, under the shadow of the Pyramids, and by the banks of the Nile. In Jerusalem, on my second visit, I had leisure to write on Mt. Olivet, under the shade of the olive-trees overlooking the historic city. Having joined my ship at Athens, amidst the ruins of the Temple of the Virgin Goddess Athena, on the Acropolis, I went on with my appointed task; also during a month's stay at Nice and Spezzia. In my hotel on Mt. St. Gothard in Switzerland I drew inspiration from the snow-capped hills, rearing their lofty peaks thousands of feet above me. I came back to Leghorn to join the "Pensacola," and there finished the principal part of this work. Few persons, except they have had a practical experience of such a life, can apprehend the difficulty, on board of a large ship-of-war, with over four hundred men as her complement, of composing one's mind for literary work. Ten days' sojourn out on an ocean steamer is as much as most people can endure. If it were prolonged for months and years, the difficulty of bringing one's mind down to the composition of matter for public perusal would be experienced. Then again, the excitement of visiting so many interesting places, some of them for the third and fourth time, where friendships are formed, reading and becoming posted in reference to all their historic points, receiving and returning social calls, the daytime occupied with sight-seeing, leaves only the midnight hour for the product of the pen.

I feel that this has been detrimental to the literary part of the book. It is sent out to hold its own or to be consigned to oblivion, as it shall seem to its readers to deserve.

The crime of Professor Homerand is a common one, and no man who takes advantage of the confidence of a woman can expect to escape retribution. God may be slow in our estimation in executing judgment, but it will surely come, with its force heightened by apparent delay.

The persons named in this book are characters whose identity will not be divulged. There are officers of the U. S. Navy now living who have known the original of Ilian, and were brought under her fascinating powers. Very often I have heard her described as the "beautiful rebel."

The original of Adrien Homerand is recorded on the books of the Navy Department as having died from yellow-fever; let him rest undisturbed.

The name of the University for whose presidential chair the great crime was committed I have thought best to conceal. There were several such institutions in 1840 whose presidency was considered a great honor.

The fifth and sixth books are from my personal experience. The psychological incidents mentioned are not uncommon, and experiences far more thrilling and out of the range of ordinary events are well corroborated. The episode in the second chapter of the fifth book was due to the morphia which had been administered to me without my knowledge. The experience which is delineated as having taken place under the shadow of the old South Church in Boston, at midnight, on the fateful 15th of November, may have been the result of an over-excited brain. My readers must judge for themselves on this point.

With this brief introduction, I ask those who take this book in hand to follow out to the end the history of Professor Homerand and all concerned with him. If one man or one woman is made happier for the perusal, I will be well repaid for my labor.

JAMES J. KANE.

UNITED STATES FLAG-SHIP "PENSACOLA,"
AT SEA, HOMEWARD BOUND, February 15, 1888.

The author begs leave to introduce to his readers the following characters, with whom he trusts they will become better acquainted as the book is read.

PROFESSOR GEORGE HOMER HOMERAND, of Boston.
JUDGE WILLIAM RATHMINE, of Boston.
MRS. H. RATHMINE, of Boston.
MISS MARTHA RATHMINE, of Boston.
MISS HELEN CLAYMUIRE, of South Carolina.
ADRIEN HOMERAND, Acting Master, U. S. Navy.
DR. HENRY RECHARD, Surgeon, Confederate Army.
CAPTAIN THOMAS JEFFORDS, South Carolina State Battery.
MRS. ELIZABETH VERDERE.
MISS ILIAN MORDINE, head of the secret service, Confederate Government, Southern Dept.
MR. and MRS. JOSEPH RENDEEM, of Fifth Avenue, New York.
MISS ALICE and MISS EDITH RENDEEM.
COLONEL ROBERT HORTENSE, of Confederate secret service.
COLONEL and MRS. ORMOND, of New Orleans.
CAPTAIN BILL HARRISON, the blockade-runner.
MRS. HARRISON.
SAM, the slave.
MR. and MRS. EDWARD HOMERAND.

Also, officers of the army and navy of the Union and of the Confederate service, and others.

CONTENTS.

BOOK I.—1840.

CHAPTER	PAGE
I.—The Professor	13
II.—The Choice	15
III.—The Decision	19
IV.—In the Balance	22
V.—After the Battle	25
VI.—The Spirit of the Red Wine	29
VII.—Sowing to the Wind	32
VIII.—The Curse of the Old South Church	35
IX.—Brain Fever	40
X.—Drifting Apart	45
XI.—Marriage Bells	49
XII.—Fall of Two Idols	53
XIII.—How the Problem was Solved	57
XIV.—Red-Letter Day	60
XV.—Adrien	64

BOOK II.—1861.

I.—The Spirits Abroad	69
II.—Union vs. Disunion	72
III.—Hannibal's Oath	76
IV.—Father Murphy	80
V.—A Vision of the Past	84
VI.—Repentance	88
VII.—The War Fever	92
VIII.—The Union Navy	95
IX.—Meeting of the Waters	99
X.—Champion for the South	103
XI.—Ship Ahoy	108
XII.—West Gulf Squadron	111
XIII.—New Orleans	116
XIV.—The Great Conspiracy	121
XV.—The Temptation	125
XVI.—The Fatal Obligation	130
XVII.—The Power of a Single Word	135

BOOK III.—1863.

CHAPTER	PAGE
I.—Grosvenor House	140
II.—The Blockade-Runner	144
III.—Yellow-Fever	149
IV.—The Warning	153
V.—Coercion	158
VI.—Under the Gray	164
VII.—Pensacola Navy-Yard	167
VIII.—Ambition Foiled	171
IX.—Battle of Mobile Bay	175
X.—On the Trail	179
XI.—Battle of Fort Fisher	184
XII.—Prisoner in the North	189
XIII.—Fate of the Blackmailer	194
XIV.—All Adrift	198
XV.—The Old Name	202
XVI.—Payment of the Bond	206
XVII.—Premonitions	212
XVIII.—The Shadow in the Glass	216

BOOK IV.—1865.

I.—The Rendeem Mansion	220
II.—Home Again	226
III.—Nemesis	231
IV.—The Exiles	235
V.—On the Boulevards	240
VI.—Echoes of the Past	245
VII.—The Veil lifted	251
VIII.—Traitor Among the Faithful	255
IX.—The Welcome Messenger	258
X.—Found at Last	260
XI.—The Mortgage-Bond	265
XII.—Hope deferred	270
XIII.—The Gambler's Curse	274
XIV.—Harvest of the Whirlwind	279
XV.—The Expiation	283

BOOK V.

CHAPTER	PAGE
I.—THE CUNARD STEAMSHIP	288
II.—RENDING THE VEIL	291
III.—THE EPISODE	298
IV.—THE DEEP-SEA GRAVE	303
V.—THE OLD VICAR	305
VI.—THE TIN BOX	309

BOOK VI.

I.—THE MIDNIGHT TOKEN	314
II.—THE SHADOW OF THE OLD SOUTH CHURCH	318
III.—ILIAN IN A NEW RÔLE	323
IV.—A DRAWING-ROOM IN FIFTH AVENUE	329
V.—MISSING LINKS	335
VI.—MYSTERIOUS SHOOTING	341
VII.—FATHER MURPHY NOT POTENT	346
VIII.—THE LAST EVENING	350
IX.—THE NEW FIRM	357
X.—THE FINALE	363
APPENDIX	367

ILIAN;

OR,

THE CURSE OF THE OLD SOUTH CHURCH OF BOSTON.

BOOK I.—1840.

CHAPTER I.

THE PROFESSOR.

The fifteenth day of November, 1840, was wet, cold, and dismal. An easterly wind swept through the streets of Boston, and in the suburbs the cold was more piercing than in the winding, narrow thoroughfares of the modern Athens. This classic name belongs, however, more properly to Cambridge, for there stands the Harvard University, whose fame has penetrated to every part of the civilized world. To be an honored graduate of this institution is equal to a title of nobility in the eyes of many of the citizens of Massachusetts. Great as she was, there were rival colleges at that period competing for the patronage of those who were seeking the best facilities to obtain a liberal education.

At the opening of our story there stood, in one of the outskirts of Boston, a granite mansion, plain and severe in its architecture, according with the taste of the older citizens of the Bay State. The house was surrounded by grounds artistically laid out and well kept. A large hall divided the mansion, leaving on the right a drawing-room handsomely furnished; on the left, in front, was a reception-room, and back of this an extensive dining-room, furnished in old English oak, and the massive plate on the sideboard was an evidence of the hospitality and wealth of the owner. The library was on the second floor front, having a large bay-window, and a small room on either side; the bedrooms looked out on the back on beautiful gardens.

This luxurious home was the property of the distinguished Professor George Homer Homerand. It came to him by inheritance. The Homerands had been famous for several generations for unusual powers of mind, showing that in their case genius was hereditary.

The professor was attached to a university in another city, but his spare time was passed at this palatial abode. Travelling back and forth was not so easy then as it had become a quarter of a century later. Business of an urgent nature had made it necessary for him to leave his classes for a week, and thus we find him at his home on this November day.

He had passed his thirtieth year, but was not married; his father, now dead, had trained him to deliberate carefully on all important matters, and, as matrimony is a most important affair of a man's existence, he had been in no hurry to take a step that cannot be retraced. It was a tradition that the Homerands were always well-mated, because they were so slow and careful in making up their minds.

A maiden aunt kept house for the professor. He had no other relative except a brother, two years younger, a lawyer, already married and settled in Hartford, Connecticut.

I have remarked that it was the fifteenth of November; dates are important factors in every one's life, but this one was particularly so in that of Professor Homerand. It was nine o'clock in the morning; a cheerful fire blazed on the hearth, as the New Englanders did not then enjoy the doubtful advantage of hot air through their houses. The breakfast-bell had rung twice, but the professor paid no heed. He had a problem to solve which involved more consequences than any previous event of his life. It was the old story of a man with two claimants for his heart. He was walking up and down his spacious library, with his hands behind his back. To say that he was perplexed would be inadequate to express his condition. Two letters, in feminine handwriting, lay open before him on the table. They had been received by the morning post. The choice was between love and ambition, not easy of solution by any means. One was of a nature akin to Mount Vesuvius, deep, powerful, passionate, and overwhelming in its intensity; the other, gentle, soft, and characterized by well-bred reserve. The first was signed Helen Claymuire, a Southern heiress of great wealth, a beauty among the beauties. She had a magnificent figure; her talents were of a high order, and had been well developed by careful education.

The other letter bore the signature of Martha Rathmine, the only daughter of the prominent and highly distinguished Judge Rathmine, of Boston. The judge was not what might be considered a rich man, although he had a large income from his profession, which he freely spent. It was an accepted fact that his daughter's dowry would consist more in social position and influence than in broad acres and stocks and bonds.

Our interest, however, is in the contents of the two letters. Long years have passed since the pens of the writers gave utterance to their thoughts. Both were aspirants for this man's love; neither suspected a rival; could the professor have but known how much misery would ensue by the choice he was destined to make—but we anticipate our story.

Now for the letters.

CHAPTER II.

THE CHOICE.

Boston, November 14, 1840.

MY OWN DARLING HOMER,—Your note of yesterday came this morning; I have read it over several times, and I am not able to account for your coldness. Once your letters were glowing with love and devotion, but this last one is brief, formal, and chilling in its tone. How have I offended you? It is a week to-day since I last saw you; to me it is more like a year. The hours and days drag their slow length along. Doubts and terrible thoughts fill my mind. You may ask, as you have done before, why should I fear, for all will yet be well? Ah, my beloved, do you remember that you promised three months ago to fulfil your solemn vow to make me your wife at the end of thirty days; and, when the **period arrived, you asked me to delay until New-Year's-Day, as it was** your family **tradition that** a **marriage on** the first day **of the** year was always a happy **one?** I consented to this, and **patiently await the** promised **hour.**

I **bring you a** family **name** honored for generations in South **Carolina; our men were** brave and honest, **and** our women faithful and **loving.** I lay at your feet a fortune of lands **and** houses that bring **in a** princely **revenue. Woman's real life is** a domestic **one; by** the decree of **her Creator, that is her ambition; her happiness** lies in her husband's love. **I am well aware** that there are exceptions to this rule. Occasionally you **will find a** woman beautiful and accomplished, **but without a heart; they are** only animated **statues, and not even to be** compared to Pygmalion's fabled Galatea, chiselled **from cold** marble, who, being **endued with life by** the **gods, loved the** man who fashioned her, **with a** pure, innocent **love, and went** back to marble when she found that her **love** was not returned. **The idea** was heroic, **but I am** afraid my love **is too ardent to be content to live on as a** statue admired only **for beauty of form, and not for** the soul that exists within.

I could not endure a rival. Do not think **me** jealous, **but it is** with heart-burning **pains that I** see notices in the papers **of your frequent** visits **to the** home of Judge Rathmine. **Rumor whispers** that **you** have been paying attention, **yes, marked attention, it is said, to his** daughter Martha. **What can this cold Puritan maiden bring you that will compare with my glowing affection, Southern born? I have had senators, judges, and generals at my feet, asking for my hand. They called me the belle of the South. I refused** brilliant **offers of marriage from others, and accepted yours.** You **have won all I have to give, and I am in your power.** Let **me see you soon, and once more hear your voice while** you tell me **the old, old story of love and devotion. Why** is it **that our last three meetings took** place **under the shadow of the old** South **Church, and at** such late **hours? My coachman and** my maid **will both think** either that **I** am ashamed to acknowledge you, **or that you** do not want your friends to know that you are engaged. Why **all** this secrecy? I am your wife before God. On your bended knees you took a solemn oath that **I** should be your lawful bride; yet only yesterday **was I asked,**

had I heard that Professor Homerand **was** paying special attentions to the **accomplished** Miss Rathmine? I was compelled to turn away to conceal my agitation. I could not conceive such a thing possible. I **do not even contemplate what I would do in** the event of such **an improbable** occurrence.

Do you know that I am looking forward to **our** tour abroad, of which you have so often spoken, with a great deal of pleasure? You said that you would get a year's leave from your University. I, too, have an eager passion for foreign travel, and long **to** see Paris, London, Berlin, and Vienna, and **beautiful** Venice, also Florence, Rome, and **Naples.** You **said once** that the dream of your life **was to visit** Athens, **to stand on the Acropolis,** and look with **your own** eyes, **and** touch **with your own hands, the work of the** immortal Phedias, **the temple of Greece's purest goddess, the** virgin Athena. Then you wanted to **visit Egypt, that** wonderful land, that rich mine of **ancient history; and** proceed onward to Palestine and Constantinople. I eagerly long for those days to come, when we can roam together at will. It **is my** thought by day, and my dream by night.

I now close, awaiting your answer with anxious solicitude.

Believe **me,** with feelings of earnest and unfaltering devotion,

Your own loving
HELEN CLAYMUIRE.

BOSTON, November 14, 1840.

MY DEAR RESPECTED PROFESSOR,—A week **ago** you asked me if I would **accept your** hand and heart **if** laid **at my feet. You** told me to take a full week **to consider this matter before I answered. You** also asked me to call you Homer, and **not professor.** I must get used **to** this familiarity gradually; I cannot **do** it all at once. In answer **to your** proposition, I respectfully beg leave to **say** that **I consider it** would be a serious breach of decorum **on my** part to state in advance what **I** would **do in** the **event of your** making a formal offer of marriage. In reference **to your** question as to what **my** worthy father would say **to such a** proposition, I can **only** make answer that he holds **you** in the very highest esteem. On several occasions I have heard him say that, in view of a prospective vacancy in the presidency of the university to which you are attached, he would, as chairman of the Board of Trustees, strongly urge that you be selected for the post, as he considers that you are best qualified to fill the important position. You further asked me if my heart was free and unfettered. To that question I answer in the affirmative, and I will give you my definition of love.

This divine quality of human nature is not the product of an hour; it is not a volcano, that opens suddenly and burns fiercely for ages, with fitful intervals of rest. Reciprocal love is a gradual assimilation of all the thoughts and aspirations of two souls whom heaven has designed should be mated for their earthly pilgrimage. It is a spiritual fire that when once kindled must be continually fed by unselfish sacrifices. It becomes bright and glowing, or dull and flickering, just in proportion to the amount of fuel, both in quantity and quality, that is used to keep up its vigor. I could not love unless it was fully reciprocated. I am one of those natures that can love but once, and if my love were misplaced the grave would soon welcome the sorrow-laden heart to its sweet repose.

We have a reception to-morrow evening, as it is my father's birthday, and a few of his choice friends will be at our dinner at six; many are invited for the evening. It was with feelings of delight that I read your letter of acceptance to attend the dinner. Will you come at five o'clock? We can have a quiet talk before the company arrives. I must now bring this letter to a close. I hope you will not find it cold and formal. I have tried to answer your principal questions. And now, until to-morrow, adieu.

I remain, with feelings of the most profound respect,

Yours sincerely,
MARTHA RATHMINE.

CHAPTER III.

THE DECISION.

LANGUAGE fails to describe the emotions which swayed and agitated Professor Homerand. In one scale **was love**, honor, wealth, and sacred obligation; **in** the other, **ambition** alone.

Why should **a man of** sterling integrity and a high **grade** of what is manly and honorable hesitate for **one moment?** The Homerand **family, for** generations past, **had greatly prided themselves on the motto of their** house,—viz., **" Chivalry to women and equity to all."** Not one member had been **known to fail in keeping up this high** standard. Wherefore, then, **this weighing in the scales,** this dallying with **the tempter?** The **solution** is found **in** the fact that the mania **of** ambition had seized upon him,—ambition to fill the presidential chair of a great university. Was this a prize to tempt a man with the probity credited to Professor Homerand to hesitate **upon a** question of honor? **Nay, more,** contemplate the committing **of a great crime in sacrificing the life,** reputation, and happiness **of a** woman **who trusted him?**

A decision was finally **reached.** The professor made up his mind as to the course which he should pursue. After his **breakfast he sat** down at his desk **to answer the two letters. He remembered** his father's favorite maxim,—" **when honor and self-respect no** longer dominate **a man's life, he** has entered upon **the downward road."** Often had he, when a boy, **heard from the** paternal **lips the** words that there must be something radically wrong **in a** man's organization when he trifled **with honor and** self-respect. Come what would, he was bound to fulfil his pledge and marry **the woman who loved** him. He knew, too, that he loved her as **he** never could love another. Yes, Helen Claymuire should **be his bride.** He **therefore** resolved to attend **the** dinner **at** Judge Rathmine's, **and frankly** explain to Martha that his hand and heart belonged **to another.** There would be no great injury **done.** She had stated in her letter that her love would be gradual, and would develop according to the fuel with which it was fed. With this decision a terrible weight was taken from his mind, and he wrote the following note as his reply:

Boston, November 15, 1840.

MY DEAR MISS RATHMINE,—Your kind favor of yesterday is before me. I will be at your house at five this evening. I have had a very difficult problem to solve this morning, and I will tell you the solution when I see you, when I purpose to lay certain matters before you which I cannot put on paper.

I will not trespass longer on your time, as I know you will be fully occupied in getting ready for the reception this evening. Your letter has been before me all the morning; every word and line is fully weighed.

I am writing now under a terrible restraint, and I know you will pardon the brevity of this note.

No more till I see you.

I am yours, with the most profound esteem,
GEORGE HOMER HOMERAND.

This letter was certainly non-committal. It was intended to prepare the way for a candid confession that honor required him to fulfil a sacred promise to another woman. She would respect him all the more, and they would be friends. He would lose the prize which had been the goal of his ambition, for Judge Rathmine had noticed and encouraged his attentions, and while he had not engaged himself to the daughter, yet the match had been the topic of conversation among their friends.

Under these circumstances his marriage to another would cut off all chance of election to the coveted position.

With a long and deep sigh as a farewell to his ambition, he folded and sealed the letter, and then betook himself to answering the other. Having decided upon the course he would pursue, he purposed to make amends for past neglect to his affianced wife by writing her the following epistle:

Boston, November 15, 1840.

MY OWN WELL-BELOVED HELEN,—Your loving letter is now before me. Three times I have read it over, and your burning words have gone like an arrow to its mark. I admit that for a season I was led away by my ambition. Knowing the power of Judge Rathmine, I was anxious to secure his influence in my favor in the prospective election for the President of the University.

I paid my court to the daughter in order to win the father. This unmanly conduct is now at an end. I have accepted an invitation to dine at the judge's house this evening, for it is his birthday. As a professor in the institution of which he is chairman of the Board of Trustees, I could not well decline his invitation. I propose to leave his house, however, as soon as I can, and will meet you to-night under the shadow of the old South Church. Let your carriage remain one block away, and mine will do the same, and at eleven prompt I hope to see you. This is the last time you will be called upon to meet me at such a late hour, and at such a place. To-morrow I purpose to call at your house and proclaim our engagment and our intended marriage on New-Year's-Day. I will at once resign my professorship. My private income is abundant for all our needs. We can spend several years abroad. I ardently long for those rambles amidst scenes made famous in classic history. I feel that I never could grow tired, especially with such a loving companion as yourself.

To visit Athens is the dream of my life, as you so fully described, I must, **perforce, be** brief now, but rest assured when I see you at your own **hotel I** will more than make **up for the** apparent neglect of the past few weeks. I say *apparent*, for never has your image been absent from me, and **you** alone possess without a rival **all the love of my heart.** And now, my lovely belle of the **South, adieu till we meet to-night, and you will then hear** the **old, old story which you say you are so anxious to hear once again.**

No one, certainly, would ever **dream** of describing you as being a marble statue, for you have one of the warmest hearts pulsating in a woman's breast, and my prayer is that I may ever be worthy of its love.

Rest assured that **my** devotion **as your husband** will fully **atone for** all my faults **as** your lover.

With earnest, undying **love, I** remain

Your own
HOMER.

CHAPTER IV.

IN THE BALANCE.

THE aphorism that

"There is a divinity that shapes our ends, rough-hew them how **we will**,"

is at times strangely at variance with facts of history.

The great apostle to the Gentiles gives his experience. "He failed at times to perform that which he knew to be right, but often did the things he would not." Is not the solution of these problems man's free agency? As to the point of how far Professor Homerand was free to follow out his convictions, I am not prepared to say. Why was he not able to do so? He had a dim perception that he was not taking a prudent step. He was going to meet Miss Rathmine on this very evening, and had significantly given her to understand that he would make her an offer of marriage.

Were coming events casting their shadows before? Not long after the two letters had been sent by special messenger he became painfully aware that two forces were at war within him, seeking for the mastery of his actions.

Much has been written about strength of character enabling a man to overcome all evil influence. Thousands have relied upon this quality with overweening confidence, and what has been the result? History tells us that men of the very strongest will and iron purpose have at times been swept away like chaff before the whirlwind.

As the day wore on the battle raged fiercely. The two influences were at work: one, which seemed to be that of his better nature, prompted him to send an apology to Judge Rathmine, stating that indisposition prevented him from accepting the invitation to his house. In his present frame of mind he certainly was not in fit condition for company. The other influence reminded him that this was the decisive night, and that if he went to the reception all his ambitious hopes would be realized. He was like a storm-tossed craft that had lost its rudder. Never in his life before had he endured such a mental conflict. He felt as if a hundred supernatural beings were in fierce conflict for possession of his faculties. One moment he would resolve not to go to the dinner, and the next he felt the despair ensuing upon the surrender of his burning aspirations.

Mechanically he dressed himself in evening attire; his carriage was ordered for four thirty; the hour had come, and he had not finally decided the momentous question. He paced up and down his library, ever and anon looking at his well-filled book-shelves, as though seeking for guidance from his silent instructors. He no longer exercised his usual calm deliberation. He was not a judge on his bench, listening to earnest pleaders for a cause. No, the battle was going on without his aid. He was the prize for which the rival powers were contending. Were they the spirits of good and evil, seeking for the mastery of a human soul? Had they means of knowing the result that would be sure to follow the course taken by the professor? For the time he seemed to have lost his free agency, and to have become a passive subject, a lawful prize for the one who should obtain a mastery over him. This condition was the result of his indecision when he drew back from his plighted word, and placed its observance in the scale against the ambition of becoming the head of a great university.

Whosoever toys and dallies with the tempter is, in ninety-nine cases out of a hundred, the sure victim of the evil influence. It wanted fifteen minutes of five when Professor Homerand slowly left his house and entered his carriage. It was a full twenty minutes' drive to the judge's house; the coachman stood respectfully at the carriage-door waiting for orders.

The conflict for mastery was more fierce and bitter than ever. Each side was urging him to utter to his waiting servant its password of victory. It may be necessary here to state that Judge Rathmine resided in the aristocratic part of Boston known as Beacon Hill. Miss Helen Claymuire had magnificent apartments at a private hotel called the "Westmoreland." It was one of those two destinations that he was pressed to give. The strain was telling fearfully, and, although a cold November afternoon, the perspiration was standing in great drops on his forehead.

"Are you ill, professor?" asked the wondering and anxious

coachman. "You do not look well. Do you think it prudent to venture out such a cold evening? If you wish, I will take a letter of excuse to the place where you are going."

The man was his confidential servant, and had long been in his employ.

"Edward," slowly spoke the professor, in a weak voice, "I am not well, and am hesitating about going out to a dinner-party. However, drive to Tremont Street and around the Common; the sharp air may do me good."

The high-spirited horses went off at a rapid rate, but there was no let up in the fearful contest. All sounds from without his luxurious carriage were drowned in the uproar of the battle within.

He seemed to hear nothing but the words, "Beacon Hill," "Westmoreland." He had neglected the opportunity afforded, to send his coachman with the letter of regret to Judge Rathmine. Now it was too late. He must give one order or the other. The Common was at length reached, and the circuit almost made of that grand historic park of Boston. The horses were walking, and the driver was expecting the order. The supreme moment had come.

A voice as of an invisible agent now rang in his ears, "Tell your coachman to drive home again." He started from the apathetic condition in which he had been since leaving his house. He lowered the carraige window to obey this last prompting. The horses were stopped, and the driver leaned over to hear the instructions. "Home" should be the word; yes, that would settle it; his lips parted and, with a spasmodic jerk, the words "drive to" came out; for a second there was a pause. "Home!" thundered a voice in his ears; "Westmoreland!" shouted another; "Beacon Hill!" seemed uttered in such a tone of authority that is used only by those who have power to enforce their command. At this critical moment a newsboy, seeing the waiting carriage, ran over to it, and cried out: "Evening paper, sir? Fire on Beacon Hill." "Beacon Hill?" answered the professor, in an interrogatory tone; "where?"

The coachman heard the words "Beacon Hill." He had been awaiting this, for it was known among the servants that the professor was expected there for dinner. The horses were driven off at a rapid speed, and the newsboy was left behind. The conflict was ended. A calm succeeded the storm; one of the forces had gained the victory. This experience of Professor Homerand is by no means a singular one. Thousands have gone through similar contests. Some have been victorious; others have fallen. Many times in the history of our world has the issue of happiness or misery of a nation hung upon a mental contest as described above. We are told that no temptation is allowed to overtake any one without a way of escape is opened. But when the bridge over which one might retreat has been destroyed, and we purpose to fight to the bitter end, we cannot wonder if we have to yield to superior forces.

CHAPTER V.

AFTER THE BATTLE.

It was twenty minutes of six as the carriage of Professor Homerand drew up before the palatial residence of Judge Rathmine. This was a granite building with large projecting bay-windows on either side, and massive stone steps led up to the hall door. At the head of the steps were a pair of Canovas lions in granite. As the professor alighted he saw at the bay-window of the reception-room the face of Miss Rathmine. As he entered the room she met him, and was about to gently chide him for being so late, when, noticing his pale, haggard expression, she said, with some alarm, "Why, professor, you look ill; what is the matter?" "Nothing," he replied; "I am not very well, and were it any one else who had invited me, I should have declined; but I was anxious to do honor to your father's birthday, and I am here."

The soft blue eyes looked searchingly into his to ascertain whether there was another attraction in that home. Did he come to pay his respects to her father, or was she the magnet that drew him? On several of his previous visits he had spoken tender words, had lighted the mysterious fires of her nature, and had made indirect proposals of marriage. They were in the reception-room on the right. No one was there;

a few of the guests were in the drawing-room on the other side of the hall, where Judge and Mrs. Rathmine were in waiting to welcome those who came. Martha had been led to expect a formal declaration of love on this eventful day, and it was for that reason she had asked him to come at five o'clock. She knew that there would probably be no opportunity during the evening for having a private talk.

It may be well to digress from our story a moment, and give a description of Miss Rathmine; her general characteristics can easily be inferred from the letter recorded in the second chapter. A pen-picture of a woman is, at best, very unsatisfactory; her true character does not appear on her face. A celebrated Scotch physician once said that for fifty years he had made women his special study; and that in forming his estimate of them he did not study their countenances, but if one or more of their letters should be given to him, he would outline them for all they were worth. This was no idle boast on his part, as he had many times proved his skill. This plan will be adopted in the history of the men and women who may figure in the plot and counterplots of this volume. The reader, if anxious for more intimate acquaintance, must study their words and actions, and their letters wherever they are recorded.

Miss Rathmine was acknowledged by all her friends to be a lovely girl. She was in her twenty-third year, of medium height, and nature had given her a well-developed form. Her hair was brown, her eyes a deep blue. She had perfect command over her temper, and no one had ever seen her off of her balance. She had been well educated, and was an excellent critic, and, having a talent for science and literature, was in every way suitable to become the wife of a scholarly man. She was dressed for this occasion in pale-blue silk, which showed off her beautiful form to perfection. Her arms and neck were exquisitely formed, and the skin of fine texture, showing generations of gentle blood in her veins. She came of good old Puritan stock. On both her father's and mother's side she was related to some of the best New England families.

This description is inadequate to do justice to one of the principal characters; but she will be better known as these pages unfold their story.

As has been already remarked, she was fully expecting a proposal of marriage. The excitement of the occasion may have aroused the full tenderness of her nature, so that a stronger man even than the professor would have found it hard to resist her charms. He was fast yielding to the impulse of the moment. When the decisive password of "Beacon Hill" had been inadvertently pronounced, he indeed acquiesced in this solution of the problem, but at the same time resolved to be true and faithful to his solemn obligations to Helen Claymuire. It was his purpose to tell Martha of his previous engagement. As they stood under the gas-light in the reception room the glare revealed to her the traces of a deep struggle of some nature in the man who was standing before her. Putting her dainty little hand on his arm, she looked up into his face. "I know you are ill," she said; "let me offer you a glass of wine." And before he could answer she hastened to the dining-room, and returned in a moment with a silver tray and decanter. She filled a glass and handed it to him, with the explanation: "This is of a rare old vintage, and my father has kept it for many years, and brought it out in honor of his jubilee year." He drank the wine, remarking that it was the finest he had ever tasted, but declined a second glass, as it was too near the hour for dinner.

He had tasted nothing since his breakfast. His mind had been in an excited state all day. The rich, rare old fluid glowed through his veins like wildfire; and this, combined with the bright eyes of Martha, began to undermine his resolution to be faithful to his first love. Judge Rathmine came into the room, and, after warmly welcoming the professor, he conducted him into the drawing-room, where the guests had assembled.

Mrs. Rathmine went into dinner on the arm of a venerable senator, and Professor Homerand took in Martha. Fifteen had been invited, and this, with the judge, his wife, and daughter, would have made eighteen. Five, however, had been prevented by illness from coming, so that the unlucky number, so-called, of thirteen sat down at the table. After a blessing was asked by a worthy divine, the feast commenced. It is strange how, in an educated community like Boston, especially on Beacon Hill, such a superstition as the fatality of thirteen sitting down to dinner should find credit.

For half an hour the conversation consisted of anecdotes confirming this phantasy; gradually more pleasant topics were introduced, and the incident was forgotten by most of the guests. The dinner was served in an elegant manner, and it was in all respects a notable feast. The professor had fully recovered his equilibrium; the color returned to his cheek, he was seen at his best, and, as a conversationalist, he had no superior.

After the dessert, the gentlemen arose from the table to allow the ladies to return to the drawing-room. As they were leaving, the professor whispered to Martha, "My long cherished hopes are likely to be soon fulfilled, provided——" Before he could finish the sentence there was a terrific crash, and the room was left in total darkness. Indescribable consternation had seized upon all the guests; that some terrible disaster had happened, and that most of those present in the room were killed or wounded, was the prevailing feeling among those who found themselves unhurt.

For a moment the stillness of death reigned; then the frightened servants brought in lights, when the cause of the disaster was discovered. It was a pet fancy of Mrs. Rathmine to have wax candles instead of gas-light in the dining-room. The gas-chandelier had been removed during the day, and a special one, with glass pendants, put up to hold candles. The workman, finding that the socket of the new chandelier was a trifle larger than the old one, had used a liberal supply of shellac to hold it in place. This answered the purpose when cold. The heat of the candles had, however, gradually softened the resin, and the motion of the company causing a vibration, down came the whole structure. Beyond breaking a few plates and glasses, and a sprinkling of the liquid wax, no great damage was done. All felt grateful that the accident was no worse. The after-dinner chat by the gentlemen was abandoned, and they went with the ladies to the drawing-room. Professor Homerand took the matter in a more serious light. He felt it prophetic of the total collapse of his ambition.

He was losing the power of will to avail himself of the avenues of escape from his perplexing entanglement. Indeed, when any one deliberately walks into temptation, he must not hope for any easy way to extricate himself.

CHAPTER VI.

THE SPIRIT OF THE RED WINE.

By ten o'clock Judge Rathmine's house was filled with the very *élite* of Boston society. The governor of the State was there, and also senators, judges, professors, and men prominent in business and politics. Many ladies were there, robed in garments of the richest fabrics. The details of a reception even as prominent as this one was would not be interesting to the readers of the present time. As we are concerned with only four persons in this large assembly, we will not linger over it.

Eleven o'clock was the hour which Professor Homerand had named for the meeting of Miss Claymuire.

The reasons for this extraordinary mode of action were twofold: it had been surmised at one time that he was engaged to her, and to call again openly, after his late special attention to Miss Rathmine, would have led his friends to suspect him of equivocal conduct. Besides this, the beautiful Southern heiress had numerous admirers. Many of them were extremely jealous of the accomplished professor, and it would have been difficult for him to obtain a private audience from her without observation.

Again, he had been anxious to prove to her that he was not so infatuated with Martha as not to be able to leave her in the midst of this grand reception. He had fully made up his mind to proclaim to his friends on the morrow his engagement to this woman, "the queen of the South," as she was termed.

She could leave her apartment in her carriage, attended by her maid, under the plea of visiting a friend at the point of death. This was her excuse at her hotel on previous occasions when she had met the professor at the same place and hour. At half-past ten Professor Homerand managed to draw Miss Rathmine to one side and explain that a friend of his would leave Boston very early the next morning, which rendered it necessary to see him at his hotel for half an hour on very important business. He would return before midnight, he promised, in time for the supper. He told her there was no occasion to mention his absence to her father, as the great number of people present would prevent him from being missed for so short a time.

He had on his arrival ordered his coachman to come round to the side door exactly at half-past ten.

Martha expressed her regret that he must go out on such a cold night, but, as he positively promised to be back in an hour, she was satisfied with the reason assigned.

"I shall miss you very much," she added, as a shade of disappointment flitted across her face. She had looked forward to this evening as a red-letter day in her life. A week ago he had asked her if she would accept an offer of marriage from him. He had now been five hours in the house, and he had not once breathed the subject, and his whole deportment was not that of a lover. Several times he had told her that he had something very serious to communicate, but it was not in the tone of a man about to declare formally his love for the woman of his choice. What could it mean? Had she offended him by the tenor of her letter? His answer did not indicate that. They were alone in the dining-room, which had been prepared for the supper, and the servants, perceiving their young mistress engaged in private conversation, left them to themselves.

"Miss Rathmine," said the professor, in a grave tone of voice, "I have something to say of an important nature."

She made no answer, but waited in an attitude of expectation. Her heart was beating rapidly; her eyes were fastened on his face. She was not willing to lose a word. It was the one period in a woman's life that she can never forget. The expectant Martha was amazed at the change taking place in the countenance of the man before her. The perspiration was streaming down his face, and he looked like one enduring a terrible conflict. It was indeed a conflict, for in a moment he realized that the contending forces, which had left him the moment he pronounced the words "Beacon Hill," had once more returned to renew the warfare.

He determined not to yield without a desperate struggle. His word was pledged to another, and he had resolved not to violate the solemn obligation. When roused he was a man of iron will, and now he felt the need of all his resources.

"Never!" he hissed through his clinched teeth.

"Never what?" exclaimed the wondering girl. "Why,

professor, you are very ill!" And she looked with a tender, anxious solicitude into his face. "Let me offer you once more some of the rare old wine." She filled a glass and handed it to him. He looked at its bright-red color; then a mighty impulse came over him to fling it to the other end of the room. For a moment he held it above his head, then, slowly raising it to his lips, drained it to the last drop. "Take another, professor; it will do you good; it will keep you from getting cold. Hark how the wind is blowing and the windows rattle! I am so sorry you have to go out. Can you not postpone your visit?"

"No," he replied; "I must go; it is important." The wineglass in his hand was refilled, and he held it up before the light; a moment later and he had drunk its contents. The conflict now ceased; the forces had retired from the field.

"You look ever so much better," said Miss Rathmine; and she smiled sweetly upon him.

"An agent more potent never yet reigned
Than the smile of a woman o'er a goblet just drained."

She had not the slightest intention to use liquor artfully to influence the man before her. She knew that he was suffering deeply from some unknown cause, and what she did nine out of ten women would have done. She offered the remedy which was at hand, a glass of wine. Had she known the true circumstances, and of the pledged word of the professor to another woman, she would have forfeited her life before stooping to an unworthy act to win him. The spirit of the red wine did its work effectually. It went like electricity through every vein; it benumbed his judgment, seared his conscience, and unloosed his tongue. His honor and self-respect were flung to the winds. His ambition to be president of his college now usurped and held the supreme place. With Martha as his wife all was gained.

As for the other woman, he would appeal to her love to pardon his desertion. She would have his heart, although Martha had his hand; that was an equal division. Helen's great wealth would enable her to cover up all scandal. Perhaps she would find some other man, and then the past would be forgotten.

Thus he cut loose from the safe moorings of honesty and self-respect to find himself adrift on a resistless current.

CHAPTER VII.

SOWING TO THE WIND.

It has been said that the downward road to evil is steep, and grows more so at every step. Professor Homerand had entered upon this pathway; whether he should halt and retrace his steps or go on to the fearful end was a problem that he had no wish at present to solve.

He had begun by sowing to the wind. The harvest might be slow in coming, yet it was certain. As we have stated in the last chapter, the spirit of the red wine had full control, and under its influence he took one of Miss Rathmine's hands and held it between both of his, and, looking into her face, said, "Martha, darling, I feel wonderfully better." The maiden blushed deeply at this tone of endearment, and her eyes were lowered before him, while he studied her features. As I have previously remarked, she was beautiful, but not demonstrative, and had an earnest, loving, truthful heart.

The professor felt himself seized by some external influence, and was no longer master of himself. His tongue moved and uttered expressions at the bidding of the force that had won the control over him.

"Martha," he continued, "do you know that this is the evening that was appointed for you to give me my answer? I love you, my own darling, and want you to be my wife. You never will have cause to regret doing so. My whole life will be spent in the endeavor to make you happy. With your love as an incentive to my ambition, I can reach the highest pinnacle of fame, and all will be laid at your feet. You shall be my guiding star and my counsellor. We have but a moment now to ourselves, for you will be missed from the gay circle up-stairs; your father will search for you, so what is said now must needs be done quickly; will you be mine for life? What say you, my sweet angel?"

Martha was under too great a strain to speak. She had been expecting this declaration, and now it overpowered her. The tears came freely, tears of joy and happiness; she laid her head on his breast, and said, in a sweet, plaintive tone,

"Will you always love me? Is there any danger that you will grow tired of me?"

"No, Martha, never; rest assured of that. I swear——" The vow was not finished, for the door opened, and Judge Rathmine came in. He did not at first take in the situation, as the room was dimly lighted.

"Why, Martha," he exclaimed, "I have been searching all over for you. Every one is asking after you and Professor Homerand." At this point he became conscious of the fact that his daughter was encircled within the arms of the professor, and a happy, gladsome smile was on both their faces. His surprise found vent in the exclamation, "Why, bless my soul, what is all this? The old, old story. Dear me, how history repeats itself! I did the same thing thirty years ago with your mother. We were at a reception, and I got her away from the company over to the dining-room, and proposed and was accepted, and had a kissing-party of two all to ourselves."

"Judge Rathmine," said the rather abashed professor, "my action this evening may seem to you a little premature, but now that it has taken place, I ask your consent to the hand of your daughter in marriage."

"Well, professor," answered the judge, "I certainly have no objections, and I hope she will prove as good a wife to you as she has been a loving and devoted daughter to me. We must inform her mother of this."

"One moment, judge," said the professor, as he took from his pocket a solitaire diamond ring, which he had placed there for the purpose of giving to Helen. He now slipped it on Martha's finger instead, saying, "Let this ring be the token of our betrothal, and with it I give you my heart for all it is worth." He then kissed the lips of the radiant maiden, remarking to her father, "We are both ready to present ourselves to her mother for her blessing, but it will be best to defer doing so until the company all take their departure." He then, in a few words, explained the appointment he had made to see a friend whom he might not see again; in fact, it was almost certain he would not for a long time, as this friend was going to Europe, and must be seen by eleven o'clock, but he would return in time for the supper.

In order not to attract attention, he would leave by the side door. A servant was sent for his hat and overcoat, and

c

he left the house. Entering his carriage, he told his coachman to drive to the Tremont House.

It would be impossible to describe the feelings of Professor Homerand as he reclined against the cushions of his finely-upholstered vehicle. He did what thousands of others do. He said it was his fate, and that it could not be helped. He began to hope that it was only a dream; yes, a dream sent to warn him. He had read of such things. Surely he would wake up and find himself in his own bed, and his heart and hands still free to fulfil his solemn pledge to Helen.

The wretched man was suddenly awakened to the stern fact that it was no dream by the stopping of his carriage and his coachman opening the door, saying, "Tremont House."

With a heavy sigh, and the tone of a man in the pangs of despair, he told his faithful servant, in whom he knew he could confide, to drive down Summer Street, into Washington, and to stop a block away from the South Church.

His mind was yet fast in the shackles of the spirit of the red wine, and hardly able to grasp the fact that he was about to meet a woman to whom he was bound by every sacred obligation. What was he to say to her? How could he explain to the fiery and impetuous Southerner the event of the past hour? He made up his mind that he would not face the ordeal, but would remain in his carriage, and send his coachman with his card to that of Miss Claymuire, and a message to the effect that severe illness prevented his coming to the appointed place, but that he would send her a letter the next day. This plan would enable him to find a way out of the dilemma. He then could return to Judge Rathmine's house, and forget all his trouble in his new-found bliss. When his carriage stopped the driver dismounted, and, opening the door, told him that he was just one block above the church.

Taking a card from his pocket, he was about to give the message to the coachman, when a muffled form appeared at the door, and a gentle voice said, "Why, Homer, you are one-half an hour late, and I was about giving you up, thinking perhaps you were ill, and could not come out this cold, bitter night. These east winds of Boston in November are too much for me." A low, agonized groan was the only response. Slowly he got out, and walked without a word till both stood by the porch of the old South Church.

THE OLD SOUTH CHURCH OF BOSTON.

They were alone. No belated pedestrian came near them. Their respective vehicles were two blocks apart, and the night was too dark for either coachman to see what was going on, or hear the words that were spoken.

CHAPTER VIII.

THE CURSE OF THE OLD SOUTH CHURCH.

To a guilty mind a low, quiet voice will impart a greater terror than the loud roar of the thunder-blast. It is doubtful whether even a spirit from the other world could have paralyzed, by its sudden apparition, Professor Homerand more thoroughly than the few words by which he was greeted at the close of the last chapter.

Yes, he was late indeed, in more aspects than one. Had this meeting taken place yesterday, how different would have been his feelings. Under the ordinary circumstances of life he was a man of strong character and inflexible will, but now he was as pliable as a child under the hand of a powerful master. Some men would have brazened it out, or thrown down the gauntlet of defiance with a haughty air. The professor, at heart, was a man of generous impulses, and he loved the woman before him as he never expected to love the one to whom he had, that very evening, pledged his word to marry. He now realized in what a terrible dilemma he was placed, and how to extricate himself with honor and credit was a more serious problem than had ever been presented to him before. To say that he suffered keenly would be a mild expression; he was in an agony of remorse. Although the night was cold, great drops of perspiration rolled from his forehead, and he trembled as if with the ague. He leaned against the iron railing of the church for support, and looked pitifully and pleadingly into Helen's face, as though seeking for mercy from the hands of one he had so cruelly wronged. The dim light of a street lamp cast its feeble glare over him, and revealed to the astonished woman a countenance ghastly pale, and eyes that were bloodshot.

"Why, Homer, my darling, you are ill. Why did you expose yourself to this cold midnight air? Why this strange fancy to have me meet you at this place and late hour? My maid, who came with me till I saw your carriage stop, and my coachman will begin to doubt my sanity. My own dear Homer, this secrecy will end to-morrow, will it not? You will proclaim to our friends our approaching marriage, and you will find what a loving wife I will be."

A small gloved hand was placed in his, and a gentle voice said,—

"Speak to me, my dear; you have not even offered a word of greeting. Tell me what is the matter; have I offended you?"

"No," replied the professor, in a voice hardly recognizable as one belonging to the eloquent and gifted orator. "I am not well. I have much to say, and don't know how to begin."

"Surely," answered she, "this is not the time nor place for a confidential communication. I have risked my reputation by meeting you here, close to midnight. This must surely be a proof of my love. You do not exhibit any sign of joy at meeting me. I have been here since eleven o'clock, and the night is bitterly cold; my servants are suffering from it, and I must return to my apartments. Cast aside this cold reserve; come into my carriage and drive to my door, and let your's follow."

There was no response to this invitation. Remorse was at work; and, now that he was in the presence of the woman whom he ardently loved, gladly would he have recalled the declaration he had made to Martha Rathmine. All that day he had looked forward to this midnight hour as the one that was to usher in a life-long period of happiness. That hour had come, and the agony of despair which he now endured could not be worse even in the abode of the lost. He cursed the wine as the cause of his present predicament. He felt it a judgment upon himself. He resolved to explain everything to Helen, and keep his solemn obligation to marry her. He would fling his ambitious project to the wind. He could afford to resign his professorship and go to foreign lands. Their united wealth would enable them to find pleasure, peace, and happiness, and he would have no stain upon his conscience.

Acting on the impulse, he seized her hand, and made a brief confession of the events of the day and evening. He told her of his internal struggles, and of the resolution which he had made on leaving his home that afternoon, to proclaim his coming marriage with her. When he had finished he calmly waited for her reply.

She stood during the recital like a statue. She was a woman of quick discernment, and saw at a glance that however strong-willed and resolute the professor might be on ordinary occasions, yet, in the choice between herself and Martha Rathmine, he was as plastic as the potter's earth, and would be moulded by the hand that kept the firmest grasp upon him. She must not, for a moment, risk the charms of her rival upon her affianced husband. Her mind was quickly made up. The case required prompt and heroic measures.

"Homer," she answered, "I have the first claim upon you, and I will not yield it to any other woman. You must decide this question to-night. There is a clergyman of one of the city churches who has apartments at our house. As a rule, he does not retire till after midnight. Let us go to him at once, and he will make us man and wife. I will not consent to another day's delay. At my feet you took a solemn and a binding oath to marry me, and before heaven I am already your wife. Further delay on your part is not only criminal, but dangerous to our future prosperity. Come." And she placed her hand inside of his arm.

He hesitated. He was in that position so often described as being at the division of a stream, where one course led to a haven of happiness and a quiet, peaceful rest, while the other led into darkness and certain disaster.

"Yes," he answered, "I will go with you and end this suspense."

He took several steps towards her carriage, and then stopped.

"Had we not better wait until to-morrow?" he asked. "Our getting married at this late hour will excite surprise, and create comment upon our conduct."

The contest, which already has been depicted, was now renewed with terrible vigor. A voice seemed to shout in his ear, "You are lost if you hesitate; go on, and marry the woman at your side." But in the other ear he heard these words: "Take not another step. Your hand is already upon the presidential chair of your university. It remains for you simply to marry Martha Rathmine, to whom you pledged yourself to-night, and the honor awaits you." But again came the rejoinder from the other side: "It is not worth the sacrifice of your honor. Loyalty to your faith will bring more happy results than can possibly accrue by disloyalty to all that a true man should hold sacred." Then it seemed to him that a thousand voices all around him were shouting, "Hurrah for President Homerand!" His conscience was cast from her throne, and he surrendered to the temptation. A few steps more would have saved him. The bell of the old South Church began to toll the midnight hour. The effect on both was electric, and there was an instant change in their manner and tone. The professor recovered at once his self-possession, and, withdrawing his arm from Helen, who held it in desperation, as though trying to save both herself and him, he said to her, in cold, formal tones,—

"I cannot consent to this hasty marriage, at this late hour; I must have further time for consideration. It would ruin my reputation. Besides, I have this night given my promise to marry Miss Rathmine. I cannot marry another till I have formally broken the match with her. Let the matter rest for a few days."

A terrible transformation took place in Helen. Hitherto he had always seen her in a loving mood. She was at all times gentle. In the even tenor of her past life no cause had given occasion to show the dreadful contrast that underlies such natures. She had loved like an angel; she could hate like a fiend.

She did not raise her voice to any unnatural pitch, as superficial persons do when angry. She spoke in low tones, but each word was uttered with energy and distinctness that carried with them no doubtful meaning. Her face was pale, her eyes flashed, and her utterance seemed to him inspired and prophetic.

"Professor Homerand," she said, "I have loved you with an idolatrous love. I have lavished upon you a wealth of affection such as seldom falls to the lot of man. In return, you basely stole from me that which every woman should guard, even if she has to go through the gates of death to save herself. You offered the atonement of an honorable **marriage.** This you solemnly swore to fulfil within thirty days. **You asked for an extension of the time. To-night you have** pledged **yourself to marry** another woman. **Were it not for my honor, I would** scorn to unite myself with **you. I have** given **you a** last chance to redeem your pledge. **This you** reject. **Your excuses and desire for delay are frivolous and** temporizing. The weakness of your character has been revealed to me in the last half-hour in such a light that no true, pure-minded woman, free and unfettered, would link her fate to yours. I again repeat, **I am** your lawful wife **before** the Almighty, **and I** will not, while I am living, surrender my claim to any **other** woman. If you fail to acknowledge me as **such before the** world, **I** will call down the curse of heaven upon your guilty head. **If** you marry Martha Rathmine you will **never win** the prize of the college presidency. The **idol you have worshipped** will fall shattered to the ground. **Your** life **will be** embittered by regret, anguish, and remorse. Marry **that** girl, and **I** call down the malediction of retributive divine **justice** upon your union. If you have a daughter as the product by that marriage, may she be cast upon the streets of Boston, and die an infamous death, her own abhorrence, and the public scorn. **You** will then curse the hour **in which she** was born. If you have a son, may he **prove a thorn in your** side, a curse instead **of a** blessing. **May** he turn **a traitor to** his country, and raise his heel against his wretched **father, and** end his weary, wandering life far **out** on the great **ocean, and** go down to his burial amidst **the roaring of the** tempest. These accumulated miseries will bring both you and your wife in sorrow to the **grave.** The choice is **now** before you. Redeem your promise, and I will forgive **my wrongs, and the** past shall never be referred **to.** Prove **a traitor,** and God will hear my prayer and will send down upon your guilty head what will be known as the curse of the old South Church."

A moment afterwards the professor heard the closing of a carriage-door and the rapid tread of horses' feet. She was gone! **but her** malediction remained! He looked up at the face of **the clock** to find pity there, but the square steeple only frowned down upon him, as if to corroborate the fearful words just spoken. Shaking from head to foot, he realized that a fearful curse was hovering over his head.

A **curse** pronounced under the shadow of the historic and venerable old South Church!

CHAPTER IX.

BRAIN FEVER.

The bells of the city were chiming **the** half-hour after **midnight when** the professor's carriage stopped before **the** side entrance **of** Judge Rathmine's house. The coachman rang **the** bell frantically. **The judge,** who was in the dining-room, anxiously waiting **for the return of his** son-in-law **elect,** and for whom the supper **had been delayed** half an hour, opened **the** door, **and was greeted with the** exclamation, "**Professor Homerand is dying! Quick, help!**" He rushed to the carriage-door, and opened it. The light from his brilliantly lighted windows revealed, in one corner of the interior, the almost inanimate form **of the professor.** His face was of an ashy **color, his hands were cold, his** eyes bloodshot, haggard, **and wild.** He was in the **condition of a** man **who** had witnessed **some terrible apparition. Among the guests** of the house were **several of the** celebrated **physicians of Boston.** Two **were found by a servant. The professor was lifted out of the** carriage, **carried into the dining-room, and laid** upon a lounge. Martha came with her mother **to extend their aid. The** stately girl gave way to no undue excitement as she saw his dangerous condition. She gently placed **her hand on his head, and said, in a low** whisper, **that no one else heard,—**

"Homer, darling, what can **I do for you?**"

These words **were more potent than medical** skill to the suffering **man.** His **reason** once more assumed her pedestal, **and,** with returning consciousness, **he** realized his surroundings **with a** promptness that puzzled the doctors. **Arising from the** sofa, he remarked,—

"**I have been ill; a sudden** attack; nothing serious. I

am better now, and, **if you** will kindly excuse **me, I** will go home. Don't delay the supper any longer on my account; I will be all right in the morning."

In the mean time, **the judge** had been seeking information **from the** coachman, **but that** astute individual (a Scotchman by **birth) was** too shrewd to betray his master's confidence. He simply said that the professor had been ill before leaving home in the afternoon, and that his going into the keen night air from the judge's house had brought on a severe chill. The professor spoke a few words in **an** undertone to Miss Rathmine, and, accepting the offer of one of the physi**cians to accompany** him, was driven rapidly home.

The strain proved too much for him to withstand, **and** by daylight next morning he was delirious. At noon his physician, **after a** consultation, decided that a severe attack of brain fever would result from this illness, and that, **if he survived, it** would be several months before he could resume **his lectures to his class** at college.

Universal was the regret among the students when news **of** his illness was brought to them. It was at once ascribed **to** overwork. It was known that he never spared the midnight oil. He was extremely popular not only with the other professors, but with the students of all the departments. He met every one with a genial smile. His memory of faces and names was wonderful. He made **it a** point to know the character of each member of his classes. A few kind words **from him** were sufficient to check the unruly spirits for which his university was so famous in those days, and many were saved from expulsion when, at a meeting of the faculty, **their** waywardness called for a stern example, but they were granted **a** further respite when Professor Homerand pleaded for them. Every one had hoped he would be the next president, and great were the expectations of improvement when this should take place. There were many candidates for the position, yet he was far ahead of all competitors, not only in talent and learning, but also in social influence. Whenever **the** subject was mentioned to him he invariably turned the conversation. It was **his idol,** but he chose to worship it alone, and was jealous of any one coming near this shrine. It had become a masterpassion. **It** was his dream **by day** and night, and yet the truth was skilfully concealed, and no one suspected it.

To fail in the attainment of this great object meant for him the extinguishing of his ambition.

He was a regular attendant at the Congregational church, but seldom spoke on religious subjects, and never would countenance any levity in regard to sacred things. He had copies of the Bible in several foreign languages, and made it a point to read a chapter every day in the different versions, finding it an excellent plan to keep up his familiarity with them. He had a rare control over his temper. In his classes, a quiet look would do more to tone down the exuberant spirits of the young men who listened to his lectures than angry words from other professors. The students often said that he was a sleeping volcano, and that it would not be prudent for any one to wake him up. The sorrow for his illness was genuine, and there was a funereal gloom over the University. As the days went by, the anxious looks on the faces of his friends told that hopes were faint of ever seeing the favorite professor in his place again.

For three long weeks the fever held its grasp tenaciously upon the sick man. It brought him to the portals of death, and several times hope was abandoned. To the physicians the case was a mystery. They felt that there was something that had not been told them. Repeatedly had they cross-questioned the coachman as to where his master had gone that night of the judge's reception: What hotel? Whom had he seen? Was there any quarrel or undue excitement? To all these questions he replied that he had driven to the Tremont House; that the person sought for was out, but was accidentally met at a short distance from the hotel. The professor had gotten out of his carriage, and walked several blocks with his friend. When he returned, he complained of feeling unwell, and wished to be driven around the Common, hoping he might feel better before he returned to the Rathmine mansion. This, the man declared, was all that he knew. No amount of questioning could elicit the real facts of the case. No word ever fell from the invalid to enlighten those who were anxious to unravel the problem. He lay most of the time in a stupor, and occasionally muttered a few incoherent words.

On the night of the 7th of December, just three weeks since the illness attacked him, the attending physician, for there was always one on watch every night, noticed that a change was taking place. The climax was reached, and his practised eyes perceived that before the dawn of morning the signet of death would be placed on the brow of the patient, or else recovery would have begun. The bell of a neighboring church tolled out the midnight chimes. The physician started at the sound. A nurse was asleep in a chair in the next apartment; servants were within call, yet the medical watcher felt a sense of loneliness come over him that he could not account for. A chill ran through his frame; his hair began to stand on end, but why he could not tell. He was sitting by the bedside, with his finger on the pulse of his charge. The door of the room slowly opened, and the curtains of the bed were agitated by the rush of air that came in. The effect on the professor was startling. He moved his head and opened his eyes, and, looking to the opposite side of the bed, said, in a quiet tone, "Why, father, what brings you here?"

To say that the physician was deeply affected would be a mild expression. He arose, and, going to the door, closed it and turned the key in the lock. Then, going back to his patient, he saw that there was a look of consciousness on his face. His eyes were open, and he was in the attitude of a man listening to words uttered by some one else. It needed but a glance to show that the crisis was safely past, and that the form before him was not likely to become unconscious clay at present.

"I am glad to see you so much improved, professor," he said, in a subdued tone.

The sunken eyes turned towards him; there was a brief struggle of the mental powers, but Reason once more quietly resumed her sway. A smile came over the face of the professor as he said, "Yes, I feel better than I did when I left Judge Rathmine's house last night."

The medical attendant smiled as he replied, "That was just three weeks ago."

"Impossible!" exclaimed the sick man, as he placed his hand on the doctor's arm and looked searchingly into his face.

"It is a fact, I assure you," was the reply; "three weeks this very night. You have been seriously ill, and must not overtax yourself. Rest and quietness will alone restore you to your wonted health."

There was a troubled look in the professor's face, and he repeated the words, "Three weeks to-night, did you assert? Then I have been delirious and unconscious. What did I rave about?" The fear agitated him visibly that he might have betrayed his secret.

Here was the opportunity to solve the mystery that had puzzled every one. The physician was certain that some secret cause of this illness had not been divulged; yet, being a man of honor, he scorned to take any undue advantage. He already held keys that would have let loose the demon of scandal in many families, had he so chosen. As the secrets of the confessional are buried in the memory of the priest, so facts that would startle society if made known lie in the minds of physicians, dormant and hidden. He therefore lost no time in assuring the professor that during his illness he had uttered very few words, and what he did say were incoherent. "Your illness," he continued, "has been brought on by overstudy, and a long rest is needed for your restoration. Judge Rathmine is of the opinion that you should go abroad for a year's travel. He has called every day, and his daughter has often been at your bedside. She has grown pale and thin, and her parents are worried about it. Your engagement to her has been made known, and your friends are waiting for your recovery to tender their congratulations. Hoping this information will put you at your ease, you must now go to sleep, and let nothing trouble you. Your affairs have been carefully looked after. Your brother came on from Hartford, and is now in the house. He has been constantly with you. Not another word till the morning."

A smile for a moment played over the face of the professor; then, as some other thought filled his mind, a troubled look overspread his countenance, and his eyes wandered all over the room as if in search of some one; then they rested for a moment on the door, then on the doctor, and again, with a searching glance, back once more to the door.

A mysterious feeling came over the physician,—an undefined dread, and a consciousness that there was a third personality in the room. He had always been noted for his cool nerve, but this was when dealing with tangible objects. He looked towards the door, expecting to see it open, when all of a sudden the candle, which had burned low in the socket, flashed up with a dying flare, and then went out, leaving the room in total darkness. It was several minutes before another light was procured.

By that time the patient was asleep, and on the road to **recovery.**

CHAPTER X.

DRIFTING APART.

It was Christmas-morn in Puritanic Boston. Bells were ringing, and the silvery echoes rolling down from lofty Catholic and Episcopal church-spires reminded late sleepers that this was a season of enjoyment. It was a memorial of that early dawn over the plains of Bethlehem, when the angelic choir tuned their harps to the glad **song of peace and** good-will to men. The snow was on the ground, and the merry sleigh-bells of those early astir awakened the juvenile population, and sent them eagerly to ascertain the contents of their stockings hung up the previous night in the fulness of childish expectation. Happy, smiling faces met at the breakfast-tables of those well-housed and clad, to whom Nature had been lavish of her bounties. To some the salutation of " a merry Christmas" had a certain **echo of irony, for over** them hung the clouds of financial misfortune. Others were mourning the death of dear ones from the family circle, who would be sorely missed on this occasion. In all the houses of Boston, from the mansions of the wealthy down to the apartments of the poorest of the poor, from the homes of misfortune, sickness, and mourning, there was no such hopeless, blank despair as that in the studio of Professor Homerand. He had risen early, and was seated in his library in an easy-chair, with a cup of coffee before him. In three weeks, intervening since the close of the last chapter, he had recovered somewhat his physical strength, but his mind had remained in the spell cast upon it under the shadow of the old South Church. He was in a mental lethargy. His face wore the expression of one doomed to die, and who is counting the few brief hours left to him. In a week from that day he was to marry Miss Rathmine. The doctors had expressed their opinion that it would be some months before he would recover the full power of his mental faculties, and that a change of air would be beneficial. They also suggested that a skilled nurse should accompany him. If he only had a wife, they said, her loving attentions would expedite matters.

His aunt, who kept house for him, was too much of an invalid to endure extended travel, and he had no other female relatives that could go with him. His friends suggested that, as he was engaged to Miss Rathmine, he should marry her, so that they could go abroad together. In the autumn he would be able to return to the University fully restored.

When this proposition was made to him, he merely answered that he was in the hands of his friends, and would follow their advice. Eagerly had he looked from day to day for some token from Helen, but none came. All Boston was speaking about his illness, and she must have heard of it. Why did she not send a message of sympathy, or write a few lines? He realized now, as he never did before, that he loved her better than it was possible for him to love any one else. It never occurred to him that it was his place to write to her. She would certainly have responded at once. Indeed, she had waited in her apartments for a token that her presence would be welcome.

Thus these two souls were gradually drifting apart, and day by day the distance was increasing. Her proud spirit was chafing under her wrongs, yet looking hourly for a message, a line, a word; and then she would have forgiven all, and made his life supremely happy. He, in moody silence, was hoping that something would intervene to save him from that marriage, the very thought of which was hateful.

One effort would have set him free. It was noon of Christmas-Day when Judge Rathmine was announced. Coming into the library, and taking the hand of the professor, he wished him a " Merry Christmas." The words seemed to the proud, gifted man of learning like bitter irony. Merry! How could any man be merry with such remorse in his heart?

" Come, you must cheer up," said his visitor. " My wife and daughter expect you for dinner; a quiet affair, only four besides our family, making a party of eight. Martha wants to have a talk with you. Just a week from to-day, and I surrender her to your care. She has always proved a loving and affectionate daughter, and I feel confident that she will be a devoted wife. Your physicians tell me it is almost a matter of life and death to you to have some one with you in your travels to nurse and take care of you. I will call for you in my carriage at four o'clock, and you are to spend the night at our house."

The professor made a few feeble protests. Only a month or so past there had been a time when, if he said no, it would have carried a conviction of an iron will, which it would be a difficult matter to swerve from a fixed purpose. That time was gone.

In his earlier years he had carefully trained his will to hold all the other powers of his mind in complete subjection; but the very moment he began to halt and hesitate between what he knew to be his proper course and that of a highly degrading action his will lost its supremacy, and the rebellion thus started in his mental faculties was not easily subdued.

Now we find his feeble negations were the prelude of yielding. He finally consented to the arrangements of the judge, who left him to make other calls. Gladly would he have remained in the solitude of his library to brood over his misfortunes. Woe unto the man who, like the professor, waits for Providence to help him, but refuses to take the first step, and help himself. Was the power of the fetters so strong that he could not sunder them by any means? One stern decision of his will would have made him a free man. He wanted to be saved by others without effort on his own part. His brain was stunned. His conscience had fiercely resented his double dealing, and the combination of circumstances had brought on his brain fever. If his friends had known the true condition of things, they would have come to the rescue. Had he only made a confidant of Judge Rathmine, all would have been well, and by sundown Helen Claymuire would have been at his side, his honor would have remained untarnished, and the future would have been bright. Indeed, he had thought of explaining matters to the judge, but his pride prevented him, and the opportunity was lost. At half-past four the professor found himself in the drawing-room of Judge Rathmine's mansion, with the fair Martha by his side, holding his hands in hers, and looking tenderly, lovingly, into his face.

His condition had called forth all the sympathy of her nature, and she permitted him to read in her countenance the depth of her love, which, under other conditions, her habitual reserve might have prevented her from doing. She spoke cheeringly of their travels and the prospect of his renewed health. She knew his aspirations, and, hoping to encourage him, she repeated the wishes of his many friends that on his return he might be elected to the head of his University. For a moment the smouldering fire of his ambition gleamed and sparkled as this new fuel was thrown upon it. The looks of other days came upon his face. He smiled, and returned the pressure of her small, delicate hand. For a moment he forgot the curse that was hanging over his head, and began to show some response to the enthusiasm of the brilliant girl at his side.

"I have a little surprise for you," she continued. "Your tradition, you once told me, was for the members of your family who got married to have the ceremony performed on New-Year's-Day. Now we also have a custom that has been in force for several generations. All our marriages have taken place in one church. You have heard that my grandfather was one of the men of the Revolution, and freely gave his money and services to that glorious cause. The year before he died, at the ripe old age of eighty, I was a girl of twelve; he said to me one day, 'Martha, when you grow up and get married, if you want my approval from the grave, where I probably will be when your marriage takes place, you must insist on having the ceremony performed in——' Where do you think?" said the happy, radiant maiden, as she glanced archly into the now smiling face of her lover.

"There are so many churches," he replied, "and many of them very old, that it would be difficult to guess the right one."

"Then I will tell you," she responded. And bringing her face close to his, to note the glad surprise that she felt sure her words would create, she repeated, slowly and deliberately, "*The old South Church in Washington Street.*"

CHAPTER XI.

MARRIAGE BELLS.

It is a difficult task to describe the surprise and amazement of the professor and Martha. One expected a piece of agreeable information; the other looked for a joyous smile at the mention of Boston's historic church.

The blood left the face of the astounded man, his hands grew cold, and a look of intense horror came over him. The smile instantly fled from his lips, and he closed his eyes to shut out, if possible, from his memory, that awful scene of the midnight of that day which was henceforth to be a dark memory in his existence.

Martha was thoroughly frightened. She rang the bell for the servant, and sent for her father, who, seeing the condition of the professor, ordered the physician to be summoned. In fifteen minutes he arrived, and found his patient in a semi-conscious condition. The application of restoratives quickly revived him, and he desired to return to his own home. The doctor would not consent to this proposition, as he was well aware that solitude only fed the disease instead of allaying it. The case demanded heroic measures. Dinner was announced, the invited guests were already in the house, and the doctor was pressed to stay. The once strong-minded man tried for a moment to gain his point, but had to yield to a will stronger than his own. Almost without knowing it, he found himself seated by the side of Martha, who handed him a glass of that old, red wine, which, six weeks previous, had been the cause of so much trouble. Once more it unloosed his tongue, brought back the color to his face and the smile to his lips. For the time being he forgot the impending curse, and became his former self. His brilliant sayings were loudly applauded. Martha was delighted at the change, and became more than ever enraptured over the man of her choice. Her father and mother looked on approvingly, and felt that their daughter was about to be happily mated to one of the most gifted men of his country. That Christmas-dinner was a grand success. At one time it had looked as though the illness of the professor would throw a pall over the whole affair.

The physician, having found a partial solution to the enigma, and a key that unlocked the hitherto entrenched doors of the professor's mind, determined to keep the advantage gained.

On the following day he went with him to his house, resolved not to leave him till he was safely married to Miss Rathmine. During the week that intervened he insisted upon his patient taking a long drive each day, and spending the evening at the judge's house. Gradually Professor Homerand's mental powers began to rally. He was conscious that, unless something occurred to set aside the plans made for him by others, his fate would be settled. Pride held him back from making a clean breast of his former engagement, and the cherished idea of his ambition was still potent to wield a controlling influence over his destiny.

There were times when he felt that he would sacrifice everything for the love he bore to Helen Claymuire. Perhaps if he could have met her and talked to her once more, then he would have married her. Oh, why did she not come or send a line? Twice he went to his desk and took a sheet of paper to write to her, asking her to come, or to appoint a place for a meeting, and he would go there, but his pride overcame his good intentions. Still, he hoped to be saved in some way. Slowly but surely the precious hours passed, and no rescue came.

The appointed day arrived. It seemed as though Nature had chosen to honor the occasion of the marriage of Boston's great professor. The snow, although deep, yet lay compact and solid on the ground. Overhead hardly a cloud was to be seen, and the sun made glad the hearts of all the people of the city. At noon the bell in the steeple of the old South Church rang out a wedding refrain, and the edifice was packed to overflowing. It was said that never before in its history was it so densely crowded with the *élite* of the city.

The bridegroom and bride moved in the highest circles of society, and were extremely popular. When the bell ceased, Martha, leaning on the arm of her father, walked up the aisle. She was robed in white silk, and a bridal veil, with orange-blossoms, fell in graceful folds around her. The professor followed with Mrs. Rathmine, who looked almost as handsome as her daughter. Six bridesmaids, all lovely in white, came after them, mated to six of the senior class of the University. They had come to show their appreciation of the professor, whom they so highly esteemed. The organ in the gallery played a wedding-march. As the last strains died amidst the vaulted roof the voice of the officiating minister was heard all over the church, as he said,—

"If any one knows of any impediment to this marriage, let him now speak, or forever after hold his peace."

The whispering among the audience ceased, and for a moment there was the stillness of death. The bridegroom grew a shade paler, and glanced uneasily around him. No one noticed this but the physician, who surmised that another woman lay at the bottom of all the professor's illness.

The silence was unbroken; no answer came to the query of the clergyman, who then went on with the service binding the one to the other, for richer, for poorer, in sickness or in health, until death should part them, concluding with the words,—

"In behalf of the civil law of the commonwealth of Massachusetts, which I now represent, and in the name of Almighty God, whose minister I am, I pronounce you husband and wife, and those whom God has joined together, let no man put asunder."

A brief prayer was then offered, and a blessing pronounced. Once more the organ filled the church with its rich melody. The newly-married pair walked slowly down the aisle to their carriage at the door. Judge Rathmine had prepared a wedding-breakfast, after which the happy couple, as they were termed by their friends, were to leave on their way to Virginia, by way of New York and Baltimore. In the spring they were to take passage from the latter port for France, to remain abroad till autumn, or longer, if it were found necessary for the restoration to health of the sick man.

The professor had handed his wife into the carriage, and turned around to answer the greeting of some of his friends, when his eyes beheld the form of Helen Claymuire standing by the church-door in almost the identical spot where she stood on the fatal fifteenth of November.

She was like a statue of the goddess Athena, calm, dignified, and haughty, with a look of scorn that pierced to the inmost soul of the guilty man, who trembled from head to foot. The indignant woman slowly raised her gloved hand towards heaven and let it suddenly fall, and, turning her back, walked away. The doctor alone witnessed this scene. He had been expecting something of the kind, and now, having obtained the secret, he knew what remedy to apply.

Taking the arm of the pale, quivering man, he said, "Professor, the excitement has been too much for you;" and, seating him in the carriage along-side of his bride, he sat opposite, and ordered the coachman to drive rapidly away.

On reaching the mansion of his father-in-law the bridegroom was more like a condemned man on the way to execution than one going in to his wedding-breakfast. The old wine was again called into requisition. The breakfast was all that could be desired, as was the reception which followed. Hosts of friends called to pay their respects. Never had the professor appeared to better advantage. It was the lull before the storm, which, though slow in developing its fury, yet, when over, left scattered upon the pathway over which it had spent its force the wrecks of many lives. At four o'clock the professor and his wife took their leave, and, amidst the hearty good wishes of all assembled, their carriage bore them to the railway-station.

The line between Boston and New York had not been long established, and the luxurious means of travelling of the present day had not then been thought of. They arranged to stop for the night at Springfield, and also at Hartford, the home of the professor's brother, where they purposed remaining two days. At New Haven a reception was tendered to them by the faculty of Yale College, and they expected to arrive in New York in five days from their setting out. We must now leave them to the excitement of their bridal trip, and the welcome received from relatives and friends, and turn our attention to the forsaken woman.

She had committed her case to the inflexible justice of God.

CHAPTER XII.

FALL OF TWO IDOLS.

"Thou shalt have no other Gods before me," was the oft-repeated injunction to the children of Israel. But of this they were not mindful, and their history is filled with the chastisement inflicted upon them for their great transgression. The present generation of the Anglo-Saxon people flatter themselves that this violation of the great commandment cannot be charged to their account. In one aspect of it, perhaps not; yet in many others they must plead guilty. The great majority have some secret idol that they bow before in worship. With some it is wealth,—gold is their god; with others it is ambition; and the prevailing sin of very many is the love of some man or woman. We have repeatedly shown that Professor Homerand had before him the presidency of his University. It would have given him power, and that became his god. Helen Claymuire had allowed her love for the man whom she had chosen to develop into a boundless confidence, bordering on idolatry. She would have refused him nothing that he could have asked. She regarded him as possessing qualities almost superhuman. His form was erected in the shrine of her heart, and she bent before it in profound adoration. When she learned from her lover that another woman was about to claim this idol for herself all the vindictive fury of her nature was aroused. During the interval of his illness her pride and love strove for the mastery. She looked daily for some token from him, even though only a line, and, deeply wronged though she was, she would have gone to him gladly. If he had only said that his love for her had not failed, all would have been forgiven. The marriage with Miss Rathmine, as announced for New-Year's-Day, made her ill, and she denied herself to all callers. She hoped that something might intervene and stop it at the last moment. She went to the church, heard the vows, and when the solemn words were pronounced making her rival the wife of the man whom she idolized, the idol that she worshipped so long fell from its proud pedestal, and was shattered to fragments. That a man so highly gifted as Professor Homerand should commit an act so base is a matter of perplexity to all honorable persons. Was his conduct the result of a brain unsettled by hard study, or was the goal of the presidency of such importance as to make it an object to be sought after by all means, fair or foul?

It must be admitted that when a man is mentally endowed, and duly qualified to stand at the head of any college where there are several hundred students, it is a laudable and worthy ambition to secure its presidency. How much more so when it is a university of national reputation! It is not a political position, to be manipulated by wire-pulling. The man who is found worthy to fill such a coveted position must stand as a giant in intellectual powers above his fellows. He must possess great executive ability, a name without reproach, a strong will, capable of governing with a firm hand the unruly and turbulent spirits of those who would quickly throw off restraint unless held in check by a master mind. Professor Homerand had all of these qualifications in an eminent degree. The other candidates acknowledged his superiority. Never, perhaps, in the history of the University, was a man so well qualified to manage and direct its affairs. His friends harped continually upon his fitness for the position, till at last, from being a mere candidate, he came to look upon the office as his right, as a sort of inheritance, and gradually, as has already been shown, he began to worship it as his idol, and it became his master-passion.

In order to secure the judge's influence he had paid court to his daughter. He had no idea at first of making love to her; he had no wish to play a double part. In an unguarded moment he had in a playful way asked her whether she would accept his hand, if he offered it, in marriage. She took the question in earnest, and the way was paved for all that followed. But no sooner had the ceremony been performed, when he found to his amazement that the idol which he had worshipped so long was losing its power. He began to waver in the desire for the long-coveted chair, and the final crisis was not long in coming.

On the evening of the tenth of January, Professor Homerand came back to his hotel in New York, where they had been staying for five days. They were to start the next morning for Philadelphia. As he entered the apartment where his wife was waiting for him to go down to their evening meal, she noticed that he was looking worried, and had the appearance of a man who is hounded down. He flung himself into an easy-chair, and, in answer to his wife's tender embrace and anxious inquiry as to his condition, he replied, in a husky voice, "Martha, I am not well."

"My darling husband, you must take me with you the next time you go out," she said. "Now let me get you a glass of wine; you know I brought some with me. The doctor told me to give it to you when you were ill."

While she was filling the glass he muttered, as though speaking to himself, "Is that woman going to follow me like a blood-hound on the trail? Let her beware; it takes two to play at curses, and if she stirs the latent devil in my heart, it will be the worse for her."

"Why, Homer," said his astonished wife, "who are you speaking about?" She had caught the words "curses" and "devil," and concluded that he was slightly wandering from nervous prostration, a condition which the physician had told her would be likely to occur if her husband overexerted himself in any way.

"My dear, take this at once." And she held the glass towards him. Well was it for her peace of mind that the single candle in the room did not give light enough for her to see the expression on her husband's face. He sprang to his feet, and by a mighty effort subdued his emotion. He became calm, and his voice was low, but it had a ring in it that startled his anxious wife. He took the glass of wine from her hand, and, holding it above his head, said, "Martha, my sweet, patient wife, forgive this little outburst of mine. I met some one to-day with whom I had an unpleasant controversy in Boston not long ago, and I allowed myself to become excited, but it is over now."

"My darling, I did not know that you had an enemy in the world."

He smiled as he answered, "Any man who goes through life without making an enemy must have a very plastic character."

"Tell me, was it not the same person whom you met the night you left our house, and came back so ill?"

"Yes, the same one; but I do not think we will meet again; our paths lie different. But now let me talk upon a more important subject. Do you know that I have drunk so much wine lately that I am developing an appetite for strong drinks? A glass of wine has been the means of a terrible curse in my family. I now take a solemn pledge before God and before you, my wife, that while I live I will not use wine or liquor as a beverage, and will only take it when prescribed by a physician. I will give you full proof that I can do without it, for you will find I am myself again without the need of stimulation. Will you let me throw this glass and the wine out of the window as a ratification of this pledge?"

"With all my heart," answered his wife, as she threw her arms around his neck, and said, " I also will join you in that pledge."

The window was raised, and a moment after a crash on the street told the fate of the glass and its contents. The evil spirit was thus banished, but it had planted seeds that would in course of time germinate and bring forth a fearful harvest.

"Martha, my dear," continued the professor, "I find that the idol of my ambition has fallen from its pedestal, and I no longer desire the position of President of the University. It is now doubtful if I will ever again occupy my professor's chair. This matter is final, and we will let it drop."

Thus fell the second idol. During the rest of the evening Mrs. Homerand was charmed to find that her husband had regained his former cheerful disposition. It was the first time that he was truly himself again since that fifteenth of November, a day long to be remembered by both.

CHAPTER XIII.

HOW THE PROBLEM WAS SOLVED.

The next morning Professor Homerand and his wife took their departure for Philadelphia, where they arrived in the afternoon, and going to one of the best hotels, they hoped to find rest and quiet. The professor, however, exhibited great disturbance as they entered their apartment. Martha had not noticed a veiled woman sitting near them on their journey, but her husband had penetrated the disguise of Helen Claymuire. How long was this to last? he thought. Was this her mode of revenge? From what he knew of her, he was surprised. It was beneath her dignity and proud haughtiness. He determined to remain in Philadelphia till things came to a climax. During his three weeks' sojourn, however, he never saw her again; so, taking courage, he went to Baltimore, where he engaged passage for Havre in a ship that was advertised to sail on the fifteenth of March. The intervening time was spent in Virginia.

Under the excitement of travel and change of scenery, and, more than all, the careful nursing of his wife, the professor was slowly but surely regaining his lost health.

He never once referred to his former ambition of sitting in the presidential chair of his university.

As he had promised her not to take any action in reference to his purpose of resigning till they reached Europe, all discourse upon the matter by mutual consent was avoided.

On the appointed day of sailing they left Baltimore in the clipper ship "War Hound;" there were a dozen other passengers who proved to be very agreeable. Fortune favored them, for they had not only a quick passage across the ocean, but fine weather. They had fully expected a stormy time, but their pathway was amid smooth seas and favoring winds. On their arrival in Havre, they lost no time in going to Paris, where, in that gay city, they hoped to spend many pleasant months. There was so much sight-seeing, so many museums of art, that time sped along almost without their knowledge. The professor had been to Paris before, and, as he spoke

French fluently, he was perfectly at home. His wife was in raptures over the novelty of mixing with a people so entirely different from her own. When the weather was fine they devoted the mornings to sight-seeing, and in the afternoons they drove to the Bois de Boulogne. Under this genial change the professor regained his full mental vigor. To his wife he was at all times kind and attentive, solicitous for her welfare, and willing to fulfil her slightest wish.

The summer passed into autumn, and they still remained in Paris. No specific plans were laid out for their future movements; they had decided not to return to America at least that year. One day, in the early part of October, Martha was reading a letter from her father, in which he mentioned the probability, almost certainty, that her husband would be elected in a short time to the coveted presidency.

"Homer, darling," she said, "pardon me if I again bring up the subject. My father has set his heart upon this matter, and, now that you are restored to health, he urges us to return home."

He paused a moment before replying, and then answered in a deliberate manner, as though each word had been weighed before being pronounced, "To-morrow, then, I will forward my resignation to the Board of Trustees, and will also decline the year's salary which they so generously voted to allow me. My income is ample for our wants, and, furthermore, I have no desire to go back to America for several years. We need not remain in Paris all this time. I am desirous to visit Germany, Austria, and Italy, taking our time, and allowing nothing to worry us. We spoke the other day about going home for a few months till after the birth of our child; but this is mere sentiment, and the prospect of a long passage, both going and returning, is not inviting enough to induce me to take it. At the same time, I have no wish that the little stranger shall see the light of day on French soil. Next to America, I prefer England. My ancestors came from Lincoln. I visited the town the last time I was abroad, and was charmed with the antique air of the place. It is about half-way between London and Edinburgh. Suppose we go there and take up our abode till you are strong enough to travel after the event. Then we can journey to the south of Italy by easy stages."

Martha answered this proposition by going to her husband's chair and putting her arms around his neck, saying, "My own Homer, the day I became your wife I took the solemn resolution that during our married life your will should be my guide, and I feel confident that in studying your happiness I will be assured of my own. We will let the presidency drop, and speak no more in reference to it. My home is where you are. Much as I would like to see my father and mother again, you will never hear a word of repining from me. I am very much pleased at the idea of going to Lincoln. The Rathmines came from Manchester, and I would like to visit that place on our way to Lincoln, or afterwards." This loving tribute touched the professor deeply, and he kissed his wife with more show of affection than he had ever before exhibited since their marriage.

"Martha, my noble wife, would you prefer to remain in Manchester? Take your choice."

"My choice," she said, smiling, "is that which pleases you best."

"I have no decided preference for Lincoln," answered her husband; "it was a mere fancy; but I will tell you how we will decide it. I will write the names of Lincoln and Manchester on two separate pieces of paper, fold them up, and put them in my hat. You then draw one out and tear it up, and the one that remains will be our place of residence for the winter." This simple way of settling what is often a difficult matter to decide was tried at once. Martha took one of the folded pieces of paper and destroyed it. She then opened the other and read the word "Manchester."

Thus was the birthplace of the coming hero of our story settled. This may seem to many readers a matter of trivial moment, yet it was one that had a very important bearing on his future life. Later on we will see how this fact was used to influence him in the turning-point of his history.

The professor laughingly said, "It rains nearly every day in winter, in Manchester, so you will have me in the house all the time. Will not that be an infliction?"

"No, indeed," was her quick reply; and as her lips were pressed to his, in proof of her sincerity, the germ of a new love began to develop amidst the ashes of the one lately buried.

In a week after this decision they left Paris for old England. Travelling in those days had not reached the degree of luxury and comfort and, what is more important, the rapidity with which it is now accomplished. Old persons say that there was more real enjoyment in the former slow mode of locomotion and transit of half a century back. Ten miles an hour by stage-coach was considered at times a breakneck pace, but in the present, sixty miles in the same period is demanded, and the cry is, "faster, still faster." Some say, "What does it matter if, once in a while, a hundred or so human beings are suddenly hurled into eternity? Does this fact deter any from going over the same course? It does not. We take our chances. The course of events move rapidly, and we must move with them."

CHAPTER XIV.

RED-LETTER DAY.

It was the tenth of November. Mr. and Mrs. Homerand were comfortably settled in handsome apartments in the most fashionable part of the ancient borough of Manchester. It was raining, not hard, but steadily, as if in accord with the staid habit of this rich and cultured city of the United Kingdom. A cheerful fire was burning in the grate, sending a glow all round the room, making a picture of home-life worthy of the effort of the best painter to rival on canvas. The professor had just returned from the post-office with a bundle of papers and several letters for himself and his wife. Some of the latter were from her school-mates, and filled with young girls' gossip, and saying how much they envied her for being in Europe and seeing the notables of foreign lands. There was nothing in any of the letters or papers out of the usual course of news, yet Mrs. Homerand noticed that her husband was restless and uneasy. She did not like to question him, and, as tea was announced, she hoped that after the evening meal the annoyance, or whatever it was, would pass away. But it did not. In two hours after he was in a very excitable condition; he walked up and down the room in a nervous manner, and, suddenly stopping before his wife, said, "Martha, I hope that the birth of our child will not take place on the fifteenth of this month."

Her eyes opened in wonder, and then, with an amused smile, she replied, "Why, I do not expect the event before December; but why do you object to the fifteenth of November? It is my father's birthday, and you know——"

"Yes," he interrupted her; "I know all that; but it was the day I was taken so ill, and the events connected with it—— Well, no matter," he continued, breaking off from his sentence; "it might be unlucky."

"Why should it be so?" Martha asked. "It was the day of our engagement, and it will always be a red-letter day in my existence."

The professor walked the floor more impatiently than ever. At last, afraid of awakening his wife's suspicions, he said, "I suffered so much from the illness contracted on that day that perhaps it has prejudiced my mind against it."

He now seated himself along-side of his wife, and taking her hand, with a smile, continued, "Martha, suppose the little stranger is a girl; what will you call her? You know it was agreed that if it was a boy I should name him Adrien, But you have not told me what, if a girl is sent to us, you propose calling her."

"Yes," she answered, "I have a name all ready. What do you think it is?"

"Well, really, the list of feminine names is so extensive that it would be difficult to guess."

"Then you give it up. Well, I propose calling our baby, if it be a girl, Helen."

The professor jumped to his feet, saying, petulantly, "I hate the name of Helen."

"Why do you hate it?" exclaimed his astonished wife. "It is my mother's name."

"Oh, I don't know," he replied; "but Helen was the cause of so much suffering to ancient Troy, and, as my name is Homer, I suppose I am prejudiced against it."

"Well, I declare," exclaimed Martha; "that is a queer reason for disliking the name. If I did not know you so well, I would suspect that some girl of that name had once held your affection, and jilted you for some one else."

To this thrust, which went deeper than she suspected, her husband replied, in a calm tone, as by a superhuman effort he mastered his feelings, " There is no name so sweet to me as Martha ;" and he kissed her with fervor.

Her affection for him was enlivened at this, and, looking into his face, she said, " Well, my dear, it shall be as you wish."

The fifteenth of November was a pleasant day. It rained a little in the morning, but cleared up at noon, and the sun came out of the cloud-banks that had hidden it for a week. The gentler sex went forth from their homes, to enjoy a sun-bath, a rare luxury at this time of the year.

The professor had invited a few friends to dinner. His fame had preceded him, and he found a warm welcome in Manchester.

In the afternoon he proposed to his wife to take a drive to the suburbs, as the day was so clear and pleasant. They drove out upon the road leading to Liverpool, and soon entered into the country. The experience of English rural life was not only a novelty, but pleasant to the American sojourners, and it was with regret that they gave the order to return to town.

As they neared the city limits a trivial occurrence was very near causing a fatal accident. They came up with a large hay-wagon, that almost blocked the highway, the driver of which refused to turn aside and let their carriage pass. A war of words commenced between the two drivers, which was ended by one of the wheels of the hay-wagon coming off the axle. The entire load fell over with a crash upon the side of the road. This startled the high-spirited horses of the carriage, and, dashing to one side, they soon ran forward in a mad gallop, tearing along the road at a fearful speed. Their wild career, however, was at length checked by meeting another hay-wagon. The driver directed the furious animals against it, and they were compelled to stop. No damage was done to the carriage, but Mrs. Homerand received a severe fright, which alarmed her husband. She was deathly pale, yet she controlled her feelings, and when the danger was over turned towards him smilingly, saying, " We had a narrow escape; let us go home at once." When they reached their house, they found several of the expected guests awaiting them. An hour after, all were present, and dinner was announced. Mrs.

Homerand had put on a white evening dress, and received many compliments for her good looks. There was a brilliant flush on her cheeks that greatly enhanced her beauty. Her husband was worried, nevertheless. He was apprehensive that the fright which she had received might produce dangerous results. There was an eminent physician among the guests, and to him he mentioned his fears. It was not long before the practised eye saw that a crisis was approaching; and he advised the professor to dismiss his guests and get his wife to bed. His foreboding was realized sooner than he expected. In a few moments later Mrs. Homerand was taken very ill. The ladies present assisted her to her chamber, and the physician contributed his skill. For half an hour there was a painful uncertainty, and the anxious husband endured intense agony. The memories of this " red-letter day" crowded upon him, and he thought of the terrible curse which had been pronounced against him. Would it reach the life of his wife, or would it pass away? His reflections were disturbed by the wail of a new-born infant. Was it a girl, and would it bear the dreaded name of Helen? Or was it a boy?

His suspense was soon relieved by the appearance of the doctor, who came into the room smiling, and said, " Professor, allow me to congratulate you on the birth of your son. Mother and child are both doing well, and there is no danger, as far as I can see at present, of any other serious result following the fright of the afternoon."

The effect of this announcement upon the professor was magical. He grasped the physician's hand with a vigor which showed how powerfully he was worked up. It was the first really happy moment he had experienced since that terrible midnight hour, just one year ago. After the arrival of the nurse the ladies who had been with Mrs. Homerand took their departure, and the doctor went with them, promising to call early next day. She was sleeping, and he would not disturb her. He drew his arm-chair up before the fire, and was lost in reminiscence. Was it possible that Helen's curse would in any way affect him or his wife or boy? He had often read of curses pronounced upon people, but they came to naught. Why, then, should he trouble himself in this matter? If it were possible in any way to atone for his crime, he would cheerfully do so. A financial compensation was out of the question. Helen's fortune was double the amount of his own. How could his sin be expiated? He had deeply repented. Was there no way by which forgiveness could be extended? His sin was not premeditated, he argued to himself, but in this he found no consolation, for his action had been deliberate and against a confiding girl. He must await the issue of the curse.

CHAPTER XV.

ADRIEN.

ABOUT an hour after the events recorded in the preceding chapter the door which led into the hall creaked on its hinges and slowly opened. The professor, thinking it was the landlady coming to inquire about his wife and child, said, without turning round, "Come in, Mrs. Brown, and congratulate me on the birth of my baby boy."

There was no response. He arose and went to the door, but found no one. A strange thrill came over him, an undefined dread, and a feeling as though some one from the dead was in the room with him. He was usually a man with strong nerves, and without superstition, and therefore not easily alarmed by anything seemingly of an unearthly character. He stood for a moment undecided what to do, when the door of his wife's chamber, which led out from his sitting-room, also opened. On going to it he saw the nurse sitting by the bedside. She raised her finger in warning not to disturb the sleeping young mother. He closed the door again, and, going to the bell, rang it. His landlady answered it in person, and as she came into the room she wished him much joy and happiness. She told him that the doctor, on leaving, had left instructions not to disturb Mrs. Homerand, and for that reason she had not come sooner; also, that she had prepared a bed for him in another room.

Again the door of his wife's room was opened. This time the nurse herself was there, and, in a low tone, she told him that Mrs. Homerand was now awake, and wished to see him.

He went to the bedside, and, taking her hand, said, "Martha, how do you feel now?"

She did not reply to the question, but, without opening her eyes, asked him what he thought of their babe, and continued, like one in a dream, "His grandfather just told me that he considered him a splendid boy, one of the old Rathmine stock."

"Grandfather!" ejaculated the professor.

The nurse again put up a finger of warning, and pointed to her head. He understood the sign; his wife's mind was slightly wandering.

"You will see," she went on, "that father has a good warm room to-night; he must be tired coming that long distance, expressly to see us, and to greet our boy. I will see you both in the morning. Good-night." And she turned her face to his for a good-night kiss.

He pressed his lips to hers, and as he raised his head that strange thrill again came over him. He could not account for the feeling, except perhaps on the ground of the excitement of the afternoon; not for a moment did the thought enter his mind that there was any thing supernatural. It might be nervousness; he did not allow it to trouble him. He left the bedside of his wife, and followed the landlady to the apartment prepared for him. Hardly had he reached the middle of the room when the door slowly opened. He looked into the passage, but all was darkness. Supposing that it was the wind, he now locked the door. He was nevertheless moved. His face grew pale, and the pulsations of his heart were quickened. He proceeded to search the apartment. He looked under the bed, a thing he rarely did, then into the closet, and behind the curtains of the window. There was nothing tangible in the room. He walked the floor, and reviewed the events of the past year. Where was Helen? His conscience reproached him; tears filled his eyes at the thought of her. Would there ever come a time when he could forget these things? It was past the midnight hour when he finally retired.

When he went to his wife's chamber, the next morning, he learned that she had rested comfortably, and her mind was clear. She spoke with a smile,—

"Homer, I had a pleasant dream last night. I thought that my father had come over unexpectedly from America, and was delighted to see his grandson. He was very pale, however, and seemed to be ill. If, now, he and mother would only join us for the winter, how pleasant it would be. Don't fail to write to them both to-day, and give them my love."

This was done, and the letter duly posted. In those days mail communications were not so rapid as they are now. The Cunard Line had sent out their pioneer steamer only the year previous.

It was therefore the 5th of December when a letter came to the professor with a deep mourning border, written by Mrs. Rathmine, giving the intelligence that her husband had died suddenly at five o'clock on the evening of the 15th of November. He had prepared a dinner in commemoration of his birthday, and while welcoming the guests he was taken with a fit of apoplexy, and died in a few minutes. Mrs. Rathmine was in great distress, and entreated that her daughter and the professor would return home as soon as possible. If, however, she added, they were not able to take the ocean voyage in winter, she would visit them abroad in the spring.

Thus, one life of that family was extinguished as a new one was ushered in. The wail of the infant had been answered by the expiring groan of the judge, who had just reached the mile-post of a half-century. Is it strange that his disembodied spirit should seek for a last meeting with his only daughter and her husband, and that it was gratified to meet also his grandson? It is not our province to express an opinion upon this matter. The simple fact is given, and we must leave it thus stated.

Mrs. Rathmine came over to England the ensuing spring, and remained with them for five years, going from city to city during the summer, and wintering in Dresden. She never fully recovered the shock occasioned by her husband's death. One cold, raw day in October she took a violent cold while watching a military display, and two weeks after passed quietly away in her daughter's arms. Her heart had been wrapped up in her grandson, and to him she left all her worldly possessions. The income of it was ample for one of moderate wants.

The next spring the professor and his wife returned to Boston, taking her remains with them, and buried them by the body of her late husband. The ensuing twelve months were spent in the Homerand mansion, but the longing for the excitement of foreign travel was too strong in both husband and wife. Again they made preparations to return to England, by the now established Cunard Line from Boston.

Since his marriage, Professor Homerand had not sought in any way to obtain information of Helen Claymuire. He had received a letter from her two years later. It merely informed him that she was very ill, and probably would not recover. A notice on the back in red ink, dated six days after the letter itself, stated that the writer had died the previous day, that the enclosed letter was found sealed and directed to him, and had been accordingly forwarded; he also received a slip from a paper, describing the death and burial of a highly accomplished young American lady, Mrs. E. Mordine, the daughter of the late Colonel Claymuire, of South Carolina. It added that the cause of death was consumption, and that she had endeared herself to a large circle of friends, who mourned the loss of one so beautiful and so amiable.

This unlooked-for intelligence made the professor very ill, and it was two months before he felt able to resume his travels. Remorse was at work, and he felt himself guilty of murder. But for the ministrations of his devoted wife, and the happy, playful disposition of his boy, he would perhaps, by some rash act, have ended his agony of soul. The face of the wronged Helen was continually before him. He redoubled his attentions to Martha, to lull any suspicions that might arise in her mind, and also, if possible, to quiet the shade of the unfortunate deceased one.

Constant travel brought relief at length, and only at times would the ghost of the past return. But conscience took care not to let him entirely forget his crime.

Thus the years went, bringing a premature old age on the professor and the promise of a noble life for his young son. In the summer of his sixteenth year the Homerands returned to their home in Boston, to enable the youth to enter the Freshman class of the University, of whose faculty his father had been an honored member.

Adrien exhibited talents that were of a high order. He was entirely free from the vices so common to youth. His home was a paradise to him, and the company of his gifted father and loving mother was preferable to any other society.

He came home every Friday evening during term-time, and returned on the Monday following. He had but one longing, and that was for the ocean. In his eighteenth year his father purchased for him a small schooner-yacht, and with some of his classmates, and an old coasting captain for a pilot and instructor, and a cook to prepare their meals, they worked the vessel themselves, and spent their vacation on the sea, going sometimes as far as the Gulf of St. Lawrence. Adrien was quick to learn, and soon became an accomplished seaman and skilful navigator.

We now enter upon a new act in our drama. New scenes, new characters, and a new history will occupy our attention.

BOOK II.—1861.

CHAPTER I.

THE SPIRITS ABROAD.

THE history of the great Rebellion gains in interest as the actors on both sides pass away, and a new generation arises who are able to weigh the mighty problems without prejudice that in the seventh decade of our century threw millions of people into fierce conflict one against the other. The blood of half a million men was shed before the decision was reached. It would be digressing from the aim of this narrative to enter upon the discussions that for years agitated all parts of the country, North and South, East and West, and which required the arbitrament of the sword to settle. One of the most powerful, prophetic representations of what war meant was given by *Harper's Weekly* in 1860. Two large pictures were published, called "The Spirits Abroad." It made a great impression at the time, but no one imagined the awful import of the war-cloud then looming over the land. The details of this great struggle have been fully written by other writers, and we can only take up such portions as relate to the individuals belonging to this story.

Adrien was to graduate in June of this year, and he had arranged to dispose of his small vessel and purchase a larger one. Ten of his friends, most of them his classmates, were invited to take a cruise in July up the St. Lawrence, to Montreal, and as far as the Great Lakes. This was looked forward to with a great deal of pleasant expectation. Adrien stood six feet, powerfully built, and was acknowledged by all to be the handsomest man in his class. He was so thoroughly good-natured, and such a polished gentleman, that he was called "Lord Chesterfield." To every one, even the humblest, he was polite and affable. Never would he speak ill of any one, and he positively refused to listen to scandal or idle gossip. A tale-bearer he despised. His manly nature recoiled from association with such thieves of character, those who take delight in aspersing the reputation of their fellows. Even the animals seemed by some instinct to know that he was their champion against cruelty. His record at college was one of the brightest in the annals of the famous seat of learning, in whose classic halls some of the most brilliant minds in the country had been instructed. He was the umpire not only in his own class, but with the juniors. Day after day was heard the expression, "Let Adrien decide the point." The young men would gather around him while, calmly as a judge upon the bench, he would patiently hear both sides of a dispute or argument, and then give his decision, which was always accepted like one of the laws of the Medes and Persians, final and fixed. His purse was freely opened to the needy student, and his assistance was tendered in a quiet way, merely as a loan to be repaid at some future time. He made the recipient of his bounty feel that it was a privilege to be permitted to lend money to one who might become a great lawyer, an eminent doctor, a celebrated clergyman, or a merchant prince. Adrien was of a sanguine disposition, and continually cheered the despondent by glowing pictures of what the future would bring forth. The silver lining of the dark clouds was soon made apparent under his manipulation. Never was his tact more needed than during the month of March, after the inauguration of President Lincoln. The spirits of union and disunion were abroad in the land, and nowhere was there such fierce controversies as in the town where the college was situated.

Many of the sons of the leading families of the South were students. They admired Adrien, and accepted his views on other points, yet on the burning question of the hour they remembered that he was of the Rathmine and Homerand stock, and therefore could not be in sympathy with the upholders of disunion. Nevertheless he prevented many severe conflicts between the young men representing the North and the South.

Often, when some of them were white with passion in the heat of an argument and ready to proceed to blows, Adrien's humorous remarks would set them laughing, and the little quarrels were suspended. The booming of Sumter's guns reached the college on the 15th of April, and the war fever spread with the rapidity of lightning. The call to arms, although it came unexpectedly, found the loyal sons of New England as ready to defend the old flag as their fathers had been nearly a century before. But the experience was a new one. It was against no foreign adversary, but a domestic one.

It was a fratricidal contest. All over the land, from the extreme northern boundary to distant Texas, in the far Western States, whose shores are washed by the waters of the Pacific, and in those whose barrier was the great Atlantic, there was but one topic of discussion, and that was war. By day and by night were the preparations hurried forward. Regiments were forming and hastening to the front. The Sixth Massachusetts, mostly from Lowell, under the command of Colonel Benjamin F. Butler, afterwards the distinguished major-general, had responded the day after the proclamation, and left on the 6th of April for Washington. Massachusetts was in the front, and her loyal sons were volunteering as fast as they could be armed and equipped. Farewells were rapidly spoken, and oaths of allegiance to the Federal government were taken by lips that afterwards were mute and cold upon the field of battle. At Adrien's college all the Southern students left at once for their homes. Among them were several who were deeply attached to him. There were two in particular, one from New Orleans, of French extraction, Henry Rechard, and the other a scion of one of the oldest families of South Carolina, Thomas Jeffords. They both sought out Adrien, and candidly told him that they proposed to offer their services to their respective States. Earnest and powerful were the arguments put forth by him to dissuade them. Never did he plead with such eloquent fervor, but to no purpose.

Failure to respond to the call of their States would brand them as cowards, and cut them off from all family associations. We have no occasion here to enter into the details of the important questions of that time and the tenor of the arguments used by both parties as justification of their course. It was not the sudden uprising from some trivial cause, such as in the past had led to fierce wars between rival kingdoms, but it extended back to the foundation of the government.

The notes that guide me in this description are not consecutive in their details, and much labor has been necessary to unravel the facts in the case. Several of the individuals connected with my story kept a diary of events, and I have thought best to publish many of the letters as they are found.

Somewhere I have read that "living, human beings are but sport for their dead predecessors." Strange as it may appear, yet I solemnly assure my readers that in some of the preceeding pages my pen has traced out the lines and characters apparently guided by some external controlling impulse. Ever and anon I hear the words "Hasten on, hasten on."

CHAPTER II.

UNION VS. DISUNION.

"The sound of the war-drum shall thrill thee at night,
As thy sons and thy brothers are borne to the fight;
The slave and the cotton shall stab thee with pain,
And the North and the South be divided in twain."

FROM lip to lip went the question, "Are you for the Union or against it?" There was no neutral ground that could be maintained with honor. Those who attempted it were despised by both contestants.

As I have already stated, Adrien was a strong champion for the Union cause, while his classmates, Henry Rechard and Thomas Jeffords, were for the South. In order to rightly estimate the conduct and character of our fellows, we must go back to the antecedents of their birth and early associations and training.

Henry Rechard was born of wealthy parents, in the city of New Orleans, in 1838. His father was an eminent physician, who had been educated in Paris. At the opening of the war Henry was in his twenty-third year. He had already graduated from the college, and was pursuing his studies in medicine. He possessed a wiry frame, and was in the enjoyment of perfect health. His hair was brown, with a slight moustache of the same color. His dark-blue eyes when in repose gave out a dreamy expression, as though the owner was living in a far-off world of his own. When roused by passion, or if his sympathies were excited by any act of oppression, the whole man seemed changed into another being, and woe betide the individual who crossed his path when his blood was up. His classmates described him as an angel most of the time, gentle and amiable in disposition, but occasionally, under great provocation, he would exhibit a character of another mould, and develop into something not prudent to molest.

Rechard was the soul of honor. He prized this quality so much that he looked upon the violation of it as the sin never to be forgiven. He was gifted with a keen penetration into human nature. His fellow-students used to affirm that he could tell what an individual had for dinner the day previous.

Next to Adrien, he was their confidant. While the other was the judge, he was the counsellor. On the 1st of May, just two weeks after the fall of Sumter, he severed his connection with his *Alma Mater*. He immediately sent his trunks to the railway station, preparatory to leaving for the South. He then waited for Adrien till he came out of the class-room at noon, and asked him to see him off.

They went together arm in arm, these two young men who were to be so strangely thrown together during the closing years of the terrible war. When they stood on the platform by the waiting train, with tears in their eyes, they clasped hands to say good-by.

"Here we part, Adrien," said Rechard. "Perhaps when next we meet it will be as enemies in conflict. I feel sure that you will enter into the service of your State, and I am certain no earthly power could swerve you from what you believe to be the path of duty. You will always be found faithful in regard to all that concerns an honorable man in the path he has chosen."

"My hand and my heart," answered Adrien, "will at all times be at your service, provided such action does not conflict with my allegiance to the Union cause. A thousand blessings on your head, and may God defend the right."

"Amen," answered Rechard, as, with his bright eyes filled

with the tears he could not keep back, he returned the pressure of his friend's hand. "If we can only meet as enemies, then I trust we will not do so until the conflict is settled one way or the other. I know that I will hear of your deeds of valor, for your star is destined to rise in the red firmament of war. Since the hour that I first met you, you have been my ideal of honor and self-respect in its highest development, and the pain at parting with you is the keenest I have ever endured. Whatever the issues may be to others, we never can be enemies. May God help us both to do our duty; and now, farewell."

A moment afterwards he stood on the platform of the moving train and waved his adieu. Thus they parted. Little did they think that, when next they should meet, the skill of the one should save the life of the other.

Thomas Jeffords first saw the light of day on his father's plantation in South Carolina. He came into the world under several disadvantages, which may serve as an excuse for some of his shortcomings: at least, he always pleaded them himself. He was of the same age as Adrien, having been born on the tenth day in the same month; and he often declared that in this stirring generation five days counted for a good deal. How the high-toned Adrien ever became attached to Tom Jeffords was always a marvel to the other students. Jeffords was in the class below him, and had very few friends in the school. He was not a favorite with any of the professors, and yet they were compelled to credit him with the term "excellent" in his recitations. He seemed to be always in luck. His class being a large one, only a few were called upon to recite each day. His classmates affirmed that he had some animal instinct by which he could invariably tell when he would be called on, and so was ready. He had a perfect command over the muscles of his face. This, perhaps, was the secret that he did not impart. When he wanted to be called upon to recite, he would assume a frightened, deprecatory air, as though dreading to be selected to tell what he knew about the subject for the day. On the contrary, when he was not prepared, he would exhibit a confident, knowing look, and keep searching the professor's eye as though soliciting a call. These tactics worked to a charm at all times, and so his record in his class was good.

He had a powerful memory and unlimited self-assurance, which carried him through the quarterly examinations. His uncle, who had brought him up, destined him for the profession of the law. I have remarked that he was ushered into the world under several disadvantages. His first wail was that of an orphan, for practically he had no mother nor father. Ten days before his birth the latter had been killed by being thrown from his horse, and his mother never got over the shock. She died before she could give birth to her baby, and the sharp knife of a skilful surgeon had saved his infantile life. He possessed a slender figure, and was of delicate constitution, but nature gave him a powerful weapon of defence in his tongue. He could utter more words to the given minute, some of them red-hot, than most boys of his age could in an hour. In regard to honor and patriotism, he had peculiar notions of his own, which will be made apparent as our story unfolds.

Tom, notwithstanding all this, had many good qualities which his profane old uncle had never sought to develop. He always prided himself on one thing,—viz., he never told a deliberate lie. He sometimes went very near the limit, but never crossed it. Tom was rather luxurious in his tastes, for which he obtained the means by telling his uncle that the expenses of a true-blooded Southern gentleman were always more than those incurred by the son of a Yankee shopkeeper. On this point the old man was weak. He sent him a liberal sum of money to liquidate all claims and pay his passage home. He directed him to leave at once that cursed abolition university, and to shake the dust of the Yankee town off his feet. Tom was so indiscreet as to show his uncle's letter to some of his classmates. A committee was at once appointed to "give him a good send-off." What the arrangements were was not made known, but a feather pillow was contributed, and a gallon of tar was purchased. "Tom Jeff" (as he was nicknamed) got an inkling in some way of the grand demonstration that was preparing in his honor, so he took the advice of Lady Macbeth to her guests,—not to stand on the order of going, but to go at once. He left the college by a back street, and was soon on his way to his Southern home.

CHAPTER III.

HANNIBAL'S OATH.

ALL who entered the service of the Federal government were obliged to take a solemn oath of allegiance. We now invite our readers to listen to an oath more appalling in its nature, and more disastrous in its consequences, than any taken by the loyal sons of the North.

In a street leading from the Boston Common, in a massive granite stone house, a scene was enacted on the 3d of May that gave rise to the details of this story. In a large front room, luxuriously furnished, sat in an easy-chair a beautiful woman. A superficial observer would have said that she was a little past thirty. A closer inspection would have shown her abundant black hair tinged with gray, and yet, judging from the absence of all wrinkles, she could not have been more than forty. Her eyes still retained their youthful sparkle. On her face, on this particular morning, there was an expression as of heavenly sweetness, but blended with a vindictive animosity that was startling to behold. On her lap lay the morning newspaper. A short paragraph in it had roused all the latent evil of her nature to its utmost activity, giving her a resemblance to the description of another woman,— viz., that she was a "beautiful devil." The only occupant of the room with her was a young girl of about twenty years. To attempt the portraiture of the latter in a single brief paragraph would be a difficult matter. She was like some great work of art on canvas or marble, that needed to be studied to be understood. Little by little, however, we shall become better acquainted with the heroine of our story. She had a book in her hand,—Pope's translation of Homer,—and was deeply interested in the exciting description of the single combat of Ulysses and Hector before the walls of Troy. She rose suddenly from her chair, and, closing her book, said, in a sorrowful tone,—

"Oh, dear, Hector is killed; I am so sorry for him."

"Hector who?" exclaimed the older lady, in an angry tone.

"Why, Hector, the son of Priam, the brave defender of Troy. Have you never read Homer, auntie? It is a charming book."

"Homer!" exclaimed her aunt, rising from her seat, and facing the girl before her with a look of intense bitterness. Her face was pale, and her eyes fairly blazed like electric sparks.

"Child," she said, "why do you choose such literature? It is not a proper book for a young lady. Homer, indeed! I detest the name."

"Why, auntie," exclaimed the astonished girl, "what could Homer have had to do with you? You look as though you would like to tear him to pieces."

"Read that paragraph," replied her aunt, fiercely, as she handed her niece the newspaper which was crumpled in her hand. The girl took the paper and read the article indicated.

"I do not see any thing extraordinary in that," said she; "I read it this morning. It only refers to the gallant conduct of Adrien Homerand. Two days ago he prevented a violent demonstration by the students at his university against some of the Southern young men who were preparing to leave for their homes. The editor declares that lasting disgrace would have rested upon the institution if violence had been offered them. You know, auntie, I love your native State, dear old South Carolina, where we have spent such happy days. At the same time, I respect the devotion of the Northern people to their cause. I think Mr. Homerand did a noble act, and I admire him for it."

"Ilian," said her aunt, grasping her arm, and almost hissing out her words, "tell me, have you ever met Adrien Homerand?"

"Not to speak to him," the girl replied; "but I have seen him several times, and I think that, without exception, he is the handsomest young man I ever gazed upon. I would like to be introduced to him."

"Curse him! and curses upon his father, and upon the whole brood of them!" shouted the now infuriated woman.

Ilian looked on in amazement. Had her aunt lost her reason? What could have caused this terrible outburst?

She was aware that her aunt had periodical fits of despondency, but never had she seen her so excited. She attempted to soothe her, and tried to put her arm around her neck. A single look from those vindictive eyes, now blazing with passion, warned her to desist. The tears came into her eyes. The woman had been as a mother to her, and had never repelled her before in such a manner.

Her aunt had been married, when a young girl, to a man very much older than herself, and he died three years later. He belonged to the old English family of the Verderes, and she had remained a widow ever since. As they had ample means, most of their time had been spent abroad. Several winters they lived on their plantation near Columbia, in South Carolina, and had come from it only a few weeks previous, and were now on their way to Paris.

Ilian was loving and demonstrative in her disposition, and the action of her aunt in refusing to allow her caresses wounded her deeply. She sank into a chair and burst into a flood of tears. This was like oil on the waters. The storm subsided. Mrs. Verdere brought a chair along-side of the weeping girl, and said, in a kind tone,—

"Ilian, my child, I did not mean to wound your feelings, but when I think of your mother's wrongs, I can at times hardly control myself."

Ilian looked up with eyes filled with tears. Her aunt gently drew the beautiful face to her bosom, and kissed her so affectionately that the glad smile came back.

"Auntie," she replied, "you often promised to tell me of my mother's history. Why not now? This is my birthday. We are to have a few friends this evening, and I was expecting to have obtained an introduction to Adrien Homerand, so that I could have invited him to our reception. All the girls of Boston are raving about him, and I——"

The sentence was never finished, for her aunt checked her with a question, uttered in a tone of voice so hollow that it might have come from the dead, it was so weird and thrilling.

"Ilian, would you, if I were murdered, invite the son of my murderer to your home, and feast him?"

"How can you ask such a question? I would kill any man or woman that dared to offer you violence." And the eyes of the young girl flashed a dangerous fire, showing the embryo passsion that was lurking beneath the fair exterior.

"Ilian," continued her aunt, "some other time I will tell you the story of your unhappy mother. One thing I will tell you now, and that is the stern fact that Professor Homerand was the main cause of your mother's death. They were engaged to be married, and he abruptly broke off the engagement, and married his present wife. I went with her to England, where she met your father and married him after a short courtship. She died in giving you birth, as I have already told you, and your father grieved so after her that he also died in a few months. She suffered so from nervous prostration that it left her no vitality to withstand your birth. In the face of all this, do you wish to have the son of the man who was the main cause of her untimely death at our house this evening, and sitting at our table? If so, I will at once obtain an introduction."

The horrified expression on the face of the girl assured Mrs. Verdere that the moment was at hand to which she had looked forward for many years.

"Ilian, have you ever heard of Hannibal's oath?"

"Yes, indeed; Hannibal was one of the three sons of Hamilcar, the great Carthagenian warrior. His father made Hannibal take an oath of perpetual hatred to the Romans, and he carried war and desolation into their midst for many years."

"Exactly; and your mother, on her dying bed, made me promise, when you were of age, to get you to take an oath of perpetual enmity to Professor Homerand and his family. Now you know the reason why I cannot, for your mother's cause, endure the name of Homer; for the sake of the dead and the love of her who gave you birth, will you solemnly promise to carry out her wish?"

"Oh, auntie, this is so sudden, and an oath like that is terrible; is there no way out of it? Was she in her right mind when she asked you to carry out such a thing?"

"Yes, as conscious as I am to-day. But you hesitate. Which do you prefer, an eternal blessing or a curse?"

"Will you not give me time to ponder this matter over?"

"No, not a moment. I am surprised that you ask for such a delay. This must be done now."

"Am I to understand that, if I fail to comply with this request, I will entail upon myself a mother's curse?"

"Yes, I have so stated."

For a moment there was silence, and then Ilian, in a low, frightened tone, said, "I swear to do as my mother wished me, by all my hopes of heaven and by all my fear of hell."

CHAPTER IV.

FATHER MURPHY.

IN a manufacturing town of Massachusetts, not far from Boston, there stood, on one of its side streets, a beautiful church edifice, built of wood, in Gothic style, and painted white. Its modest tower did not seek to rival its more pretentious neighbors by rising into the clouds. It was surmounted by a cross of golden hue. The bell was soft in tone, which did not jar upon the ears like that of others in the same place. The good Catholic priest who was its pastor called it a chapel. He might have termed it a church, for it could seat five hundred people. But Father Murphy was not ostentatious, either in private or public life. Many of his parishioners declared that he was too modest, and that this was a virtue not appreciated in this forward age. He had travelled over a large part of Europe, and had visited many of the States, going as far as California. His church, proud of their pastor, had two years previously raised a liberal sum of money and sent him on a visit to Rome. A six months' tour had been rich in experience, and his parishioners reaped the benefit. Travel, and its consequent mixing with all sorts of people, had broadened his mind. He was liberal in his views; being thoroughly honest himself, he gave others credit for being sincere in their belief, although they might differ from him in doctrine. His manner was genial to all, rich as well as poor. A high, square forehead was a token that Nature had been lavish in mental gifts, but one quality he lacked, and that was ambition. Yet he was active and energetic in church work, and zealous in the performance of the multitudinous duties of a pastorate, but he had no desire to rise to a higher position. Time and again he was told that his great talents were wasted in the small parish over which he gently ruled. He ought to be a bishop. To this he invariably replied that he preferred his quiet work, and hoped to live and die with his present charge. His chapel was opened each day from sunrise to one hour after sunset; and every week-day afternoon he was always found there to give a word of counsel or comfort to any one who might seek him. They came regularly, the old and young, and the middle-aged; men of business came when things went wrong, and always went away with a glow of sunshine in their faces; mothers sought his advice when the burden and cares of their household were too heavy, and on their return home their children would exclaim, "Where has mother been, she looks so happy?" And so it was, year after year. By the sick-bed he was found when needed, but he never intruded his services when not desired. The worthy priest was careful to avoid all occasion for scandal, by seeing every one in the church. He would go from pew to pew, talk, encourage those present, and then retire to his modest cottage attached to the rear of the chapel, where a widowed sister kept house for him.

One afternoon in the latter part of May the sky, which had been clear all day, became darkened by a heavily-charged cloud, which passed rapidly over the town and opened suddenly its flood-gates; it did not rain, it poured. Pedestrians sought shelter wherever they could. A lady, richly dressed, was caught in the shower two blocks away, and by the time she reached the vestibule of the chapel she was drenched through. As she stood there Father Murphy came towards her, and, bowing with that ease of manner which only the true gentleman can exhibit, expressed his regret that she had been caught in the unexpected rain, and invited her into his house, where his sister would be at her service. The lady at first declined, saying that she was anxious to reach her home in Boston, and was then on her way to the station. She was a stranger in the place, and came by the noon train to get some information about a private matter. Just then the whistle of the locomotive was heard, and the priest smiled as he said,—

"I am afraid you will not get the four o'clock train, and there is no other before six, which is a slow one. It will therefore be fully four hours before you can reach your home, and to remain in your wet garments that length of time would endanger your life."

The lady accepted the offer of hospitality, and went to the cottage, where the sister took charge of her.

The pastor returned to his chapel, to find twoscore people assembled, most of them refugees from the storm. He had a smile and pleasant greeting for each. At five the cloud passed over, and the sun far in the western horizon filled all the landscape with the golden beauty of its parting rays. It was a glorious scene, and the priest stood in the rear of his chapel, admiring the grandeur of the picture which no painter could produce. At last he remembered his guest. It wanted thirty minutes to the time when the next train would leave for Boston, but the station was only five minutes distant. When he entered his parlor he found her waiting to express her thanks. Her outer garments had been dried before the kitchen fire, and his sister had furnished a change of under-linen, and she was now anxious to get home. The experienced eye of Father Murphy read at a glance that the woman before him was no ordinary person; that she was wealthy was apparent from the texture of her apparel and the two large solitaire diamond ear-rings which shone resplendent from her ears. Her choice language and dignified, yet extremely courteous, behavior, were evidences of superior education and birth. She earnestly invited the priest and his sister to visit her in Boston before she sailed for Europe in the middle of June. She was not a native of the old Bay State, but came from South Carolina. She hoped that the outbreak of civil war had not extinguished kindly feelings in their hearts for those who, through no choice of their own, first saw the light of day in the far-off South, and who, as a sequence, were deeply interested in the welfare of the seceding States.

Father Murphy and his sister had both been born in Massachusetts, and their patriotism was fully aroused, but here was a woman, and a beautiful one at that, who was their guest, and how could they have any but the most friendly feelings for her? Both took her hands, and assured her they hoped that the acquaintance formed through the accident of a thunder-storm might develop into the bright sunshine of a life-long friendship. The lady handed her card, on which

was written " Mrs. Elizabeth Verdere, —— Street, Boston."
" Just off the Common," she said.

"I know the place and the house very well," said Father Murphy; "I have been there before."

A grave look came over his face, and a deep sigh escaped him, as though the memory of some past event of no pleasant nature had been brought up in review before him. Suddenly he said, as if seeking to change the topic, and prevent any question being asked,—

"You do not, I suppose, belong to our mother church?"

"No," was the answer; "I was brought up in the Episcopal fold; I am satisfied with its teachings, and hope to live and die in that faith."

"Well, we will not discuss religious dogmas, especially if you want to catch the six o'clock train."

Mrs. Verdere laughed, and a smile of such sweetness came over her face that Father Murphy and his sister were completely captivated. Her curiosity had been aroused by the strange look that came over his face when she mentioned the place where she lived. In a gentle, insinuating tone, as they walked to the station, she asked,—

"Is there any marvellous story attached to the house in which I have my apartments? My niece has a peculiar penchant for houses in which great tragedies have been enacted. Ilian is a strange girl, and an earnest student of psychic problems."

"Is that your niece's name? It is quite classical. It sounds like a derivation from the *Iliad* of Homer. What a wonderful man that poet was."

It was well for the good father's complacency of mind that he did not see the face of his companion as he mentioned the name of Homer. A dark cloud came over it that told of suppressed passion.

"You ask me about the house where you live," he continued. "Five years ago a dreadful scene took place in it. I was well acquainted with one of the families involved. I was called to hear the dying man's confession. He owned the place, and was living there with his widowed mother. It is a long story; but here we are at the station, and there is the whistle of the locomotive."

"Was there a murder committed on the premises?"

"Yes; the young man referred to had deceived a girl of good family under promise of marriage. She heard that he was about to marry another. She called at the place and waited for him in their sitting-room, which is on the second floor front. When he came home she made a demand that he should keep his promise and marry her. This he flatly refused to do. She then took a revolver from the bosom of her dress and shot him. He died three days after."

"That was my—I mean that I am now occupying that identical room. Good-bye; a thousand thanks for your hospitality and kindness."

The next moment the worthy priest was alone on the platform, and the train had passed out of the station.

"There is some design of Providence in this meeting," he said to himself, as he walked back to his home.

CHAPTER V.

A VISION OF THE PAST.

ON the morning of the fifth day after Mrs. Verdere left Father Murphy's house he received a letter by the early morning post, written in delicate handwriting, and highly perfumed. "Some lady fair, seeking advice," said his sister.

The following were the contents:

BOSTON, June 2, 1861.

REV. THOMAS MURPHY:

REVEREND AND DEAR SIR,—My aunt, Mrs. Verdere, to whom you so kindly extended your hospitality five days ago, is very ill. She took cold from the rain-storm that overtook her in your town. A high fever has resulted. No serious danger is anticipated. She has expressed a desire to see you, if you care to come as a friend. You evidently made a deep impression upon her during the short time she was with you. It is best to state in advance that my aunt is a member of the Episcopal Church, and has no intention of severing her connection with it. She is anxious to hear something more of the tragedy connected with the apartments where we are now living. I join with her in sincere thanks for the hospitality extended to her. I sent your sister a package by express yesterday, containing the clothing loaned to my aunt and a few tokens of our esteem.

With best wishes for your welfare, I remain, with feelings of gratitude, ILIAN MORDINE.

P.S.—As you know our house, it is needless to give the number.

"I like the open frankness of this note," said Father Murphy, "and I will go at once and see Mrs. Verdere. Her guardian angel may have led her to our home for the purpose of bringing her into our fold. I am glad of the opportunity to express my thanks in person for the valuable presents which came this morning."

Shortly after the noon hour the worthy priest stood before the house he knew so well. In answer to his ring, a servant-girl came to the door. Taking his card and reading the name, she surveyed him from head to foot. There could be no mistake in the man. He was a priest all over, and the girl perceived it at once. In answer to his inquiry for Mrs. Verdere, she replied that the lady was very ill, and the doctor, who had just left, had given strict orders to admit no visitors. "Besides," she continued, "Mrs. Verdere is a Protestant, and——"

"Take my card at once to Miss Mordine, and say I am here in answer to her letter."

The decided tone in which these words were uttered gave the girl to understand that the man before her must be obeyed. She at once opened the door, which she had previously kept half-closed, and asked him to wait in the parlor. His temper was slightly ruffled, and he walked the floor to regain his composure.

"These New England country-girls," he said, half aloud, "are brought up to look upon a priest as prowling around seeking to make proselytes. They perhaps may learn that our religion is not forced upon unwilling recipients; we offer it, but do not thrust it upon any one. A time may come——"

"Glad to welcome you, Father Murphy."

The priest turned round at this cordial salutation, and a

vision of loveliness burst upon his gaze. He had seen many beautiful women in his own State; had looked upon fair faces in London, Paris, Berlin, Vienna, and in sunny Italy; but never in all his travels had he seen the equal of the radiant girl before him. Her abundant hair was of a rich golden tint, her eyes were deep blue, and had a magnetic power that brought the beholder at once under her sway. For a moment the priest wondered if he was not dreaming, and that he beheld some angelic messenger. The silvery tones of her voice seemed to confirm this as she continued,—

"I am delighted at being able to tender you my thanks for your service to my aunt, and for the kindness of your sister to her."

"Do not mention it," he replied, feeling, for the first time in his life, embarrassed before a woman.

"I assure you," he went on, "the obligation rests upon my side. It was a pleasure to be of service in any way to Mrs. Verdere. I am deeply grieved to learn that she took cold from the rain, and hope the indisposition may pass away in a few days."

"It is not likely to prove serious," said Ilian. "It will delay our departure for Europe a week or so; if you will come to our sitting-room, up-stairs, I will inform my aunt that you have arrived, and I am certain she will be deeply gratified by this visit from you."

Ilian turned and led the way. The priest followed her into the hall and up to the second floor. At the door of the sitting-room she asked him to wait inside while she went to prepare her aunt for the interview. As he entered the room so well-remembered a vision of the past flashed upon him with a strange power. He saw before him in fancy a man of about thirty years, handsome and well-endowed, having all the advantages of wealth and education. He was listening with a scornful smile to a demand made by a girl with a pale but determined face, dressed in the height of fashion. In low words, but with a terrible meaning, she said, in a firm voice,—

"So you positively refuse to fulfil your sacred obligation to make me your wife, after having basely deceived me, and now wish to cast me aside like a useless toy?"

"What nonsense, Bertha," he replied, "to urge this matter further. I gave you my final answer last week, and I purpose to adhere to what I then stated. I have agreed to provide for you, but I cannot make you my wife."

"Then you regard your word of honor of no value?"

"It does not count in a case of this kind."

"Can nothing induce you to change your purpose in this respect?"

"No; I do not think any argument that you can bring forth will do so. I may as well tell you now, and settle the matter for good, that in a week from to-day I expect to marry Julia."

"Then take this as a wedding-present from Bertha."

She took a pistol from the bosom of her dress, a loud report was heard, the man staggered, and, putting his hand over his breast, exclaimed, "My God, Bertha, you have killed me!" and then fell heavily to the floor.

"My aunt is ready to receive you," said Ilian, who had again appeared at the door. "Are you ill, Father Murphy? You look dreadfully pale. Let me offer you a glass of wine."

"No, no; a thousand thanks. It is only the association of this room with the terrible deed committed here five years ago this month. It all seemed to come back before me."

"You must tell me all about this affair some time, I am anxious to hear it. Was it in this room where the shooting took place?"

"Yes; right where you are standing."

"What day of the month was it?"

"The 2d of June. This is the fifth anniversary."

"Do you believe, Father Murphy, that the dead ever come back to rehearse old scenes?"

"That is a difficult question to answer. We know comparatively nothing of the capabilities of the spirit after it leaves the body."

"I merely ask the question because you seem to have just had a rehearsal of the events that took place five years ago to-day. How do you account for it?"

"The power of memory, I suppose. We will talk it over another time. I will go in and see your aunt now."

CHAPTER VI.

REPENTANCE.

When Father Murphy stood by the bedside of Mrs. Verdere, he was greatly shocked at the change that had taken place in her appearance. The fever was making sad havoc with the beautiful woman before him. To his mind came the words of the prophet Isaiah to King Hezekiah,—" Set thine house in order, for thou shalt die and not live." He felt the conviction that she would never rise from her bed, and that the end was near. Why he felt so, he was unable to tell.

" Ilian," said the sick woman, " I wish to have a private talk with Father Murphy. Let no one disturb us."

As the door closed she turned to her visitor, saying, " Can you give me any details of the tragedy of this house?"

" The subject is very painful," was the answer, " and the particulars are too long to go over now."

He became visibly agitated at the remembrance of the rehearsal of the terrible scene he had just gone through.

After a moment's pause Mrs. Verdere asked, " Do you not think that the girl was justified in the course she took ?"

The priest crossed himself as he answered, in a tone of horror, " My God, no ; how can murder be justified ? What did this girl gain for the blood which she shed ? She was at once arrested, and, after the death of her victim, was placed on trial for murder. The friends of the murdered man spent money lavishly to make her conviction of a capital crime certain. She was vilified, and false witnesses were brought forward to testify to her previous bad character. She narrowly escaped the death-penalty, and was condemned to ten years in the State prison, and died there two years after. How much better to have left her case with God,—" Vengeance is mine, saith the Lord ; I will repay."

" Vengeance is slow on the Lord's part," replied Mrs. Verdere. " Twenty years ago I called down on the head of a man who wronged me the solemn curse of Heaven, and, instead of being cursed, he has been blessed and has prospered. Would that I had taken my own revenge."

"Don't you remember the ancient oracle,—'The mills of the gods grind slow, but they grind fine.' How do you know that this man of whom you speak has not been punished? Remorse may have made his life a burden to him, and yet to the world he perhaps keeps it hidden."

"I would rather do my own grinding; and I would take care that it was done very fine."

"But this is not Christian charity."

"The man deserves no charity."

"Admit all that; but don't you think your Maker could attend to this matter better than you can? Make me a confidant; tell me your story; perhaps I can suggest some remedy."

The long pent-up fires burst forth, and she poured into the ears of the priest her sad history. She told the tale of her wrongs, and her weary waiting for the curse of the old South Church to fall upon the guilty one. Father Murphy had listened to so many strange tales in his time that he showed no sign of wonder. When the sick woman had finished, he took her hand in his and asked, "Are you willing to risk going into the presence of your Maker with these feelings in your heart?"

"Yes," was her answer; "but I am not going to die till the curse has been fulfilled. I propose to live and see it all."

"But in case your present illness should terminate fatally, you would ask God to forgive you your trespasses against him?"

"Certainly I would."

"But how can you expect it, when you harbor such thoughts of enmity against another?"

"Mine is an exceptional case; and when I see the curse accomplished in all its particulars, then I will forgive him, and not before."

"If this is your determination, I can do you no good till you are in a different frame of mind. My office as a priest of the church would be of no benefit. I also doubt whether any Protestant clergyman can do anything for you till there is a radical change in your disposition. I must now say good-by, and I leave you in the hope that when next I see you your heart may be in a softer mood."

" It never will be till the tenor of my curse is complete."
" I hope for better things," was the parting reply.
The bell at the bedside was rung, and Ilian answered it in person.
" My dear Father Murphy," said she, " lunch is prepared for you, and I will esteem it as a great favor if you will accept of our hospitality."
Pressing the hand of Mrs. Verdere, and with a silent prayer for the help of heaven, he went to the dining-room. Half an hour later he had left for home. In his devotions he remembered the rebellious heart crying for vengeance and wondering why it was so slow in coming. Two days afterwards, while in his chapel in the afternoon, speaking to those who came to seek his counsel, a telegram was handed to him:

BOSTON, June 4.

Come at once. My aunt is dying, and wishes to see you.

ILIAN.

It was half-past four, and there was no train that stopped at his town until half-past six. An express train, however, passed through at four forty-five, which might be stopped if the case was urgent. He went to his cottage, told his sister of the message, and went to the depot.

The station-master was a New England Puritan of the old type, but the genial smile and hearty greeting of the priest could always win its way to his heart. When he was shown the telegram he took up a red flag and waved it furiously in front of the train now rapidly approaching. The ponderous locomotive slowed up and came to a full stop. The priest sprang upon the platform, and, waving his thanks to the station-master, was soon out of sight.

The state-house clock was tolling the hour of six as Father Murphy again stood at the door of that fatal house, as he termed it. Ilian answered the bell in person. A smile lit up her tear-stained face as she saw him.

" You are just in time," was her greeting, " The doctor left a few moments ago, and promised to return in an hour; he thinks my aunt will not survive beyond midnight, and I am in great anguish over the news. I had not expected a fatal termination.

As he reached the sick-chamber, a single glance told him that the end was not very far off. The dying woman was perfectly conscious, and recognized him as he took her hand. He knew the moments were precious, and no time was to be lost.

"Mrs. Verdere," he said, "before two hours will have passed you will stand at the judgment-bar: are you willing with all your heart to forgive Professor Homerand the evil that he has done you, and leave the judgment of the whole matter with God?"

The mention of this name aroused all the dormant fire of her nature; her eyes flashed defiance and rebellion; for fully five minutes not a word was spoken. Slowly the evil passions subsided; a look of calm resignation and a soft, sweet disposition spread over her face, and she replied, "Father Murphy, you have conquered; I yield, and I freely forgive Professor Homerand, and I hope to be forgiven."

"No, my child. It is not I, but the Saviour who won the victory over the powers of darkness. In the name of Christ I bless you, and commend you to His mercy."

"Ilian, come to my side," called the dying woman. "Before God and before man I now recall the obligation that I made you take a month ago. Consider it null and void. It was wrong on my part to ask you to bind yourself to any such malediction; you are therefore free from it. I have left you all my property, and you will be the sole heiress of a vast fortune. I now commend you to the care of God. You will find all the information you want about your father in the tin box containing my papers. I am getting very weak, and feel faint."

At this point her breath became feeble and her words disconnected.

"Ilian," she continued, "open the tin box—velvet lining—full record—the oath—is void. If you wish the last blessing of your dying———"

The sentence was never finished. There was a gurgling sound in her throat. Death had come sooner than was expected. The spirit of the former Helen Claymuire left its earthly tabernacle and went to the bar of final reckoning.

Two days after, all that was mortal was laid away to rest in one of Boston's great cemeteries. The burial service was read by an Episcopal clergyman, and only a few friends were invited. Some relatives from New York came on, among them a Mrs. Rendeem, who was her cousin, and with whom Ilian returned after all was over.

CHAPTER VII.

THE WAR FEVER.

The month of July, 1861, was an inauspicious one in this memorable year. The battle of Bull Run had been fought, and the Northern forces had retired from the field. The prevalent idea which seemed to exist throughout the States north of Mason and Dixon's line was that war meant the killing of enemies in battle. When General Sherman's interpretation was made known, that war was not only killing, but being killed in return, then a large number who objected to the latter feature of it retired from the contest.

Many had loudly urged that it would be far better to let the seceding States go out of the Union than to shed the blood required to preserve the compact. But all hopes of peace were finally swept away, when the news of the defeat of the Union troops occurred on the field of Bull Run in July. The Southern leaders, flushed with victory, increased their demands. But two courses were now open to the North. One was a dishonorable peace and the dismemberment of the union of States; the alternative, a bloody civil war, lasting for years. Abraham Lincoln was the first President in the history of the Republic who was inaugurated under the auspices of fixed bayonets and artillery, with troops drawn up in line of battle. There was now no choice but to accept the challenge of the South, and leave to the arbitrament of the sword what statecraft had failed to decide. The call for three-months' volunteers was due to the fears of those who desired peace at any price. It was now found to be a mistake; a proclamation was sent out calling for a first instalment of three hundred thousand men, to defend the Union standard by sea and land. It was carried on the electric wire through every city, town, hamlet, and village along the shores of our great lakes and beyond the Mississippi, across the broad prairies of the distant West. The fiery message spread through all ranks. The people accepted the gauntlet of defiance thrown to them by the South.

Not only the native-born but the naturalized citizen came forward to defend the flag that gave them protection. The war fever spread even across the border, and thousands of Canadians entered the service of the Union. The ploughman left his furrow, the smith dropped his hammer on the anvil, young men forsook their desks and counters, their shops and factories, their offices, homes, and firesides, and hurried to the rendezvous. Clergymen left their pulpits, judges their benches, lawyers their clients, physicians their practice, merchants their traffic, and students came from schools, universities, and academics. From every profession and trade, from every calling and rank in life, came the tens of thousands who withstood the ordeal of battle on many a hard-fought field. Many of the leading officers in the army and navy resigned their commission and went South; but their places were quickly filled. The North was thoroughly aroused, and fulfilled the prophetic poem of Mrs. H. W. Booth, written in Europe twenty years previous, of which the following is an extract:

> "The North in her might, like a whirlwind shall rise;
> And the notes of the cannon be borne to the skies;
> And though the warm blood of her heroes be shed,
> The light of her freedom shall never be dead;
> The stars and the stripes in Excelsior shall be
> Proud Liberty's banner from land and by sea;
> And the Union, though spurned by the slave-holders' scorn,
> Shall be guarded by Northmen for ages unborn."

The commencement exercises in all the Northern universities were held amid great excitement. Wherever there were Southern students, they left, and the war fever seized those who remained and were able to volunteer. Adrien Homerand, in deference to his father's urgent solicitation, had refrained from offering his services till after his graduation. But the very next day he left for Washington, and through the influence of Senator Sumner, his father's friend, he was introduced to the Secretary of the Navy. He brought with him a certificate from the Board of Trade of Boston, testifying to his superior seamanship, both practical and theoretical, and also his skill as a navigator. An appointment as an acting master was given to him, with orders to report at once for duty on board of the United States steamer ——, then fitting out at the Brooklyn Navy-Yard. The fame of the father reflected its lustre upon his son, and the memory of his grandfather, Judge Rathmine, was still held in kindly remembrance by many old friends in New York. The best society was thus opened to him. He was flooded with invitations to balls and receptions. He devoted all his time, however, to become thoroughly proficient and acquainted with the duties of his place. The art of naval warfare was new to him, but his active mind quickly mastered the details of the management of a ship-of-war, and the division to which he was assigned command on this vessel soon far excelled all the others in rapid movement and efficiency. His commanding officer, in the report to the Navy Department on the condition of his ship prior to sailing under sealed orders, stated that Acting Master Adrien Homerand was the most perfect example of a naval officer that he had ever sailed with. This encomium from the stern old martinet could only have been won by very rare qualities in any officer on his ship.

Adrien's voice was deep and far-reaching, and could be heard in the remotest part of the vessel. The topmen aloft on the royal yards, and the men in the fire-room, and in the inmost recesses of the shaft-alley, heard his trumpet-tones distinctly. His words of command were always given in a concise, seaman-like manner that carried no doubtful meaning to the ears of those to whom they were addressed, and made them vividly conscious that the sooner the orders were obeyed the better for them. He never used profane or vulgar adjectives in the performance of his duties, nor, in fact, at any time; never, under the greatest provocation, would he curse the men on deck. Those who have served as watch-officers on ships of war know by experience that occasions often arise when it requires an effort almost superhuman to keep one's temper. In the ward-room men are often associated with such diverse temperaments, and with conditions of living in all its phases so different from life on shore, that, unless great forbearance is exercised by all, a condition will ensue, termed, in signifiant nautical parlance, " a floating hell."

This would have been the case with his ship, but for the tact of Adrien. He exercised the same influence over his messmates that he had previously done at college, and before the vessel left New York harbor he had become the umpire in all matters of dispute, and his decision was considered final.

For the benefit of those who have no knowledge of life on a man-of-war, I will enumerate the divisions or messes into which the hands are divided. Among the crew, twelve men, as a rule, form a mess. Then there are several petty officers' messes. The boatswain, gunner, carpenter, and sail-maker, who are warranted officers, constitute the "forward officers' mess." The junior commissioned officers comprise the "steerage mess." In the wardroom of the senior officers are small state-rooms, about seven feet square, opening into the larger space; in these boxes, as they have been termed, they must sleep in a berth twenty-seven inches wide, and in drawers beneath it they keep all their clothes, consisting of four styles of uniform, hot- and cold-weather clothes sufficient to last for a three years' cruise, often without an opportunity to have them washed. In this box each officer has a bureau, washstand, and chair. It is astonishing how much material can be crowded into a space of the above dimensions. There is also a captain's mess, and the admiral's, when the vessel is a flag-ship.

CHAPTER VIII.

THE UNION NAVY.

At the outbreak of the Rebellion the Federal naval authorities found themselves with only a few available ships. Part of these were old sailing-craft. They had no full-powered screw-ships. What they had were auxiliary steam power. Orders were given at once to purchase all merchant vessels suitable for blockade and fighting. Contracts were made for a large number of steamers of all kinds for the branch of service intended,—deep-sea cruising, river, and inland waters. The regular navy formed but a nucleus, and acting appointments were given to officers of the merchant marine.

The ship to which Adrien was attached was one of the best-equipped vessels of the naval service; in fact, she was considered one of the best of her kind afloat. A week before the appointed time of departure, while the ship was at anchor off the battery, on a clear, bright day, just as Adrien was relieved as officer of the forenoon watch, one of his old classmates came over the side, and, grasping his hand, said, " I want you, old fellow, to do me a particular favor."

" Certainly, I am at the disposal of one whose cordial friendship in our school-days will always be a source of pleasant recollection."

" A thousand thanks for this compliment. I am the bearer of a peremptory mandate from my sisters and my cousins, that you, Adrien Homerand, report yourself in uniform to-morrow evening, for dinner at six o'clock. After which you must answer to the charges, preferred by a dozen or more young ladies, that you have on sundry occasions slighted their invitations, and absented yourself without leave from so many receptions where you were expected. You are also directed and invited to bring with you as many of your messmates as can be spared from duty."

" Well, my dear fellow," replied Adrien, " I am glad I can bring reinforcements. I suppose the plea of duty before pleasure will not be accepted ?"

" Hardly, with young ladies. We expect also to have with us, for the reception, a Southern girl of a style of beauty so rare that she might have come direct from Houriland. All the young men say that she is more angel than human."

" Who is this divinity that possesses such wonderful charm ?"

" She is a second cousin of my mother, but I am forbidden by my sisters to tell you her name; they want to surprise you."

Adrien introduced his friend to his brother officers of the wardroom as Mr. John Rendeem, a classmate of his. He was invited to stay for lunch, and consented. Five of Adrien's messmates accepted the invitation for the following day, and made the incautious promise to defend him from the charge of preferring the stern routine of a ship-of-war to the fascination of young ladies' society. Mr. Rendeem laughed as he told them that they would find it a difficult undertaking.

"I would like to assist you," he said; "but I am pledged to be neutral."

After lunch their guest was shown all over the ship. He expressed his astonishment at her ponderous battery, and felt confident she would make a grand record. When he left the vessel he extended a cordial invitation for all of the officers to pay a visit to his father's house when convenient.

On the following evening, at the hour appointed, six officers, clad in the brilliant uniform of the Union navy, ascended the steps of the marble mansion of Mr. Joseph Rendeem, the merchant prince, on Fifth Avenue. As they were ushered into the drawing-room they found a large company assembled, over half of them young ladies, daughters of the best New York families. Brass buttons and gold lace are at all times magnets which attract the admiration of the fair sex, and more so when to them are added charm of youth and single-blessedness. The eyes of the naval officers swept rapidly around the room in search of the star of first magnitude from the South, of which young Rendeem had spoken. All the ladies present were beautiful, yet none outshone the others. Adrien in particular seemed to seek for her. His young host noticed his eager gaze and surmised the object. Coming to him, he told him that the fair Ilian would not arrive before nine o'clock.

"Ilian!" remarked Adrien. "Can this be the Miss Mordine of whom I have heard so much?"

"I think she is, for she came from Boston two months ago with my mother. A Mrs. Verdere, a Southern lady of great wealth, was her aunt, and Miss Mordine inherited all her vast fortune. She stayed at our house for three weeks, and then went for a short visit to Mrs. Hortense, the mother of the manager of her property in New Orleans, at present residing in this city."

"Well, I am delighted at the prospect of seeing this wonderful beauty. Why did she not come for dinner?"

"She is in deep mourning, and only consented to come for an hour when she heard that you were to be of the company. Because of the difficulty experienced in getting you away from your ship, she made it a condition that she must first hear that you were actually here. A messenger has already been sent to inform her of your arrival."

"That is strange; for I have never met Miss Mordine, although I have heard wonderful stories of her intellectual power."

"No description of her can do her justice; she is one of those rare girls who must be seen to be appreciated. In the three weeks that she was at our house I tried to study her, but found something new each day."

"I am anxious to know something of her history. You mention that she is a relative of your mother; where was she born?"

"She was born in England, and it is stated that her mother died in childbirth, and her aunt, who was her mother's only sister, brought her up. They have lived mostly abroad. Now, my gallant hero in blue and gold, you already exert more influence over her than any other young man, for she was always talking about you."

"But we never met."

"She saw you on three occasions in Boston, although you knew it not. As your old classmate, I have been doing ample justice to your character, and now she knows you as well as I do."

"Many thanks for all this, but I am afraid that I shall not come up to the high standard you have measured for me."

"Do not worry on that point. Do you know, I think you both are splendidly mated? I will stand aside for you; but for no other living mortal would I give up my chance to win her."

"John, do not do that; I am not a marrying man; I am wedded to my new profession."

"Wait until you see and hear her, and then good-by to all benedict notions. I speak from experience."

"Who will escort her here this evening?"

"One of the managers of her estate, a Colonel Robert Hortense, a fire-eater of the first class, a red-hot secessionist. Where he got his title of colonel, no one knows. There is a great deal of bark about him, but not much bite, I fancy. He is always talking about what he is going to do when he gets back South. I cannot bear the sight of him. He assumes the air of a guardian to Miss Mordine, and tries to dictate whom she must see and whom to avoid."

"Perhaps he stands in your way as a rival," said Adrien.

"Oh, no; I do not rate him so highly as that."

At this point they were interrupted by several young ladies, and one of them said,—

"Look here, cousin John, we object to councils of war being held without participation by ladies, and we especially protest against your monopoly of Mr. Homerand. He must answer the complaint of neglect of our society, and we are now going to take charge of him."

At this point dinner was announced. Adrien was mated to Miss Alice Rendeem, and the other officers were given charming convoys.

CHAPTER IX.

MEETING OF THE WATERS.

THE Mississippi River at one point is divided by a long island. At the upper end of this island the river is compelled to separate; its reluctance to do so is shown by its turbulent motion, as though protesting a division of its power. At the lower end, however, the meeting of the waters takes place silently, without noise or demonstration. Its united force forms a compact body that carries along every object that comes into contact with its current. This is the analogy of the meeting of Adrien and Ilian, in the house of Mr. Joseph Rendeem, on the eventful evening now to be described.

She had consented to come to the reception given by her cousin, Mrs. Rendeem, conditional on the attendance of Mr. Homerand. Her excuse for this was that she was anxious to meet him. His father had formerly been distinguished, and the son was also celebrated. At this time Ilian was in suspense as to whether her oath was binding, or, as her aunt had expressed it on her dying bed, was null and void. That there was some mystery deep and far-reaching between her aunt and Professor Homerand she was well aware, but the secret had not transpired. Perhaps Adrien might possess some clue. Accordingly, although it was hardly within the bounds of fashionable propriety to go into society so soon after her aunt's death, when she learned that he had accepted the invitation to be present at her cousin's house, she resolved to go there. She made her preparations carefully. The evening was cool for the time of year, so she arrayed herself in a black velvet dress fastened high to the throat. A pearl necklace encircled her dainty throat; solitaire diamond ear-rings and a diamond coronet in her hair were all her ornaments. Eight o'clock found her sitting in the drawing-room of the house where she was staying, waiting for the clock to point to a quarter of nine. Colonel Hortense was the only occupant of the room with her. He was leaning against the mantel-piece in a very unenviable state of mind. As he is connected with our story, a brief description of him may be proper.

Robert Hortense was born in Columbia, South Carolina. His father was one of that large class of persons who insist that the world owes them a living, and who, therefore, take life as easy as possible. He had inherited a small fortune, and he eked it out by genteel gambling. For a gentleman of his grade, a business or a profession was out of the question. He died when his son was fifteen, and his widow, by judicious management, educated her boy as a soldier of fortune, to be on the alert for a favorable opportunity for a rich marriage or some lucky master-stroke. She was a firm believer in the aphorism that all things will come to him who can but wait. Her faith was at length rewarded. In his twenty-fourth year the manager of Mrs. Verdere's estate in South Carolina died, and she procured the position for Robert. This was in 1860. The situation was a lucrative one. Her success encouraged the mother to hope that a marriage might be brought about between her son and Ilian, the niece and heiress of the richest woman in the South. Robert Hortense was slightly built, with light hair and a ferocious moustache of the same color. He had prepared himself for all incidental occurrences by becoming an accomplished swordsman and an unerring marksman. This stood him in hand, for he had already figured in five duels. In the first two he had wounded his adversary each time, coming out of the ordeal untouched. In the third he appeared upon the field with a bright and cheerful smile, and asked that, as he was a little out of practice, he should be granted the privilege of firing one shot at a target, just to get used to the smell of gunpowder. His antagonist was, of course, to do the same. His second thereupon fastened the ace of hearts to a tree and, handing his principal a loaded pistol, counted off twenty paces, and young Hortense, firing at the word "three," sent the bullet through the centre of the card. As he had long practised this feat, it was no difficult performance. He then took the ace of diamonds from his pocket and handed it to the other second, for the benefit of his principal. The exhibition of such accurate shooting and the significant obliteration of the heart on the card was too much for the nerves of his antagonist, and he promptly apologized. The same result followed in the fourth challenge. It was about this time that Hortense assumed the title of colonel, on the ground that a man who has been four times on the field of honor was entitled to such distinction. In the fifth challenge this by-play did not work, for his antagonist did exactly the same thing, and, furthermore, told him that he could cut his name on a target with pistol-shots without any difficulty. This information was not at all assuring to the colonel. The agreement was to fire at the word "three." Hortense had in the two first encounters fired at the word "two." His nerves were not as steady now as they had been when facing men who were not as skilful as himself. He began to consider whether it would not be as well to apologize instead of running the risk of suffering daylight to be sent through his thin body. Matters were hastened before he could decide, and at the word "one" a bullet grazed his temple, and his own went twenty feet wide of the mark. His opponent expressed regret at his own bad marksmanship, and insisted upon another shot, to redeem his credit. The colonel, however, was perfectly satisfied, and after some discussion the principals shook hands. Hortense was not so ferocious nor anxious afterwards to fight more duels. Thus we present him to our readers.

As already stated, Mrs. Hortense had persuaded Ilian to reside with her for a short period. She was living in a handsomely-furnished house, as Ilian, on her aunt's death, had generously doubled the colonel's salary. It is needless to say that, when Mrs. Hortense received Ilian under her roof, she urged her son to make good use of his time, and win, if possible, the young heiress's hand and fortune. On this very evening of the Rendeem party he had endeavored to persuade her to stay away from the reception. Finding that she would not, he had boldly proposed an offer of marriage. He anticipated no difficulty. The girl was young and inexperienced, and how much it would tend to relieve her mind from the burden of her grief to engage herself to a handsome young man of good business habits, and one who was acquainted with all the details of her property. He would take all responsibilty off her shoulders about her large estate. Then, again, his mother would take the place of her aunt, and instruct her in all the duties of a wife. He proposed, but was refused in such a quiet way that he could find no pretext to take offence. Ilian pleaded that it was out of the question to think of marrying so soon after her aunt had been laid in the grave. As she spoke of that dear one who had filled a mother's place to her, tears filled her eyes. The colonel was afraid that if he pleaded any further at present he might injure his case, so he turned the conversation to a subject in which they both felt a strong interest,—the war.

They were deep in this discourse when the carriage was announced. They then left the house for the Rendeem party. While both the colonel and Miss Mordine were in full sympathy with the Southern cause, they were too refined to show partisan feeling in a company composed mostly of Northern people. When they were ushered into the drawing-room all eyes were riveted upon Ilian. The gentlemen hastened forward to be introduced, all except Adrien, who, with one elbow resting upon the mantel-piece, was engaged in conversation with Miss Alice Rendeem, the subject, of course, being the Southern belle, as the ladies termed her.

"What do you think of her, Adrien?" asked his fair companion. She was thus familiar with him, for they had known each other for several years.

For a moment he closely scanned Ilian as she was replying to the many flattering words from those who were being introduced; then, slowly answering the question, he said, "Fascinating and beautiful; a perfect model of nature's handiwork; she is, without exception, the handsomest woman of her style that I have ever seen; but, after all, I prefer brunettes;" and, looking into Miss Rendeem's face with a smile, he added, "especially when they are from the North."

Alice Rendeem was a brunette of the purest type, while her sister Edith was a blonde. There could be no mistaking this direct compliment.

Adrien continued: "Miss Mordine has dangerous eyes; they magnetize, and will yet bring sorrow and trouble to more than one man's heart."

This answer was prophetic, and was also well timed, for he at once made a firm friend of Alice, and soothed the jealousy that a handsome woman feels when a star of superior magnitude comes into her sphere.

Mrs. Rendeem now came up and insisted upon introducing Adrien. Slowly he approached Ilian. As his hand touched hers, a cold chill ran through his frame and a foreboding of evil oppressed him.

Thus the waters met. They had not yet joined all their forces, but the current would only be again separated by death. The meshes of Adrien's fate had been woven by others.

CHAPTER X.

CHAMPION FOR THE SOUTH.

NEVER in the previous life of Ilian had her beauty shone out with such dazzling splendor as after her introduction to Adrien Homerand. Whatever conscientious scruples she may have had in reference to her oath of hatred to the Homerand family, there was no desire on her part, on this eventful evening, to begin her work by hating the son. To say that he was completely carried away would be a mild expression. What the feeling was that filled his heart he did not take time to analyze. He was conscious that a new power had either come into activity within him or taken possession of him from without. Whether it was love or infatuation he cared not; sufficient was it that at his side stood a lovely, radiant girl, with a rare gift of language and a pair of eyes in whose depths of azure shone an intellect not often found in feminine mould. Those eyes beamed on him with such intensity, that, with all his noted presence of mind, he was so overcome that he could hardly answer the questions put to him by a bevy of girls who now surrounded him. They asked him if he would plead guilty to the charge of having, on a number of occasions, declined pressing invitations to sociables, and also to special parties made up for his benefit, but at which he failed to appear. At any former time he would have felt equal to the almost herculean task of holding his own against a dozen girls, but now his intrenchments had all been carried by a single glance of the magnetic eyes of a being whom he then felt was more akin to an angel than our common humanity. Adrien turned to Ilian with a look which was at once interpreted as a desire that she should answer for him. Indeed, she had such a power over other women that there was no feeling of jealousy or envy exhibited towards her. On the contrary, they felt proud of belonging to a sex that could produce such a marvel of beauty, both mental and physical. She therefore quietly answered for Adrien, and said, "Any man who can, in days like the present, set an example of strict adherence to the duties of his position in preference to wasting his time, which belongs to the government that employs him, is a man that every true woman would be proud to call a friend."

The sweet smile, childlike in its expression, that accompanied these words had such an effect, that a number of young ladies at once promptly came forward to take his hand. One of them, however, echoed the sentiments of the others as she said, "Of course, this only applies to naval officers, and not to young men in general; for, if it did, what would the young ladies do for society?"

This created great merriment, and expressions of "Certainly," "Why, of course," were heard on every side, the young men being as enthusiastic on this point as the girls. In fact, they were more so, as they were somewhat jealous of the influence of brass buttons and gold lace.

It was long after midnight when the party broke up. Adrien accompanied Ilian to the door of her residence, much to the disgust of Colonel Hortense, who sat in the carriage, listening with jealous ears to the conversation of the couple before him. The impulse of a deadly hatred sprang up within him, for he now realized that all his chance of winning the hand of the great heiress was gone. Only by the death of his rival could he hope to marry the girl that he loved for her wealth, perhaps, more than for her beauty. Another agent potent for evil was thus raised on Adrien's pathway. After leaving Miss Mordine and the colonel at their residence, the driver of the carriage, which belonged to her, was instructed to take Mr. Homerand to the Battery. Here a boat awaited him and the other officers, who reached the place shortly after he did. A new impulse was added to his ambition, and he became more zealous than ever.

In the afternoon of the second day after the reception Adrien and the other officers who were with him called to pay their parting respects to Mrs. Rendeem and her daughters. Their ship was under sailing orders to proceed to Sandy Hook, in order to test the compasses and exercise the crew in the evolutions of a ship-of-war. A week was to be spent in this way, after which they were to return to their anchorage off the Battery and await assignment to duty, which they expected would be in the waters of the Gulf of Mexico and vicinity. They found Miss Ilian Mordine at the Rendeem mansion, and an hour was spent in pleasant conversation. Ilian was in her brightest mood. She had the rare gift of talking upon half a dozen different subjects at the same time with that number of persons.

The principal topic was the one then most prominent before the public mind,—the right of the Southern States to withdraw from the Union. Ilian alone held to the affirmative, and such was her power of persuasion that the paymaster of Adrien's vessel, who was of the party, said, playfully, "Miss Mordine, may I use St. Paul's quotation?"

"Certainly, was the reply."

"Well, your logic has such weight that almost you persuade me to be a rebel."

Several of the others aquiesced in this statement.

Miss Edith now came forward as the champion of the negative side. "Paymaster," she said, "where do you get the authority for this quotation? I am afraid you do not read your Bible very often. In the first place, St. Paul did not use any such words. It was King Agrippa that uttered them, when the great apostle made his defence before him; and some commentators insist that he used them sarcastically; and he did not say that he was almost persuaded to be a rebel, but a Christian. Now, what is your answer? Surely, you were not ironical?"

This ingenious turning of the conversation redeemed the

day for the Northern party, and the paymaster felt as though he had been completely quashed. The laughter at his expense was loud and boisterous. He enjoyed it as much as the rest, and declared that he would be very careful how he quoted Scripture hereafter.

Miss Edith followed up her advantage by saying, in a merry tone, to Ilian, "Now, fair cousin of mine, you must not sow the seeds of rebellion in the hearts of these Northern officers. I will stand forth as their protector."

Ilian laughed good naturedly, and looked round among the gentlemen for one to support her in setting forth her view of the case. Her eyes rested upon Adrien. As he met her gaze a cold chill flashed over him with the speed of electricity. There could be no mistaking her appeal. Her words as she set forth the rights of the seceded States had made a deep impression upon him. He now remembered that he was a citizen of the old Bay State; also that he was the son of Boston's great professor and the grandson of the honored Judge Rathmine. His answer was dignified, yet blended with a smile which would have charmed many a woman,—

"Miss Mordine, your arguments in favor of the South have been ably presented, and I admit that I feel the force of much of what you have spoken. If the issue rested between us alone the war would end at once. But, as you are well aware, the controversy has gone from the hands of the statesmen who have argued these points for many years, and the issue must be settled on the field of battle. We are now compelled to say farewell for a period, as our ship leaves at daylight in the morning, and we have to be on board by sundown this evening. When we return next week we all hope to have the great pleasure of hearing more of such skilful arguments, and we will feel honored if you will visit our ship."

As Adrien took Ilian's hand to say good-by, he noticed a change of expression in her eyes. Her manner, however, was apparently as cordial as ever, and, with a smile, she said to him and the other officers, "He laughs best who laughs the last."

A moment afterwards they had left the house and were hurrying to the Battery to meet the sundown boat.

That night Ilian retired early to her chamber, but not to

sleep. She walked the floor, pondering the momentous question which was agitating her mind. Was her oath binding, or was it null and void? The clock of a neighboring church struck the midnight hour, and still she was engaged with the problem, should she hate Adrien for her oath's sake? Her happiness, she was vividly conscious, was bound up in his life. There was no doubt in her own mind of the fact that she loved him. And now was the time to destroy the germs of this affection, if she felt that she must not marry him. As the very thought of marriage suggested itself to her, there came a fearful revulsion of feeling that she could not account for. What course should she pursue now? More than at any former period of her life she felt the want of a mother to advise and direct her. Among her friends there was no one to whom she cared to unburden her heart. She must rely upon her own judgment. It is at all times a difficult matter for even a superior mind to sit in calm judgment upon one's own feelings and render an impartial decision. Ilian felt this as she tried to weigh the question of her attitude towards Adrien. Hate him she could not. No, not if a thousand oaths demanded it. Love him she must, and yet marry him she dare not. Why? yes, why? But to this question there came no answer. Weary and perplexed, she lay down upon her bed, and her dreams were troubled. Adrien had refused to stand by her in the controversy of the afternoon, and she felt annoyed at him for it, and yet his answer could not be found fault with. She dreamed that she was standing by the sea-shore, and heard his voice call to her from over the deep for help, but she made no movement to render him any aid. Why should she do so? He would not take her side when she appealed to him for aid. Again she dreamed that she was herself alone upon the ocean, drifting about helplessly, and the night was dark and dreary, and the wild waves were dashing against her frail craft. She called upon Adrien to help her, as the boat was sinking; then came a heavy sea and swamped it, and she went down, but strong arms raised her out of the stormy waters, she was folded in a loving embrace, and was back once more in a warm room; when, as the light fell upon the face of her preserver, it was not that of Adrien, as she had fondly hoped, but her dead aunt, and she heard her name called, "Ilian, darling, I am ever watching over you; go to sleep, my child; you have been dreaming." And so she slept on through the night, peacefully and calmly.

> " Peaceful be the maiden's sleep;
> From the dreams of terror free;
> May all who wake to weep,
> Rest again as sweet as she."

CHAPTER XI.

SHIP AHOY.

THE night was clear, the moon being three-quarters full. The United States ship-of-war —— was at anchor off Sandy Hook, and Adrien Homerand had the watch from eight to twelve. As he walked the deck, his thoughts were full of Ilian and of her remarkable mental ability in presenting the cause of the South. Nine o'clock had just been reported to him, and the bell struck two notes. This was the signal for quietness throughout the ship. A few minutes after, the quartermaster of the watch reported that a small steamer was heading towards them, apparently a navy-yard tug, and no doubt bringing important orders from the commandant of the navy-yard. This was reported to the captain. Adrien mounted to the bridge, and his powerful voice could be heard far over the waters, " Steamer ahoy ! What steamer is that?"

" The ' Ajax,' from the navy-yard, with despatches and supplies for your ship. I will come along-side."

This announcement brought all hands on deck, and the most intense excitement prevailed. The orders, coming so unexpectedly and at so late an hour, meant, no doubt, that the ship must go to sea, perhaps in the morning. The tug was soon fast along-side, and fresh provisions and supplies were rapidly passed on board. A long official document was handed to the captain. Ten minutes after, the word was passed along the deck by the boatswain and his mates, "All hands up anchor for sea."

Great was the disappointment among the officers, as all had expected another week off the Battery. Several receptions had been arranged for. Adrien, in particular, had invited a number of friends, including **the** Rendeem **family** and Miss Mordine. He had looked forward to meeting the latter with feelings of eager delight. **Now, by this unexpected order to go to** sea at a moment's notice, **his air-castles were levelled to the ground.** The captain called all his officers into his cabin, **and informed** them that he **was** instructed by **the Navy Department** to proceed to sea at once, and cruise for **five days** between Cape Henry and Cape Hatteras, in search of several vessels reported as flying the Confederate flag. They had already captured, so far as known, three schooners bound home from the West Indies. No details were given of the size or rig of the vessels, but one was said **to** be a large steamer, heavily armed. The captain further told them that he had sealed orders which were to be opened on the fifth day.

"**Now,** gentlemen," he continued, "as we are liable at any **hour,** after passing Sandy **Hook, to** be engaged in conflict with one or more **of these** piratical vessels, I will expect you to get **your** divisions into fighting **trim as soon** as possible, and for **that** purpose it will be necessary **to** drill all night. As we **have** three hundred able-bodied men on board, we can give **a** good **account** of ourselves in any ordeal of battle."

In half an hour from the time that the orders were received, the ship was under way and steaming out to sea. The wind was moderate, **but** there was **a heavy** swell, which made her roll heavily, and created a scene that **baffles** description. Over one hundred of her men, who were landsmen, were stretched all over her decks sea-sick, and were mixed up with the ship's stores and fresh provisions. Divisions were drilling, sail was being made, the supplies were stored in the hold, and expletives were frequently used by both officers and **men that** certainly would not adorn a Sunday-school volume. The moon went down at eleven, and the night became very dark. By this **time something like** order was restored, and the drilling went on.

Under the persuasion of **the** officers, most of the sea-sick **men** were working for all **they** were worth. The sea had moderated, and the vessel was speeding along at ten knots an hour. **Just as the** midnight bell was tolling, a startled cry rang through **the** ship,—"Sail ho! close aboard." The engines were stopped, and a large steamship loomed up on the starboard beam a hundred yards away. Battle-lanterns were burning at all her gun-ports, showing that she was a man-of-war, and ready for action. Not a gun had been loaded on Adrien's vessel, and all felt that they were completely at the mercy of one of the enemy's ships. They were unprepared to fight, too near to attempt to run, and not close enough to carry her by boarding. The excitement was intense. The stranger hailed, "Ship ahoy! What ship is that?" No answer was returned, but the captain passed the order to load with five-second shells and heavy charges. Again was the hail given; still no answer. A third time it was repeated, in a quick, angry tone, which, to a seaman's trained ear, meant that, if not answered at once, something more expressible than words would follow. The guns being now all loaded and pointed at the unknown craft, the desired answer was given slowly and deliberately, in order to gain more time for the training of the battery,—

"This is the United States sloop-of-war ———. What ship is that?"

For fully a minute there was no reply. Strong men held their breath, as each passing second might reveal the flash of the stranger's guns, and the crashing of her shot would send many brave fellows into eternity. The suspense was terrible. At last came the words, pronounced with a suspicious intonation,—

"This is the United States ship 'San Jacinto.' Send a boat on board."

Language fails to describe the relief to all hands at this intelligence. As the captain of the "San Jacinto" was the senior, a boat was sent on board with an officer to convey the news of the privateers. It had been anticipated, however. They had heard of it two days previous, and had taken Adrien's ship for one of these vessels. The "San Jacinto" went on her way, and was soon lost in the darkness.

Naval officers may criticize this incident as gross carelessness. It should be remembered that this was at the beginning of the war, and neither ship carried mast-head or side-lights. Each was searching for an enemy's vessel, and in the darkness came close aboard unexpectedly. Many worse mistakes were made before the war was ended. At the end of the appointed five days the sealed orders were opened, and found to contain the following instructions:

"SIR,—If you fail to come up with any of the enemy's vessels within five days after leaving Sandy Hook, proceed with the ship under your command, and report to flag-officer William M. McKean, on the United States ship 'Niagara' for duty in the West Gulf Blockading Squadron."

Four days afterward, the ship anchored off Key West, remaining there a week. Word came the day before leaving that a small privateer had come up one dark night with the United States frigate "St. Lawrence," and mistaking her for a Northern merchant ship, had boldly fired into her. The great frigate opened her ports and returned a single broadside from her port battery, after which she lowered her boats to pick up the survivors of the saucy craft. All they found was a few pieces of broken spars. The crew of the ill-fated privateer had been swept out of existence in a second of time.

This story has been denied. It is said that the "Petrel," which was the name of the schooner, endeavored to escape from the "St. Lawrence," but that the latter fired upon her and sunk her.

CHAPTER XII.

WEST GULF SQUADRON.

WITHIN a week after leaving Key West, Adrien's ship had reported to flag-officer McKean, and was assigned with several other vessels to blockade the passes of the Mississippi. There the days and weeks dragged slowly along. Occasionally there was a little excitement to relieve the tedious monotony. On the 12th of October the rebel ram "Manasses" came down to attack the squadron, but was driven back, as was also a flotilla of gun-boats. Autumn and winter passed away with only a guerilla warfare carried on along the coast blockaded by the West Gulf Squadron.

As this story does not aspire to be a history of the war, except as the several incidents come within the experience of our principal characters, I must pass on to the month of February, 1862, when flag-officer David G. Farragut relieved Commodore McKean. Important operations were to be undertaken,—a bold effort was to be made to capture **New Orleans**. That city was defended at the head **of** the passes **by two** strong fortifications called **St. Philip** and Jackson. The "Hartford" was the new flag-ship. **She was what was then** called **a spar-deck** sloop-of-war, and carried **a heavy battery of twenty-four guns.** In the month **of April, a** large squadron was assembled **below the forts; it was the most** powerful one that **had mustered under the Union flag.** There were altogether seventeen ships-of-war, **and a fleet** of twenty **mortar-schooners, each** carrying **a thirteen-inch mortar, and a flotilla of six gun-boats attached to the latter division.** The mortar flotilla was under the charge **of Commander** (afterwards **Admiral) D. D.** Porter. The whole number **of** vessels amounted **to forty-three.** There were other ships in the West **Gulf Squadron,** but they drew too much water to cross the bar **at the mouth** of the river.

On the 18th of April the bombardment **of** Forts St. Philip and Jackson was begun, and early **on the morning of** the 24th **the** squadron steamed up **to the** doomed forts, and at close quarters threw in heavy charges of **grape and canister, and one by one passed them going up the river.**

The Confederate flotilla was **met above the forts and destroyed, and at noon of the 25th Flag-officer Farragut anchored before the city with his fleet. Everything in the defenceless place was now in the** utmost confusion. **Up and down the levees great destruction of** property **took place,— steamboats, ships,** cotton, in fact, everything combustible, was **set on fire by the frantic and** excitable inhabitants. Captain **Bailey, whose ship, the forty-gun** frigate "Colorado," was **unable to cross** the **bar, but who** had command of one of the **divisions, was** sent ashore to demand the surrender of the city, **and that the Union** standard **be** hoisted upon **the** public **buildings.**

The rage **and mortification** of the Creoles, who were **the bulk of** the **population, would be hard to** describe. **The insults which they showered** upon **the landing-party was of no avail, and the mayor, finding an evasive answer would not be accepted, and as all the Confederate soldiers had been withdrawn,** sullenly surrendered the **city. Once** again the United States flag waved **over the** mint, **the first time in twelve months.** It **was hauled down the** following day by a few hot-headed fanatics, who thus foolishly endangered the safety of the city. A landing-party of marines and seamen was sent on shore, the flag was rehoisted, and the building guarded until the arrival of General Butler, on the 1st of May, with a large force of troops. The place was then turned over to him. Martial law was proclaimed,—a new *régime* was established in the history of the great Queen City of the South.

The news of this brilliant victory created great rejoicing throughout the Northern States, and a corresponding depression prevailed all through the South. Many thought the war must now come speedily to an end, and that peace was certain to follow. Very few, comparatively, foresaw that three long, weary years of harder fighting than had yet taken place would intervene before the sound of the war-drum would cease in the land.

We will now go back to Adrien, whom we have neglected during these eight eventful months. His ship had been engaged in all of the fighting that took place, and he received the commendation of his captain before all hands for the high state of discipline and splendid training of his division. He received the offer of the command of one of the small captured gun-boats from Flag-officer Farragut, but his commanding officer prevailed upon him to remain where he was. He valued his services too highly to part with him.

From time to time Adrien received many letters, not only from his father and mother, and his numerous friends, but especially from Miss Alice Rendeem. She had fallen desperately in love with him from the hour at their reception in September, when he told her that he preferred Northern brunettes to Southern blondes. Alice, who was herself a beauty of a high order, had fondly cherished the remembrance of this complimentary speech. Perhaps, if the Southern star had not crossed his horizon, he might have laid his heart at her feet, and certainly she would have made him a most excellent wife; but it was not so written in the book of his fate. He had received only one letter from Ilian since their last meeting. It was brief, and in answer to one that he had written to her from Key West, in which he expressed his regret at the unexpected departure from New York. Her letter was non-committal; she told him that, compelled by the demands of her large estate, she was going to risk a journey to South Carolina. Only her maid and Mrs.

Hortense and her son, the colonel, were to accompany her. She had procured a pass through the lines, and would set out on the following week. Later on, Miss Rendeem informed him that she had received a few lines from Ilian dated from Charleston, in which she informed them that she was going to New Orleans to look after her property there. This was the latest news, and it was five months old. If she was then in the city, he reflected, he might see her; perhaps she would send him word where to call upon her, as she knew the ship to which he was then attached.

General Butler had restored order in New Orleans. Adrien went ashore nearly every day when the weather was fine. His uniform, however, was a barrier to the obtaining of information. He called upon several real-estate agents, and inquired whether they knew where Miss Ilian Mordine resided. As she held considerable real estate in the city, he doubted not that her whereabouts would be known to them. He was invariably met by the ironical inquiry whether, on the supposition that the Yankee fleet were going to remain until the day of judgment, he wished to purchase a residence. At last, however, fortune favored him. Towards the close of May, as he was walking up Canal Street one day, he met a Confederate officer in uniform, with his arm in a sling, looking pale and dejected. The face seemed familiar, and he stopped; so did the stranger. The latter frowned, then relaxed, and held out his hand, saying,—

"Adrien, is it thus we meet? You in blue, and one of the victors; I in gray, wounded, and a prisoner on parole. A year ago we were at college, and classmates, and now we are——"

"Friends, the same as we were in the days gone by," interrupted Adrien, as he grasped the unwounded hand of his college chum.

"Ned Burrow, my dear fellow, I am delighted to meet you, and profoundly grieved for your misfortune. Tell me where you were wounded."

"At Fort Jackson. I was in command of one of the divisions; a shell came in through the casemate and exploded; a piece of it wounded my left arm and breast. I was paroled when the fort surrendered, and am now living at home with my mother and sister. My father is up the river in command of a regiment."

"Ned, my heart for you is the same as ever, and if I can be of service in an honorable way, command me."

"Ten thousand thanks. I may need your kind offices for my mother and sister. The hand of General Butler is heavy upon our city and its inhabitants."

"My father is a friend of the general," said Adrien, "and I know that he will grant any reasonable request I may ask. Will your mother and sister permit me to call upon them?"

"My mother would receive kindly any friend of mine; but my sister, Lulu, is what you would call an uncompromising little secessionist. I am afraid that she would not extend a cordial greeting to an officer of the Federal navy. However, the ice must be broken, and it may as well be done now as at a later period. Come with me to our house."

On the way, Adrien asked Ned whether he knew Miss Mordine, and where she was."

"Certainly I do," he replied; "she is in Charleston. Are you acquainted with her?"

"Yes; I met her several times. Her last letter informed me that she was going South, and I was anxious to meet her again."

"Then she has written to you? That fact alone will open for you the door of every Southern home. You were always in luck at college, and your good fortune follows you."

Ten minutes' walk brought them to a large brick house, the outward appearance of which indicated it as the residence of cultured people. The first glance in the hall and drawing-room, as the massive door opened to the ring of the young master, confirmed this impression. Ned welcomed Adrien to his home, and asked him to wait in the parlor till he had himself prepared his mother and sister for the interview, which we will describe in the next chapter.

CHAPTER XIII.

NEW ORLEANS.

During the civil war the women of the Southern States were the most unrelenting and bitter in their demonstrations of hostility to the North. Nowhere was this fact more conspicuous than in New Orleans. General Butler has often been severely censured for the harsh measures which he employed to repress the abominable insults offered at times to persons belonging to the Union army and navy; but what he did in this matter was for the safety and welfare of the city. I mention these facts as a prelude to the reception which Adrien received at the Burrows mansion.

Mrs. Burrows came into the drawing-room with her son, and, after being introduced to Mr. Homerand gave him a cordial welcome. She told him that Ned had often spoken about him, and that the reputation of his worthy father was known all over the South.

"You are the first Federal officer who has crossed our threshold since the war began," she added; and she gave him greeting, not only for the sake of the old college days spent with her son, but also from the welcome intelligence that he was a friend of Miss Mordine's.

At this point Mrs. Burrows was interrupted by the entrance of her daughter Lulu. The young lady was of medium height, with dark hair, piercing black eyes, and a small mouth. She was one of the belles of the city, and was decidedly handsome when smiling, but when she was angry she was, to say the least, not at all attractive. Her mother and brother both spoke,—

"Lulu, this is Mr. Adrien Homerand, who is also the friend of——"

Lulu did not give them time to finish. The sight of the blue uniform, brass buttons, and gold lace acted upon her like the proverbial red flag to a bull. The frown on her face settled deeper, and was like a heavy, dark cloud descending upon the landscape. A storm was brewing, and it came. The long pent-up wrath of her nature had been seeking some victim on which to explode, and now found vent.

"Mother, I am surprised that you should forget the dignity of a Southern lady by giving a welcome to a Yankee officer beneath our roof. Father to-day is at the head of his regiment, perhaps in battle, and here we have one of his bitterest foes. Ned, I cannot find words to express my indignation at you for bringing this man here. He is one of the officers of the fleet by which you were wounded, and that terrible shell may have come from his ship. Your wounds are not yet healed, and yet you associate with those who come with fire and sword to invade our native State. I am ashamed to own you as my brother."

"Lulu, this gentleman is my old classmate."

"Then so much the worse, for now he is your enemy, and holds you by the throat."

Adrien was aware that the best way was to let the tempest exhaust itself. Then, looking full into her face with all the power of his great brown eyes, he said, "Miss Burrows, pardon me if I have intruded upon these premises. Your brother and myself were very closely associated at college. I have often heard him speak in glowing terms of his beautiful sister; I felt I almost knew you, and was anxious to see you. I am here as your brother's guest, but if my presence is distasteful to you, I will beg leave to withdraw. I hope you will pardon me if I say that your lovely lips were never made to utter unkind words."

This reply brought a gleam of sunshine into Lulu's face. Women, as a rule, are not proof against flattery, and she was no exception. The frown disappeared from her face, and her mother finished the sentence that the impetuous girl had interrupted,—

"Lulu, Mr. Homerand is a friend, and also a correspondent, of Miss Ilian Mordine."

"Then," answered the girl, now radiant, "I bid you thrice welcome. I hope you will pardon any thing I may have said that would wound your feelings. I have been sorely tried since the occupation of our city by the Federal troops. This very morning two of the minions of Butler forced their way into the house and threatened to turn us out, to confiscate all we have, and to use these premises as an office for the provost marshal. Their language was insolent, and I have been chafing under the insult all day."

"Let me assure you, Miss Burrows," replied Adrien, "that General Butler is too much of a gentleman to insult defenceless women. Many things that he knows nothing about are done by his subordinates in his name, but the odium is cast upon him. I will call upon him to-morrow morning; he is a warm friend of my father's, and I feel sure that hereafter no one will molest you. I will also be your bond that no disloyal demonstration will be made from this house."

It is needless to say that Adrien spent a very pleasant afternoon and evening. He stayed for dinner, and entertained his hostesses with descriptions of his meeting with Ilian and also the Rendeem family. There was also much to say about the old college days and of their former classmates. Dr. Rechard, he was told, was at Vicksburg, surgeon of a regiment, and he also learned particulars of the others who had left the University before Commencement, all of whom had joined the Southern army. So far as heard from, two had been taken prisoners, and one besides Ned was severely wounded.

It was late when Adrien rose to take his departure. He was warmly invited to visit them as often as possible. As he took Lulu's hand, she said, with an arch smile,—

"I hope you do not think unkindly of me for my rather violent reception of you."

"It would be impossible for me to do so," was the reply. "You remember that I told you that your lovely lips were not made to utter unkind words. Now I know it as a positive fact."

Mrs. Burrows, with tears in her eyes, thanked him for his kind offer to see the general in the morning, and Ned insisted upon walking down to the levee with him. Adrien kept his promise, and called upon General Butler on the following forenoon. He was cordially welcomed, and obtained an order which set forth that any one molesting Mrs. Burrows or her family in any way would be severely dealt with. This was sent to her house by an orderly. Adrien made frequent calls at the Burrows mansion, and other doors were opened to him that were closed to his brother officers.

The summer of 1862 passed away in New Orleans and

vicinity without any special occurrence of note. The yellow-fever, which, it had been confidently predicted, would commit terrible ravages in the ranks of the Northern invaders, failed to make its appearance. This was owing, no doubt, to the efficient sanitary measures which General Butler had employed. He taught the inhabitants of New Orleans most salutary lessons in hygiene. A future generation may render him the gratitude for this which he so eminently deserved. He certainly received none from those whom he directly benefited. Never had a city been so well governed. The very name of Butler was a terror to evil-doers.

If space permitted, the author, who was in the Gulf Squadron two years and a half, and in New Orleans during the whole time of General Butler's administration, could give numerous citations from his personal experience in support of this statement. There was a strong under current of ill-feeling exhibited in New Orleans on all safe occasions against the officers and men of the Union forces. Many families were very bitter and vindictive.

One night, late in the autumn of that year, an adventure took place that has much to do with the publication of this story and the unfolding of its secret in its present form to the public.

The popularity of Adrien had spread in a wonderful manner. Invitations poured in upon him, and he was a welcome guest in the homes of the leading citizens. His brother officers chaffed him a great deal about this. Another significant fact was that the five officers who had gone with him to the Rendeem party in New York were often included in these select invitations. The paymaster especially was made much of. There were times when Adrien was asked to bring some of the others belonging to his vessel who were not of the above five. No other ship was thus favored. This partiality was attributed to the fascinating manner of their "Count Chesterfield." Whenever he was off duty in the evening, he went to a reception.

On the particular night above mentioned, about eleven o'clock, he was returning to his ship. As he passed a lonely street near the levee he saw, by the feeble rays of a gas-light, an officer of the Union navy with his back against a fence and a small revolver in his hand. He was keeping at bay half a dozen ruffians armed with bowie-knives. **Adrien heard, amidst** their uttered curses, the words, " Death to the Yankee hound." Without a moment's hesitation he came up in **the rear of** the scoundrels, and before they were aware **of** it three **of** them were knocked to **the** ground by blows from his powerful fist. Then, placing himself at the side **of** the officer, he said **to him, "** I will stand **by you for all I am worth."**

There **was no cause for further action. The attacking** party fled in all **directions, leaving two of their number** prostrate upon the pavement.

The **two** officers **walked together to the boat-landing. The** stranger **said to** Adrien, **" I am indebted to you for my life; may I know** your name?"

" With pleasure. I am Acting Master Adrien Homerand, **of the** Union navy. Whom have I been able to serve?"

" **I am an** acting ensign attached to the United States steamer ' Tennessee.' Our vessel is made fast to the wharf, **and we** have several spare state-rooms on board. Can I offer **you one for the** night?"

" **No,** thanks; I **have the** midnight watch, and must go **on board."**

" **Well, then, can I have** the pleasure of your company to **lunch to-morrow at noon?"**

" Certainly, **I have no** other engagement, and **I will be** pleased **to meet the brave** defenders of the ' Varruna.' I believe **they are all on your** ship."

" **Yes; they were** transferred **to the** ' Tennessee ' **when the city was** captured. **I joined her in** September, **but was not on the ' Varruna.' "**

From that hour there sprang **up** between these two men a **warm friendship that was to last until** death parted them. **The survivor, the author of these** pages, will carry to his **grave the tender recollection of that** manly form, **over** whose **head the dark clouds of** adversity **were then hanging.**

CHAPTER XIV.

THE GREAT CONSPIRACY.

A WEEK after the adventure recorded in the last chapter the acting ensign was the officer of the forenoon watch on the steamship "Tennessee." A young man came on board and asked for him. He gave his name as Henry Ormond, and explained that he was the bearer of an invitation for a reception to be given by his mother. Mrs. Ormond said in her note that, while she had not the pleasure of knowing him personally, yet her friend, Mr. Adrien Homerand, had mentioned the exciting incident of the previous week, and had also spoken in such flattering terms of him that it would give her much pleasure if he would come with Mr. Homerand on the following evening. The invitation was promptly accepted. Mr. Ormond was invited to remain for lunch, but declined on the score of urgent business. He was a typical young Southerner. While affable and genial to one who had been invited to his mother's house, he was cold and haughty to two other officers who were introduced to him. Perhaps he considered his position in society compromised by going on board of a Yankee war-ship. That same evening the acting ensign went on board of Adrien's ship and showed him the invitation.

"Glad you received it, my boy," said Adrien; "it is to be a swell affair. Go in uniform. Mrs. Ormond believes in every one being true to their principles, and would rather see you in uniform than in citizen's clothes; her husband is colonel of a regiment of Louisiana volunteers, stationed near Mobile. She is a native of the State of New York, and is a diplomat of the first water. Admiral Farragut is invited; so is General Butler, and a number of officers, both of the army and navy. The influential Northern connections of the Ormonds make them very popular; and the family is one of the best in New Orleans."

The next evening was bright and beautiful, with a full moon. At nine o'clock the drawing-room of the Ormond mansion was filled with the leading citizens of New Orleans and the ladies of their families. Brilliant uniforms were conspicuous, and good feeling prevailed. Admiral Farragut and General Butler sent regrets at being unable to be present, but they were well represented. Mrs. Ormond gave a very cordial welcome to the acting ensign as he was presented by Adrien. She assured him that she would be glad to see him at any time when he found it convenient to call.

"Mr. Homerand," she continued, turning to that gentleman, "I have a surprise in store for you this evening. You will meet an old friend who will come on purpose to see you."

"Is it a lady or a gentleman?"

"Whom would you like to see the most, Dr. Rechard, your old college chum, or Miss Mordine?"

"Both of them. Will they be here?"

"No, only one; which would you prefer?"

"Well, I suppose if a choice were given me, and I could only take one, I would say Miss Mordine."

"Your eyes have already betrayed you, and there is no supposition about it. Like a sensible man you would vote for the woman every time. Do you know I think you are very fortunate in having such an interest taken in you by the beautiful, the wealthy, and accomplished Miss Mordine?"

"What! Is the fair Ilian in the city? and will she come to this reception?"

"Ah!" said his hostess; "you must be on very familiar terms with the young lady, to call her by her first name."

"I heard the name used so much in the Rendeem family, and forgot myself."

"Yes, I understand; I will not betray your secret. Your face tells its own story. Here she comes; I must go and greet her."

All eyes were now centred upon a young lady approaching to pay her respects to the hostess. She was escorted by an elderly, clerical-looking gentleman, to whom she bore a strong resemblance. "An uncle of her late mother," whispered Mrs. Ormond, as she left him to go and welcome her guests. Adrien had always, since the hour when he first met Ilian, thought her beautiful; but now he was lost in wonder and amazement. "Angelic" was the only term that he felt was appropriate to express her magnificent appearance. She was dressed in a costume of pale-blue silk, cut square in the neck, exhibiting her splendid throat, which was encircled by a diamond necklace. A coronet of the same precious gems sparkled in her golden hair. Her eyes were searching inquisitively amidst the throng. When they fell upon Adrien, her whole face lit up at once with a brightened expression. Mrs. Ormond alone knew of its cause, and her generous heart rejoiced that both were apparently so well suited to each other. This was confirmed when in a few moments the hands of the lovers had clasped and the sparkle of both their eyes told the old, old story; they loved, and their love was reciprocal.

We have not space to tell of all that took place during the rest of the evening. The remembrance of it to the author is like one of those dreams of paradise which are sometimes permitted to mortals where youth and beauty meet, and unalloyed joy and happiness are the products of the hour.

The ball was a great success. The bitter feelings that afterwards became so intense between the North and the South had not yet developed as keenly as they did two years later. Mrs. Ormond was, indeed, as Adrien had expressed it, a diplomat of the first water, and her object in bringing so many officers of the Federal forces in contact with the best families of New Orleans was to ameliorate the harsh conditions that were at times forced upon the citizens as the result of martial law. In this she had been successful. A conspiracy, however, had been gotten up without her knowledge, that would, if it had been carried out, brought down upon the city perhaps its entire destruction. The complete history of this plot has never been made known; but one fact has been vouched for. Not one of the individuals engaged in it ever distinguished himself in any way during the remainder of the war; nor was there a single prominent name among them. It was confined apparently to a few hot-headed young fanatics, who never once gave thought to the disastrous consequences that would be certain to fall upon innocent individuals. The plan of the conspirators was to take the opportunity afforded by the ball at the Ormond mansion, in order to assassinate General Butler and several of his obnoxious officials, and then make prisoners of Commodore Farragut and the prominent officers present. It was purposed to convey the prisoners through the lines by night, a raid being made for that purpose. The signal of success was to be three red rockets. The immediate evacuation of New Orleans was then to be demanded from the Federal forces, under threat of executing Flag-officer Farragut and the officers captured with him.

This project was so wild and visionary, that it is a wonder so many could be found to give it countenance. The unexpected absence of both General Butler and Commodore Farragut from the ball checkmated the attempt to carry out the plot. If it had been tried, the result would have been fearful to contemplate. Blood would have flowed like water, the city of New Orleans would have been utterly destroyed. The secret leaked out after the supper. Several of the conspirators were made incautious by a too free indulgence in champagne, and expressed their disappointment at being unable to carry out their project. The remarks were overheard by young Ormond. Alarmed at the proposed breach of hospitality, he hastened to his mother and told her what had been contemplated. Mrs. Ormond was indignant beyond expression. She sought out Ilian and asked her advice. It was a serious moment. If the plot should come to the ears of General Butler, he would at once take vigorous measures and arrest the prominent individuals then in the house. Ilian's eyes flashed the scorn and anger which she felt at the attempting of such base measures in the name of the South. Prompt measures, however, were necessary. She sought out a gentleman whom she knew, and together, within fifteen minutes, they ferreted the secret. The ringleaders were then quietly warned that if they did not escape beyond the city limits by noon of the next day, they would be delivered up to the provost marshal. They left without ceremony, not daring to remain within the power of the dreaded military governor. There was a rumor that they were members of the band called the "Gray Tigers."

With her feelings wrought up by the indignation she could hardly keep within bounds, Ilian came to Adrien and said, "The South is fighting an honorable war for her rights, and needs no assassin's knife to enable her to keep out of the Union. If that is resorted to, the years that she will have to repent in sackcloth and ashes will be long and bitter."

"Amen to those sentiments," answered Mrs. Ormond.

This plot was only made known to five individuals then present. They thought it prudent to guard the secret. It was after four o'clock when the party broke up.

CHAPTER XV.

THE TEMPTATION.

ADRIEN, as the favored friend of the rich heiress, was the lion of the hour. Invitations were showered upon him from every direction. He made the condition, in accepting them, that his brother officers should be included.

Commodore Farragut, who was now made a rear-admiral, believed that conciliation was a better method for the restoring of fraternal union than stringent coercion. He encouraged the social feeling between the officers of his fleet and the families of New Orleans.

It had been fortunate for Adrien that the ship remained so long at New Orleans. Rumors, however, were abroad that she was soon to have a tour of duty on the blockade. He resolved, accordingly, to make the best use of his time with Ilian. Although no declaration was made by him to that purpose, it was plainly manifested that his love was returned. Two weeks following the Ormond ball he resolved to bring matters to a climax. He had seen her every day since her return, but she parried all attempts he made to come to a definite understanding.

It was a beautiful afternoon, and Ilian was anxious to do some shopping, so they walked up Canal Street together. He was on the watch for the opportunity which he felt would come.

"Why do you look so sad?" was the gentle inquiry, as her brilliant eyes looked into his.

"Because our ship will probably leave for the blockade off Mobile next week."

"Do you wish to go? Do you prefer the prospect of the dreary monotony of lying at anchor ten miles from the land to that of daily promenades in the Queen City of the South, to say nothing of the receptions every evening?"

"How can you ask such a question? The very thought of it is a torture. How can I be happy away from ——" Here he hesitated.

"New Orleans?" suggested Ilian.

"No; that was not the word."

"Oh, what was it?"

"You know."

"How should I know? You never told me."

"Ilian, are you blind?"

"No; I do not think I am."

"Let me explain," was the passionate rejoinder.

"Not in the public street; but go on. What was the place you said you could not be happy away from?"

"It was not a place."

"What was it, then?"

"It was you. Ilian, my darling, I love you, and the prospect of going away from you, even for a short season, is maddening, especially as that Colonel Hortense, who arrived three days ago, is hanging around you all the time."

"You have nothing to fear from him; but let me ask, if you feel as you say you do, why go to the blockade?"

"How can I prevent it? I am attached to the ship as one of her regular officers, and we are short of our complement; and my commanding officer would not approve of my application for leave, and would oppose my being detached."

"The remedy is very simple."

"What is it? I am anxious to know."

"Resign your acting appointment."

"Resign! You surely do not mean that. What would become of me?"

"In what way?"

"Well, financially."

"Your father is rich, and you have your grandmother's inheritance in your own right."

"Yes, that is true; but my prospects in life would be ruined."

"I do not think so. There are many lucrative positions in this city open to a man of your genius and education; besides, I have a host of friends, and my influence would be at your service. You have felt it already."

"In what way? I know that the mention of your name has been potent."

"Have not the doors of the best society been open to you exclusively? Have you not entered homes and been made welcome where no other officer of the army or navy has entered except when they came as your friends, and then **only with you?"**

"**Ah!**" said Adrian; "this, then, explains the problem that has puzzled so many in the fleet. Now I understand it. I am indebted to you for all the favors I received. You wrote to these persons."

"I did; and more even than that,—the chief of police had instructions to look after your welfare, and see that you were not molested."

"Then I was shadowed by a detective, who was my unseen body-guard?"

"Yes; **and** on several occasions it stood you in good need, for you were followed by some of the ruffians who infest the city, and, had it not been **for** my precautions, **would have** been stabbed in the back, robbed, and perhaps killed."

"How about that evening three weeks ago, when I helped my friend, the acting ensign, out of a bad scrape?"

"The two men whom you left prostrate on the pavement were taken to the station-house, and before daylight the other four were arrested, and by noon next day they were in the chain-gang under a year's sentence by the provost marshal."

"I did not hear of this before."

"There are a great many things that I **have** done for you that you do **not know** of."

"Then you must surely care for me."

"Have you **any** doubts on this subject?"

"I am trying to reconcile this statement with the advice you gave me to resign, and thus ruin all ambitious hopes in the navy."

"Did you not just declare that it **was** torture to you even to think of leaving me? So I suggested a simple remedy."

"If I should take your advice and leave the navy, will you become my wife?"

"Not until the war is ended. I have taken a **solemn** vow not to wed any man till peace is declared between the North and the South."

"Suppose the war should last for twenty years?"

"It would be the same should it last fifty years. **My vow will be kept.**"

"Will you be my wife when the war is ended?"

"Place your resignation in my hands as an officer of the Federal navy, and I will answer this question to your entire satisfaction."

"I dare not forsake the standard of my country in the hour of her need, when traitors, with arms in their hands, are seeking to destroy the constitution."

"Do you call those brave men traitors who, on the field of battle, are upholding the sovereign rights of their native States?"

"Yes, I do; because the allegiance due to the Federal government is paramount to all others."

"Adrien, you just said that you could not desert your country. It is not in danger."

"Not in danger! What do you mean?"

"England is your country; you were born in Manchester."

"Yes, I admit that; but I am a citizen of Massachusetts, and the son and grandson for several generations of good old New England stock."

"Well, we will not discuss this matter any further. Return to your ship, and go to the blockade. Colonel Hortense makes a devoted cavalier."

"Great heavens! Ilian, do not mention that man's name in that way, or I will rend him limb from limb. Why are you so cruel?"

"It is you that are cruel. I am anxious for you to stay in New Orleans, and you refuse to do it."

"Yes; because you demand it at the price of all that I hold sacred,—my honor."

"Why do you persist in that way? Do you not suppose that if I thought for one moment that you would forfeit your honor, I would be the first to leave you?"

"Then tell me in what way you look upon this matter. I have sworn allegiance to the Federal government and obligated myself to maintain the integrity of the Union. If I should resign my appointment as an acting master in this present crisis, would I not be stigmatized as a coward, or a faint-hearted man."

"Not by any means. Are there not already a number of officers, both of the army and the navy, who have resigned and returned to their homes? and who would dare to call them cowards?"

"They may have had good and sufficient reasons for so doing; but I have none."

"I understood you to say a few moments ago that you loved me; and now, when I ask for a small proof of the earnestness of your love, you absolutely decline, and then coolly say that you have no reason for resigning."

"You surely do not wish me to give as a reason for leaving the service that I am in love, and eager to be near the object of my devotion."

"There is no occasion to give any reason. You have already served seventeen months and taken part in the greatest naval battle of modern times. You will have a war credit for gallantry that will cling to you while you live. Tender your resignation, and, if you must give some excuse, say that your private interests require your time. I have influence at Washington, and I guarantee it will be accepted with regret and also with thanks for what you have already done."

"But my father and my mother, what will they say? They will ask for explanations; and my classmates of my college, how will I answer them after all my speeches about standing by the colors until peace is declared?"

"Are you not of age, and free to dispose of your own time? What is the bond that binds you to your college so closely that you dare not take a step in life without weighing the factor of its displeasure?"

"Ilian, I am surprised to hear you talk in this manner so lightly regarding my filial duty to my parents. You cannot be ignorant of the just pride felt by those who have been honored by a diploma from the university where I was a student for four years. Then, again, there is the fact of my father's long service years ago as a professor. Can you wonder that I hold in high esteem the good will of that college? No, I cannot resign; I dare not grieve my father, who has labored so hard in my behalf ever since I was born. My loving, patriotic mother would rather see me dead upon the field of battle than have me live with the stigma of coward and traitor to the Union cause. In my veins on both my father's and mother's side flows blood that was freely shed in the war of the Revolution and the war of 1812, and it will never be said that I was the first to bring the blush of shame to the cheeks of my kindred."

"Adrien, all this would make a very good fourth of July oration delivered on the Boston Common, and my answer to it is, that I have weighed you in the balance, and you are found wanting. I was anxious to have you near me as my friend and protector until such time as I can become your wife, when my vow is fulfilled, but you scornfully decline all this. Colonel Hortense told me yesterday that if I would only give him some hope, he would wait ten years, and be my willing and obedient slave all that time."

"Ilian, if I thought you capable of entertaining a serious thought for such a sycophant as this so-called Colonel Hortense, I would regret the hour I ever offered you my hand and heart."

"Adrien, you are excited. This will never do on the public street. Return to your ship, and weigh over carefully what I have said. Here we are at my residence. I will not ask you to come in, for in your present temper we might have a quarrel. When next you come to see me I will expect you to hand me a certified copy of your resignation from the Federal navy. The original you are to state, upon your word of honor, has been duly handed to your captain to be forwarded to Washington. I will look after the rest. Adieu."

A moment after the door closed upon her.

CHAPTER XVI.

THE FATAL OBLIGATION.

It would be difficult to find language to describe the feelings of Adrien, as he rapidly walked down to the landing to go off to his ship. He realized more than ever how deep was his love for Ilian. Was it possible that he could ever give her up? Yet the conditions for seeing her again were of such a nature that he could not accept them. As he reached the deck of his vessel the first greeting which he received was the information that the ship was under orders for sea on the following day, and that the last mail would leave at five in the morning. It was now nearly six o'clock, and he had the watch from eight to midnight. This would give him time for reflection. The night was a grand one, and most of the officers stayed up late to enjoy it. The moon, although only quarter full, shed its soft light over the city, and made every one anxious to be on shore to enjoy a promenade; but as the ship was under sailing orders, all were required to remain on board. They were bound for the blockade off Mobile, and it would probably be six months, if not longer, before they returned to New Orleans. It was eleven o'clock when Adrien got rid of his talkative messmates, who enjoyed chaffing him, especially as he was so reserved and totally unlike himself. When alone he carefully weighed every argument that had been presented to him by Ilian during the afternoon, but could find nothing to justify him in leaving his country's service in the hour when she needed her stalwart sons to uphold her honor. He therefore framed an answer which he would write and send by the early morning post. At midnight, when his relief took the deck, he went below to his room and wrote the following letter:

U. S. Ship ———, off New Orleans, November 25, 1862.

Miss Ilian Mordine:

My very dear Friend,—Your ultimatum given to me this afternoon made the condition that to see you again I must resign from what you termed the Federal navy. On my return to this ship I learned that orders had been received for our departure to-morrow morning for duty on the blockade; consequently I am unable to go ashore again at this place until our return, an event which may not take place for several months.

I am certain that you will give me credit for loving you for yourself alone, and not for your wealth. You are aware that I am the sole heir to an estate almost equal to your own. You ask me to give a proof of my love by sacrificing what I believe to be my honor. I stand ready to make every other sacrifice in the world. I therefore now tell you candidly and plainly that I cannot resign my position in the naval service until I can honestly feel some justification for so doing. My term of service is for the war, and only when peace is declared will I be willing to lay down my sword and take up the avocations of civil life.

My love for you will never change while my spirit remains a tenant of this mortal body. My heart is too full of emotion to write a longer letter. As I fully believe in you, and trust you in all things. I ask as a return that you will repose in me the same confidence. I will anxiously look for your answer whenever you find it convenient to write. Send it to this ship on the blockade (off Mobile).

I remain your most devoted lover,
ADRIEN HOMERAND.

By eight o'clock next morning the ship had left New Orleans far behind, and was steaming down the muddy waters of the great river. Adrien, as he stood upon the poop-deck, thought how different was their peaceful passage now compared to that fearful night just seven months back, when amidst the awful storm of exploding missiles and battle-smoke they made their perilous way past the heavily-armed forts and the all-consuming fire-rafts. It was a scene never to be forgotten. Brave men held their breath as the flash of the loud-roaring guns revealed the terrible carnage of war. Now no hostile shot menaced their progress. They went over the bar, and in twenty hours dropped their anchor seven miles off Fort Morgan. The duties of blockade life thus commenced once more. In ten days Adrien obtained a reply from Ilian. Its contents brought the sunshine once more into the sphere of his life. All on board noticed the change, and he had to run a gauntlet of questions in consequence.

NEW ORLEANS, December 2, 1862.

MY OWN DEAR ADRIEN,—Your letter reached me the evening of your departure. I did not fully realize the value of your friendship until I found your ship had sailed. Do not think me selfish when I desired to keep you near me in New Orleans. The only way I saw open for that purpose was to persuade you to resign from the navy. I do not blame you for the course you have taken. Your manly, straightforward letter has opened my eyes more than ever to the combination of noble qualities which you possess. I would

UNITED STATES FLAG-SHIP PENSACOLA.

have answered your letter the hour I received it, but I was afraid to trust myself to write until now. I have not been out since the day I left you so abruptly on the sidewalk. Can you forgive me for the rude, unkind way in which I parted from you? If I could only have known that I was to be deprived of seeing you for some time, I never would have acted in the childish way I did. I have been so used to having my own way that perhaps I am spoiled; yes, I admit it. I have refused to see any of my friends on the score of illness. Colonel Hortense called several times, but he did not see me. Yesterday I sent him a note asking him to attend to some business for me in Charleston, and I just heard that he passed the "picket lines" in safety. My business will, I hope, keep him away for several months.

I had an offer conveyed to him of a command of a company of calvary, which he declined. He wants to be colonel of a regiment. He is all the time talking of what he will do, but does nothing.

I must now close, hoping this letter will reach you safely. Don't be surprised if in the course of a month or so you should be ordered upon special duty in this city. Write by return mail. I remain yours, faithful until death.

ILIAN.

The correspondence between Adrien and Ilian was kept up as often as the mails permitted. Life on the blockade was dull and dreary beyond expression, especially after the gay life at New Orleans. All the ships lay so far from land that they were exposed to the heavy swell and fierce winter gales. There was nothing to relieve the monotony except the visit of the supply steamer with fresh meat and vegetables and the mail from the North once a month; occasionally they also received a mail from New Orleans. Thus the winter and spring passed away, and on the 15th of April Adrien unexpectedly received orders detaching him from his ship and instructing him to report for special duty to Admiral Farragut.

On arrival at New Orleans he found the admiral up the river in the flag-ship "Hartford," and all communication with him cut off. So he reported to the senior officer in charge, Commodore Morris, commanding the United States ship "Pensacola," then at anchor off the city. He was permitted to make his abode on shore. The Navy Department desired to be kept apprised in regard to the movements of certain vessels belonging ostensibly to Union citizens, but which were suspected of blockade-running. He was, therefore, assigned to this duty.

When he arrived he learned that Ilian had been absent for some time, but she returned on the 3d of May. Their meeting was a joyful one. Adrien made a renewed offer of his hand and heart. His proposal was accepted by Ilian with the condition that the marriage should not take place till the war was finally ended, also that Adrien would grant a request which she would make known to him at the end of thirty days, and to consist of only a single word.

"Just a whim of mine," she said, with one of her most enchanting smiles. "You know that women have to obtain all their promises before marriage; the men are so indifferent afterwards, as a rule."

In vain Adrien protested that he would be more tractable when he could call her his little wife; but he added, however, that if he could do any thing now to please her fancy, he would do it.

"I am going to bind you with a solemn promise," said she, "that my little request shall be granted at the time specified."

In the artlessness of his nature, and the utmost confidence that he reposed in her to whom he had pledged his vows of life-long love and devotion, he accepted both these conditions, and gave his sacred word of honor to grant her request of a single word, whatever it might be. He then placed a solitaire diamond ring on her finger, and the compact was ratified. Never was his horizon so clear nor his prospects so favorable. He wrote a full account to his father and mother, but did not give the name of his intended bride, but would do so later; and in the mean time he would remain true to his purpose of staying in the navy until the war was over.

CHAPTER XVII.

THE POWER OF A SINGLE WORD.

It is an old adage that "lovers take no heed of the flight of time." The 3d of June came before Adrien was aware of it. This was the day appointed for him to comply with Ilian's mysterious request.

He had never for a moment surmised what this word would be; some girl's notion perhaps, or a "whim," as she expressed it. Yet he knew that Ilian was no ordinary girl; a request of only one word could not be a very difficult one to perform. It was playfully agreed that as the clock struck the hour of noon a slip of paper should be handed to him, with the request written on it, and according to the agreement it was to be granted at once. For several days he found pleasure in chaffing her on the impossibility that any woman should confine a request to a single word. He said jestingly that he would adhere to his promise, but that if two or more words were written, or afterwards uttered or even implied, he would consider the request null and void. Then again the one word must be complete in itself, and convey an adequate meaning; there must be nothing ambiguous about it.

"Why, Adrien," was her response, "you remind me of the conditions in the *Merchant of Venice*, where Shylock was told to take his pound of flesh,—that it must be of exact weight, and that if the scale weighed a feather's weight more or less than the bond called for he should die."

"Well, the fact is, my dear," said he " I am rather sceptical about the ability of womankind to confine their requests to one word; a Webster's Dictionary hardly suffices some of them."

"May I ask what is the standard by which you judge our sex? You have no sisters at home for a criterion, and you are too young to have seen much of woman's nature. I suppose that your knowledge is gained from novels and books in general. Most of these are written by men, and what do they know about the feminine mind? When women write books they are more interested, as a rule, in the men folks, and have no time nor disposition to analyze their own kind."

"Am I right in the inference from what you say that woman's nature is an unexplored mystery?"

"Hardly unexplored," she replied, "but positively misunderstood. Perhaps some day I may write a book on the subject."

"Let me help you; it will be a charming task."

"But I ask again, where is your knowledge and experience to come from?"

"I will take yours for a starting-point," said he.

"I am afraid," said Ilian, "that the product of your work as far as I am concerned will be all inferences and deductions, based upon unsound premises. I would like to see a book written upon woman by a man in two stages of his existence,—one estimation of her written six months before his marriage, and the other one year after his wedding-day."

"Do you imply that your lovely sex change so radically in so short a time?" he asked.

"No, I do not; but the adjectives by which men refer to them are different; just now you said 'lovely.' Many men use the same term when making love, but later on employ a more emphatic one. Am I not right?"

"It is my turn to ask where you get your experience?" he rejoined. "Is it from books?"

"No, not altogether; I keep my eyes and ears open. Of course, I am speaking of men as a class. There are exceptions to the rule, and I believe that you are one of them. Now, after this disquisition upon the lovely sex, as you call them, we will turn back to where we started from,—the fulfilment of my request of a single word. The clock is striking the hour of twelve, and here is the piece of paper with only one word, which I think complies with all your demands."

It was a very small slip, and was rolled up tight. For a moment Adrien mused and said, "I wonder if it is a diamond necklace; I know you have a penchant for gems of pure water. No, that would be two words; diamond alone has no relative meaning. What can it be?"

"The surest way to find out, my dear, is to open it." She placed her little hand upon his shoulder and brought her face provokingly near his; of course, he kissed her, and her beautiful eyes glowed with a strange fire. If he had not been so blind in his love, he would have noticed that she was now a shade paler than usual, and that her frame trembled slightly. Slowly he unwound the tiny morsel of paper, and his eyes became riveted upon the single word that met his gaze. It was full of unutterable meaning to him. Its power held him in its grasp and convulsed his frame. An agony of soul which cannot be described took possession of him. He leaned upon the mantel-piece, and his emotions found vent in the exclamation, "My God! has it come to this? I am ruined!"

Again he took up the paper, which he had grasped tightly in his hand as though it had stung him and he was anxious to crush it. Once more he looked at it to be sure that there was no mistake; no, there was none; for that single word read "Resign."

"Ilian," he said in a despairing tone, "surely you do not mean to ask me to leave the service of my country in this dark hour of her history, when she has sore need of every arm. Tell me that you only wrote that word to try me, and that you will not insist upon the fulfilment of my promise."

"I insist upon nothing, my dear Adrien," said she. "You gave me your word of honor that you would grant a request of one word. You have it before you. If you decline to do it, that is the end of all our transactions."

She then went to the bay-window of the drawing-room and looked out upon the street. The house was a magnificent residence and luxuriously furnished. It had lately come into her possession by the inability of its former owner to pay a large mortgage advanced upon it by her agent. He had notified her that he could not even pay the interest, and offered to surrender it to her for what was due. Her generous nature would not let her take advantage of another's misfortune, so she gave him her check for a liberal difference and moved into it herself. She had a large staff of servants, but lived quietly and unostentatiously.

After a lapse of ten minutes Adrien went to the window where she was standing, and, with a voice choked with emotion, said, plaintively, "Ilian, cannot you help me out of this dilemma?"

Turning to him, she was startled and alarmed by the change of his countenance. "Yes, I will help you, my darling. Let the matter stand over for another month, and we will devise some means that will be satisfactory to us both. By the way, you are going off this evening on some secret duty, are you not?"

"Yes, I will be gone five days or more, up the river. I am going on a scouting expedition."

"Be careful of yourself; you may get caught, and you know the fate of——"

"Spies, you were going to say. Do not fear for me, for at present I am not going outside of our lines."

"Perhaps," said she, "I can help you if you will tell me where you are going, or at least I can prevent harm coming upon you."

"I gave my word to Commodore Morris this morning," he replied, "not to mention to a soul where I am bound, and no one besides him knows my mission. I hope, however, to be back not later than a week from to-day. I am like a man under sentence of death who has received a month's reprieve."

"Why do you take such a gloomy view?" she asked. "You have now nearly two years of a splendid war record, of which any man might be proud."

"That makes it all the more difficult to think of resigning. My parents will be disappointed, and my classmates will say that I preach one thing and practise another. Ilian, I am ambitious."

"Ambitious of what? she demanded.

"Of rising in my profession."

"Trust in me," said she, "and I will raise you to a height you never dreamed of before."

"To be your husband is high enough for any ordinary man; yet the day on which I call you my wife I would like to have a naval rank of which you will not be ashamed."

"I purpose to marry the man and not the rank," she answered. "Brass buttons and gold lace have no attraction for me. You say that you are ambitious; so am I, perhaps more than you are."

"In what way, may I ask?"

"Mine lies buried in my own heart, and I will use all my wealth to accomplish my object, with the hope begotten of youth and the experience of past success. I *shall win*."

"You have my best wishes, and I have faith in your ability and judgment," was his reply.

"Full success can only be obtained by your co-operation."

"I dare not make any more blind promises or engage myself in any enterprise until I redeem my almost forfeited word of honor."

"I will not ask you now. So *au revoir* till you come back. Candidly, I am too staunch a Southern woman to wish you success in your secret expedition, but I do hope that you will return safely."

She gave him a smile of such power that even the stern old military war governor, General Butler himself, would have been melted by it. And thus they parted.

BOOK III.—1863.

CHAPTER I.

GROSVENOR HOUSE.

The upper part of the city of New Orleans, on the opposite side of the river, is called Algiers; perhaps from the affinity of its inhabitants to many of the traits of the Arabs in the great city of the same name on the African coast. It was not celebrated either for its purity, honesty, or health. He was a temeritous man who trusted himself there after sundown. About two blocks from the river's edge was a frame building with the rather high-sounding name of "Grosvenor House." It was owned by an Englishman whose reputation was not of the best odor on the police records. He was powerfully built, with a short neck, and had an arm that could strike a blow equal to a sledge-hammer. He called himself Bill Harrison. His patrons, when they had money in their pockets to pay for what they obtained at his table or bar, called him "Bill, old boy;" but those who were short of funds addressed him as Mr. William Harrison. This always drew from him a smile, and the announcement came with it that their rooms were needed for a friend "just from England, you know." He was very popular, but no one cared to arouse him or to test the limit of his forbearance. One afternoon, about sunset, he was standing at the door of his house, in his shirt sleeves, intently watching a schooner of very fine lines that was being hauled alongside of a wharf situated about four hundred feet from his inn. He heard footsteps at his side and a voice, in a quiet tone, ask if this was Mr. William Harrison, the proprietor of the Grosvenor House? Without turning his head to look at the one who spoke, he replied,—

"Yes, I am the man; but I have no vacant rooms, and my table is full."

"When you have taken the bearings of that piratical-looking craft with her raking masts, you will be kind enough to put your helm a-starboard and luff to the wind, in order that I may get a good look at your figure-head."

These words, uttered so quietly, yet with such a clear ring in the tones, convinced him that a man not of common quality stood before him. He took off his cap and, turning round, surveyed the stranger. No one had ever before presumed to use such authoritative language to him. The man was tall and well-proportioned, with large eyes, a high forehead, and an open, frank expression that won confidence and respect at once. He had the appearance of a seafaring individual, and one whose place had long been on the quarter-deck. All this and much more the astute Mr. Harrison took in at one glance, and then, in a respectful tone, asked in what way he could be of service to the gentleman before him.

"I want a room and board for a week, provided you will take English gold, for I have no other," was the answer.

The landlord bowed lower than he remembered to have done for many a long year, saying, "My house is at your service; and allow me to welcome you to New Orleans; I suppose you are a stranger here."

"Yes, I am; and I do not care to have my coming heralded all over the neighborhood. I am here on a speculation. I want to take a load of cotton over to England, and I may need your services, for which you will be well paid."

The landlord rubbed his hands gleefully as a new idea came to him, and then suddenly responded, with a sigh,—

"Ah, I am sorry to say that cotton is very scarce here."

"But not in Mobile, is it?" asked the stranger.

"No; but the blockade is stringent and hard to evade."

"What will prevent me from buying a schooner, loading her with freight for Havanna, and slipping into Mobile some dark night, and then out with the cotton for Bermuda?"

"It has been done before," said Harrison, "and can be again, especially when backed by English gold and energy."

"We will talk this matter over at another time; I am hungry now, and want my supper. Can you get me a grilled steak and whatever else you have handy? No Yankee dishes for me."

"My wife is a first-class cook, and will serve you up as good a meal as could be found in London."

"All right, pass the word, for I am all ready to stow it away. Let me ask, before I forget it, is that schooner in the market that is hauling along-side the pier?"

"No," Harrison replied; "she belongs to a firm in the city, and is bound for Mobile to load cotton for Havanna. There is a chance for a command, for the man who had her last trip is down with the yellow-fever, and will not be able to go out this trip."

"I did not know you had any cases of that scourge."

"It is not prevalent now, but there are a few cases imported from the West Indies, and mostly developed by hard drinking. By the way, captain, what is your name?"

"My name," said the stranger, "is Andrew MacKenzie. I was born in Manchester, but my folks are from Scotland. Dumbartonshire is the old camp of our clan. I have been a ship-master for some time, and I am not a novice in blockade-running; in fact, have had considerable experience, and I would prefer that the Yankee authorities should not know I am in the city."

"Rest assured, captain, no one will disturb you here. If you would like the command of that schooner, I can get it for you. I am the agent for the owners. You can have a share of the profits without any risk of your own money. They will think themselves fortunate in having an experienced man like yourself for her master."

"Well, I will think the matter over. I can refer to the Cunard Steamship Company and other large shipping firms in Liverpool, London, and Glasgow."

"Why, captain, your face is your passport. The reference required will be the other way. The firm I represent will have to give you a reference. Consider it settled. I do not mind telling you that I myself am interested in her ventures. On her last trip she cleared an immense profit for all concerned."

"Can you get a clearance without any trouble?"

"Oh, yes; we cleared her in water-ballast for Havanna; she was duly inspected and passed, and was overhauled at Southwest Pass; also by three gun-boats off the blockade; and yet she got into Mobile with a valuable cargo."

"I don't understand how that could be done, if she was in ballast."

"I did not say that she was in ballast, but only cleared as such."

"Then the officers who overhauled her must have been very careless."

"No, not by any means," answered Harrison; "she was well searched each time, but as they could find nothing, and as her papers were duly signed by General Butler, they had to let her go."

I must admit, you interest me very much, Mr. Harrison, and I will be very glad to obtain the secret. I am aware that much money can be made by a cargo into Mobile and a load of cotton out. He needs to be a sharp man who can get the weather-gauge of those Yankee officers on the blockade, for they are like blood-hounds on the trail."

Here Bill Harrison indulged in a hearty laugh, and, placing his hand familiarly on the shoulder of his guest, said,—

"Captain MacKenzie, let us have some good old port that has not been tainted by duty paid on it, and I will explain the *modus operandi*."

It was only on very rare occasions that the landlord of the Grosvenor House touched either wines or liquors. He had seen the evil effects of them on so many men that, while he dispensed the fiery liquid to his customers, he abstained himself. The wine was opened, and they sat down to taste it while the dinner was preparing. He drank a large glassful to the health of his new guest, then another to old England, and again to the Confederacy. He did not observe, however, that Captain MacKenzie adroitly emptied nearly all his into a large spittoon at his feet filled with sawdust.

"Mr. Harrison," said he, "this wine is worthy of the Grosvenor House. I had no idea such rare old vintage could be found in your cellar."

"Oh, captain, perhaps something besides wine could be found there. Let us fill up again for the success of your new command."

"Once more the glasses touched, and the contents of one went into the sawdust. It was harmless there. Harrison's tongue was now thoroughly unloosed.

"Captain," said he, "it is a proud day in my life when I have the great and well-known Captain Andrew MacKenzie as a guest under my roof. My wife will wait upon you, and your dinner will be ready for you in a few minutes. There is a private parlor for your exclusive use, and I will send in no bills."

"Oh, no; I cannot accept that. I have plenty of money." And a handful of English sovereigns was laid on the table.

"Put up your money, my dear captain; and if I don't make every sovereign in your pocket increase fifty-fold before a month is passed, then my name is not Bill Harrison. From Manchester you said you came? I have been there many a time. I was born myself in Sheffield. We will have plenty of time to talk over old England before the 'Emily Sutton' sails with her new master."

"Is that the name of the schooner that you want me to take?"

"Yes; and she is called after as pretty a girl as ever turned the head of youth."

"You have not told me, Mr. Harrison, how the 'Emily Sutton' managed to hide her valuable cargo."

"Don't call me 'Mr. Harrison.' I would prefer that a great captain like yourself should say 'Bill Harrison,' or, better still, 'Bill, my boy.'"

"Just as you wish. Bill, you level-headed old bull-dog, explain about that mysterious cargo."

"That is the style; give me your hand. Now for the racket played on the Yankee blockaders."

CHAPTER II.

THE BLOCKADE-RUNNER.

BILL HARRISON filled the glasses again.'

"Captain MacKenzie," he said, " I suppose you know it takes a diamond to cut a diamond. The idea of our hidden cargo originated with a Yankee from Connecticut. I told you that the 'Emily Sutton' cleared in ballast. She had about two hundred casks, filled with water apparently, which we stated were to be used for a cargo of molasses from the West Indies. Each cask was divided into three compartments. The middle one, being very narrow, was filled with water; the two end ones were lined with tin and filled with ammunition, rifles in sections, medicine, and other valuable articles needed in the Confederacy. These were all placed in position and the casks headed up, and when stowed the water was put in the middle one; a large bung for each one was arranged to come out easily, and a tin dipper was provided to draw water out by the inspecting officer. When she cleared from Mobile, compressed cotton was placed in the end compartments, so that if overhauled nothing would be found. On her return trip last time she put molasses instead of water in the centre compartment, and slipped into Mobile a second time, discharged a valuable consignment, and then brought a lot of cotton here. We have her nearly ready with merchandise purchased in New York. If you can get her into Mobile going and coming from Havanna, it will be a matter of five thousand pounds in your pocket. You ought to be back here in a month, or five weeks at the utmost. We will pay you twenty-five per cent. of the value of the net profits of the round trip. She will be ready to sail this day week."

"Your offer is so tempting, you generous old Briton, that I must perforce accept."

"Then I greet you as Captain Andrew MacKenzie, commanding the Confederate schooner 'Emily Sutton.' Come, your dinner is ready. There is your special servant while you are my guest. Come here, you black scoundrel," addressing a tall, powerfully-built mulatto, who stood with a white apron on, waiting for orders. "You see this gentleman here?"

"Yes, massa, I sees him."

"Well, then, if you don't promptly obey all orders he gives you, I will break every bone in your black body; do you hear?"

"Yes, Massa Harrison, I hears."

"If you don't do something more than hear, I will be into your wool."

"Yes, sah. I waits on de gentleman to his utmost satisfaction."

The dinner was admirably served, far beyond what might

have been expected from the outward appearance of the Grosvenor House. At an early hour the guest desired to be shown to his room, on the plea of being tired. Everything so far had succeeded beyond his expectations. Nothing seemed likely to mar his project, and only his fatal obligation to Ilian stood in the way of his happiness; for " Captain MacKenzie" was no other than Acting Master **Adrien Homerand**. The next morning he was duly installed as commander of the " Emily Sutton," and superintended her preparations for sea. Several times he expressed a desire to be introduced to the other owners. Harrison made evasive answers, saying that everything was left in his hands; and finally acknowledged that he himself was the chief owner, and the others merely attended to purchasing her cargo and getting the clearance-papers, for which he paid them a percentage of the profits. A first and second mate and a crew of four men and a cook were shipped. Some repairs were needed, which would be finished to allow of her sailing at the proper time. Adrien purposed to send word of the whole proceeding to Commodore Morris, and also to inform the senior officer on the blockade in regard to the false casks of water; as no doubt other vessels were adopting this shrewd plan of smuggling goods contraband of war. Before doing so, however, he wished to obtain further details of other individuals engaged in blockade-running; also, what Bill Harrison meant when he vaguely hinted that he had something more than wine in his cellar. Three days passed rapidly, and Adrien had gained much valuable information. But he could not fathom the mystery about his landlord. After the first night Harrison had not been so communicative. He had allowed himself then to be pumped dry, in a measure. He was profoundly respectful to his honored guest, as he continually called him, and kept him well supplied with wine and other luxuries, but refused to touch any himself, on the score that a single glass awakened a morbid appetite, and therefore he restrained himself. At times he would assume the arrogant manner of a man who had both power and wealth at his command. Money he certainly had; yet he would draw a five-cent glass of beer with as much apparent desire to please as though his whole living depended upon this petty trade. Adrien had closely scanned the servants of the house, to see if there was one whom he could safely interrogate. They all exhibited a great dread of their master, and some fled in abject terror when he came near them. They were a mixed lot, slaves and poor whites. The staff was larger than the house needed, and it was evident that they had at times other work to do besides the duties of the hotel. Well-dressed people came there, stayed for a short time, and left. This was noticed especially after dark. The mulatto detailed to wait on Adrien was the one he finally selected as the most likely to give him the points he needed.

He was called Sam, and declared that he never had use for another name. He often said, "What for a nigger want two names? One mighty unhandy to have when de police am after you, and de debil don't want no name to find you. No, sah; one name am enough for dis nigger, sure."

On the morning of the fourth day he came into Adrien's bedroom to take his orders for breakfast, and the pumping process began, with what result the sequel will show.

"Sam, how old are you?"

"Lord a massa, dat am a mighty home-question. Hab you de idea ob investing in dis ere nigger?"

"Well, I don't know; do you suppose your master would let you come with me to Mobile and other ports?"

"You hab a powerful sight ob influence wid Massa Harrison; but it am de opinion ob dis ere woolly head dat it would not pay to ask dat question ob him."

"Why so? I have taken a great fancy to you. You are a very intelligent man, far above the average; and as I am now in the employ of Mr. Harrison, your services on the 'Emily Sutton' would be to his interest and all concerned."

"Dat am de way you look at dis question; but Massa Harrison he looks at it in anodder light; besides, he don't own dis child; he am de boss and de superintendent only."

"Who is this owner you speak about? does he reside in New Orleans?"

"It am a lady, but I dare not mention de name; and I am sure dat she nebber consent to dis nigger going to English territory. I am acquainted wid too many ob de mysterious goings-on ob dis house and de business in general to be let go out ob dar sight."

"What are the mysterious phases of this house?"

Here Sam closed the door, and, looking cautiously around, came nearer his questioner, and said, in a low voice, "Massa Harrison hab a long whip and a powerful site ob arm, and dis nigger's skin am too tender to risk massa's anger. A preacher said de oder day dat ignorance am sometimes bliss; in dis case I assure you, Massa MacKenzie, dat you am a blissful man; better you remain dat way. I serb you to de utmost ob my ability, and I don't nebber done gone and forgot your kind words,—dey am a scarce article in dis house. And, captain, it am de solid opinion ob your servant before you, dat you better sail wid dat schooner as soon as possible, and perhaps if you don't come back it am to your advantage. Must go now; Missus am suspicious, and if I stay too long. she come to de key-hole and examine what am going on. You can trust dis nigger. Your kindness am deep-rooted in my heart. Don't let on to Massa Harrison I been speaking so long; de smell ob dat whip am bad fur nigger digestion."

Adrien was puzzled; the problem was deeper than ever. It was true he had discovered one of the potent agents of the blockade-running, and could stop the "Emily Sutton;" but the Grosvenor House was the rendezvous for something more than the mere sending of contraband goods into Mobile. If his identity was discovered, or even suspected, he never would escape with his life. How should he send information to Commodore Morris? The mail was too risky, and besides there was no branch post-office nearer than two miles; and if he attempted to go there he ran the risk of being discovered. Every time he had gone out for a short walk he was "shadowed" by a rough-looking white man who was generally hanging round the kitchen. He knew that this was the work of Mrs. Harrison, for she was suspicious of every one who came around the house. The two mates and the crew of the schooner were men of Harrison's type, and in his confidence; and any attempt at treachery on the way down the river would be resented by them.

Adrien at this time had not seen his landlord since the previous afternoon. Harrison had gone to the city, remaining away all night, arranging matters for the departure of the "Emily Sutton." Adrien dressed himself and went to his breakfast, but could not eat. The day was sultry, yet he felt cold.

As he sat at the table he was taken with a severe chill. At first this gave him no alarm. He took some quinine that he had provided himself with. The chill changed to fever; so he went back to his bedroom and laid down. Sam went with him and bathed his head. His blood now seemed to be all on fire, and he wondered whether he had an attack of yellow-fever. He had been down a good deal in the hold of the schooner investigating the secret of the false casks. He might thus have contracted the fever there, or perhaps in the cabin, as her former captain was then at death's door with the disease. He now felt that he could not return to the "Pensacola," nor to his apartments in the city; yet if he remained where he was, he might in the delirium of fever betray his identity, which would be certain death. He sent Sam for the landlady.

CHAPTER III.

YELLOW-FEVER.

NOTHING has such power to appal a seaman as the mention of yellow-fever. The fierce howling of the gale as it sweeps through the rigging of his ship is music to his ears. The flash of the lightning and roar of the thunder do not unnerve him in the least, but he quails before "yellow-jack." Adrien knew and realized his double danger. He was fast losing that power to act promptly in a time of danger, which had previously been his distinguishing trait.

Mrs. Harrison came to his room. She was a tall, angular woman of English birth, and her one absorbing passion was her suspicion of every one around her. She made her servants miserable by constantly accusing them, first of one thing and then of another. She had not taken kindly to Adrien, and had worried her husband with the assertion that Captain MacKenzie was a Yankee spy. Only the morning before, he, wearied with her suspicions, had broken out on her with not very choice adjectives, and asked her if she thought him such a fool as not to know an Englishman from a blasted Yankee. This had increased her vindictive feeling for her guest, and it was in this frame of mind that she answered his call. In a few words he told her of his condition, and asked her if she thought these were symptoms of yellow-fever. At the mention of the dreaded name she turned deadly pale. A single glance sufficed her. The man before her was very ill. Almost for the first time in her life she accepted the facts without indulging in her weakness of suspecting something or other. At heart she was sympathetic, and the sight of suffering roused all the generous impulses of her nature. She perceived at a glance that prompt measures were of the utmost importance. As it was beyond doubt a case of genuine yellow-fever, she knew what to do, having lived so long in the South and seen many cases of it.

"Captain MacKenzie," she said, "if you have any friends in New Orleans, you had better send them word of your condition, for I think that before six hours are passed you will be delirious. The captain who commanded the 'Sutton' on her last trip died this morning, and I believe he might have been saved if he had obtained proper nursing. Yellow-fever is easy to manage if taken in time, and a good nurse is more essential than a doctor."

"Yes," replied the sick man; "I had a letter of introduction to a Southern lady of wealth and position, and called upon her, and she received me very kindly; but I did not tell her where I was going, or what I purposed to do."

"What is her name, and where does she live?" she asked.

"I do not think that I would be doing the proper thing to mention her name to a stranger."

"Well, all I have to say is, that your life is now at stake, and you need all the friends you have. My husband and myself will do whatever we can to aid you, but I think it would be far better if you were removed at once to a more healthy neighborhood. Sam will take a letter to any of your friends."

There was no time to consider about the judiciousness of letting his landlady know of his acquaintance with Ilian. He had barely strength to write in a trembling hand the following note:

GROSVENOR HOUSE, June 6, 1863.

Miss ILIAN MORDINE,—I am down with yellow-fever just developed. Must be removed to other quarters. Can you help me? CAPTAIN ANDREW MACKENZIE,
of Manchester, England.

P.S. The servant who takes this note is called Sam; he will tell you all particulars. A.

This note was handed to Mrs. Harrison to read while he directed the envelope. His eyes were becoming dim, and a terrible nausea was felt in his stomach. He now lay down and wondered whether Ilian would risk the danger of contagion, and come and see him. The landlady read the note, and exclaimed, "What! do you know Miss Ilian Mordine? Pardon me for suspecting you for a Yankee spy."

It was Adrien's time for amazement. He asked, "Do you know her?"

A smile was the only answer, but it was full of deep meaning. She told Sam to take the note, saddle a horse out of the stable, ride at full speed to the ferry, cross over, and deliver it to Miss Mordine.

Adrien began to explain the locality, when Sam interrupted him, saying,—

"Captain MacKenzie, I know dat place better dan you do. I's mighty glad you hab de honor ob knowing dat illustrious lady dat——"

"Sam, leave at once," said Mrs. Harrison, "and don't lose a minute on the road." And she gave him a look of mysterious caution that the sick man did not fail to notice. More mystery and more problems, he thought. But the great problem now was how to battle successfully with the pestilence that had taken hold upon him. Mrs. Harrison covered him with blankets, sent for some ice to put on his forehead, gave him the usual preparatory medicine, and sat by his bedside and encouraged him.

After the lapse of two hours, carriage-wheels were heard, and half a dozen persons entered the sick-chamber. The fever-stricken patient now barely recognized any one. He heard the voice of his landlord asking how he felt, and then there was a soft voice that thrilled every fibre of his nature, and he was conscious that Ilian stood by his side. Stooping down she whispered in his ear, "**Adrien**, my darling, **I will keep your** identity secret, and will nurse **you** myself. We will remove you at once to more suitable quarters. I have brought an old friend, **Dr.** Rechard. Do you recognize him?"

"Yes," was the faint reply **and** the strong man's reason was swept from **its** pedestal by **the fierce fire** of the malignant fever; delirium followed. He **did not realize that** powerful **arms** lifted him **tenderly from his bed and carried** him, all wrapped in blankets, **to a** carriage; **nor that a** gentle hand bathed **his** burning brow **and spoke sweet words of** comfort. **Nor did he know** that a skilful surgeon **held his head in his arms while the** carriage with closed blinds dashed swiftly **over the streets. He was** not conscious when he was carried **into a large, cool room,** and placed **in** a soft bed, and watchers **ware installed to** help him to fight in the battle for his **life.** For three days **and** nights Adrien was wildly delirious; **the** best medical skill was obtained **for** his benefit; Dr. Rechard seldom left **the** room. On the afternoon of **the** third day a consultation was held. Three out of the four doctors declared **that the** patient would **pass away in a few hours.** Doctor Rechard alone had hope of his recovery. **He based his judgment upon his previous knowledge of Adrien's former habits of life, and the fact that he** had never indulged **in any of the** excesses of **youth. He** had been temperate **in both eating and** drinking, was **regular in** his meals and **methodical in his habits,** and had inherited a sound physical system. **The other** three physicians were older men, **and** had more experience. Doctor Rechard was **a** young **man of** unusual **talents.** Finally, at **the** conclusion of the consultation, he affirmed that **the** best medical authorities maintained that where the organic, **the** physical, and moral laws by which we are governed are properly **observed** in all their **aspects,** it tends as a powerful factor **to** help recovery from severe illness, especially where **the** patient is in **the** prime of **life.** "These facts," he added, "should preponderate in the balances of life and death in the present case." Upon one point they all agreed, and **that was,** that a change would take place in the **patient's condition by** midnight; and that if his reason was restored, it would greatly tend to aid recovery.

The afternoon was a stormy one; the rain fell in torrents,

and the atmosphere was close and heavy. At nine o'clock in the evening Dr. Rechard and Ilian sent the other nurses to bed, preferring to be alone with the sick man, especially as a crisis was expected. They both knew of the mysterious phenomenon which for several generations surrounded the Homerand family. This was manifested when any of their number was nigh unto death. Adrien had often spoken of it, but could not account for it.

CHAPTER IV.

THE WARNING.

It is not within the province of this work to explain any of the phenomena that may be recorded. The author is not taking any steps that would lead into the domain of the marvellous. It has been noticed times without number, that when human life draws near the border-land, in many cases there is a peculiar influence manifested that cannot be accounted for. It may be that, as the immortal spirit finds itself becoming gradually freed from the limitations of its earthly tabernacle, it can receive impressions from the dawn of a new life. As to the much-discussed theory of the power of our departed relatives to aid or to warn us in times of special danger, I do not propose to discuss it. That such things have taken place is well authenticated. By what law this is effected, or whether these things are in accordance with any law of our being, I am not prepared to explain. Neither can I answer the question why they are the experience of the minority, and not of the majority of mankind. There may come a time in the future history of our race when it will be possible for the living to hold open and undisputed communication with those who have left this life. But so far the veil is too thickly woven to be pierced by human eyes, and our ears are too dull to hear again the voices of the former days from lips now silent in the grave. I hope this digression from the thread of our narrative will be a sufficient explanation of the words of warning conveyed to **Adrien Homerand** which we are about to relate.

It was a few minutes after eleven o'clock. Adrien, who had been in a stupor for some time, suddenly opened his eyes and at once recognized both watchers. In a very weak voice he asked whether it was a dream, or did he really behold Ilian and his college friend, Rechard. He was assured on this point that it was reality, and then it was briefly explained to him that he had been very ill of yellow-fever, and utterly unconscious for over three days, but that now everything pointed to recovery, provided he was careful not to exert himself unduly. The next moment his eyes seemed fixed in a gaze of wonder at some object at the foot of the bed; then he turned them as though some one was coming to his side. There was now noticed a stillness of expression, as though listening to some one speaking. A smile gradually spread over his face, and he went off into a gentle slumber. By the next morning the fever had left him, and Dr. Rechard's hopes were realized. The patient was saved.

Six days later Adrien was seated in an arm-chair. It was his first day out of bed. His recuperative powers were of a high order and his mind had recovered its normal condition. He had been told that he was the sole occupant of a small, furnished house belonging to Ilian. She had purchased it a few days previous to his illness for the use of a distant relative, a widow lady, whose husband had been killed in battle, and was expected from South Carolina. The apartment he occupied was a large bedroom looking out upon a neatly-trimmed garden. Two servants had been detailed to wait upon him, and every wish had been gratified, but he had been forbidden by Dr. Rechard to read the newspapers, as war news might be detrimental to him. Books, however, were furnished in abundance, and Ilian read to him every day. It was eleven o'clock of this day when Ilian came as usual. He noticed a peculiar expression on her face, and it was evident that she had come for some fixed purpose. He felt a dread of coming disaster in a manner that he could not account for. She locked the door to prevent intrusion, as she expressed it, and, drawing a chair in front of his, she greeted him kindly, but her manner was somewhat constrained. He had never seen her in this humor before. Taking his hand, she said, in a low voice, while her blue eyes searched his face as though to make sure of the truth of his answer to her questions, and her small mouth gave indications of an inflexible will,—

"Adrien, what and whom did you see, six nights ago, when you returned to consciousness?"

"You and Dr. Rechard."

"Yes, I know that; but you also saw some one or some object besides, and you heard some communication."

"I repeat that I saw you—at least your counterpart. I was fully aware that you and the doctor were on one side of my bed, when a form like yours came first to the foot, and then to the other side from the place where you were sitting. Perhaps it was your mother, for she bore your likeness and was a shade older."

"What did she say to you?"

Adrien closed his eyes, and after a moment replied, without opening them,—

"It must have been the force of imagination."

"Tell me what brought such an amusing smile to your face."

"I will do so if you press for an answer; and then it will be your turn to smile. I thought that this beautiful woman, who had your hair and eyes, but a very sad look, as though she had suffered, said to me, 'Ilian is your evil star. Beware of her ambition. She has designs upon your peace and welfare. Flee from her.' The absurdity of this statement made me smile. I closed my eyes and refused to listen to any more calumnies on you, my darling, and I immediately fell into a dreamless sleep."

Ilian, at this information, turned deathly pale, and arose from her chair, went to the open window, and looked out upon the garden. Adrien heard her say, as if speaking to herself, "Is this a warning? shall I desist? No, I cannot retreat. After all, it is only a sick man's fancy."

She returned to her chair and seated herself again before him. There was a fixed look of stern determination on her face that made him feel uncomfortable. Slowly but distinctly she said, "Adrien, do you remember the solemn promise you made on the 3d of May to grant my request of a single word?"

"Yes," was the reply; "I have not forgotten it; and you

promised to help me out of the dilemma with honor and credit to myself."

"I have done so; and in a week or so more, when you are fully recovered, I will tell you how it was accomplished, and, in fact, the only way."

A look of intense relief and joy came into Adrien's face, and, with tears, he replied, "Oh, Ilian, what a load you have taken off my mind; you have made me supremely happy."

"I will not weary you to-day with too many questions, for I am anxious to avoid taxing your strength too much; but I will ask you about my cousin, Alice Rendeem. In your delirium you repeated a conversation that you once had with her, when she asked you what you thought of me, and you replied that you preferred Northern brunettes to Southern blondes."

"I did not know you then as I do now; besides, that was two years ago."

"I doubt very much whether you know me now. I hardly know myself. My master-passion is the love and devotion I bear towards the cause of the South. Dark days are coming upon her. Vicksburg cannot hold out much longer. General Grant has that place in a regular bull-dog grip, and he will not let up for one moment. When that falls, the Mississippi will be in full possession of the Northern forces; and perhaps, after all, our great sacrifices will have been in vain. I must leave you now for a while, and will come back this afternoon and read to you."

Four days more went by without any special incident. It was early in the forenoon. Ilian had called to say that some special business needed her presence, and that it would be five in the evening before she returned. Shortly after, his two servants asked permission to go out to make some purchases, and he was thus left alone. He went down to the parlor and sat in an easy-chair to read. The weather was sultry, and he fell asleep.

It seemed to him that the door-bell rang, and that he went and opened it. There to his amazement, stood his grandfather, Judge Rathmine. It was as though the portrait which hung in his father's drawing-room in Boston had suddenly become endowed with life. The expression on the face was a serious one, "Adrien," he said, "leave this house at once. Go and report yourself to Commodore Morris. The delay of an hour may be fatal to all your hopes of happiness. I obtained special permission to come and warn you, provided I did not attempt in any way to interfere with your free agency. Ilian's mother gave you one warning; I give you another, and it will be the last. You must ask no questions, for I cannot answer them; farewell!"

Adrien tried to speak, but he could not utter a word. With a great effort he found utterance in a groan. He opened his eyes, and it was a dream, for he was still in his chair. "Only the effects of the morphia which I have taken," he said to himself. He walked up and down the room, thinking over the strange warning. Should he heed it? He ought to report in person on board of the " Pensacola." He had been told before this that Dr. Rechard had reported his illness in due form to the Commodore, and had also written to his father. At this moment he heard a carriage drive slowly up the street. He went to the front door and opened it. The carriage stopped, and the driver asked him if he would like to take a drive? Here was the opportunity to report to Commodore Morris. His hat and coat which he had worn at the Grosvenor House were in his bedroom. He now had on a silk wrapper, the gift of Ilian. He also had ample funds. He could drive to his own apartment, put on his uniform, report what he had discovered, stop the " Emily Sutton," and raid the Grosvenor House. This was his duty, and he felt strong enough to do it. If necessary, he could be back long before Ilian was expected. But would this be the proper way? Would it be a manly course to sneak out of her house as though he was afraid of her? Was she not his affianced wife? Might not such a proceeding show a want of confidence? He resolved that he would notify her, and on the morrow would leave and report himself to Commodore Morris. He answered the driver that some other day he might accept his offer, but not now. The door was closed. He went back to his chair and took up his book, but he could not read. The warning was vivid before him. Once more he fell asleep, and was awakened by one of his servants, who stood before him with a large tray of refreshments. It was now two o'clock. The afternoon glided away, and he looked for the return of Ilian. How bitterly he repented afterwards that he did not heed this counsel **of his grandfather so** mysteriously given. But how was it possible **that the** judge, who had been in his grave twenty-two years, could come back? Did he do so? Was it not a phantom of dreamland, a mere coincidence? Things **just** happen so. Some persons explain it in that way.

CHAPTER V.

COERCION.

Precisely at five o'clock Ilian drove up in her carriage. Adrien met her at the door, and they went into the parlor together. At first he thought of telling her the dream, but decided **not to do so.** He informed her, however, that he purposed **to report for duty to** Commodore Morris **on** the following day.

"Impossible!" **was her reply;** "**Dr. Rechard tells me that it** will not be prudent for you to go on duty for at least two weeks, and advises **that** you go into the country. I have a **house** vacant **on Lake** Pontchartrain, and we will **take you there to-morrow. The commodore** does not want **you to come on board till all** danger of contagion from **the fever is** passed. **Dr. Rechard called upon** him a few days **ago about** your **affairs, and** he was very uneasy, being afraid **that the** doctor **might have the** contagion of the fever in his clothes. **No, I** am satisfied that if you **went on board the** 'Pensacola' **now, they would be** terribly frightened. Two or three weeks **will give you** time to recuperate."

"**The naval law** compels me to have a **sick-leave** officially signed. I cannot leave the limits of the city without it. I will **go to my** apartment to-morrow, and will report by special messenger."

"Adrien, **I am in great trouble and need** your help."

"**Command my services. I owe** you my **life.**"

"What would be the use? **I have** asked several favors of **you,** and you have declined, **even** when you had solemnly promised to do what I asked **you.**"

"Has not that matter been settled?"

"No; for you may decline the compromise."

"Do not fear on that point; I will take an oath on it."

"That is just what I want you to do. First, let me say that I did not think you would condescend to play the spy, and worm yourself into the confidence of Bill Harrison. If I had known that you were going there the day that you left me, I would have taken steps to prevent it."

"All is fair in war as in love."

"Is it? Perhaps you would not think so if it were applied to you. I heard from Harrison of the great acquisition he secured in a man to command the 'Emily Sutton,' but I never for a moment suspected that you were the individual."

"What was wrong in my action? I had been detailed by Commodore Morris to find out who were connected with blockade-running. I followed out my instructions, and will send my report to him with full details to-morrow."

"Are you fully decided on this course?"

"Certainly; such are my instructions."

"Then, Captain Andrew MacKenzie, as you called yourself, allow me to say that no such information as you propose will be given by you to Commodore Morris, or to any other Yankee officer. I must bring matters to a crisis sooner than I expected."

"Who will prevent it, I would like to know?"

"I will, by every means in my power."

"Will you have me fail in my duty to my country, and render myself liable to court-martial?"

"What do you call your country?"

"The Union government in general; Massachusetts in particular."

"You were born in England."

"True; but, as I have told you before, my ancestors for several generations were born near Boston; besides, I have sworn to uphold the Federal constitution, and my oath must be kept at all hazards."

"Well, so have I taken a solemn vow to uphold the Southern cause, and mean to keep my oath. Now answer me, did you not purpose to deliver the 'Emily Sutton,' with her two mates and crew and all her valuable cargo, into the hands of the Union authorities to be adjudged a prize?"

"Yes, that was my intention, and I will ask for a prize-crew to-morrow, and go myself and bring her to anchor alongside of the flag-ship 'Pensacola,' and also investigate the contents of the cellar of the Grosvenor House."

"Perhaps under proper persuasion you will do nothing of the kind, or in any way disturb the traffic and business of Bill Harrison. As for the 'Emily Sutton,' it may interest you to know that I have received word this morning that she arrived safely in Mobile, and will be out again in a few days with cotton for Havana. As for Harrison himself, perhaps the next time you meet him it will be to hail him as a comrade in arms, as the business carried on here has been removed to other quarters. Captain Harrison has received his commission from Richmond to command a company of English volunteers, and will report to Colonel Ormond at Mobile for duty with his regiment."

"What are you thinking about? Are you losing your senses?"

"Not at all; I mean what I say. Let me ask you another question. Are you aware what would have been your fate if your identity had been discovered by Harrison, and all your treacherous intentions become known to him?"

"Why do you use that word? I was there in the legitimate discharge of my duties."

"Please answer my question."

"Well, there would have been an end of my command of that schooner for Harrison & Co.'s interest. A few hard words would have followed, and I would have returned at once with a prize-crew from the 'Pensacola,' and those triple-department casks and their valuable contents would have gone north instead of south."

"What a nice programme you have drawn. Now let me give one not quite so rosy. In less than twenty minutes after it had become known that the so-called Captain Andrew MacKenzie, of Manchester, England, the famous blockade-runner, was no other than the distinguished Acting Master Adrien Homerand, of the Federal navy, you would have been at the bottom of the Mississippi with a dagger in your heart and a rope heavily weighted around your neck. Indeed, the very morning that you were taken ill Harrison received word that an officer of the Union navy had been detailed to investigate his business. I will further inform you **that at the very moment when** I received your note **stating you were ill, a counsel of war was sitting, and had resolved to demand** satisfactory **references** from you. **Harrison vouched for your being a full-blooded** Englishman, and scorned **the suggestion that you were a Yankee spy.** I did not recognize your writing, **as your hand** must have been unsteady from illness; and it was only when **I was privately questioning Sam that it suddenly flashed upon me that Captain MacKenzie and you were the same person.** I **caused you to be removed to this house at once, thereby saving you from vengeance. Dr. Rechard will tell you that it was the nursing which you received here that kept you alive; so that twice I saved your** life, once forfeited as a spy, **and again as a victim to the fever."**

"Ilian, I acknowledge my gratitude, and **my whole** life will be devoted to your service."

"I do not credit that statement. If I were to ask a single proof I would not get it."

"How can you thus doubt **my** love and devotion?"

"Because it is all in promises, and **not in deeds.** Have you forgotten that you forfeited your solemn pledge to grant me a request of a single word?"

"That **one word** meant the forfeiture **of** my honor and **all** that I hold sacred."

"Nonsense; this is all moonshine."

"But, my dear, you told me that you had a compromise that would solve the problem of how to keep my word and **yet not resign.**"

"I did; and I now repeat that my request of **one word can be granted, and yet** you need not resign."

"I am curious to know how."

"**It is easy enough.** I will waive my claim to your resignation for the compromise I mention."

"Oh, what a load you have taken off my heart. I love you now with a thousand-fold **more fervor** than I ever did before."

"How long will that fervor last?"

"**Till** death shall separate us."

"The substitute of my claim to your resignation is a simple one; and all **your** honor and past service will be saved, and **your war record remain** untarnished **on** the books of the Navy Department."

"Tell me what it is, and I will cheerfully comply with it."

"I must have a stronger word as a guarantee than 'cheerfully.'"

"What can I give you?"

"You failed me once in a solemn promise; now I want a binding obligation that you will not dare to break."

"If I am not to be called upon to resign, why all this formality?"

"Because great interests are at stake. In return for twice saving your life, and giving up my just claim to your resignation from the naval service of the North, do you solemnly promise and swear before your Maker that you will accept the substitute and fulfil the compromise?"

"I cannot take that oath till I know the tenor of your request. You surely do not ask me to walk blindfolded into any snare which would involve my peace of mind and shipwreck all that I hold dear in life."

"No; I will not ask you to walk blindfolded. I will state my request in advance, and then you *must* take the oath that I have demanded."

"'*Must*,' did you say? Is not that a dictatorial word?"

"Yes; and I repeat it, *must!* Now for my ultimatum."

"Ultimatum! Am I dreaming?"

"No; you are wide awake and in full possession of your faculties; but listen. You have of your own free choice assumed the name of 'Captain Andrew MacKenzie,' a friend of the South; therefore, under that name you must enter our service and take a solemn oath of allegiance to the Confederate cause. I have procured you the command of a company of artillery in the regiment of Colonel Ormond, and in two weeks I expect to see you under the gray, drilling your men at Mobile."

"Ilian, have you gone mad?"

"No; I have every reason to believe that my reason is upon her pedestal and my judgment upon her throne."

"How can you reconcile this preposterous request with your assertion that you waive my fatal obligation to resign? My God! do you want to brand me as a deserter?"

"Not at all. You do not understand your present relations to the Federal navy."

"You speak in enigmas."

"Then I will solve them. Ten nights ago three physicians gave up all hopes of your surviving for more than a few hours; in fact, you were virtually a dead man. Therefore the next morning, at my request, Dr. Rechard officially notified Commodore Morris that you had died of black vomit, and had been buried at daylight. An unknown man who had died of this disease in one of the small hotels of the city, and who was attended by a friend of Dr. Rechard's, gave us the opportunity to procure a body, and it was buried under your name. A kind letter of sympathy was also written to your father. Word was sent to your late ship on the blockade. The newspapers have printed your obituary. Now do you understand that Acting Master Adrien Homerand is dead and buried? A tombstone of white marble was this morning placed over his grave. I have announced to my friends that I am not at home. To-morrow Dr. Rechard will come with us to the house that I have mentioned, by Lake Pontchartrain, till you are able to join your regiment."

"Oh, Heaven help me!" was the exclamation of the astounded man. "My loving father and my fond mother! how can they bear the awful news? It will break their hearts."

"Thousands of other parents, both in the North and South, are weeping for sons as well-beloved as you are."

"How was it possible that you could be so cruel?"

"Did you not remark a little while ago that all was fair in war as in love? I did this to save your life. You are strongly suspected of being a spy possessed of important secrets about blockade-running. The secret service of the Confederate government, who have a branch in this city, informed me at noon that a strict watch would be placed on this house; and at two o'clock their men were guarding it with orders to kill you instantly if you should attempt to leave before your identity was fully established. Harrison pledged his life as security that you were what you assumed to be. I also gave a guarantee to that effect, and that you would take command of a company in Colonel Ormond's regiment. Only that will satisfy them. Do you now swear to accept the compromise and serve the South?"

"I cannot do it; I will die first."

Ilian remained cool, calm, and collected. She took from

her hair what appeared to be a large hair-pin with a cross handle, drawing from its sheath a fine dagger with a blade five inches **long,** which looked like a darning-needle. She placed its keen point to Adrien's throat, and said in a low voice, that carried a conviction of her purpose,—

"I love you better than **any** other mortal being, but I love the **Southern** cause more; and for that I would sacrifice my life and **yours.** Harrison's life **is now a hostage** for your oath **of fidelity, and your silence on the points that** you have **gained must be secured. Swear, therefore,** to comply with all I **have demanded, or I** will claim the forfeit of the life which I **have twice saved."**

Adrien was still weak from the fever. **For a moment he** hesitated. The point of the blade entered the skin; the steel was cold. The animal instinct of life overpowered all other considerations. Slowly he uttered the words, "*I solemnly swear to do as you bid me.*"

Then he became unconscious.

CHAPTER VI.

UNDER THE GRAY.

THREE **days** after the closing scene **in the last** chapter Adrien had sufficiently recovered to be able to leave for Lake Pontchartrain with Dr. Rechard and several servants. Ilian and her **maid** joined **them two days** afterwards.

When she saw her **lover become** totally unconscious, after taking **the oath required of** him, she was in an agony **of remorse, lest the coercion** had killed him. Several hours had passed **before his symptoms** yielded to Dr. Rechard's treatment. His memory **was** partly affected, and for fully a week the past was almost a **blank.** The **quiet rest by** the lake-side gradually **restored him, but** he manifested a great reserve toward Ilian. It **was hoped that in time this** would wear **away.**

On the 15th **of** July he and **Dr.** Rechard left for Mobile. He found his commission as captain of artillery awaiting him;

and the doctor also accepted an appointment as surgeon to the regiment of **Colonel Ormond, to whom Adrien** was ordered to **report for duty** under **his command.** He was then holding a **strong position near the** city **of** Mobile. The colonel gave a **very hearty** greeting to the new-comer. **Dr.** Rechard explained that Captain MacKenzie had served for several years **as a** junior officer in the navy of his country **and was** proficient in the drilling of men and handling of batteries. **The** inference of course was that meant the English naval service. Dr. Rechard was not willing to depart from the truth, and only his love for the South and his faith in the wisdom of Ilian's **course of** action **induced him to** aid in the deception practised. She **had exacted** a solemn promise from him that he would serve with his college friend in all his campaigns, and herself promised **to** render **all** needful assistance. She **had** returned to **New Orleans, but was expected** shortly in Mobile.

Young as she was, her influence was widely felt through the **Southern States.** Having both talent and money, she soon **became** an important auxiliary **in the war.** Her specialty was the secret service of the Confederate government. She had been seeking to control the Southern branch of this important service. The official at the head of it in New Orleans was one of that class of men who have no faith in woman's power to hold secrets, and he worked against her.

On the 10th of July her wish was granted. The **whole** Southern department of the secret service was placed **in her** sole charge.

It would be difficult to describe the feelings of Adrien when, dressed **in** the gray **uniform of** the Confederacy, he took charge of **his** company of artillery and gave his first orders of command. None of his old friends would have recognized him. His beard, which he had formerly worn full, was **now** trimmed to the regulation English side-whiskers. This altered his appearance very much. His cheerful gayety **of** manner had left him. He was **still** kind and courteous, but **had a** sad **and** wandering look, that left the **impression** on the beholder **that he was not** quite sure **of his own** identity. **This was attributed to the** fever and the fact that he had **not been** acclimated.

At times, indeed, he was not sure of who he really **was. It** was like a dream. He brooded so much over his change of position that at last he came to accept the fact that, during the fourth night of the fever, the spirit of Adrien Homerand had left its bodily tabernacle, and another, that was called Andrew MacKenzie, had entered the vacant mansion with its cultivated mental faculties. This being the case, there was no treason in the new-comer serving the South. This solution of the cause of the change of his condition was fostered by Dr. Rechard, and also by Ilian, who came to Mobile a week later. She was not long in finding out that the deep love and devotion once exhibited by Adrien was not manifested by Captain Mac-Kenzie. His eyes never more sparkled with joy at her approach; the voice that had so often brought music to her soul was no longer that of the former days. Even the footsteps were changed. In the privacy of her own room she shed bitter tears as the conviction was slowly but surely forced upon her that in the hour when she had coerced her lover into taking a position so utterly at variance with his principles of honor and duty, that same hour he had substantially died, and that this was a being with the old form, but a strange tenant had taken possession of it. Would he, the Adrien of the olden time, ever return? It was now she knew how deep had been her love. Day by day its force increased, but he remained the same. Nor was this all, Dr. Rechard informed her that there was great danger that his personal identity might be revealed if she was heard to call him by that name that was woven in all the fibres of her heart. There were many of his college-mates in the Southern army, and the name of Adrien was so peculiarly the property of the son of Boston's great professor that unpleasant inquiries would be set on foot. "Above all," continued the doctor, "we must be careful of Tom Jeffords, who is captain of a battery in a South Carolina regiment lately come into this neighborhood. This fellow was very intimate with Adrien at college. He is a born detective, and if he should discover this, his silence would be a costly purchase; therefore, for the credit and safety of all concerned, the name of Adrien must remain in the grave where his friends suppose that he was buried."

This was the keenest pang of all. How could she substitute the name of Andrew for one that had so often thrilled her with delight? Yet even this would have been endurable if there had been any response from the man whom she had won for the Confederate cause, who was now lost to her as a lover.

For the present, therefore, the name of Adrien must lie in abeyance, and we will follow the fortune of Andrew MacKenzie under the gray uniform of the South.

Many readers will condemn in unsparing terms the conduct of Ilian, and assert that she was cruel, and perhaps use even harsher terms. Before a judgment is rendered as to her action, it will be best to wait until all of the facts in the case are presented. It is a difficult task at this late day, so far removed from the times of the civil war, to explain the intense patriotism of the Southern women to the cause which they had espoused with so much zeal and fervor. It is a well-known fact that long after the men were convinced of the hopelessness of the contest against the almost unlimited resources of the Northern States, the women would not listen to any compromise short of actual independence; and they endured terrible privations and made heroic sacrifices, that have never been emblazoned on the pages of the history of the greatest civil war that ever occurred for many generations. Ilian gave her money, her time, and she would have given her life if necessary to have won the independence for which they were fighting.

CHAPTER VII.

PENSACOLA NAVY-YARD.

WE now turn to the baptism of fire that was to inaugurate the new departure of the son of Professor Homerand. We can speak of his deeds; but the agony of his soul is beyond the power of our pen to depict.

In the month of August, 1863, General G. T. Beauregard, commanding the Confederate military forces of South Carolina, Georgia, and Florida, determined upon a raid for the destruction of the stores in the Pensacola Navy-Yard. He had been informed that about a million dollars' worth were accumulated there, and perceived at once that their loss would be severely felt by the blockading fleet. Colonel Ormond was ordered accordingly to send a company of artillery to report to the general commanding the raiding forces. When assembled they numbered four hundred cavalry and four hundred infantry, and a battery of field-pieces under Captain Andrew MacKenzie. The only difficulty anticipated was in crossing the mouth of a narrow bayou not more than three feet deep. Then came a short stretch of sandy beach leading into a wooded tract two miles in length, at the end of which was one of the navy-yard gates. The wall of the yard continued into the water of the bay, but this was an easy matter to ford. The only defence of this gate was a twelve-pounder howitzer and a marine guard of fifty men under the command of Captain George W. Collier. There were also a number of war-ships at anchor off the yard; a single gun-schooner, the "Maria A. Wood," with a battery of two long thirty-two-pounders and one pivot twenty-four-pounder, constituted the sole protection of the mouth of the bayou and the sand-beach. There was a picket guard of colored troops along the bayou, but persons continually passed and repassed.

The general commanding the Confederate raiding force was well acquainted with all of the details of the defences of the yard. On a cool September morning he arrived at the eastern edge of the mouth of the bayou. The thick woods at this point prevented his presence there from being known to the Federal forces. It had been previously arranged that as soon as darkness set in the cavalry should silently cross the bayou and dash on through the woods, and some should ford the water round the walls, open the eastern gate for the rest to enter, and then set fire to all the buildings and storehouses. They felt confident that the gun-boats would not fire on them, as the hospital was full of patients with yellow-fever: and long before they could be removed to a place of safety the work of destroying the stores would be accomplished. Strict orders were given that the hospital was not to be molested in any way. The infantry were directed to capture the few pickets along the bayou, and hold it against any superior force from Fort Barancas. The battery of artillery was to sink the "Maria A. Wood," this being the only vessel that was reported to them as being there. But two days previous, in answer to the representations of the executive officer of the gun-schooner, a mortar-schooner had been sent up from the navy-yard to assist in guarding the mouth of the bayou. This additional vessel was a serious obstacle to the well-planned raid. Captain MacKenzie informed his general that he felt confident that he could sink or disable one of the schooners, but that to engage two of them was a serious risk, especially as the "Maria A. Wood" was a vessel of five hundred tons, and well manned and drilled. He also told him that unless the vessels were sunk or driven off very few of the cavalry would return alive through the sweeping fire of grape and canister which both vessels could concentrate on the beach and waters of the bayou.

At ten o'clock the executive officer of the mortar-schooner, not dreaming of any hostile force being so near, took a small boat, with only the captain's steward, to hunt for wild turkeys, which were plentiful in that locality. Both were captured before an alarm could be given of the presence of the enemy. The statement of the officer that the vessels could concentrate six heavy guns on the beach besides the destructive thirteen-inch mortar was not encouraging to the Confederates. Nevertheless the general determined to make the attack that same night. Captain MacKenzie had learned that his old friend, formerly the acting ensign of the "Tennessee," was the executive officer of the "Maria A. Wood." Upon receiving this information, he was greatly perplexed. He felt that he could not fire on her. He also knew the destructive power of the long thirty-two pounders at close quarters. They were only a thousand yards off, and his battery of six pieces consisted of only twelve-pounders. He urged the necessity of sending for reinforcements. A council of war was held, and finally decided that this was the best course. So they went into camp twenty-five miles from the bayou. Captain MacKenzie volunteered to stay behind and intercept any crew that might be sent for the captured officer. Fifty men from one of the infantry companies were placed under his orders for that purpose.

When night came on they concealed themselves in ambush close to the landing-place, and their watching was rewarded about eight o'clock by hearing the regular stroke of the oars of a man-of-war boat, which came to the beach close by the place where they lay. Both of the gun-boats had their crews at quarters, and were ready for action. Captain MacKenzie counted eighteen men besides the officer in the boat. It was his intention to rush in as soon as they had landed, kill the officer, and make the men prisoners. He believed that the schooners would not fire on their own men. But the officer of the boat had received strict orders not to land. He was directed to hail the beach, and, if no answer was returned, to come back and wait for daylight. As soon as his voice rang out on the night air, Captain MacKenzie recognized it as that of his old friend of the "Tennessee," now the executive of the "Maria A. Wood." How he longed to be able to speak with him, to make a confidant of him, and tell him how he had been compelled to take a solemn oath to remain in the Confederate service till the war was over. This, however, was impossible, unless he could make him a prisoner. The sound of that voice re-echoing among the trees brought back in vivid force the consciousness of his former position. It acted like a magic wand to dispel the cloud that hung over his mind. His men urged him to give the order to fire on the Yankee officer standing in the bow of the boat, his body clearly defined by the starlight. He was a splendid target, and a score of rifles were drawn on him. It was a terrible moment for the Confederate captain. How could he give the order to shoot the man whose life he had once saved, and whom he valued as a true friend? No; he would not do it. He whispered to his men that he would brain the first man who dared to fire without orders. Half of his command were already creeping down with bayonets fixed, hoping to carry the boat and the crew by storm. To have peremptorily ordered them back would have disclosed the ambush. A moment afterward, however, the boat pushed off from the beach and returned to the vessel.

Captain MacKenzie was too strict a disciplinarian to allow the violation of his orders to pass unnoticed. On reaching the encampment the guilty ones were severely punished, and it was soon made known that the English captain was not a man to be trifled with.

The next day news reached Fort Barancas of the close proximity of a large body of the Confederates, and a strong force was immediately posted on the west side of the bayou. Notice was sent to the gun-boats to that effect. They opened fire and shelled the woods. The contemplated raid, however, was made that night. The general commanding the raiding forces determined to make an effort to storm the navy-yard. Captain MacKenzie was sent with his battery to hold in check the troops from Barancas, and was assisted by two hundred infantry, while the remainder were to hold the mouth of the bayou. On reaching that point, however, it was discovered that two steam gun-boats had been sent up from the lower station. The Federal picket gave the warning signal, and the fierce bombardment of the four vessels convinced the raiding-party that the favorable opportunity was gone. Before they reached a place of safety a number of men were killed and wounded by the far-reaching shells. The retreat was nobly covered from the pursuing Union troops by Captain MacKenzie, who stood the brunt of the battle. Thus ended the great raid, which, if carried out a week earlier, might have been successful. The destruction of the navy-yard and its valuable stores would have been an important factor in prolonging the war, and, perhaps, in obtaining the longed-for recognition of the Southern Confederacy by France, as much would have been made of it. Captain MacKenzie returned with his battery to Mobile, and was warmly greeted by Colonel Ormond and the other officers of his regiment.

CHAPTER VIII.

AMBITION FOILED.

ILIAN kept herself well informed of the movements of her lover. A dread had taken possession of her, lest he should be killed in some action with the Federal forces. This would have been a disaster that would have crushed her. On his return to Mobile she received a letter from Dr. Rechard that gave her a detailed description of their expedition, and also the indifference to danger manifested by Captain MacKenzie. When his battery was covering the rear of the retreating raiding forces, a shell from a thirty-two-pounder had taken a man's head off at his side, yet he never appeared excited. His coolness was the theme of admiration of all the troops.

This was any thing but pleasant reading to Ilian. Was it possible that he was seeking death on the field of battle? She had not won him from the Union navy for any such purpose. She could not understand the change which he had manifested. Apparently it was not from the fever. For on the morning of the day she had coerced him into taking that terrible oath he was bright and cheerful. The next day he was able to leave his bed, but the whole man was transformed. A new spirit seemed to have taken possession of the stately form. There was no longer any opposition on his part to any of her wishes. His manner was that of a prisoner to his jailer, meekly obedient and without comment. She now had a period of three months of trial for her pet scheme. The final success of the Southern States she had never doubted. She fondly hoped that the name of Captain Andrew MacKenzie would rise to the zenith of the war-horizon as a star of the first magnitude. At the close of the fratricidal contest, with the rank of lieutenant-general, he would clasp her as his bride and tell her how much he was indebted to her forethought for his exalted position in the Confederacy of the Southern States, and a grateful country would call him to the presidential chair. All this, and more too, she had pictured to herself. Now, when all had gone so smoothly in the grooves prepared by her, she was rudely awakened from her dream by the information contained in Dr. Rechard's letter. Could it be possible that the man whom she hoped by her help to raise so high was seeking death in battle?

Ilian was a woman of infinite resources, and she determined at once upon a course to pursue: first, that Captain MacKenzie should be promoted; and, secondly, to keep him out of the range of the Federal bullets till such time as he had recovered the full vigor of his mental condition.

The Confederate authorities of Richmond had early in the war learned to appreciate the great value of the services of Miss Mordine. Her vast wealth was freely employed to aid and establish the right of the Southern people to deliverance from the bond of the Federal Union. Several of their great leaders who, in the beginning of the contest, were disposed to uphold the Union, had been convinced by her able and clear presentation of the just claims of one or more of the States to withdraw at any time from the compact of federation by a two-thirds vote of their citizens. The strength of her logic was not only in her tongue, her eyes were powerful agents that few could resist. She not only sustained the courage of her own people, but she greatly disheartened the officers of the Union army and navy whenever they could be reached. As an "interviewer" she had no equal, and when any secret expedition was planned she generally contrived by adroit questions, seemingly innocent, to obtain knowledge of all the particulars needed. If any one of the other sex thinks this description of Ilian and her power to obtain State secrets overdrawn, let him try the experiment. He may be possessed of valuable information, and a young and handsome woman about one degree removed from the mundane conception of angels in form and temperament desires to obtain it from him. How long will he stand up against her art? There will have to be a radical change in man's nature when he finds himself proof against all the fascination which a beautiful woman with superior talent can bring to bear.

Such was Ilian, and her influence was felt in every department of the government at Richmond. On the evening of the day that she received the letter from Dr. Rechard she sent a letter from New Orleans to the Secretary of War asking for the promotion of Captain MacKenzie to the post of major of his regiment, which was then vacant. She also asked for a complimentary letter recognizing his gallantry in the face of the enemy. By the return of the mail she received information that both requests were granted. At once she hastened to Mobile to witness the reading of the official order of promotion, which in highly flattering terms referred to the services of the brave captain. She keenly watched his face as he received the congratulations of his colonel and brother officers, and also the cheers of his men, who had become devotedly attached to him. He acknowledged their greetings with a smile, and replied that he was sorry that some one more worthy had not been selected for the high honor which had been conferred upon him. When Ilian took his hand and expressed her joy at the advancement of the brave Major MacKenzie, she realized for the first time in her life that there was one man who was not under the power of her magnetism. Her eyes filled with tears and her love for him increased a hundred-fold. All this had no effect

15*

upon the major. He merely bowed, and then in a tone which was not intended to be ironical, but was quiet and dignified, replied, "It was indeed a great honor to have her approval of his actions, and he hoped to prove more worthy."

With a smile that would have melted the heart of the most cynical woman-hater, she told him she looked for a time, and that not far distant, when she could behold the triple stars of a lieutenant-general on his shoulders; and that then when the war was over she would be ready to redeem her promise; "but not," she added, with her sweetest manner, "for the stars, but for the man himself who wore them."

For a moment there was a gleam of sunshine on his face, as though the recollection of some pleasant dream came before him; then followed that inexpressible look of sadness which was habitually there, and he asked, with an inquiring look,—

"To what promise does Miss Mordine refer?"

This was the first time since their engagement that he had made use of this formal term; and now he had apparently forgotten that she had promised to marry him.

This was too much for her to endure. Her first impulse was to throw herself into his arms and call him by the name of Adrien, which she treasured in her inmost heart, and to ask him whether he had forgotten his Ilian and her vow to be his loving little wife. But they were in the presence of his regiment, and in order to control her feelings, which were ready to break down all barriers, she drew herself up to her full height, and in a haughty tone replied,—

"I am sorry that my promises are of so little importance to Major Mackenzie that he has to ask for information of their purport. Perhaps others may be more interested in what I offer to do." And, bowing coldly, she left him.

Colonel Ormond now came up, and, with a look of intense surprise, remarked,—

"Why, major, you have offended Miss Mordine."

"Have I? In what way?" was the innocent answer.

Dr. Rechard whispered in the colonel's ear, "Perhaps it is a lover's quarrel, and it were better not to interfere."

Thus was her ambition partly foiled, but it was to be totally checkmated at a later period. Ilian, however, gained her point in keeping the major out of danger, for he was assigned to the command of one of the small forts at the head of Mobile Bay.

She made up her mind to adopt new tactics. She would for a while keep away from the major, and then perhaps he would learn to appreciate her services.

In the performance of his duties in strengthening his fort, and keeping on the alert at all times, the autumn of 1863 passed gradually away. Rumors were current from time to time that Admiral Farragut proposed to attack Fort Morgan, pass the batteries, and thus hold the route by water to the city of Mobile. Every preparation was made to resist.

CHAPTER IX.

BATTLE OF MOBILE BAY.

I CANNOT undertake to give a detailed account of the great historic battle of Mobile Bay, but only refer to such portions of it as come within the experience of Major MacKenzie. A very able description, however, is given by Commander A. T. Mahan, United States Navy, in his book called *The Gulf and Inland Waters*. I will take the liberty of copying a few remarks, which will serve our purpose:

"The city of Mobile is thirty miles from the Gulf, at the head of a great bay of the same name. The entrance from the Gulf was guarded by two works,—Fort Morgan, on Mobile Point, and Fort Gaines, on Dauphin Island. There were also other small forts at different points. The most formidable was Fort Morgan, already mentioned. It was five-sided, and was built to carry guns in casemate and barbette, and had a water-battery facing the channel. The total number of guns were about fifty, nearly all of heavy calibre.

"In the waters of the bay there was a little Confederate squadron under Admiral Franklin Buchanan. The most powerful ironclad built by the Confederacy was his flag-ship, and called the 'Tennessee.' The preparations for the defence of Mobile Bay was not confined to the forts and ships. Torpedoes were thickly planted, and a long line of pile obstructions extended from the point of Dauphin Island to within two hundred and twenty-six feet of Fort Morgan. Thus prepared, they awaited the coming battle."

We now turn back to Ilian. Shortly after the promotion of the major in October she had gone North. She passed the lines without trouble, visited Washington and New York, where Colonel Hortense was installed in charge of the bureau of the Confederate secret service. She remained a few days with Mrs. Hortense, and her son once more renewed his offer of marriage. She told him that she had postponed the consideration of matrimony till the war should end. After finishing her business in New York she went to Boston, and there made particular inquiries as to how Professor Homerand and his wife had borne the loss of their son. She was informed that the regret was universal at the untimely fate of Adrien. His father had aged very much and seemed to have lost all interest in the war, and had lately gone to Europe with his sorrowing wife. She also paid a visit to the grave of her aunt, and while standing by the side of the marble shaft that marked the place, she reflected upon her Hannibal oath. If it was still binding, it had been fully carried out. The senior Homerand and his wife were exiles from home, bowed down beneath their terrible calamity. Their son, whom they mourned as dead, was a deserter from the flag he had sworn to defend, and bound by a terrible oath to remain where he was. If, on the contrary, the oath was null and void, then she had done nothing amiss, but had won from the Union forces a champion for her beloved South ; and as he was born in England, no such stigma would attach to him as it would if he had been a native of the North. Besides, if the Southern independence was won, then no one need ever know his past history. Thus she reasoned. The logic must stand or fall on its own merits.

Late in December Ilian again returned to Mobile.

It was a great disappointment to her to perceive that while Major MacKenzie was enjoying sound physical health, yet his mind was still clouded. His great hobby was the remarkable proposition that two spirits could exchange their earthly tabernacles regardless of sex, as they were in their own function independent of the body, which, indeed, was merely, as Professor Holmes once expressed it, an omnibus for the carriage of the spirit across the continent of this life, and so was liable to be invaded at any time by one or more other beings of the same nature. On all other points his arguments were clear and logical. As he was a genial companion, no particular attention was paid to this peculiarity.

When his duties permitted, he mixed in society, won a host of friends, and was a special favorite of the ladies. He had a fine, cultivated voice, and sang frequently in French and German. His greatest hit, however, was the old ballad called "A fine old English Gentleman, one of the Olden Time." None ever tired of hearing him sing it.

On New-Year's-Day of 1864 a grand ball was given in Mobile in honor, as it was termed, of the brave defenders of the South. Major MacKenzie was the lion of the evening. Ilian came on from New Orleans to attend it. For the first time she felt the pangs of jealousy. Judges and generals were bowing at her feet, delighted if they but gained a smile, while the man who held her heart was indifferent to her attractions.

When the gallant major was asked by one of the ladies how he liked the handsome dress of Miss Mordine, he replied that he had not noticed it. He was surrounded by the belles of the evening, with whom he laughed and chatted in his brightest mood; but when Ilian spoke to him he would only bow and express how much he was indebted to her. She could not tell whether he was sarcastic or not.

Her mortification reached its culminating point when supper was announced. She had mentioned to him that several gentlemen were anxious to take her in to supper, but that courtesy was reserved for her dearest friend. She then looked smilingly into his face, but he would not take the hint. He simply said, "What a highly-favored man that friend must be!" She employed every little feminine art to induce him to escort her in to the table, but of no avail. At last, at midnight, when the meal was announced, she saw him offer his arm to a handsome woman and go with her into the dining-hall.

Jealousy and offended dignity, when united in a woman of such a temperament as Ilian, produce a condition of mind very difficult to describe. Two days after Major MacKenzie received orders to report for special duty to the officer com-

m

manding Fort Morgan, and it was only at rare intervals that he was permitted to visit Mobile.

Thus passed the spring and early summer. On the 1st of August the Confederate forces were made aware that the long-expected battle for possession of Mobile Bay was at hand.

The day before the fleet entered, Major MacKenzie was transferred from Fort Morgan to the command of a small fort, supposed to be far above where the severe fighting would take place.

Ilian was at this time in New York engaged upon secret service. She had only seen the Major once since the New-Year's ball. His manner was courteous in the extreme, and he appeared anxious to please her, but there was no beaming of love in his eyes. Her heart was bursting, and there was no one in whom she could confide except Dr. Rechard. That secret of her coercion was too terrible to trust to any one else. When the news came to her that the victorious Admiral Farragut was about to open fire from his formidable fleet upon the forts in Mobile Bay, she was in the utmost distress, lest that life which was now dearer to her than her own should be sacrificed in the combat. At her request he had been transferred, as she thought, to a place of safety. She herself hastened to return to the theatre of conflict; but before reaching her destination the battle had been fought and won, and the standard of the Union floated over the forts and captured vessels of war. The city of Mobile still held out. On her arrival she sought for a list of the casualties, and her eyes eagerly scanned the page,—first the killed, then the wounded, and following the prisoners, lastly the missing. The first name that met her gaze on the latter was that of Major MacKenzie. His fort had been shelled and carried by assault. The shock was too much for her already overstrained nerves, and she swooned away.

When Ilian recovered consciousness Dr. Rechard was standing by her side. In answer to her inquiries, he stated that when it was found that the fort could not hold out, Major MacKenzie had instructed him to leave with such of the wounded as could be taken in a boat which was in the rear of the fort. This he had done. There was another boat in waiting for the major. But when it arrived on the opposite side filled with fugitives he was not in it. It was reported that he had been too badly wounded to be removed, and he must therefore have fallen a prisoner into the hands of the Union forces. This was three days ago; but he had received word this morning that a wounded Confederate officer was lying very ill at a negro cabin ten miles from the city, and he was just preparing to investigate the case and find out who the officer was, when news was brought of her return.

Both realized the awful fate that would be meted out to the major if he was made a prisoner and his identity discovered. Ugly rumors were floating round New Orleans that Miss Mordine had won several Northern officers from their allegiance, who had resigned and were supposed to have gone North, but instead had joined the Confederate army.

Horses were immediately ordered, and within an hour Ilian and Dr. Rechard were in the saddle bound for the place where the wounded officer was said to be.

Who he was will be described in the next chapter.

Note.—It was at first my purpose to give a brief description of the celebrated battle of Mobile Bay, and while I will speak of it in the next chapter, I think it best to refer my readers who may feel interested in it to the work already mentioned at the commencement of this chapter, by Commander A. T. Mahan, **U.S.N.** It is published by Charles Scribner's Sons, and is of deep interest and will repay reading.

CHAPTER X.

ON THE TRAIL.

THE sun was shedding its parting rays over a small negro cabin, in front of which the owner, an old man, was chopping wood. He was interrupted by the unexpected appearance of two foam-covered horses that drew rein before him, and a gentleman and a lady dismounted. They had come, they told him, to offer assistance to a wounded officer who was then in his cottage. The old negro planted himself firmly in front of the door-way and demanded credentials that they were friends. When convinced on this point, he told them that his son was the body-servant of the commanding officer of one of the forts in Mobile Bay which was carried by assault, and in the confusion had taken his master away in a skiff which he had concealed. He took him in a different direction from the other boats, and finally brought him here. He had gone to Mobile to find a Dr. Rechard.

"That is my name," said the gentleman.

As they entered the single room of the cabin they saw a bed in one corner with an occupant whose head was bound with a cloth. By his side sat an old colored woman with a bowl of gruel in her hand, and they heard her say, "Now, honey, you must done gone and took dis 'ere refreshment, for you am pow'ful weak." Then looking up and seeing the two strangers at the door, she exclaimed, "Lor' a massa, here am de friends dat you expect."

The sick man raised himself in the bed with a frightened air, as though dreading capture, and, recognizing who had come, spoke in a voice in which surprise, joy, and excitement were mingled.

"Dr. Rechard, my tried and true friend, thrice welcome. I need your help and skill as never before. Ilian, my own darling, have you come to me? How I have longed in the weary hours of my sickness to hear your footsteps and to listen to that sweet voice of the dear long ago! It seems to me that I have been in a dream; perhaps I am dreaming now, and will awake and find myself——"

Before he could finish she had clasped him in her arms, and her tears fell fast. The doctor withdrew to wipe his own eyes and leave the united lovers alone. The colored pair displayed unbounded delight. Paradise is said to be a place of happiness, because it is in extreme contrast with the trials and miseries of earth. Ilian now felt the force of this. After fourteen months of weary waiting, to hear her name called by that voice that was woven in the essence of her life, in the very hour when she was uncertain as to whether he was living or dead, or what was possibly worse, a prisoner, she had not only found him alive, but his mind was restored and he called her "his darling Ilian." Their happiness, their brief foretaste of an earthly paradise, is too sacred. We may not intrude.

The following morning he was removed by easy stages to Mobile. He had been wounded in two places by fragments of a nine-inch shell, one on the left side of his neck and the other on his left knee. The hurts were not dangerous, but would prevent him from going on active service for several months. A week later he was able to walk around by the aid of a crutch. Ilian was his daily visitor. Her lover had recovered from his mental depression, and she was superlatively happy. He had forgiven her for her act of coercion, as he was convinced from what he had been told that if he had not taken the course he did he would have been assassinated that night, and it would have fared badly with Bill Harrison also. The man was kind to him, had treated him nobly, and had gone security with his own life to the secret-service agents. The major looked upon the matter as belonging to the fortune of war, and could see no way out of it till the contest should end. This, he was aware from all he heard, was likely to occur before long; and then in Europe a new life could be begun, and he would make up some story to his father and mother that would satisfy them. He had not entered into his present position with his own volition, and he must patiently await his release.

He related to Ilian the awful agony of the hour when he saw the famous flag-ship "Hartford," followed by the "Brooklyn" and other ships of the squadron, cross the bar and repeat the tactics of the passage of the forts at New Orleans over two years previous. He witnessed from the parapet of his own fort the terrific combat with the ironclad "Tennessee," and saw the stars and stripes float from her stern. He had received instructions that in case the fleet succeeded in reaching the bay, and his fort was attacked by a superior force, to evacuate and fall back on Mobile. He noticed several ships approach to open fire on his works; and at the same time he discovered a large body of men marching on his flank. Resistance before such overwhelming odds was useless. He only had ten guns of small calibre, so he gave the order to spike them and leave. Before all could depart he observed his old ship steaming up, and she swung her broadside to him and opened fire on his fort by divisions. He saw a number of his old messmates, and he would not return their fire even if he could. He stood still, hoping that death would come to his relief. As the third sheet of flame burst from the sides of the powerful ship-of-war a five-second shell burst almost along-side of him; two of the fragments struck him, and he became unconscious. When he recovered his senses he found himself conveyed in a rough litter by half a dozen of the colored men who had been employed in throwing up breastworks. He had spoken kindly to them, and now in return they were taking him to a place of safety.

Congratulations were offered by his numerous friends, for he and Dr. Rechard were the only ones of his regiment that escaped capture. Colonel Ormond was wounded and a prisoner. Among those who came to see him was Tom Jeffords, whose company to a man had been captured. Tom had escaped; how, no one could tell. His own statement was that he had cut his way through the Yankee hordes and thus reached Mobile. The most singular part of the affair was that his uniform was faultlessly clean and showed no signs of rough usage, and his sword was not even marked, as some thought it should have been when a valiant soldier has fought his way through masses of the enemy. He silenced further criticisms, however, by the blustering assertion that he would shoot, scalp, annihilate, rip up, and exterminate generally any individual who dared question his statement. Tom stood six feet high, weighed two hundred pounds, and carried a pair of revolvers, a bowie-knife, and a short carbine slung over his shoulder; and with a long sabre at his side he was a formidable antagonist. He was always well mounted, and rode splendidly at the head of his company of artillery in all parades and drills. Persons were therefore very careful in expressing their doubts of his wonderful escape, as they felt that in an encounter with "the mounted arsenal," as he was called, they would be at a fearful disadvantage. There were three persons of whom he was afraid. One was Dr. Rechard, his college-mate; Major MacKenzie inspired him with respect that amounted to almost a dread which he could not shake off; and Miss Mordine he always avoided.

Dr. Rechard had cautioned the major and Ilian to be on their guard. He had found Tom prowling around and asking questions of the servants. This was more than Ilian would endure. At her instance he was transferred to another district. Orders came for him to report for duty to Colonel Lamb, who was commanding at Fort Fisher. This would take him far away. He came one afternoon to say good-by to the major, and found him alone. The servant told Jeffords that his master was asleep and he could not disturb him, but Tom, in a peremptory manner, commanded him to inform Major Andrew MacKenzie that Captain Thomas Jeffords, of the South Carolina State Battery, wished to see him on important business. This opened at once the door of the sick man's chamber. He strode in with a haughty air, and took a seat without being asked, holding in his hands his orders for duty at Cape Fear. For a moment the major was a little uneasy, not knowing what Tom's sharp scent might have discovered. The keen gray eyes of the captain were fixed searchingly upon the man before him, as if trying to trace some resemblance to another face, and also to read, if possible, his inmost soul.

Slowly he said, "Major, do you know that you strongly remind me of a former classmate of mine at college in the North, whose name was Adrien Homerand? He joined the Federal navy as an acting master, and was reported to have died of yellow-fever a year ago last June in New Orleans."

If the crafty captain expected that this announcement would startle the major he was doomed to disappointment. The only answer was a yawn. The major in a careless way asked him, "Was this the important business that justified him in waking a sick and wounded man out of his afternoon sleep?" Then in an indignant tone he added, "What interest is it to me if I do resemble a score of Yankee officers? I held my ground against them in battle and bear the marks of the conflict."

Tom was out-manœuvred. He tried to retreat gracefully.

"No offence, my dear major," said he. "There are some splendid men in the Federal service."

"How do you know?" was the quick rejoinder. "Have you been holding personal communication with them, or has the remembrance of their faces as seen in battle left an indelible impression on your memory?"

This was a home-thrust, and the irony of it was felt. The intending biter had been badly bitten. He rose in some confusion, saying that he had been ordered to leave that very afternoon for Fort Fisher. He was expecting a remittance from his uncle in Charleston, and needed some money to settle a few bills, and had called to know if his comrade in arms would lend him a hundred dollars, which he would return on his arrival at his destination.

The major arose from his bed, and, going to a desk in the room, took out the amount and laid it on the table. The captain placed it in his pocket, saying,—

"Many thanks, my dear major. Shall I give you my note of hand for this loan?"

"No; your word of honor will be sufficient."

"Oh, you can have that cheerfully. I hereby give you my word of honor that I owe you one hundred dollars." And with this he bowed himself out.

As the door closed upon him he heard, in a muttered tone, the words, "A cheap riddance."

"Ah!" he thought to himself; "cheap, is it? Then I will increase the price next time."

By evening he had left Mobile far behind him. Dr. Rechard was very indignant when he learned of this visit, and Ilian was furious. Now, however, that the fellow has left, she hoped for a season of rest. But no sooner was one cause of annoyance gone before another came to take its place.

CHAPTER XI.

BATTLE OF FORT FISHER.

At sundown of the evening on which Tom Jeffords took his departure for Cape Fear Colonel Hortense reported himself to Ilian. This was unlooked for. She had left him in New York in charge of the secret-service office, and now he had returned when he was not wanted. He informed her that he had met Captain Jeffords at a way-station where the train had been delayed. They only had a few minutes for conversation, but the captain had told him that Adrien Homerand was not dead, and——

"Stop at once this miserable gossip," was the stern command of Ilian, and her eyes flashed a dangerous fire. "You know as well as I do that he is dead, for you stood by his grave in New Orleans, and did you not then make a remark for which I have never forgiven you? Do you forget that you said you wished you could put your foot on the grave of every officer of the army and navy of the Union forces?"

"But, Miss Mordine, I am not alone in this sentiment."

"Admit that; but you were aware that Mr. Homerand was my friend, and you should have respected my feelings."

"I am deeply sorry if I have pained you; but tell me, who is this Major MacKenzie, whose fame is all over the South?"

"An English gentleman who has united with our cause, and who has the sterling qualities of Englishmen in general; he strictly minds his own business, and does not seek to pry into others' affairs. Now, colonel, you have just come in time, when I need some trustworthy agent to go to New Orleans to look after certain interests there. I value your services more than you can tell."

"Ah! Miss Mordine, I am happy to hear you say so. And when this war is over may I hope——"

"Yes, you may hope, as I do, for many things. Now, can you set out to-night?"

"I am ready to go at once."

"So much the better. I want to send a letter to Mrs. Ormond, whose husband is wounded and a prisoner, also a letter to Mrs. Harrison, of the Grosvenor House, to send me Sam, who is my property. He is a very shrewd man, and will be of service. By the way, did you succeed in getting Harrison released?"

"I did, and he is now in England. You remember that when he was arrested after the death of Mr. Homerand he was sent North on the charge of being engaged in smuggling goods into the Confederacy. It was a fortunate thing that the arms and ammunition were removed from his cellars in time, or they would have been seized. I had a letter from him just before leaving New York, and he expected to sail with a fine steamer to run the blockade into Wilmington. I thought it best to leave New York, as Pinkerton's men were getting a little too inquisitive about my business, and I heard likewise that they have suspicions about you. I think it will be best for you to keep away from there at present. I will call in an hour for your letters."

16*

The following morning Ilian received a letter from the Secretary of War, at Richmond, stating that a promotion to the rank of colonel of artillery had been sent to Major MacKenzie, and he was assigned to special duty under General G. T. Beauregard. Slowly, but surely, she thought, is the ladder being mounted, and the stars of a lieutenant-general were at the top.

It was late in October before Colonel MacKenzie could mount his horse, and when he did so he left the pleasant circle of friends who had made life so agreeable for him in Mobile. Ilian at the same time went to New Orleans, and from there to New York. Sam had been given to the colonel for his body-servant, and the one who had saved his life when the fort was captured was taken into the service of Ilian, and had a home for life in her house at New Orleans. Dr. Rechard was also to report for duty with the colonel. Little did they expect what was before them.

In the month of December, 1864, Major-General John J. Peck, commanding the forces in the State of North Carolina, sent word to General Beauregard that a large Federal fleet, including five heavy ironclads, all under the command of Rear-Admiral David D. Porter, was forming in line of battle to attack Fort Fisher, which commanded the main entrance to Cape Fear River, and was the chief defence of Wilmington. The fort was held by Colonel Lamb, one of the ablest men in the Southern army, and no fear was entertained that the fortress could be taken. It was heavily armed and nearly three miles in extent. It was an oblong square, bounded on the west by the river, and on the east by the Atlantic; on the south was the channel, well protected by torpedoes. The north face was a narrow strip of woods. On the 27th of the same month word was again sent to General Beauregard, stating that the last of the Federal troops had that day re-embarked on their transports and sailed for the North. The fort had sustained without material damage a heavy bombardment from the largest fleet that had yet gathered under the Union flag. Admiral Porter had given up the attempt, and was retiring with his squadron. Colonel Lamb reported that the bombardment had made known the weak points in the defences, and urgently asked for reinforcements, as another attack would most likely be made.

Colonel MacKenzie was sent with such troops as could be spared, and reported on the fifth day of January. Colonel Lamb gave a genial reception to the brave Englishman, and assigned him an important point in the defence of the fort. Almost the first man the colonel met was Captain Tom Jeffords, who was profuse in apologies for not having sent back the one hundred dollars, but promised to do so the next remittance he got from his uncle.

The following day a blockade-runner, closely pressed by the blockading fleet, anchored in the river off the fort, and her captain came ashore to pay his respects to Colonel Lamb. Colonel MacKenzie was anxious to see the man who had so cleverly evaded the strict watch, and was surprised to find that it was no other than Bill Harrison, of the Grosvenor House, who, as soon as he caught sight of his old friend, as he termed him, grasped him warmly by the hand and expressed his great joy at meeting him. This was his second trip, and he hoped to make another from Bermuda, and would then retire from the business. On his way back to his boat he was intercepted by Captain Jeffords, who asked him if he knew any thing of the antecedents of Colonel MacKenzie.

"Yes," was the reply. "The colonel comes of as pure English blood as can be found anywhere. 'Know him,' did you ask? Yes, and I am proud to know him."

This did not satisfy Tom. His suspicions were aroused. If he could verify them, he would demand a high price for keeping silence.

The next morning he met the colonel, who was drilling his men and preparing for the second battle, which was near at hand. Tom resolved upon a bold attack; going up to him he said, in a loud tone that was overheard by those around,—

"Colonel MacKenzie, there is a rumor that an ex-Federal naval officer is fighting under our flag, and a large reward is offered for him, dead or alive, by Admiral Porter."

"Is that so?" was the quiet reply. "Well, I must say you have more of the Yankee inquisitiveness in you than any man I ever met, but you have not their dash and bravery; for our experience of their fighting qualities has convinced us that cowardice is not one of their failings, and that is more than I can say for other individuals that I know personally."

"Is that slur meant for me, sir?" cried out the captain, putting his hand on his sword.

"Better reserve that virgin blade for initiation when in the course of the next few days the Union forces will make the attempt to storm our works," was the sarcastic answer.

"You will hear more of this later on," retorted the baffled captain, as he retired amidst the laughter of the men who had overheard the dialogue.

The expected battle was renewed with a vengeance on the 12th of January. A fleet composed of over fifty vessels of all grades, from the large double-banked steam-frigates and ironclads down to the heavily-armed gun-boats, anchored in three lines of battle before the doomed fortress. For three days the shells poured in like hail. The explosion inside of the works of the fifteen-, eleven-, and nine-inch shells was so terrible in destructive force that all the guns on the sea-face were disabled. Colonel MacKenzie never once sought the shelter of the bomb-proofs; his courage and coolness animated his men. Captain Jeffords, however, was laid up early in the fight with a wound in the leg, which he kept carefully bandaged.

On Sunday, the 15th of January, the assault was made. Two thousand blue-jackets and marines from the fleet, who had landed early in the forenoon, charged at three o'clock up the sea-face of the fort, expecting to carry it by assault, but were driven back with great slaughter. Cheer upon cheer rent the air, the excited defenders all coming out from their bomb-proofs, Captain Jeffords being one of the most demonstrative. A few minutes later a terrible cry was heard,— "The Yankees have stormed the fort and have carried seven redoubts! To arms, and repel the assault!" Tom at once fled, regardless of his lame leg, and reached cover.

When the naval contingent was repulsed the Confederates had supposed it was the main assault, and were not aware of the presence of over seven thousand troops, under Brigadier-General Terry, who, coming on the flank, had carried everything before them. It now became a hand-to-hand conflict. The carnage was fearful; the blue and the gray bit the dust together. The Southern troops were outnumbered, but they bravely contested each foot of ground, and retired slowly before the overwhelming odds. Colonel MacKenzie held his position for a while. Then came a fierce bayonet charge, like a tidal **wave, and** the grays went down before it. The colonel **felt a sharp pain,** and was borne backwards **and** trampled upon **by the surging** masses of struggling men. He was left where he fell. **He** saw not the flag which he had so gallantly defended lowered in the dust. **Neither did he see the** Union standard as it floated in the evening breeze, **the emblem of** victory, over every point of the strong walls of **the** captured fortress. He heard not the shouts of the victors, the answering steam-whistles of the ships-of-war, nor the loud cheerings of their crews, many of whose gallant shipmates were then lying dead upon the sands. The fort had been bravely defended. When the animosity **of** party and the excitement of sectional spirit shall have passed away, future generations will give Colonel Lamb and his brave **troops the praise that is their due for the stubborn defence made against a formidable** array of war-ships **and a superior force of veteran** soldiers.

After the battle **the wounded of both** sides were sought **out and attended** to at once. The blue and the gray shared equally in the ministrations of the surgeons. **Dr.** Rechard, finding **that the colonel** was not among the prisoners, was permitted to search for him, and found him, apparently lifeless, under half a dozen slain. Tenderly he was borne to a casemate, but when the surgeons looked at him they said,—

"Too late; he is dead."

CHAPTER XII.

PRISONER IN THE NORTH.

By the side of the blood-stained officer sat the faithful ser**vant Sam.** With **his** eyes filled with tears, he was eagerly **chafing** the hands and seeking **to** call back life. Every half-hour Dr. Rechard **came** to see if there was any sign of returning **animation.** He could not believe that the spirit had fled. Once before he had brought him back when he was almost across the dark river. All of the surgeons were hard at work through the night, as the number of the wounded on both sides was very large. By sunrise next morning Dr. Rechard found an opportunity to make an examination of the wounds of his prostrate friend. A bayonet had gone through the fleshy part of the arm above the elbow. A bullet had entered the left side near the heart and come out at the back. But whether the organ of life was pierced could not be ascertained. His head was cut in several places from being trampled upon. Sam washed his wounds, and the doctor bandaged them up; some brandy was poured down his throat, so that if any life was left it would soon manifest itself. Shortly afterwards there was a spasmodic contraction of the body and a slight pulsation, followed by regular breathing, weak in its effort, but proving that the heart had not been touched. At nine o'clock the wounded man opened his eyes, and, recognizing his faithful attendant, said, in a low voice, "Sam, is that you? Where am I?"

"Yes, Massa MacKenzie, dat am me, sure; and you am a prisoner in dis fort, and am pow'ful wounded. Dis 'ere nigger's heart am clean broke, a-fearing you was dead. Here comes de doctor. When he sees dat your eyes am open, and hears dat voice again, he hab a smile on his face something like my ole mudder hab when dis child am gone back to New Orleans arter dis 'ere war am ended. Lor' a massa, I t'ink it am ended now; heap o' men killed. But de Lord am good to some peoples. Dat 'ere Captain Jeffords, he am alive, and don't get no wounds; somebody done gone and took dat bandage off his leg and put it on some one dat am wounded, sure; and no make-believe like dat captain."

The doctor did indeed smile as he took the hand of the colonel, and the tears flowed freely down his cheeks when he heard the utterance of that voice which he had feared was silenced forever.

"Is the fort taken?" was the colonel's eager question.

"Yes; it was carried by assault. The attack of the naval brigade on the sea-face was not the main body, and General Terry, at the head of his troops, came from the woods and swept everything before them. Last night Colonel Lamb and General Whiting were made prisoners, being wounded, and the Federal troops are now in full possession."

For a few moments the colonel was silent. Then he asked, "Is there any danger of my being discovered?"

"No, not any; for none of your friends would recognize you."

"But how about Tom Jeffords?"

"I have looked after him. I told one of the Union colonels that I hoped he would not take Captain Jeffords as a specimen of Confederate officers. He replied, 'By no means.' His qualities had been gauged by his cowardice, for he was dragged out of a bomb-proof, and begged for his life, pleading that he had always been a strong Union man. He was cut short and told to shut up his infernal bosh. You are aware that the Federal people hate a coward, and detest a man who is parading his Union principles, yet strikes a blow whenever he can. Jeffords will be sent North with the first batch of prisoners, and I hope never to see him again. Both of us will also go North as soon as your wounds permit of your being removed."

The naturally strong constitution of Colonel MacKenzie aided in his recovery, and he made rapid progress. One afternoon, a week after the capture of the fort, while he was lying in a cot in a casemate, surrounded by a number of other wounded men, several naval officers from the fleet entered the apartment. As this was a daily occurrence, no attention was paid to them by the others, but Colonel MacKenzie eagerly scrutinized their faces to see whether he could recognize any of them. On one of them his gaze was fast riveted. It was no other than his old friend, the acting ensign, whose life he had saved in New Orleans, and whom he had not seen since that night of the raid on Pensacola Navy-Yard. If his friend should recognize him, the consequences would be certain death. Far better, then, to have lain in the traverse where he fell than to face trial by court-martial and suffer execution for desertion. His friend came straight up to him and asked if he could do any thing for him. The agony felt by the colonel at that moment showed itself on his countenance. The officer, observing it, said,—

"You are suffering; command my services. Would you like a glass of water?"

"Yes," was the faint reply.

The water was procured, and in a few moments his friend left him, having failed to recognize him. This fact was very assuring to the colonel. If his bosom friend failed to detect in his face any resemblance to the acting master of two years ago, **then** he was safe.

Dr. Rechard, when he heard of this event as it was related **to** him **in a** whisper shortly after, replied, "Why should he recognize you? He thinks you dead and buried. Take courage, and all will be well."

In the middle of February Colonel MacKenzie, with other wounded Confederates, was sent North, where, on arrival, he was taken to **a** hospital for **treatment.** While there he was visited by Ilian, whom he **had not seen for** four months. She informed him that she had been reported to **Mr.** Stanton, the Secretary **of** War, and by his orders was sent to Fort Lafaye**tte for a** month. She had been finally released upon giving her **solemn** promise not to return South till the war was over. **She** was **now** endeavoring to procure the exchange or release **of the** colonel **and** Dr. Rechard. Then they could sail for Europe. She was closely watched by detectives of the secret service of the Union, and twice had been interrogated by Pinkerton himself, the chief of the service. Every luxury that money could purchase was now placed **at** the disposal of her two friends.

On the 31st of March orders were received **to send Colonel Andrew** MacKenzie **and Dr.** Rechard to Elmira, **where there** were a large number of Southern prisoners. They set out **under** guard that evening by the North River steamer **for** Albany. **On** their arrival there the colonel was found to be **too** much exhausted **to** continue **the** journey, and for nearly a month he was dangerously ill. The wound in his left side gave **him severe pain.** Ilian wrote every day from Washington, and strove hard to procure their release. She had ascertained that the author of the letter that had caused her arrest **was** Tom Jeffords, and added that she would not forget it **when her** turn came.

On the 3d of May the colonel had sufficiently recovered to **proceed to Elmira, where they arrived late at night.** The next morning he was disquieted and alarmed at receiving a **visit** from Tom Jeffords, who **expressed** delight at meeting an old comrade with whom **he had fought** side by side **in the** great battle of **Fort Fisher, and ended** by asking the loan of **one** hundred dollars, with the reiterated promise that it, with the other loans, would be repaid when the long-delayed draft came from his uncle. He obtained the amount, and for a few days the colonel was at peace. Tom now felt certain that he had struck a paying claim, and he resolved to work the mine for all that it was worth. If he could only verify his suspicions, then there would be big dividends for the purchase of his silence. He surmised that Sam would be a good subject to get points from.

Meeting him alone one day, he said, "Sam, do you know it does my heart good to meet an old veteran like yourself! When we stand together in battle the color of one's skin does not make any difference in stopping the enemies' bullets."

"Dat's so, Massa Jeffords," answered Sam; "and some folks has a pow'ful way ob getting out ob de range, and dey lets 'em strike oder people."

The captain turned red at this allusion to his own conduct at Fort Fisher. Sam, he perceived, did not take kindly to flattery, so he tried other tactics.

"Sam," said he, "your master, Colonel MacKenzie, is very much like an old friend of mine, a college-mate who went into the Union navy as an officer and suddenly disappeared; in fact, was reported to have died of yellow-fever. If, now, you will help me find out whether your master is the same person, once called Adrien Homerand, I will give you a thousand dollars. This will make you a rich man."

Sam's eyes fairly flashed fire as he indignantly retorted, "What you done gone take dis nigger for? You tinks I was anoder Judas what betrays his master. I hear you one day in Fort Fisher make dat inference to de colonel, and I don't gone and forgotten de answer. Now, Massa Jeffords, Colonel MacKenzie am an Englishman ob eddereation, and he hab proved his bravery in de battle by standing at de head ob his men. He am no bomb-proof hider what looks after his precious careass when de bullets and broken shot am flyin' 'round. I consider dat my dignity am lowered by de furder conversation wid a man who am covered all over wid de cotton ob de bales he hugs so close in de day when de fightin' am going on."

With this parting shot, Sam turned on his heels and left the captain indulging in profane language which we dare not repeat.

Tom from time to time borrowed more money from Colonel MacKenzie, for which he gave him further "words of honor" to repay.

CHAPTER XIII.

FATE OF THE BLACKMAILER.

On the morning of the 10th of June the Federal officer commanding the detail of soldiers guarding the Southern prisoners sent for Colonel MacKenzie, and told him he had just received telegraphic news that the orders for his release and also that of Dr. Rechard had been sent, and would probably arrive by the noon mail. He would be free in the mean time to leave the prison, and he would himself be happy if he would take breakfast with him. The colonel's arm was still in a sling, and he looked pale and haggard.

After breakfast he went back to his room and told Dr. Rechard of the good news, and added that he purposed to go to Buffalo at once in order to get away from Jeffords. He would await his arrival there with the release-papers, and Ilian could join them there or in Canada. The doctor did not think it prudent for the colonel to go alone, but he urged it strongly, pleading that it would throw Tom off the scent if they left Elmira singly. It was then agreed that they should meet at the National Hotel, in Buffalo, that evening. Not being burdened with extra baggage, he then set out for the gate with his pass in his pocket. Half-way across the parade-ground he met Tom, who boldly demanded another hundred dollars.

The colonel replied that he only had ninety dollars to his name and could not spare it.

"Perhaps," was the sneering answer, "you will spare a much larger sum to defend yourself from the charge of being a deserter from the Federal navy."

A scornful glance was the only reply of the colonel.

"Well," continued Jeffords, "Pinkerton will let me have the money I want. I hear that one of his agents is in town and pays liberally for information of this kind."

"Then go to him," was the laconic answer. The colonel turned to go back to his quarters. It would never do to let this man know that the order for his release was coming.

"Oh, colonel, I was only joking," said Tom, who followed him. "The fact is, that I am nearly wild. I have been gambling, and have a chance to win back all I have lost, and a cool hundred will just do it."

It was a critical moment to the colonel, and a delay might be dangerous. He decided to lend the money. "Well, captain, here are ninety dollars. It is all I have, I assure you, on my word of honor."

"No use," said Tom; "I must have a full hundred."

"Here are a pair of sleeve-buttons," was the answer. "You can borrow ten dollars on them. I value them highly." Well he might, for they were set with diamonds and were a present from Ilian.

Tom took them, together with the money, and in a few minutes afterwards the colonel was outside of the prison enclosure, a free man. He hastened at once to the railway station. There he realized what had escaped him in the excitement of getting rid of Tom Jeffords. He had not a dollar to pay his fare. He walked up and down the station in a bewildered state of mind. To go back to the prison and get money from Dr. Rechard would be to expose himself to further blackmail from his relentless persecutor. But without money and in the uniform of the Confederacy, how could he get to Buffalo? A few minutes later a train from the South came in, and it would remain half an hour before starting. He resolved to try the conductor for a free pass. Going up to him, he told him that he had lost his pocket-book and was anxious to get to Buffalo, where he had friends. He showed him his permit for leaving the prison. There were half a dozen Union officers on the platform, who, seeing a Confederate colonel with his arm in a sling and learning his condition, went up at once and took his hand, saying,—

"Colonel, we met in the field as enemies, now we meet as friends. Our pocket-books are at your service."

A large crowd gathered round, and fifty persons offered to pay for his ticket. The station-master, hearing of his case, wrote out a complimentary pass to Buffalo. The loan of money was freely tendered on every hand. This he absolutely declined, but accepted the offer of refreshments. He was escorted to the railway coach, and, amidst a grand ovation, the train moved on. This exhibition of kindly feeling should have convinced the most rabid fire-eater of the **South that the Northern people had not** been inspired by any malicious or revengeful disposition. We must now return to the prison.

Two hours after the colonel's departure, **Tom Jeffords, with** a flushed face **and** his eyes blazing with excitement, **sought** the apartment of **Dr. Rechard.** He found **him alone, busily** writing. Without any attempt at courtesy, he said, abruptly,—

"**Doctor, I have** just heard that Colonel MacKenzie has **been released from prison.**"

"**Yes,**" was the calm **reply;** "**and** he sails **in a few days for his home** in England."

"**Home** in England **be** hanged!" **was the savage reply. "You know as well as I do that** his home is in Boston with his father, **Professor Homerand.** I hope you don't take me for a fool. **Now listen** to my ultimatum: I got ninety dollars and a pair of sleeve-buttons this morning from your 'colonel,' as you call him, and I have lost it all and must have more. Silence is golden, and mine **must be purchased. I** want my **freedom** and **five** thousand dollars in **gold coin.** Then I swear **to keep** silent forever. **If you fail I will give** this written **statement of** facts which **I now hold in my hand to** the officer **in command of this prison. The colonel has** not gone so far but that he can be promptly arrested. **You will** also be tried for enticing a Union officer away from **his duty, and in the present temper of the** Northern people **you will** both suffer **the death**-penal**ty.**"

Dr. Rechard saw the danger, **and** felt that he must at all hazards save his friend. He told Jeffords that he was wrong in his surmise, and as to five thousand dollars, that was absurd. He was willing to help an old comrade of the war, but the **sum** named was too large.

"**Then** here goes **for** Pinkerton. He will pay me **my price.**" **And the captain,** holding in his hand the incriminating state**ment, started for** the commandant's quarters, situated by the **side of the large gate,** which then stood **wide open,** but was well guarded by sentries.

The doctor **rushed** after him and cried **out,** "Stop, Captain Jeffords! **Don't take that rash** step."

One of **the** sentinels near the doctor's apartment, seeing a prisoner running towards the gate, and hearing the call for him to stop, **at** once supposed that an escape was intended.

He brought his rifle to his shoulder and called, "Halt!" The captain, thinking it was the doctor repeating his demand, told him to go to a "certain hot place." The orders in regard to prisoners were very strict. The sentry had no other option but to fire, which he promptly did.

The report of the musket rang all over the prison enclosure, creating the greatest excitement. Tom Jeffords suddenly halted, reeled, and then fell prostrate on his face. Dr. Rechard, with great presence of mind, hurried up to him, and adroitly taking the paper from his clinched hand, put it in his own pocket. He then felt his pulse, but it had stopped. Blood was issuing out of his mouth and nostrils. The bullet had gone through his heart, and the spirit of the blackmailer went to the bar of judgment.

When the officer of the day came up and asked for the cause of the shooting, Dr. Rechard told him that he was himself writing a love-letter, and the dead man had snatched it off his desk in order to show it to his brother officers for the purpose of ridicule. As he called him back, the sentry, naturally supposing that he was trying to escape, had fired to frighten him, and the bullet had finished his career.

A court of inquiry was at once ordered to investigate the matter. Dr. Rechard went to his room, wrote a love-letter to some imaginary girl, and then crumpled it up. This was produced in the court, and created a smile of amusement when it was read.

The verdict was short, viz., that Captain Thomas Jeffords had met his death in pursuance of military orders in consequence of disobeying the sentry. At sundown he was buried.

The commandant sent for the doctor at noon and handed him all the discharge-papers, and offered any assistance in his power. In speaking of the dead man, he told him that he had no regret for the affair. He heartily despised him for several base acts of cowardice while in the prison.

"I hope," said the doctor, "that you don't take him as a sample of the men who fought for State rights."

"Far from it," the officer answered. "I have had a large experience with Southern officers, and I can testify that, as a rule, they are gentlemen, generous to a fault, and brave in battle; and now that the war is ended, I hope fraternal feeling will prevail."

"Many thanks for your good opinion," replied the doctor, "and also for the extreme courtesy shown me in this place."

As Dr. Rechard was leaving, a telegram was handed to him. It was from Ilian, and informed him that she would be due at two o'clock. She wanted the doctor and the colonel to meet her, prepared to go on to Buffalo.

His preparations did not take long. He met the train punctually, and gave Ilian a full account of all that had happened. They sent a telegraphic message to the colonel at Buffalo that they would be due there about nine o'clock.

At ten minutes before three both were speeding on their way.

CHAPTER XIV.

ALL ADRIFT.

WE must now go back to Colonel MacKenzie. He received every attention possible from the conductor and the Union officers on board the train. On his arrival at Buffalo they offered to pay for a carriage, but he declined. His friend's house was only a short distance away, and he preferred to walk there. Bidding them all good-by, and with many thanks for their kindness, he left the station. He was very much excited by the apprehension of what Tom Jeffords would do when he should have learned that he had left the prison. It would be unsafe, he thought, for him to go to the hotel appointed by Dr. Rechard. Detectives might be waiting there to arrest him. Accordingly, he wandered up one street and down another, looking anxiously into the faces of the policemen whenever he met them. His uniform attracted attention, and he expected to hear each moment one of them say, "I arrest you for desertion."

When it became dark he found himself near the lake. The tall masts of the shipping loomed up in the starlight. Before him was a gate leading into a lumber-yard. It was partly open. He went in and sat down. He was ill and weary, and thought whether it would not be better to throw himself into the lake and there find rest from his troubles.

Sleep came to alleviate his sorrows. He slept soundly, but his dreams were troubled. He imagined that Captain Jeffords had obtained proof of his identity and informed against him. His arrest and trial followed. He saw the faces of his former messmates in the court-room, with his commanding officer as president of the court. After the evidence was taken, he heard them one by one pronounce the verdict "Guilty." Sentence then followed, viz., "That Adrien Homerand, *alias* Colonel Andrew MacKenzie, should be beheaded, and his head placed on the prison-gates at Elmira for a warning to others." He realized being led to execution; the chief boatswain's mate of his late ship held a sharpened cutlass to perform the decapitation. Close at his side he saw the mocking face of Tom Jeffords jeering at him, and asking how many hundred dollars he would give to save his life. Slowly the bright blade was raised, and he bowed his head to receive the stroke. Quickly the steel descended, but the executioner brought it down on the neck of Tom Jeffords, whose head rolled at his feet. He immediately seized it with his hands; it felt soft, and then seemed all of a sudden to go to pieces.

There was the headless form before him, but all the witnesses had suddenly vanished; even the executioner had gone. What could it mean? He was wide awake and standing on his feet; the moon lit up everything with a pale light, and showed him the lumber-yard and in his hands a red handkerchief. "A dream, after all," he said to himself. But who was this man by his side? Raising a coat which covered his head, to his astonishment he saw that it was a sailor, and the fumes of liquor that came from him gave evidence that he was sleeping off a drunken carousal. The bundle he had held in his hands, and which in his dream he thought was the head of Jeffords, contained a blue shirt and trousers. They were lying at his feet. The man had apparently entered by the same gate as himself, and seeing some one else asleep, had lain down beside him with the bundle for a pillow. A bright idea now came to the colonel. He would exchange his uniform for the sailor's clothes and then go forth and seek employment on some vessel, and thus reach the Canadian shore. It took but a few minutes to make the transfer; the man being of his own size, they fitted to a charm. He carefully wrapped the uniform up and placed it in the handkerchief, and exchanging his felt hat for the sailor's cap, he left the lumber-yard. He walked down to the end of a long pier, where he found a large schooner called the "Michigan," of Cleveland. He sat down to await some sign of life on the vessel. His left arm pained him so badly that he had to keep it in a sling. It was not long before the sun came up, and with it he heard voices on the schooner. From the orders given he knew that she was about to leave. The captain, seeing a dignified man with a pale face and in the garb of a sailor, came to him and asked if he was seeking employment. He replied in the affirmative, and that he was formerly a ship-master, but had met with a great deal of misfortune and had sprained his arm. He would, however, do what duty he was able. The captain told him he needed a second officer, and if he would take the position he would be glad to have him do so. The offer was accepted, and he was at once installed. Able seamen were scarce, competent officers more so, as the war had furnished them other employment.

The new second mate was not long in giving a sample of his qualities. His voice and manner commanded respect and obedience, and before the schooner was five miles from port the captain congratulated himself upon his lucky acquisition of such a thorough officer. The vessel was bound for Cleveland, and we must now leave her to plough her way over Lake Erie, and return to Ilian.

The doctor and herself, with her maid, arrived at Buffalo in due season, and were bitterly disappointed at not finding the colonel at the hotel. They supposed he had gone to some other house, and concluded to wait until next day before searching for him. Early in the morning messengers were sent to every hotel in the city, but no news could be had of him. The case was laid before the chief of police, and a reward was offered for information. The conductor of the train certified that he had left the station immediately on arrival, but from that moment no trace could be had of the missing colonel. At noon word was brought that a man had been arrested dressed in sailor's garments, but with a Confederate officer's felt hat and a suit of clothes evidently belonging to a colonel of artillery, and hence was supposed to be an escaped prisoner of war. The doctor went to the police court, and saw at a glance that the prisoner was a genuine sailor, and a man-of-war's man at that. In looking at the uniform, he at once recognized it as belonging to Colonel MacKenzie. The frank manner of the seaman gave credibility to his statement of who he was and how he became possessed of the colonel's uniform.

When the officer who made the arrest preferred the accusation before the police justice against the sailor of being an escaped Confederate officer, the look of amazement on his face was intense.

"That be blowed for a yarn!" was his answer. "What racket are you on, anyhow? I have been shipmate with all sorts of queer characters in my time, but I am blessed if ever I was shipmate with a rebel colonel. Some one has swapped those gray duds for my mustering-suit; I have just been discharged from the United States steamship 'Brooklyn.' My discharge-papers were in the pocket of that suit. I arrived here yesterday direct from New York, and sent the balance of my things home to Detroit by express. I had perhaps a little more whiskey aboard than I could very well carry, so I shortened sail and came to anchor in a lumber-yard. At daylight this morning I got under way and shaped my course for the railway station. I did not notice that my head-gear had rebel colors flying. When this 'ere bobby hove to along-side and demanded my clearance-papers, I opened my bundle and found my blue clothes had turned gray and my papers were gone."

The explanation of Dr. Rechard threw light upon the subject. He said that Colonel MacKenzie had been very ill, and no doubt in this condition had gone to the lumber-yard, exchanged clothes with the sailor, and perhaps sailed in some vessel.

The seaman was at once discharged, and the doctor paid him fifty dollars for the colonel's uniform and to compensate for the annoyance. This so delighted him that he volunteered to join in the search for the lost man. He struck the trail with a seaman's instinct. In one hour after he brought word to the doctor at his hotel that the schooner "Michigan" had sailed for Cleveland at seven o'clock, and, before leaving, her captain had shipped a Mr. Andrews for second mate, and, moreover, that his arm was in a sling, and he was dressed in blue shirt and trousers of the kind worn by seamen in the United States navy. The schooner would reach Cleveland in about forty-eight hours. Another fifty dollars was paid for this information, and a promise made him that the discharge-papers would be mailed to the post-office at Detroit when recovered from the colonel. The sailor went on his way, rejoicing at his " prize-money," as he called it.

Ilian and the doctor left the following morning for Cleveland to meet the vessel on which they had no doubt the colonel had sailed. They were both of them mystified at his conduct, and supposed it was owing to aberration resulting from his severe illness. Indeed, Ilian was ill herself. All her well-laid plans had failed. General Lee had surrendered, Jefferson Davis was a prisoner at Fortress Monroe, and the war had virtually come to an end. Over half of her fortune had been spent in the Lost Cause, and her dream of the triple stars of a lieutenant-general on the shoulders of her lover was utterly dissipated. The man whom in the hour of his illness and weakness she had coerced away from his duty to the flag that he had sworn to defend was now a fugitive from the terror of that retribution that was due as a penalty for his crime. She asked herself the question, " Is life worth living now?"

CHAPTER XVI.

THE OLD NAME.

On one of the piers bordering on the lake in the stately city of Cleveland a crowd of people had collected, watching a large schooner hauling into her berth. It was early in the morning, but the day was clear and beautiful. A carriage with a handsome span of horses had been waiting for fully an hour. The occupants were Dr. Rechard and Ilian. They were anxiously looking at the vessel. It was the " Michigan," and if they were on the wrong track it would be necessary to retrace their steps to Buffalo. The minutes seemed hours. "All things will come to him who has but patience to wait," was Dr. Rechard's consoling words to some remark of his fair companion.

" Yes," she answered, " but that word *patience* signifies a rare virtue, and I am afraid I have but little of it. Supposing the colonel is not on that vessel, what then?"

"But he is on her," cried the doctor. "Look! is not that his form on the poop? Listen! can you forget that voice?"

"Stand by to take this stern-line! make fast!" he was shouting to the men on the pier. "Haul in, my lads; haul in merrily! belay all!" were his orders to his own crew.

Ilian's eyes filled with tears of joy, and a feeling of happiness such as she had not known for a long time glowed at her heart. She had found once more the man of her choice; and nothing but death, she resolved, should part them again.

When the schooner was made fast, a gang-plank was put on board. The captain and his crew were amazed to see a beautiful woman, escorted by a dignified gentleman, rush into the arms of the second mate, and heard them address him,—

"My dear colonel, we are delighted to have found you."

While Ilian and the colonel were having mutual explanations, the doctor told the captain that the whole affair was a result of a wager. His friend, he said, was a great yachtsman, and consequently proficient in nautical affairs. He had made a bet that he would ship as an officer with his arm in a sling for a trip on the lake, and had done so, and would divide a hundred dollars among the crew. The amount was accordingly handed to the captain for that purpose. The doctor had also brought with him a light overcoat and hat for his friend to hide his sailor-clothes. When he put them on he bade the crew good-by, as also the first officer, and then shook the captain warmly by the hand, thanking him for all his kindness.

The captain, with a puzzled expression, replied, "Mr. Andrews, I am glad you have won your bet, and I must say I never thought it possible for any yachting man to handle a vessel and give orders in such a seamanlike manner as you have done. In thirty years' experience as man and boy, I have never seen your superior on a ship's deck. I am proud to have had you on board."

Thus they parted, the crew giving a hearty cheer for their departing officer.

On arrival at their hotel a tailor was sent for, and by evening the colonel, for the first time in two years, was once more in citizen's clothes.

Ilian then, in the presence of the doctor, said to him, "**Two years ago you** took a solemn oath to keep the name of Andrew MacKenzie till the end of the war released you from the obligation. That time **has now come,** and Colonel MacKenzie will hereafter live in history only, while Adrien Homerand comes to the front as a living being. My own darling, I welcome you back."

Her hand was placed in his, a pair of dark-blue eyes filled **with** tears looked into his face, and a voice as sweet as a chime of bells said, **in a** plaintive tone,—

"Adrien, **will you** forgive me for my act of coercion and for the **suffering** that it has entailed upon you? **I myself** have **suffered.** I have never known an hour of peace since that **fatal day.** Yet I did it to save you from certain death. **If you had not taken that** oath you would have been assassinated by sundown. Oh, say that you will forgive me and take a terrible load off my mind!"

Slowly the beautiful head was pillowed on his bosom, and **the answer** was whispered into **her ears,** "Ilian, my own sweet, lovely one, **let the** past be buried **in oblivion.** I freely forgive as I hope to be forgiven. **May I now ask** for the payment **of the** bond? **The war is ended, and** I claim you for **my promised bride. Will you be mine?**"

"**Yes,**" was the low response.

"**Delays are** dangerous; **let the** marriage take place **to-morrow, and our** joint friend, **Dr.** Rechard, to whom we **both owe so much,** will witness our union."

"**With all my heart,**" said the doctor; "but after the wedding **I will have to leave** you to return to New Orleans. **In the** mean time, **I am** entirely at your service."

"Dr. Rechard," said Adrien, "there are two problems that have been **on my mind all** day since I left the schooner. One, as I have already **told you,** was the reason I shipped on board of her, viz., how **can the silence** of that blackmailer be purchased effectually? The other is, what excuse can I make to **my father and** mother **and to** my friends for the announcement **of my** death two **years ago, and** how can I satisfactorily explain my whereabouts **during the interval?**"

"Both are already solved **for you.** In fact, they are easy of solution, and all the details of the last problem are prepared. **It** was my purpose to have **told** you all this after dinner. I did not do so this morning, as your mind was too much worked up, and further excitement would not be beneficial. Make your mind easy in regard to Tom Jeffords; his eternal silence has been assured."

A doubtful shake of the head showed **Adrien's** feeling in regard to this assertion; then, with clinched fists, he said, "I will never trust that man while he is living, and I cannot feel safe till I can place five thousand miles between us."

"Is that all the distance you want? I am under the impression that there are many times that amount of space between you. Tom's tongue will never again ask for the price of his silence. He is dead and buried."

"Great heaven! how did that happen?" Adrien asked.

The information was duly given, and also the fact that the sleeve-buttons had been recovered.

"Then I can breathe freely for the first time in many months," said Adrien. "What a frightful incubus has been removed from off my mind!"

"Now," said the doctor, "about the second problem. All is fixed on that point, as I just stated. I have written a letter to your father, which you are to mail to-morrow, after you are married. It states that in June, 1863, you became possessed of important secrets of the Confederate government. You were taken a prisoner while on special duty and kept in close confinement. An attack of yellow-fever gave the opportunity of spreading the report of your death, and during the two years of your captivity you were under a solemn obligation not to make known your place of imprisonment or to betray the secrets that had come into your possession till the war should be ended. The individuals concerned in this matter then took you to Buffalo, so as to be near the Canadian border. You were to be set free on the 21st of June, and proceed to New York by way of Cleveland and Erie. You also expected to bring home as your bride a young lady who saved your life and nursed you in the yellow-fever. Now, my dear Adrien, this is substantially the truth of the whole affair, and will satisfy your parents; and if you go abroad for a few years, the excitement of your return will die out and prevent any unpleasant cross-questioning. I shall be glad when all is settled, for I hate and despise falsehood. Telling one lie very often necessitates telling three more to cover it

18

up. I do not believe that the end justifies the means, or that it is lawful to tell a lie though good come out of it. I am sorry to say that I have been compelled for the sake of others in the last year or so to depart from the strict facts of history, but I now turn over a new leaf, and propose for the rest of my life to stick to the truth, the whole truth, and nothing but the truth."

The two problems having been solved, the wedding-eve was spent by all of the three united friends in talking over the past and planning for the future. The sky of their horizon was clear and there was no sign of the coming storm,—to the bride and bridegroom the irony of fate, to the friend the deep anguish for the misfortune of the two persons whose history was interwoven with his own. The hours passed away, midnight came, and they retired to rest.

The author wishes he could end his story here, and say that the hero and heroine were married and lived to a happy old age, blessed with children. That is the usual ending of novels. In real life it is often the contrary. I have spoken of the irony of fate; what is it? Citations: First, a soldier of the late war who passed unwounded through a hundred engagements and was discharged at the close was killed on his way home by a railroad accident. Second, a sea-captain who had followed the sea for forty years was drowned in a pond only seven feet deep. Other citations will be found in the further history of Ilian and Adrien.

CHAPTER XVI.

PAYMENT OF THE BOND.

THE morning of the 21st of June was ushered in with a clear sky, and gave tokens of an ideal summer day. Ilian, Adrien, and the doctor met at the breakfast-table in a cheerful frame of mind. They each had a peculiar dream the night previous, and for a while the subject of conversation was dreams in general, their nature, their origin, and their tendencies. The doctor was requested to tell his dream first.

"I thought," said he, "that Adrien and myself were out walking. A heavy fog set in, and we lost sight of each other. I wandered all over the city in search of him; then I came back to the hotel, but could not find him, so I continued the search. Somehow I found myself back in New Orleans, and then it seemed that several years had passed; but I never saw you again. This dream, I judge, was a sort of reaction after our hunt for you in Buffalo."

"Doctor," said Adrien, "let me ask you, do you believe in presentiments or premonitions, as they are called?"

"No, I do not," replied Dr. Rechard; "most of such feelings are the result of indigestion. If you had an unpleasant dream last night, it came, no doubt, from that lobster-salad which we had for dinner."

"Then you do not accept the theory that coming events cast their shadows before?"

"Certainly not."

"But there are some startling citations that can be brought forward to substantiate this notion."

"Merely coincidences; nothing more. But let us hear where your mind wandered last night in dream-land."

"Well, I dreamed that Ilian and myself got into two different boats, as a single one was not able to support us both. We lashed them together for greater safety, and pushed from the shore to cross a stormy river. Half-way over, a violent wave broke our fastenings, and we drifted apart and lost sight of each other in the darkness. The agony of the moment awoke me from the dream."

"Well, I do not wonder at such a dream," answered the doctor; "you two have been separated from each other so often during the last four years. Now, however, that you are to be married within three hours, there will be no more drifting apart. I must say, Miss Mordine, that you look too gloomy for a bride on her wedding-day. Have you also been a victim to the lobster-salad, or did your dream accord with Adrien's, and you dreamed that you found him again?"

"No, it did not. My dream was very unpleasant; and I think it better not to relate it, as it refers to a past episode that I prefer should be forgotten."

"Ah!" exclaimed the doctor; "I knew that salad would

leave unpleasant results behind. But go on. Now that you have excited our curiosity, we object to being left in a state of expectancy."

"All right; but if a cold chill comes over you when you hear the dream do not blame me."

"'Cold chill,' did you say? Well, it will not be out of place, for a cold wave would be very refreshing this warm morning. Now we are all attention, and I will use this fan to ward off the chill which you prognosticate."

"In my dream," said she, "I thought that I was in New Orleans, and was rehearsing that oath of coercion. I held the dagger hair-pin to Adrien's throat to make him swear to join the Confederate cause, when some one violently pushed my arm, and the steel went into his neck. I looked around to see who had dared to do such a thing, and beheld the mocking face of Colonel Hortense. I raised the dagger to drive it into his heart, when he warded off the blow, and it went into my own breast. I looked to see whether Adrien was hurt, but he had vanished. Then I seemed to be alone in a wild valley, and I was calling, with tears streaming down my face, for Adrien to come and show me the way out. At last I heard his voice from one of the highest peaks, which was capped with snow, and the clouds were around it. I at once began to climb up to where he was, and, after a wearisome toil, I had almost reached the spot, when my foot slipped and I went over a precipice and had the terrible sensation of falling, when suddenly I was caught by a strong hand; but before I could recognize my deliverer I became unconscious, and awoke to find it was all a dream."

"A happy ending, was it not?" said the doctor to Adrien.

"Yes, indeed; and when we are married to-day, and embark at noon on the sea of matrimony, we will never be separated till death shall call one or the other."

"Amen to that, I say; and may my blessing rest upon you both! Hereafter I will, as a medical man, strongly advise people on the eve of being married to avoid eating lobster-salad, and then they will not have the blues."

"By the way, doctor," said Adrien, "did you ever hear that poem by Lieutenant Holm, United States navy, written twenty-five years ago, off some island in the Pacific Ocean? It coincides with my dream."

"Look here, my dear fellow, I object to any more indulgence in indigo."

"But I assure you, doctor, that the poem is a beautiful one."

"Well, we have just time to hear it before getting ready for our visit to the minister's; but I warn you, if it is a doleful one, I will put an end to the recital, or I shall begin to feel that I am going to a funeral instead of a wedding. When my matrimonial morn comes I expect to be as jolly as——"

"An undertaker," chimed in Adrien.

"Well, hardly; but go ahead with your sea-poem."

"I dream that I am a bright seamew
    At home on the ocean spray;
I dream, I dream that the song is true
    We chanted the other day.
I dream that the earth is a fairer green,
    The ocean a purer blue,
That love is reality; woe but a dream,—
    Would that my dream were true!

"I dream, I dream that the curse will pass
    Away from my maddened brain,
As the shadows that flit o'er yon wavy grass,
    Or as the mist that follows the rain.
I dream, I dream that a golden cloud,
    Like a rainbow that spans the sea,
Comes floating along on its misty shroud,
    And bears thee away with me.

"To the siren isles in the placid main
    That rock in the pearly sea;
Oh, never was aught so fair, I ween,
    As those islets seem to be!
Embowered in a fragrant cocoa grove,
    Infringing the purple sky,
Enjoying a transient dream of love,
    We lay us down to die.

"Again I dream of the ocean-foam,
    And again I dream of thee;
But the shadows that flitted in myriads come,
    Shrouding in storm the sea.
On the breakers drifting to and fro,
    As dark as dark may be,
Dismally, wearily, on we go
    On separate waves of the sea."

"Splendid poem, I admit," said the doctor; "but I have no idea that the last verse of it will be your experience."

"I like that poem very much, Adrien," said Ilian. "Do you not remember I told you a dream which I had in 1861, when you left me to return to your ship? I thought that I was in a boat drifting far out to sea, and I called on you to help me. Now I propose we leave dreams and turn to something practical. We must prepare for the ceremony. I once thought that I never could be married except in church, and with white wedding-raiment and veil and orange-blossoms and at least six bridesmaids. Now I am content to be married in a pearl-gray travelling-suit, with my faithful maid, who has never left me during the last four years, as witness. I was in hopes that Sam would have been here in time. Here comes a telegram. It is for you, doctor, and I hope it contains no bad news."

The doctor laughed when he read the slip of paper. "It is from Sam," he said. "It is very concise, and reads, 'Sam will be on hand eleven o'clock.' (signed) 'SAM.' You remember, Adrien, I sent him to Washington two days before you left Elmira, as they did not consider him a prisoner of war, to hunt up Colonel Hortense. I received a despatch from him the morning we left Buffalo. It said, 'Colonel am gambling like de debil, but his money am gone.' This I fully expected, and it accounts for the large losses incurred by Miss Mordine."

"Why do you persist in calling me by that name?" she demanded. "I prefer that you should call me Ilian."

"I will do so after you are married, and I have your husband's permission."

"Doctor," said Adrien, "we are both so much indebted to you that we never can repay your kindness and devotion. I shall always regard you as a brother, and Ilian will be your sister. In reference to our programme, I will say that two carriages will be at the door at half-past eleven, and after the ceremony there will be refreshments at the minister's house. I ordered them to be sent there. Our baggage will go to the station and wait for us. I am sorry that you must tear yourself away so soon; but you have promised to dine with us at our hotel at six o'clock."

"I will do so; but at seven thirty I must leave for the South, as, besides my own affairs, I have to look out for the property of your bride, as Colonel Hortense has been discharged from his stewardship. He has squandered in some way over one hundred thousand dollars. *Au revoir* until half-past eleven."

The Rev. Dr. Bowman, who was one of the most distinguished preachers of Cleveland, had festooned his large drawing-room with flowers and made every preparation for a grand wedding. The table in his dining-room was laden with a substantial repast, provided by the best caterer in the city. In the centre was a large wedding-cake. Mrs. Bowman and her two daughters were arrayed in their best; they were to be the only witnesses, besides those who were to come with the bridal party.

At noon precisely they came. One carriage containing Ilian and her maid and Adrien and the doctor; the other carriage had gone to the station with Sam in charge of the baggage.

The ceremony was short; the worthy doctor was noted for this, and consequently had many such interesting duties.

After the usual preliminary questions came the final part. "Husband and wife I pronounce you in the name of Almighty God, and none may separate you till death shall come," were his closing words, followed by a brief prayer. Congratulations were offered to the newly-married pair. It was the happiest moment of their lives. They walked arm in arm to the dining-room; Dr. Rechard followed with Mrs. Bowman, although he looked as though he would have preferred to have escorted both her handsome daughters instead,—perhaps because he was a bachelor. We cannot linger over the wedding-breakfast. At ten minutes after one the party left. The happy husband slipped a five-hundred-dollar note into the minister's hand, who, when his eyes caught the figure on the bill, called out,—

"Many thanks; come again; glad to see you at any time."

Amidst waving of handkerchiefs they drove to the station. Sam met them, his face radiant and full of smiles as he said, "I congratulate you both. I's always expected to see dis 'ere day; may de joy nebber end."

A few minutes later and they were on their way to Erie. The bond had been paid.

CHAPTER XVII.

PREMONITIONS.

The journey and arrival at Erie occurred without incident. Sam and the maid were cautioned not to mention any thing at the hotel about the wedding, as the married couple were adverse to be subject to the comment usually bestowed upon bridal parties. Their apartments, having been written for in advance, were ready for them, and at six o'clock they sat down to a luxurious dinner. Dr. Rechard laughingly objected to any lobster-salad being brought on the table.

"Ghosts," he said, "always follow weird dreams, and lobster-salad two days in succession would surely bring them. Besides," he added, "I have to travel all night, and might see some myself."

"You surely, doctor, don't dread meeting any of your former patients," remarked Ilian.

"Oh, dear, no. But, jesting aside, one's imagination can easily be worked up to a high pitch. For instance, I have heard of persons who went into a bedroom in the evening when the light was dim, and afterwards asserted that they saw the face of some dead friend in the looking-glass; of course, there is nothing in it; merely the force of one's imagination."

"Doctor," remarked Adrien, "I am afraid that you are like many medical men, rather sceptical."

"Not by any means," he replied. "I am not a sceptic, although I want proof of a positive kind for any event out of the ordinary course of things. There are many strange phenomena that cannot be explained, and I am not one of those people who must have ocular and palpable proof for everything presented to my notice. If certain statements are well corroborated by persons competent to judge of the facts at issue, I accept their testimony. I do not believe in spiritualism with the preposterous claims they put forth. They may do some wonderful things that I cannot fathom. So do the wizards, such men as Hermann and others of his class, who claim sleight-of-hand and optical illusion and nothing more."

"Doctor," asked Ilian, "do you believe that our departed relatives, who during life had our interests at heart, would be willing to let us walk into danger without some warning, even were it only given in dreams?"

"I will reply to your question by asking another. Where do you get the authority for supposing that in their disembodied state they linger on this planet? There is nothing in the Bible upon which to found such a belief."

"I concede that point; but is there any thing in the Scriptures which positively asserts that they do not sometimes come back to warn of approaching danger? There are cases recorded in that book which prove my point."

"That is a problem of theology or psychology to which it is difficult to give a satisfactory solution; and, to tell the truth, I am not anxious for any experiments of that nature. I am satisfied with the humdrum routine of my daily life."

"The last four years of the war, just past, was hardly a humdrum affair in your experience," remarked Adrien.

"Well, no; but I don't expect another such period while I remain on this sphere. But now we have on hand the sundering of our pleasant association. For the past two years Adrien and myself have not been separated, and in a few minutes I must leave you both and turn my face to the South. I expect to feel the separation keenly. Adrien, my dear boy, our four years of college-life wove the bonds of friendship that only death can break. Now that you and Ilian are at last united, I will depart with the assurance that many years of happiness are in store for you. I shall expect to see you often in New Orleans; and whenever I visit the North, or wherever you decide to make your home, I know I shall be a welcome visitor."

"Indeed you will," said Ilian, as she rose from the table and took the doctor's hand. She added, "I feel the poverty of the English language, because I cannot find words adequate to express my feelings at the moment of separation from one whom I hold in the sacred light of a brother. May your every step be blessed; and Adrien, I know, will let me give you a sister's parting kiss."

"Certainly," said he. "I will now go to the station and see the doctor off, post my letter to my father, and call upon some tailor and order several suits, and will leave you to talk over the new dresses with your dress-maker, whom you instructed to be here at seven thirty. It will probably be half-past nine when I return, as I have to make some purchases; then we can take a walk on the lake-shore. How happy my father and mother will be to get this letter from Dr. Rechard! I hope to see both of their dear faces by this day week, and we will have a grand welcome home. It seems like ten years since I left the mansion of my parents. They will have two children to gladden their hearts instead of the one they thought was dead and gone."

A moment after Ilian was left alone.

The parting at the station between the two college-chums and companions of the last two years was of such a touching nature as it is almost impossible to describe. Their hearts were too full for utterance; tears were in their eyes.

"Doctor," said Adrien, "you seem to have something on your mind."

"Yes, I have," he answered; "but it must be owing to the excitement of the last week. The feeling is a new one to me."

"Can you describe it? Your face has a troubled look."

"I have a presentiment, that I cannot shake off, that there is trouble coming between you and Ilian. I never believed in such things before; now it has taken full possession of me. Ever since the narration of our dreams this morning, and especially that poem you quoted, which seemed almost prophetic, I have been under a strange influence. Telegraph to me at once if you need me, and I will come even were you at the extreme limits of the globe."

"All aboard!" shouted the conductor. The locomotive gave the warning whistle, and, standing on the rear platform of the railway-carriage, the doctor waved his hand until out of sight. It was some minutes before Adrien could tear himself away from the spot where his true and noble friend had stood but a moment before; the pressure of his hand was still felt. Could he only have known that never more in this life would he see the face of the genial Dr. Rechard, the agony of parting would have been greater. Happy for mortals that the future is hidden from their eyes, and that hope never ceases as a factor of human happiness while life or reason are with us. Adrien walked slowly away from the station and went to the tailor recommended by the proprietor of his hotel, where he ordered two suits of clothes. Thence he went to several shops and made a few purchases.

We leave him thus engaged, and go back to Ilian and see how she employed her time while waiting for her husband. The dress-maker called and made an appointment for the next morning, so she had plenty of time for a review of the past four years. She sat by the window of her bedroom enjoying the cool evening breeze. Her thoughts went back to the month of May, 1861, when she was in Boston with her aunt,—the day that she took the fatal oath of hatred to all the Homerand family; and then again she thought of that hour, a month later, when her aunt on her dying bed recalled that oath and declared it null and void. Often since that time had she weighed the momentous question, whether, after having taken such an oath, any human power could release her from it. There was no definite limit to it; the words used were, "perpetual hatred," and it was the exact meaning of the term "perpetual" that had caused her much anxiety, providing her aunt had no power to annul the obligation. At times this subject came up for her consideration, and it had generally resulted in the decision, after a weary struggle, that she was released from the vow. Her love for Adrien had much to do with the matter. But the problem would not rest. It was like some evil spirit that could not be exorcised by any art she possessed. Once more this troublesome question was taking full possession of all of her mental faculties. "Admitting that the oath was binding," she said to herself, "what was then really implied in the term 'perpetual hatred?'" Surely it was not in marrying one of the persons involved in the execration. This she had done that very day, yet it was in conformity with a solemn promise to do so when the war was ended. If her aunt could come back from the dead, what would she say? Surely if she had been wronged, there had been ample revenge. Could the most vindictive person wish for more than had been accomplished? The only son of the man who had wronged her mother, in what way she knew not, had been torn away from his allegiance to the flag that he had sworn to defend, and for two years had been placed in a position which, if found out, would have procured for him an ignominious death. Even now he was making arrangements to leave his country for fear of discovery. The father, who was the prime cause of the death of her mother, was he not punished by the two years of mourning for his son? Yes, the oath had been fulfilled, and there must be a truce to all this hatred. It must end forever. From this time on she would accept the fact that she was released from the fatal obligation, and would devote her whole life to the happiness of the man whom she loved and who had suffered so much to prove his devotion. She would also love the father, and be to him and to his wife a loving, devoted daughter. Certainly her aunt must approve of all this, and from that other sphere would bless her. Ah! if she could only have a test of this, it would set the seal of her happiness. Could she get one? A moment she pondered, and then a bright idea came into her head.

She at once set about to try it.

CHAPTER XVIII.

THE SHADOW IN THE GLASS.

I AM very confident that the method employed by Ilian which I am about to describe and the result which she attained can be explained by purely natural causes. I might declare it a psychological problem easy of solution by well-known laws. Ilian seemed to think differently, and acted upon her own motion. That in this case she was right in the course pursued will be made apparent before the story is finished, but I certainly would not advise any one else to make deductions of a supernatural agency from any experiments or experiences of their own of a similar kind.

For several months Ilian had not looked upon the portrait of her dead aunt. It was beautifully painted in a locket which was in her trunk. She now went and took it out, and returned to the window and fixed her gaze upon it. The starlight gave the face a strange look; in fact, it seemed to frown upon her, and for several minutes as she looked upon it the frown grew deeper. This troubled her, so she concluded to call her maid and ask her opinion of the portrait. A wardrobe stood at the other end of the room with a large mirror in the door of it. She left the window and walked towards the door to ring the bell. Her eye still rested upon the locket. Passing the wardrobe she looked at it, and there in the glass she saw the full outline of her dead aunt's face. The expression upon it was terrible to behold. She was naturally brave and fearless, but this unexpected event was more than her nerves could stand. For a moment she stood gazing at the face, then sank to the floor trembling in every limb. She did not faint, but hid her face in her hands, and thought of what Dr. Rechard had said that very day upon the force of imagination, and of persons in fancy seeing the face of some dead person in a looking-glass. She looked again, hoping to find that frowning face gone, but it was still there, and the countenance had an expression that filled her with awe and terror. She felt there could be but one meaning, and that was that her oath was still binding, and hence, although she had promised to wed Adrien, yet she had not bound herself to live with him. Death was preferable than to come in contact any more with that angry face before her. Her resolution was formed. Yes, she would leave the hotel at once. For fully five minutes she sat on the floor with her head between her hands reflecting on what was best to do under the circumstances. Finally she determined to go to New York by the express train leaving at half-past nine and give the matter a full trial of three days. She could then examine the papers left by her aunt, which were in a tin box at her bankers, and also some papers of her late mother. Perhaps these would throw some light on the subject. This investigation she had long purposed to undertake, but her heart was too full of her loss after her aunt died; and then the four years of the war had left her no time to do so. After this decision she looked once more upon the face in the mirror and the frown was gone; there was the sweet smile instead represented in the portrait; gradually it faded away, leaving only the polished surface of the glass.

Ilian was a girl of rapid decision, and hastened at once to carry out her resolve. Calling for her maid, she told her to pack her trunk and prepare to leave the hotel in half an hour, as an urgent message just received required her to take the nine-thirty train for New York. Sam was also sent for, and told to assist her, and he was likewise directed to remain

with his master, who would follow in three days. Both
servants were too well trained to ask any questions, and as
they were used to her sudden movements, they conjectured it
had some reference to the secret service. At nine o'clock the
carriage was at the door. She sent for the landlord, and told
him that a case of life and death called for her immediate departure for New York, and handed him a roll of bills, telling him
to take his charges out of it and hand the balance to her
husband, who would follow in a few days after he finished
some pressing business. The carriage left the hotel, and Sam
was seated beside the driver. At twenty minutes past nine he
saw his mistress and her maid comfortably seated in a coach
of the New York express. She then told him not to wait,
but to hunt up his master and give him the letter which she
put in his hand; she directed him where Adrien was likely to
be found. Sam promptly left the station and went to the
promenade on the lake, where he found his master smoking a
cigar.

Adrien, seeing his servant coming, said, with a smile,—

"Sam, I suppose your mistress sent you to hunt for me,
thinking I was lost, but it is just half-past nine, and I was
not due at the hotel before."

"To tell de truth, Massa Homerand," said Sam, "dis nigger am mystified. I don't gone and quite understand de
situation ob affairs. I guess der am some trouble in New
York, for missis just left for dat place, and tole me to gib you
dis ere letter."

As the letter was placed in his hand a chill came over him,
and a terrible foreboding of ill took possession of him. The
letter he opened and read by the aid of a gas-lamp.

ERIE, June 21, 1865, 8.30 P.M.

MY DARLING ADRIEN,—Never in my life before were you
so dear to me as at this moment, and yet never was I so
wretched and unhappy. What I have to tell you will seem
like the force of a morbid imagination, yet to me it is an
appalling reality. While waiting for your return this evening,
I saw my aunt's face in the mirror of the wardrobe in our
room. The frown on it was terrible to behold. This in
itself would not have induced me to take the step I am about
to do; it is something of a deeper import, and I am in the dark

respecting the foundation of it. I am leaving here for New York by the nine-thirty train to examine some papers left by my late aunt. Follow me in three days, and then this mystery will be cleared up.

I will tell you now what I purposed telling you to-morrow. In the month of May, 1861, my aunt required me to take an oath of perpetual hatred to all the members of your family. A month later, on her death-bed, she recalled this oath and declared it null and void. She told me that your father had been the cause of my mother's death, but gave me no particulars. I now hope to solve the mystery when I reach New York. I will tell the landlord of this hotel that a case of life and death calls me unexpectedly away, and will leave a large amount in bills for your credit. I will go directly to my cousin's, Mrs. Rendeem. It will be best to say nothing of our marriage to any one at present, till we know our conditions. As I have only a few minutes left to prepare for my journey before the time of departure, I will not give you full particulars till we meet again. Take good care of yourself, and believe me now, as I will be till the hour of my death,

Your devoted and loving wife,

ILIAN.

When Adrien finished reading this letter he folded it up and placed it in his pocket; then, taking Sam's arm, he went back to his hotel, perplexed and sick at heart. He was crushed, but endeavored to find consolation in the thought that it was but a dream, and the waking hour would bring the glorious sunshine into his life again. With his deep sorrow, alone, we must now leave him.

BOOK IV.—1865.

CHAPTER I.

THE RENDEEM MANSION.

It is four years since we last met the members of the Rendeem family. Mr. and Mrs. Rendeem were about the same. Such a short period makes very little difference to individuals who have passed the half-century mark. John, their son, who had gone to the war a second lieutenant, had returned the major of his regiment, with a brilliant war-record. Alice Rendeem, who was just twenty when we first met her, was more beautiful than ever. Her sister Edith was three years younger, and was a girl of rare talent and brimful of patriotism, as illustrated by her defence of Northern principles on that eventful evening at the period recorded in a former chapter, when Adrien's ship sailed from New York. During the war she had been an active member of several aid societies, whose object was to nurse and assist the sick and wounded Federal soldiers. She became so interested in the work that she was anxious to study medicine. It was some time before her father would consent to this. Her great beauty brought many admirers to her feet, but she would not listen to an offer of marriage. Her sister Alice was engaged to a rich young man, who had been captain of one of the companies of her brother's regiment, which had just been disbanded. With this preliminary statement we once more introduce the Rendeem family, who will from this time become active personages in this narrative.

On the 22d of June, as the ladies of the house were about sitting down to their one-o'clock lunch, a carriage drove up to the door, and a lady thickly veiled ascended the steps, and a moment after was ushered into the drawing-room. The servant who received her came to the dining-room and announced that the visitor had declined to give her name, but wished to see Mrs. Rendeem at once. The kind-hearted lady had many such callers, as her charity was well known. It was half an hour before she returned with a smiling face and said to her daughters,—

"Who do you think our visitor is? I have persuaded her to stay for dinner."

"Some worthy head of a Union aid society," answered Alice, gayly, "who wants——" Here she stopped, as a warning look from Edith told her she was treading on dangerous ground."

"No, it is not," replied her mother; "and our visitor wants nothing more than two hours of strict seclusion in order to look over some papers. But knowing the impatience of young ladies, she will first devote half an hour to your company."

"How condescending," replied Alice; "perhaps——"

Again she was cut short by her sister saying, "It must be Ilian." And she was out of the room and up into the drawing-room before Alice could realize it.

"Yes," said her mother, "it is indeed Ilian. She appears worried half to death over some matter. I never saw her looking so ill before. I wonder——"

At this point the good lady found herself alone, for Alice had vanished to join in giving a cordial reception to Ilian; for no one was more welcome to their home than "the charming little rebel," as they often playfully called her.

She told them that she had just arrived from Buffalo. She had left her baggage with her maid at the Fifth Avenue Hotel, and had gone to her banker for a package of papers belonging to her late aunt. She desired to look over them, and then she would be at their service. "I suppose," she continued, "you have heard all about Adrien Homerand?"

"Yes, poor fellow," they answered; "he died two years ago, and his father and mother are nearly heart-broken over it. Why, you told us all about it at your last visit."

"That was a false rumor," Ilian replied. "It now transpires that he was sent on a secret expedition, and obtained valuable information on some important point in reference to blockade-running. He was taken prisoner and kept in close confinement. He had an attack of yellow-fever, which gave the opportunity to spread the report of his death. The war being over, he has been released, and is on his way North."

"Are you sure of this, Cousin Ilian?" said Alice, as her eyes filled with tears. "I wish I had known of it sooner."

"Why sooner?" was the rather cool answer, and the eyes of the two women met in searching inquiry. They were rivals for the love of the same man. One had won it and then left him; the other, thinking he was dead, had pledged herself to another man, while her heart was buried, as she supposed, in the far-off grave of her first love.

Ilian had long ago read this love in her cousin's eyes; and although she now felt that her oath forbade her from living with him as his wife, yet no one else must have him; besides, he was her lawful husband. The secret, however, would be well guarded.

"If I had only known this a month ago," continued Alice, "it might, perhaps,—but no matter, it is now too late." And she went to the window that her tears might flow unrestrained.

"Ilian," said Edith, who had been endeavoring, if possible, to read the inmost soul of her cousin, "I have always thought that very little went on in the secret service of the Confederate government that you did not know."

"Oh, Edith, how can you talk this way? It was just such rumors that caused my arrest, and I may yet be compelled to leave the country, for Secretary Stanton is very bitter against me."

"Not without reason, fair cousin; but come, now that the war is ended, we will forget the past. I am sorry if I have hurt your feelings." And she laid Ilian's head on her own breast, for she was weeping, but faster and faster flowed the tears.

Mrs. Rendeem came into the drawing-room, and with both her daughters endeavored to soothe their guest. It was well for her she was able to shed tears, for it was a great relief to her overstrained feelings. She was urged to lie down and postpone the examination of the papers to some other time.

"Do let us send for your trunks," said Mrs. Rendeem. "Why did you go to the Fifth Avenue Hotel? You have always been a welcome visitor here."

"Do not ask me why. I cannot leave the hotel for important reasons, and must return this evening. I have much to attend to which can only be done there. I will, however, remain with you for dinner; it is possible that I may sail the day after to-morrow by the Cunard steamer for Liverpool."

"But, my dear child," urged Mrs. Rendeem, "wherefore this haste to leave your country? The strife between the North and South is ended, and no one will molest you now."

"There you are mistaken. Secretary Stanton is under the impression that I possess valuable information about the late Confederate government; and if he could by any means force it from me, he would do so. I am liable to be arrested at any moment."

"Papa has considerable influence with Secretary Seward, of the State Department," said Edith; "and I know that he will gladly use it to prevent any annoyance to you, now that the war is over."

"The fighting may be ended," said Ilian, sorrowfully, "but the bitterness engendered on both sides will take many years to efface. No; I would prefer to go abroad. I would like to stay and meet Adrien Homerand, but I am afraid I cannot do it. I will, however, accept your kind offer and lie down, for my head aches."

Tenderly soothed by loving hands, Ilian was soon asleep. But the respite from sorrow and trouble was only brief. It seems strange that a girl who had what all women crave, was nevertheless, by some unknown combination of circumstances, unhappy, and looking for death as the only balm for her sorrow-laden heart. In her gift of life were united great wealth, peerless beauty, a sound organic system, a very high grade of talents, and the matchless charm of youth. Over all these was thrown the mantle of purity and virtue. She did not fail to recognize the fact that she was highly favored by a kind Providence, and was eager to be happy and enjoy these choice boons of her Creator. Was the failure to do this the result of error on her part, or had she no voice in the decrees of her fate? Who can answer?

It was five o'clock when she awoke. She was soon joined by her cousins, and preparations were made for dinner. Edith threw her arms round her neck and kissed her, saying, "Now, sweet cousin, war topics are forbidden, so we will not talk about them. Papa and John have returned and are anxious to see you."

As they descended to the drawing-room, Mr. Rendeem came forward to greet her.

"Thrice welcome, my dear Ilian," said he, and he tenderly embraced her.

"Uncle Joseph," said she, gratefully, "one of your genial smiles is more potent to heal than a chemist's shop full of drugs."

Another kiss rewarded this compliment. John Rendeem also extended a welcome, and looked very much as though he would have liked to have followed his father's example. The dinner that ensued was one long remembered in the Rendeem family. Ilian for the time forgot her curse, that terrible oath that was sapping the foundations of her life, and enjoyed a brief season of reunion with her kindred. It was nine o'clock when she arose to depart. Again and again was she pressed to stay, but with tears in her eyes she pleaded not to be urged, as it was essentially necessary for her to return to her hotel. John told her that he would escort her. It was only three blocks away, and he insisted upon carrying the tin box containing the valuable records. After leaving the house he said he must walk a little slow, as he had touches of rheumatism from sleeping so much on damp ground during the war. Nevertheless, he took her three blocks out of her way, on the plea that the walking was bad in the other streets. It is needless to say that John Rendeem was desperately in love with his fair cousin, and no doubt under other circumstances this love would have been returned, for John was a peer among his fellows. Unlike many of the gilded youths of New York, he felt that there was a higher purpose in life than to spend his father's money foolishly. The very day after his return from the war he went to the counting-house and took his old place, resolved to relieve his father as much as possible from the details of his pressing business. He was correct in his deportment, and loved his home and the society of his mother and sisters better than that which was to be found in the fashionable clubs of the city. His father idolized him, and leaned upon him as the prop of his declining years. Daily, morning and evening, they were to be seen going and coming from their business; and many a mother with marriageable daughters looked with great favor upon the manly form of the stalwart John Rendeem. But his heart was not his own. Four years ago it had gone out to his charming cousin, and now that she was by his side he improved his time, and made propositions to visit sundry ice-cream saloons, and urged the healthful exercise of walking in the moonlight ; it was, in fact, a sure cure for rheumatism. When they, finally, reached the hotel he told her that he had not felt so well for a long time, and expatiated upon the delicious cream and water-ices in a French restaurant three blocks away,—just a minute's walk.

"Only a minute?" said Ilian ; " while we have taken over half an hour to walk six blocks?"

" Yes, I know that," he answered; " but I was stiff in my limbs. Now I am limbered up, and the moonlight is perfect; just the ideal night for rambles with ice-cream thrown in."

Ilian told him that if it were not for her headache—she could have said heartache also—she would cheerfully extend their pleasant promenade, but that to eat ice-cream with her head ready to split would keep her awake all night. To-morrow, perhaps, she would take a walk. She bade him a kind good-night, and he was compelled to be discreet, for they were in the vestibule of the hotel. He would have liked then and there to utter the words that have made so many happy or miserable,—" I love you ; will you be mine?" He fully resolved, however, to make this declaration on the following evening, and he went his way with his heart full of delightful expectations. The pressure of a small gloved hand was still felt; but, alas for human hopes! it was many years before he again held that hand in his own. The evening which he fondly hoped would come, with its ice-cream and moonlight walking, was a long time off. Ilian returned to her room and dismissed her maid. After putting on a loose-flowing robe, she prepared herself for the examination of the papers in the tin box.

With what result the next chapter will show.

p

CHAPTER II.

HOME AGAIN.

We left Adrien at his hotel in Erie. The brain-trouble that had attacked him two years before, when Ilian forced him to take the oath in New Orleans, had again returned. He was not yet fully recovered from his wounds, and this, with the sudden unlooked-for departure of his wife, left him crushed and in despair. He remained in his room, where his meals were served, and Sam was devoted in his attentions. The morning of the third day after Ilian's departure he received the expected letter, but it gave him no hope. A presentiment had taken full possession of him that he had parted from her forever. For fully an hour the letter lay untouched. It seemed to him that he knew its contents; why, therefore, read what was known? At last he opened it, with the same fortitude that a man summons up when about to undergo a surgical operation. He spread the letter before him and read as follows:

New York City, June 23, 1865.
Fifth Avenue Hotel, 2 a.m.

Adrien, my best Beloved,—My heart is breaking under its heavy load, and I see no relief except in the grave. The gulf which opened up between us two nights ago has widened to a mighty chasm, over which I cannot cross under penalty of a curse that I dare not incur. For the last four hours I have been examining the papers in the tin box left by my aunt, but the mystery is deeper than ever. I found half a dozen pages of a diary torn out of a book and tied with a string. They were evidently left in the box by mistake. The handwriting bears a resemblance to that of my late aunt, but was probably that of my dear mother. It is dated January 1, 1841. I now send you a copy; the first part was written in the morning of that day. It is as follows:

"This is the day long expected and anxiously looked for, but it has no bright expectations for me. It is not in the power of my large fortune to buy the peace of mind which I have lost. But will he dare at the last moment to wed the cold Martha Rathmine and forfeit his word solemnly pledged to me? Before God I am his wife: have I not the right, then, to forbid the performance of this marriage? Shall I do it, or let it go on? What a grand revenge that would be to stand before the trembling groom and tell his haughty bride that the man she holds by the hand is my husband,—yes, mine,— and never shall be given to another while I live! Oh, how I love that man! What a feeble word that is to express my feeling! It was more than love, it was idolatry. I worshipped him, I bowed before him; I could have endured his anger at times if only he was mine without a rival. Who of the many hundreds that will be gathered in the old South Church to-day will suspect that the great Professor Homerand, the highly gifted son of Massachusetts and the pride of the far-famed university, is guilty of perjury, and by his act of taking another wife while I live violates all his sacred obligations of manhood? Yes, I will go to the church and be guided by circumstances——"

Adrien, my husband, is it possible that all of this terrible record stands as a fearful blot against your honored father? I will again quote from these notes of the same date:

"Midnight of New-Year's-Day.

"Oh, my God, how shall I bear all the agony of this hour! My brain is reeling under its terrible load, and I see no hope but in madness or death. I sat in the church to-day thickly veiled, and saw the man I once worshipped walk up the aisle, and heard him pledge himself to another when he was already mine. I saw his pale, frightened face in an agony of terror when the officiating minister asked if any one knew of an impediment to this marriage to make it known. Oh, how I wanted to raise my voice in a thunder-tone and say, I forbid it, for he is my husband. But I dare not expose my own shame. So I had to let him pledge his false vows of love, for I knew he did not love Martha Rathmine. He could not, because his heart was mine. When the blessing was pronounced upon the wedded pair I wanted to pronounce a curse. I stood at the door as he handed his Martha into the carriage. He turned round and saw me, for I raised my veil and lifted my hand to heaven to indicate that the curse would come down upon him and his wife and children; and I now utter a curse upon any relative of mine who shall dare to attempt to set aside that which I have registered in heaven. How shall I face the future, which to me is without any ray of hope?——"

Adrien, there is no more; the balance of the notes I cannot find. I have searched all the papers, and yet I feel that the missing links have not been destroyed. Was ever woman placed as I am? I love you, my darling Adrien, with the whole energy of my nature, and yet that awful curse registered by my mother rises from the past and creates a formidable barrier between us, which no mortal power can remove. There is but one course; we must never meet again on this side of eternity. I have made up my mind to leave by the Cunard steamship which sails early to-morrow. I will write to Dr. Rechard and explain to him as much as may be necessary. In some quiet place in Europe I will live alone with my maid. I solemnly charge you by all the love you bear me not to search out my residence. If I can ever explore the mystery of my birth I will let you know. But as no human power can recall the curse that separates us, we must patiently wait until we are both freed from the limitations of this life, then, in a purer, brighter sphere, there may be eternal happiness in store for us. When you arrive in New York go directly to the Rendeem mansion. Telegraph to John Rendeem when to expect you, and he will meet you. Our marriage must never be made known. Dr. Rechard will hold fast the secret, and Sam you can rely upon. Send word to your father from New York of your arrival. I would advise you to go to Paris, and amidst its gay scenes try to forget all the misery I have caused you. I will to-morrow place to your credit at my banker's twenty thousand dollars, and I will instruct him to pay you ten thousand dollars every year. This belongs to you as your right. It is possible that this may be the last letter I will ever write to you. But come what may, my love for you will never change. I am now, as I expect to be up to the hour of my death,

Your loving, but heart-broken,

ILIAN.

Thrice was this letter read, and the strong man bowed his head in the agony of grief which his faithful Sam sought in vain to soothe and restrain. For two hours he never moved or spoke. At last he rose from his chair, and, going to the window, looked at the sky as if to read a solution of the problem contained in Ilian's letter. Turning to his servant, he said, in a tone of voice hardly recognizable as his own,—

"Sam, pack up my trunk, pay all the bills, and let us leave at once for New York." He laid his pocket-book on the table saying, "You will find money enough there."

"Don't got no bills to pay in dis 'ere hotel," was the reply. De landlord say all paid, and he got a heap ob money for your credit."

"All right," said the unhappy man; "you keep charge of everything; I am too ill to attend to finances."

Within two hours they were speeding to New York, where they arrived early next morning. Adrien decided to go directly to the Fifth Avenue Hotel, where, after registering, he looked over several pages of the register and saw Ilian's name. In a careless tone he asked the clerk whether Miss Mordine had left.

"Yes; she sailed yesterday for Europe," was the answer.

This was what he expected. He sent a telegraphic despatch to John Rendeem announcing his arrival, and also one to his father saying he was very ill and asking him to come on at once. He then went to his room, where he made preparations to cover his tracks for the past two years. Sam had already been instructed by Dr. Rechard on this point, but further explanation was necessary. He felt that he was fortunate in having such a faithful valet. Sam was indeed shrewd, and no amount of pumping could get any thing out of him that was necessary to keep concealed.

Adrien had now somewhat recovered from the shock of Ilian's two letters, and the instinct of self-preservation aroused him as nothing else would. If his false position were discovered, even though the war were ended, yet, in the present temper of the Northern people, the death-penalty might be inflicted, or there would be a long term of imprisonment. And how could his father and mother bear the awful information that their only son had deserted the flag of his country? He made up his mind to follow Ilian's advice and go to Paris. Every day was dangerous; New York was filled with Southern officers, and some of his old comrades might recognize him.

An hour later John Rendeem was announced, and the meeting between these old college friends was cordial in the extreme. John lamented the sudden departure of Miss Mordine. He remarked that he had made an appointment with her for a walk on the evening before her departure, but that she had sent word to his mother that she would be out of town all day till late in the night, and yesterday they received a note saying that she was about to sail for Europe to escape the annoyance of the secret-service agents.

A few minutes after the arrival of John, Adrien received a message from his father stating that he and his mother would be due in New York by six o'clock, and would go directly to his hotel and meet him there. A pressing invitation was given by John Rendeem to go to his home, but this was declined. Adrien said he would be glad to welcome his family if they would call upon him. Two hours after, John returned with his father and mother and two sisters. The welcome was a grand one, for Adrien had virtually risen up from the dead. Alice shed tears freely as she took his hand, and said, in a quiet tone,—

"If I had only known you were alive a month ago."

"Why a month?" he asked, with a smile.

"I will tell you some other time."

The ladies agreed to stay for lunch and keep him company, and tell him all the news about his old friends. John said he would meet the train from Boston. The time passed pleasantly, as there were so many questions to ask and to answer. He was urged to come to their home and stay for at least a week, and they would nurse him. But he was firm in his resolution to remain where he was. It was more than likely, he said, that he would return to his home in Boston, next day, with his father, as he needed the rest and seclusion of the home of his boyhood, and his dear mother never would consent to any one else nursing him but herself. As soon as his visitors left he took a much-needed rest to fortify him for the interview with his parents.

At half-past six a carriage drove up to the hotel and the genial John Rendeem entered the room, saying,—

"Adrien, my dear fellow, I have brought those whose hearts are made supremely happy, because their son, whom they mourned as dead and buried in a far-off Southern grave, is once more alive to cheer them in their declining years. I will now leave you alone with them."

The next moment the dignified, gray-haired Professor Homerand was embracing one that was dearer than his own life, and exclaiming, "Adrien, my son, am I dreaming, or do I really hold you in my arms?"

Then his mother came to him, and, with the tears fast flowing down her face, put her arms round his neck and laid her head on his shoulder; her heart was too full for utterance. All she could say was,—

"Thank God! a thousand thanks! my boy has come back to me from the dead. Oh, Adrien, Adrien, is this indeed a reality?"

We must leave them alone for a while; the scene is too sacred for intrusion. It was a foretaste to them of a celestial home; it was the one bright gleam of happiness that shone like the parting rays of the setting sun in the horizon, before the ushering in of the dark night, when the evil-doers come forth from their hiding-places.

As Adrien had predicted, they left next afternoon for Boston by the Fall River line, taking Sam with them, and once more the old mansion opened its doors to the heir who was mourned for as being dead.

The wanderer was at home at last.

CHAPTER III.

NEMESIS.

Professor Homerand was worried over both the mental and physical condition of his son. The war-service had wrought a vast change in him. Several physicians, who were called upon to advise as to the best course to pursue for restoration to health, unanimously recommended a long tour abroad. There was an expression of fear upon his countenance something akin to that of a man hounded down by officers of the law. When his friends and relations called to express their congratulations, he looked eagerly into their faces to see if they suspected the plausible story which he had invented to account for his mysterious disappearance for the past two years. His mother was the only one who had power to soothe him when the spirit of restlessness was most active. He longed to make her a confidant, and tell her the true story of his entrance into the Confederate army, but he dreaded wounding her maternal pride. She was proud of his war-record, and he doubted whether her love for him would stand such a strain as to learn the fact that the boy she idolized had incurred the dreadful stigma of a traitor and deserter. The Rathmine blood would boil in terrible indignation at such a taint upon the fair name of their family. Adrien quailed before the portrait of his grandfather, Judge Rathmine, which hung upon the walls in the drawing-room. He had been fully warned by him in a dream in New Orleans, on the day of that awful scene, but had delayed obedience to it till it was too late. He thought the eyes followed him with a fierce glare, and the lips seemed to his overwrought imagination to be continually pronouncing the word "traitor." The professor noted with pain that his son avoided him as much as possible. He attributed this to the long illness which he had suffered during his captivity. A few days after his return home Adrien made up his mind to ask his father to solve the problem of his relation to Ilian's mother. He asked in a careless way whether he had ever met Miss Mordine, of whom the papers were speaking so much, and who was styled the great rebel female spy.

"No," was the reply; "I do not know any thing of her except from newspaper reports. Her aunt, Mrs. Verdere, died in Boston just at the opening of the war; but, my dear boy, I heard from Mrs. Rendeem that you met this beautiful rebel at her home just before you sailed for the West Gulf Squadron in 1861, and we had rumors here that you were very intimate with her at New Orleans when your ship was stationed there. Do you know that your mother and myself surmised that she was the fair bride that Dr. Rechard referred to in his letter two weeks ago, and which was the most welcome intelligence that I ever received? Our hearts overflowed with gratitude when we heard that our dear boy was alive and on his way home. Why do you not give us some information about the young lady who nursed you through your illness in yellow-fever and whom we expected you would bring **back**, and **we** would have two children to sustain us in **our old** age?"

"**Our** prospective marriage, **as I** have repeatedly **told you**," said Adrien, "**I have promised** to keep **a secret for the** present. Her family are opposed to the union of their daughter with the son of Professor Homerand."

"Oh, yes," replied the professor, "I suppose it will take some time for that bitter feeling to die out. The life-long friend of Senator Sumner cannot be acceptable to the fire-eaters of the South. I was too old to go to the war myself, but I freely gave my influence **and my** money, and you went, my dear Adrien, as my representative. When the news came of **your un**timely **end**, **your dear mother and** myself **thought** we would sink under the **blow. I never knew how much I** loved you until that bitter **hour came.** But tell me **some of** the particulars of your being made prisoner; **you must have been** betrayed. Had Miss Mordine any thing **to** do with it?"

"I cannot go into any of the details at present," Adrien answered. "I am bound by a terrible oath."

"But is there no limitation **to** this oath?" his father asked.

"Yes, there is," replied the son; "and the time will come when I can tell you all. One of the stipulations was that I should not make known any of the facts of which I had become possessed to either the War or Navy Departments; **I also** obligated myself to leave the country within **a month** after my return home, and to remain abroad at least five years, and the record of my death was to stand unchallenged **on** the books of the Navy Department."

"The secrets you held must have been very important," the professor remarked.

"Yes," Adrien answered; "they were of vital importance."

"There is one thing I would like to know," his father asked, "if your oath **will** permit,—did Miss Mordine have any thing to do with these matters of making **you a prisoner or your** release?"

"Why do you ask such a question?"

"Because," said the professor, "**it is well** known that she was the moving spirit of the secret service of **the** Confeder-

20*

ate government. Furthermore, her great beauty absolutely blinded some of our leading men, from whom she obtained valuable information, which she used for the Southern cause. I have it on good authority that even the stern and matter-of-fact Mr. Stanton was not at all times able to withstand her smiles and her tears."

"Why, father, you interest me," Adrien exclaimed. "I had no idea she was so celebrated. Who was her mother?"

"That I do not know," the professor replied. "Her name, Ilian, is a singular one. It was chosen by me over twenty-five years ago to give my own daughter if I ever had one. I supposed I had a monopoly of that name; but it seems not."

"Did you ever mention this fact to any one?" Adrien eagerly asked.

The eyes of the son sought those of the father to read, if possible, the secrets of the past. The gray-headed professor, however, had not trained himself in vain for quarter of a century. His thoughts went back to the woman who should have been his wife, and he wondered if her love had been so great that when she married another man she would call her daughter, if she had one, by the name that he had often spoken of as his pet hobby. Then again he thought of her sister, whom he never met. She had married, and perhaps the name was given to a child of hers. He resolved that if he could only meet Ilian he would investigate this matter.

Adrien observed that his father had gone into a revery, and presently repeated his question.

"Yes," was the response; "I did many years ago; but why should I resuscitate dead facts that have lain so long buried, but not forgotten? There are many men, Adrien, who have skeletons in their closets and a Nemesis in their heart exacting the full measure of retributive justice for some deed of the past, committed perhaps in a thoughtless hour when passion usurped the place of reason. I thank God, my dear boy, that you have been spared tribulation of this kind. You have, no doubt, suffered from illness and deprivation of your liberty, and your bright naval career was arrested almost in its zenith, but you had the satisfaction of knowing that you made a sacrifice for your country and flag. This may never be acknowledged, but you do not need a pecuniary reward. I have a large fortune which is yours; so that you will not want in any way. Make up your mind now to enjoy the good things of life, and this little affair of your heart may be settled before long, and you can be restored to the woman of your choice. But nothing of what I said must be mentioned to your mother."

Thus was the wedge fairly inserted, and Nemesis was on the trail.

CHAPTER IV.

THE EXILES.

TEN days after Adrien's return home he received the anxiously-expected letter from Dr. Rechard, as follows:

NEW ORLEANS, June 28, 1865.

ADRIEN, MY DEAR COLLEGE CHUM,—Ilian's letter and also your own are at hand. I am bewildered at what has taken place; I cannot understand it. I arrived here feeling quite unwell, but will go on and see you if I can help you in any way. After carefully reading both your letters I have come to the conclusion that there is some family mystery between you that perhaps your father may be able to clear up. Why not question him upon this subject,—better still, make him a confidant? Tell him candidly without any reservation of the past two years, and be guided by his advice. In a crisis like this there is no one so reliable as one's father, and especially a father like yours. The more I think of it, the more I am convinced that he can supply the missing links for the chain of evidence needed to solve the problem of Ilian's departure. I am glad that you have decided to go abroad as soon as possible; perhaps you may meet your wife; and after all is made clear and satisfactory to her I know she will cling to you while life lasts. Her present place of sojourn I do not know, except the fact that she left for England.

I have charge of her interests here and in South Carolina. The war damaged her property very much and Colonel Hortense neglected it. I hope, however, with care, to make it more valuable than ever. I am to send the income of her property to her banker in New York; and she asked me as a great favor not to seek by any means to find out whither she had gone till further instructions.

Write to me, my dear Adrien, as often as you are able. I assure you I feel more than language can express our separation, after being so constantly together for two years. I think it fortunate that you have Sam with you. You will find him a devoted fellow, and the trip abroad will be of great advantage to him, for he has latent talents of a high order. Since my return I saw his mother, who, as you are aware, was one of Ilian's slaves. She is to be handsomely provided for while she lives. She told me that Sam's father was one of the leading surgeons of New Orleans, who owned her and promised to educate the boy. No doubt he would have done so, if he had lived, but he was thrown from his carriage by a runaway horse and killed, and so Sam and his mother were sold with the rest of the slaves. There is, therefore, a good foundation of brains to build upon.

In regard to yourself, I admit that this is a dark period in your history; but take courage from past experience. Three times in the last two years I have seen you nigh unto death, and yet you came out of the ordeal with renewed vigor.

This city is fast recovering from the war. Colonel Ormond has just returned from a Northern prison. He was in Fort Warren. He is about to resume his old business of law, and his son will study with him. Mrs. Ormond is as charming as ever. I told her the other day that you had returned home, having been a close prisoner, and that the rumor of your death was a false one. I do not know whether she suspected the truth, for she asked, with a smile, if Ilian had any hand in it? Colonel Ormond, not having seen you when you were in the Federal navy, of course did not recognize you under the gray. I saw him yesterday, and he told me, when referring to his comrades, that he was delighted to hear that the gallant Colonel Mackenzie had recovered from his wounds and sailed for his home in England. Colonel Hortense arrived here the day after I did, and had the audacity to ask for a year's salary in lieu of notice of being discharged. His mother was arrested by Pinkerton's agent in New York and sent here. Your friend Ned Burrows is at home and fully recovered from his wounds. His sister Lulu is to be married to a Federal army officer. Who would have thought such a thing possible three years ago? But love makes no distinction in politics.

I must now bring my letter to a close. Do not fail to write to me from Europe, and I will promptly answer all your letters.

With best wishes for your welfare and earnest hopes for your speedy recovery,

I remain,

Your true friend,

HENRY RECHARD, M.D.

This letter encouraged Adrien to hope for a solution of the mystery, and that he and Ilian would yet be able to live together in peace and harmony and free from all overhanging curses. He had strong hopes of meeting her abroad, and that a settlement could be effected.

It was just two weeks from the time of his return home that he left it again; but this time in company with his father and mother, and Sam as their servant.

They went directly to the Cunard steamship, and with only a few friends to see them off they embarked. Among those present was Mr. Thomas Homerand, the professor's only brother, and his wife. They came on from their home in Hartford for that purpose. He was a lawyer of some standing. He was several years younger than the professor, and had also inherited a goodly share of the genius and talent of the family.

He had no children, and purposed to leave all he had to Adrien, whom he loved with a deep affection. He was a man of considerable wealth and very charitable. He maintained a high code of morals and ethics, and a transgression on this point was in his mind an unpardonable sin which found no forgiveness though sought with tears. He placed a letter in Adrien's hands which was not to be opened till land was out of sight. Both the brothers were in a very serious frame of mind. They shook hands, and with tears in their eyes said "farewell." The parting of the sisters-in-law was also a sorrowful one. The uncle and aunt both embraced Adrien, for he was almost as a son to them.

Sam was the only one of the party who did not partake of

the sadness that marked the occasion. **He was** at the very climax of his glory. His light mulatto face was radiant with the excess of his joy, his eyes flashed **with** keen delight, and his hungry soul felt that his great opportunity was at hand. The shackles had been removed both from body **and mind, and** it was no longer a felony to teach him to read, **to write, and** develop the talents which his Maker had intrusted to him.

"Sam," **said the** professor, "do you not dread sea-sickness? This will **be your** first experience of ocean travel, will it not?"

"No, **Massa** Homerand," replied he; "**dis** child hab some awful feelin' in de stomach before."

"When was that?" the professor asked.

"De time dat Massa Adrien and de rest **ob de prisoners came from Fort Fisher.**"

"Fort Fisher!" the professor exclaimed, with surprise. "**I** thought you came by land **to** New York?"

A warning glance **from** Adrien reminded Sam that he was treading on dangerous ground. **This was** noticed by the professor. He quickly **surmised that there was some** mystery of which he had been kept **in** ignorance, and quietly resolved to try the pumping process on Sam at **the first convenient opportunity.** Sam, however, **was** equal to the occasion.

"Massa Adrien was delibered wid **some** odder prisoners to de Federal folks at Fort Fisher, **and we don** gone and come **North** in **de army** transport, and he **hab agreed to go to** Canada as he don **told you,** but dat was changed, and **dey let him come home. Lor** a massa, I thought dis 'ere nigger die sure **when** dat 'ere vessel rolled, **and arter two hours I don** gone asked some of de sailor-folks to throw dis child ober **in** de sea, life was **not worth de** living, and den dey all laughed, **and** don't got **no sympathy.** You don't suppose dis 'ere steamer cut **up** such **nonsense?**"

A roar of laughter **from** the Homerand family and their friends greeted this **inquiry.** They **were** very much amused at the earnest inquiring **tone** of Sam, **and it** had the effect of bringing the **sunshine to all of** their **faces.** The tears were wiped away and good-byes were said with less of the **grieving** tone that had characterized **their previous conversation.**

Slowly but majestically the **ocean-bound** steamer left her pier, and **the friends with their** waving handkerchiefs were soon lost to view. Adrien now **felt** that he was an exile indeed;

not banished by any decree of his government, but by the fear of what that government might do if all should be made known. He had no settled plans in view except to live somewhere without fear of detection. Could he ever safely return to the land of his fathers, made doubly dear to him now that he was looking with tear-dimmed eyes upon the fast-receding shore? Before him was the great ocean, and on the other side of it the woman whom he hoped to meet, who was his lawful wedded wife. Why had cruel fate parted them thus?

What a boon hope is to the human heart! On the following morning he opened his uncle's letter, and found a draft on a London bank for five thousand dollars, with words of encouragement and earnest wishes for a full restoration to health.

The passage across the Atlantic was made without any particular incident worth recording. The weather was favorable, with light winds and smooth seas. Sam had some more "terrible commotions ob de stomach," as he expressed it. He was a great favorite with all the passengers, and every evening after dinner he amused them by relating incidents of his slave-life and of his war-experience. The late Captain Tom Jeffords received a good deal of withering sarcasm. Sam was a keen observer of human nature, and cowardice in a man excited his abhorrence. Dr. Rechard was not mistaken when he said that he had talents of a high order which only needed the opportunity to show what was in him.

Professor Homerand now resolved to develop these faculties by a course of judicious instruction. With such a master, one of the ablest of his day, and a pupil with a burning zeal for knowledge, the reader will not be surprised at the development and the rise in social position that followed.

When the Homerands arrived at Liverpool a stay was made there for a few days, as there is much to see which is too often neglected by the average tourist. A visit was paid to Manchester, and the house pointed out to Adrien where he was born. From thence they went to Chester, that grand old town which has no other equal for its style of architecture in the kingdom. London was duly reached, and the purpose was to remain a month before going to Scotland. A week after their arrival Adrien was taken very ill; in fact, he had never been well since his arrival home. His wounds did not heal. He told his parents that he got them in a desperate attempt to escape from his prison. In addition to his **physical** ailment his mind also suffered, and at last he was prostrated by a severe attack of brain fever. Sam was untiring in his attention, and seldom left the sick-chamber, taking his intervals of rest in an arm-chair. He was afraid lest his master in his delirium might disclose the secret that would bring disgrace upon the family if made known. **A** strong constitution finally prevailed, and after two months the disorder yielded to the treatment employed, but the full recovery to his normal condition was slow. It was late in the autumn when the professor and his family left for the south of France, there to spend the winter.

CHAPTER V.

ON THE BOULEVARDS.

I KNOW of no extreme so great and the change it has upon both body and mind than to leave London in November and journey to the far-famed Riviera. It is not one particular place where this is felt, but it extends from Marseilles to Vintimiglia. I draw the line here, for beyond this you come to Genoa,—delightful enough in spring and autumn, but a villainous climate in December and January. I speak in this matter not by hearsay but experience. I would not advise any tourist to miss seeing Genoa; but if a pleasant impression of it is to be carried away, then avoid it in the two months which I have named. Nice is perhaps the best patronized among all of the charming towns and villages on the northern side of the Mediterranean. Here our sojourners took a furnished villa on the Cornica Road leading to Monte Carlo, that garden-spot of the world which nature has so richly adorned, but man has made a hell. I never went near it, but I heard so often such enthusiastic descriptions of it that I seem to know it by heart. The drive to Monaco from Nice, over the Cornica, has been described in such glowing terms that I refrain from its praise as described to me during my four visits to Nice.

Professor Homerand was in hopes that the quiet rest of their villa would completely restore Adrien's health. He was moody and melancholy, and his parents soon became conscious that there was some secret of his life which he had not made known to them. Every effort was put forth to induce him to make a confidant of either his father or mother or both, but without avail. They believed that Sam possessed the clue, but no amount of coaxing or promises were of avail. His answers were good-natured, and he attributed the condition of his master to the severe strain upon him by reason of his wounds and imprisonment.

Adrien sought for excitement to relieve the agony of heart at the loss of his wife in the very hour when he had supposed that all his trials and troubles were at an end. He tried the fascination of the gaming-table at Monte Carlo. It made no difference whether he lost or won; what he wanted was something to divert his thoughts. As a rule he went alone, and it was often late at night when he returned.

In the mean time Sam was making rapid progress in his studies. This afforded occupation for the professor, who had not become aware of the strong passion for gambling, which was gradually taking possession of his son, for he made no mention of the fact in any way.

The winter and spring passed without any other special incident, and in May they took their departure for Paris, where in handsome apartments facing the Champs Elysées they settled down to enjoy the attractions of that metropolis. Adrien spent most of his time by day on the Boulevards watching with keen interest the faces of the promenaders and the occupants of the endless line of carriages, hoping that he might catch a glance of Ilian. He knew her fondness for Paris, and trusted he might be able there to see her once again. At times Sam aided him in this search; but they were not rewarded by even a glimpse of the lost bride. Thus the summer of 1866 passed away. The falling of the autumn leaves heralded the approach of winter.

In December and January the climate of Paris is somewhat akin to that of Genoa, but not so trying to a foreigner. Again Adrien lost large sums at the gambling-tables. These losses he represented to his father had been incurred searching for news of his affianced wife. Day by day the professor besought his son to make a confidant of him, and tell who the lady was, the cause of their separation, and why the marriage did not take place. At times there was a fierce contest in the bosom of the son. Two potent agents sought to gain control over him. One advocated a frank avowal of the mystery of his life; the other urged procrastination. The latter prevailed, and, taking his father's hand, he would say,—

"Do not urge this matter now; some other time I will tell you all."

It was the 15th day of November, the day so fateful in his father's history, and also his own birthday. A few friends had been invited to dinner, and Adrien, who had been awake all night under some strange restless influence that he could not account for, went out at noon accompanied by Sam for a walk. When they reached the Hotel Bristol Adrien told his servant to watch the carriages as they passed; also to see who came and went from the hotel. He himself, he said, would go to the Grand Hotel. It seemed the very irony of fate for the man who had watched day by day for six months, that in five minutes after he left the Hotel Bristol the object of his search drove up to the door and alighted with her maid. She had been in the city for a week, but was not aware that the professor and his family were still sojourning there. As her foot touched the pavement from the carriage-step Sam stood respectfully before her, and in a quiet but firm tone said,—

"Mrs. Homerand, my heart rejoices to see you once more. The sight of your face will bring back the light of other days to my master, your husband."

To say that Ilian was astounded and amazed would be but a feeble expression, not only at meeting Sam, but at the altered expression of his whole demeanor. A year ago, when last she saw him, he was an uneducated slave but lately liberated; now he was dressed in a fashionable suit of clothes, his manners and dialect of negroism had gone, his language was correct and showed careful culture. He made a movement as though to leave her, and Ilian surmised at once his intention to give notice to his master; this she resolved to defeat.

"Sam," she said, "I want to have a talk with you in my *salon*; come up with me for a moment."

He hesitated between the obedience due to his master's

commands to notify him without the slightest delay, should he see Mrs. Homerand, and his devotion to the lady who had given him his freedom, and was the means of placing him in his present superior position.

The latter seemed to him the better impulse; so he followed after her, exchanging on the way words of greeting with the maid. When they were alone in the *salon* she offered him a glass of wine, hoping that this would unloose his tongue, so that she could obtain all the details that she needed. Sam had been tried this way before, not only by the professor and his wife, but by others anxious to get clues of his master's life. Wine only put him on his guard, and, as already stated, he was proof against the blandishments of flattery. Ilian in all her experiences had never found any one who could hold back any secret she wished to obtain; and with a man who only a few months back had been her purchased slave she expected confidently that there would be an easy victory. The case was of vital interest to her and she resolved to use her best arts.

"Sam," she said, "I see that your year's instruction under the great professor has been productive of grand results, yet not more than I should have expected with a pupil like yourself, who has been gifted with great talents that only needed developing."

Sam bowed at this compliment, and placed himself doubly on guard.

"I suppose you have taken another name now?" said Ilian.

"Yes," he replied; "I have taken the name of Andermatt, and am called by every one Samuel Andermatt; but to you, my late mistress, I am still Sam, at your service."

"Why the name of Andermatt?" she asked, with a hesitation of manner and a searching look that was noticed by her keen-eyed visitor.

"Because," said Sam, "Professor Homerand said that it was a level and beautiful plain high up in Mount St. Gothard, and only reached after a toilsome journey, and suggested the name for me as indicative of the rich mental pasture that would reward my efforts up the rugged hill of learning. No doubt you have visited the place."

"Yes, I have," was her reply; and the next moment she was angry with herself for her admission, for it was the spot where she had remained secluded so long, and she was hoping to return thither the following summer.

"But tell me, **Sam**," she continued, "how is it that the professor and your master are still in Paris? I heard they had gone to Nice for the winter."

"We did expect to leave here on the first of this month," Sam answered, "but Mr. Adrien, your husband, was anxious to remain here longer."

"I suppose that when you leave this hotel you will notify him that you have seen me?"

"It is my duty to do so."

"Sam, I believe that ingratitude is not one of your faults. You surely have not forgotten my former services to you."

"Never will I forget how much I am indebted to you in the past, and I know and fully realize that but for you I might to-day have been a freedman in New Orleans working for my daily bread, and without any higher aspiration than animal delight, whereas I am now on the highway of learning, and am able to read and speak three foreign languages,— French, German, and Italian."

"Then, if I should ask you not to inform your master that you have seen me, what would you say?"

"My reply would be, that no lady, no loving and loyal wife, would call it ingratitude for a servant to be faithful to her husband's interest."

"Your master has, then, made you a confidant in all his private matters?"

"He has, and also permitted me to read the last letter you wrote him."

"Then you must be aware that for me to live with him as his wife is impossible till the mystery has been cleared up. Why does he not seek to obtain from his father the clue to this?"

"I have never yet presumed to advise my master as to what course to pursue in this, his relation to you as his wife," Sam answered, with an air of conscious dignity. "I guard his interest to the best of my ability and keep the secrets confided to me; and neither his father nor mother have been able to obtain them from me."

"Will you take a letter to him if I write one?" Ilian asked.

"With pleasure," Sam replied; "I know that the sight of your handwriting will stir the impulses of his heart as nothing has done for many a long day."

Ilian wrote a few lines and gave them to Sam. As he was leaving she took from the white cuffs on her wrists a pair of diamond-crested sleeve-buttons and handed them to him. For a moment he hesitated, but she said,—

"As your master's wife and your former friend, take them as a token."

He bowed and left, but resolved never to wear them. He felt that it would be desecration to do so. He would cherish them while life lasted as sacred relics.

Ilian was disappointed. She had expected to gain the knowledge which she wished, but had been overmatched at all points, and that by a man formerly her slave. Her plans were quickly formed. She called for her bill, and in fifteen minutes had left the hotel with her luggage, having brought only one trunk with her. She left word for any one who might call that she was going to London, but she went directly to the Lyons Station. Late at night she and her maid got off at a small town near the great manufacturing city of Lyons.

For the present she felt secure.

CHAPTER VI.

ECHOES OF THE PAST.

SAM, on leaving the Hotel Bristol hastened to the Grand Hotel, but could not find his master. He searched the *salon* and gave fees to several of the waiters who aided him in the search. The *concierge*, who had been out, returned in twenty minutes after Sam arrived and stated that he had seen Mr. Adrien Homerand walking arm and arm with a friend upon the Boulevard. Sam surmised at once that he had gone to one of his favorite gambling resorts, and he set out to find him.

At the very first one that he entered he saw his master with a flushed face, staking and losing heavy sums. He had been drinking and was at the mercy of several sharpers, who, under the pretence of playing at cards, were robbing him outright. Prompt action was necessary, and without hesitation he went up to Adrien and whispered in his ear,—

"I have important news for you."

This interruption enraged the sharpers, and one exclaimed,—

"Adrien, my boy, tell that infernal nigger of yours to mind his own business and go home and blacken up your spare boots."

Sam drew himself up to his full height, and then, reaching over, he pressed his hand against the breast of the man who made this insulting remark, and with a slight shove sent him backward, chair and all, then whispered in Adrien's ear once more,—

"I just met your wife at the Hotel Bristol, and have a letter for you."

This news thrilled through Adrien like an electric shock. He was sober in an instant. Rising from the table, he seized his hat and made for the door, leaving all his money behind him upon the table. Sam, however, swept it into his hat, as also the pile that was on the opposite side belonging to the man whom he had upset on the floor, coolly remarking,—

"This money is my master's, and you have cheated him out of it. I will see that notice is given at once of this to the commissary of the police. Good-day, gentlemen." And bowing to the others in the room, he followed Adrien.

No one dared remonstrate, for Sam stood six feet high and was of massive proportions. His eyes flashed a dangerous fire, which impressed the beholders with the fact that it was wisest for them to let him alone.

On arriving at the Bristol, Adrien, who was well known to the manager, was informed that Miss Mordine and her maid had left the hotel nearly an hour previous and gone to London, having received an important telegraphic despatch that rendered her immediate departure imperative. He was ushered into the *salon* lately occupied by her, and, asking for writing materials, he was left alone with Sam, who gave a full account of his interview with Ilian. Adrien then took from his pocket the letter that she had written and read as follows:

HOTEL BRISTOL, PARIS, November 15, 1866.

ADRIEN, MY **UNHAPPY HUSBAND**,—I use this term because I know that you have suffered keenly since the evening of our marriage, when I was compelled to leave you under the threat of my mother's curse. My sufferings have been as great as yours, and perhaps greater. My love for you has grown stronger, and there are times when I feel that I can no longer bear the fearful strain, and consider whether it would not be better to risk the curse than live this life of torture and anguish. Can the penalty of the curse be greater than what I now suffer? When I thus hesitate, an undefined dread comes over me, and a horror that I cannot repress overshadows me, and compels me to flee **as far as I** can from you. Yet I love you as woman never loved man before. I beg of you by all that you hold sacred do not **try to find my** hiding-place; **for if you pursue me** I **may have to seek in death** the **relief which I cannot find in** life. Ask **your father for the clue** to the terrible mystery that is around **our lives, and send** me the information through my banker. He tells **me** that you absolutely refuse to take the money which I set **apart** for your use. Why treat me thus unkindly? The funds are yours, and if you love me you will make use of them.

By the time that this letter reaches you **I shall** be far away. Will we ever meet again? It is a question that I often ask myself, and an answer comes to me from **an** unknown source that makes me sick at heart.

I was astonished at the improvement in **Sam's** education in so short a time. Treat him kindly, for **he is** thoroughly devoted to your interests.

I remain, your sorrowing, heart-broken wife,

ILIAN.

After reading this letter Adrien sat for an hour in his chair without moving, pondering over its contents. At last Sam spoke,—

"Master Adrien, shall **we not return home?** You know **that a** reception is to **be** given this evening in honor of your birthday, and that your father and mother will be bitterly disappointed **if you** are not there."

With a deep sigh, that indicated how much he was suffering, Adrien arose, left the hotel, and **took a** cab to his apartments. Outside of his family circle, he never let any of his friends know that there was a fire within that was slowly but surely destroying the foundation of his life. At the dinner-table on this particular evening he exhibited almost a boyish exuberance of spirits. He kept the company amused with humorous anecdotes, and during the evening he sang some of his best songs, and his fingers rattled over the keys of the piano with a power that fairly thrilled the audience. The professor and his wife were delighted. They believed the spell to be broken that had for so long a time held their son under its baneful influence. Sam, who waited upon the guests, was the only one who was not deceived. He dreaded the reaction that was sure to follow on the morrow, and resolved to intimate to the professor that very evening that if he hoped to keep Adrien in his present frame of mind they must leave Paris the very next day. This he did after the friends had gone home. Adrien had retired to his room, and Mrs. Homerand had also gone to her chamber. The professor had great faith in Sam's judgment, and, after hearing what he suggested, instructed him to pack up the trunks and they would set out the next day for Naples. Mrs. Homerand, when she heard of the proposition to leave Paris, did not acquiesce. She felt that as the gayeties of Paris had effected such a change in their son it would be foolish to leave. She was so emphatic upon this point that her husband yielded, and seeking Sam's chamber, countermanded the order for packing the trunks.

The following morning Adrien resolved to follow Ilian's advice, contained in her last letter, to obtain from his father the key that would solve the vexatious problem that was wearing out two lives. At ten o'clock in the forenoon he suggested a walk in the Champs Elysées, and reaching a retired place they sat down. Adrien opened the subject at once without any preliminary talk.

"Father," said he, "my wife was in Paris yesterday, and left at once as soon as she heard I was here, but she sent me a letter."

"Your wife, Adrien!" exclaimed his father. "You never told me that you were married."

"No, I am aware of that; but I did tell you that, when the proper time came, I would unburden myself to you."

"When and to whom were you married?" his father asked.

"On the 21st of June of last year, to Miss Ilian Mordine," Adrien replied.

"Then she left you. What was the cause?" the professor asked.

"You, my worthy father, were the cause assigned," said he.

"I?" exclaimed the professor, in astonishment. "I never met the young lady."

"I know that," said his son; "but you met her mother, and, I believe, her aunt also."

"There must be some terrible mistake," the professor answered. "I do not remember that I ever met Mrs. Verdere or Mrs. Mordine. I am sure I did not. What was her maiden name?"

"Perhaps you can tell that," suggested Adrien.

The professor grasped the arm of his son, and his face became an ashen color. With a hollow voice he said,—

"Adrien, I command you by all the respect due to me as your father, tell me if you are keeping back any knowledge you may have obtained of my past life."

"No, I am not," Adrien declared. "I am in the dark; and you alone can give me light upon the subject."

"Why did your wife marry you if she knew of anything to prevent your living together? Why wait until you were married?"

"She had sworn to marry me when the war was ended, and she fulfilled her pledge; but she was bound by a previous obligation which her aunt had made her take of perpetual hatred to you and your family. This oath was recalled by her on her dying bed; still, Ilian had doubts whether her aunt had power to release her from this 'Hannibal oath,' as it was termed."

"How long did you live together as man and wife?" the father asked.

"We were married at noon," said Adrien, "and in the evening I went to the railroad station to see Dr. Rechard set out for New Orleans. On my return to the hotel I found my wife gone, leaving a short letter, which was followed by another from New York, saying that she had made an unexpected discovery of some papers of her aunt's, disclosing certain facts, and it was imperative that we should not meet again. The following day she sailed for Europe."

"Where were you married?" his father asked.

"In the city of Cleveland, by the Rev. Dr. Bowman, and after the ceremony we took the train for Erie, at which place my wife left me."

"Why did you go to Cleveland?" the professor demanded. "You came by steamer, you told me, from Wilmington, where **you were** set free, and landed in New York. Why did **not you** notify me of your arrival?"

"Because **my movements** were directed by others who had control **of** my actions."

"Will you let me see the letters that Ilian, your wife, **wrote to** you?"

"Certainly. They **are in** my trunk at my room; but," added Adrien, "I must exact a promise that my mother know nothing concerning what I have told you."

"That was the very promise I was going to exact from **you**," said his father. "But tell me what was the tenor of **the** reason assigned by your wife for taking the 'Hannibal oath,' **as** you term it, and also for leaving **you,** her husband, the first evening of your marriage."

"Her oath was exacted on the ground that you had been the means of her mother's death. The papers which she discovered after our marriage were leaves of a diary written in Boston in **1841, on** New-Year's-Day, and referred to your marriage **to** my mother, and of a solemn promise which you had given to marry another woman."

"Was there any name attached to these notes?" the professor inquired.

"Yes. On the margin of one of the pages, written in red ink or in blood, was a woman's name," said Adrien.

"What was it?" **his father** eagerly asked.

"Helen Claymuire."

"Was this Ilian's mother?"

"That matter is in doubt. **You** alone hold the clue."

Adrien was frightened at the effect of these words on his father, who would have fallen **to the** ground if he had not supported him. His eyes seemed **to** be fixed on some object, and he kept exclaiming, "The curse! the curse! it is working. My God! what will it develop?"

"A passing cab was hailed, and the two reached home in a few minutes. The illness of the professor alarmed his wife, who sent for a physician. On his arrival he declared the case to be premonitory symptoms of apoplexy, and advised a change of air. He suggested that they should go to Marseilles, take steamer to Naples, and there spend the winter months.

The following day the professor expressed a strong desire to leave as soon as possible, and on the morning of the third day they set out for Lyons, where, after two day's rest, they continued their journey to Marseilles. Here they took a steamer to Naples, where a charming villa was rented, and Adrien devoted himself to the restoration of his father's health. The propensity for gambling was held in abeyance, and he spent his time in reading books to his father. The subject of Ilian was avoided by both. Sam continued his studies, making wonderful progress. He expressed a desire to study medicine, and books of that profession were procured for him. Six months were thus passed pleasantly and quietly. The professor was very slow in recovering from the shock. He had grown ten years older in appearance and dreaded to be left alone.

The curse was maturing. How much of it had been fulfilled he was destined soon to know.

CHAPTER VII.

THE VEIL LIFTED.

In the middle of May the professor and his family left Naples and went to Rome, where they stayed a month. Thence proceeded to Florence and Venice, resting four weeks in each place. After that they went to Munich, and in September they came to the beautiful city of Vienna, where they settled down for a protracted stay. Adrien, feeling that his father no longer needed the close attention which he had given him for the past ten months, sought once more the dangerous pleasure of the gaming-table. Sam, who now spoke German fluently, attended the lectures of one of the universities and also one of the medical colleges. His progress was something unprecedented. His memory was wonderfully retentive, and his capacity for languages and scientific studies was unequalled by any of the students with whom he associated. His skin had actually grown lighter. In fact, he had seventy-five per cent. of white blood in him, and had been matriculated as a Creole from New Orleans.

The fame of Professor Homerand had reached Vienna years before, so that his *protégé* was well received.

Adrien, was now left to his own resources, and during their five months' stay he developed into a confirmed gambler. He had entire charge of his father's finances. The checks on Boston were signed for him in blank, the professor never for a moment suspecting that his only son would use the money for any but legitimate purposes. His losses at the gaming-table were very heavy. In a single month he made away with fifty thousand dollars. A large portion of his father's wealth had been invested in government bonds, left with his banker in Boston. Thus Adrien had funds to draw on without limitation. He was his father's secretary, and all the professor's letters passed through his hands, and of course everything relating to the fast disappearing fortune was suppressed. At last he was compelled to avail himself of Ilian's offer and draw all the money which she had placed to his credit. In a short time, this, too, was lost. The passion for play had full mastery over him.

Sam soon became aware of this fact, and repeatedly urged the professor to go to some other city. But Mrs. Homerand objected to roving about, and as Vienna was a charming place, she easily prevailed upon her husband to stay. In February, however, of the following year they set out for the North, going to Prague for two weeks and resting at Dresden for two months; and from that city they went to Berlin, where Mrs. Homerand proposed to make a long stay. Sam, she said, would be greatly benefited by the opportunity of studying there. But Sam was of too noble a character to benefit himself at the expense of Adrien. He had noticed that when they made short sojourns in each place, the passion for gambling did not manifest itself. It was only when the novelty of each place wore off and time hung heavy that he plunged into gambling. At times he won largely, but in the end he lost all his gains and much more besides. Sam finally disclosed these facts to the professor, and urged that one month should be the limit of their stay anywhere.

Yet neither Sam nor the professor had any conception of the enormous losses sustained by **Adrien**. Whenever the subject was referred to, he would answer that the amounts were trivial and not half what many men of his age spent for fast horses. His final argument was that the excitement of the gambling-table made him forget the misery of the past. This silenced his father's gentle reproof. The subject of Ilian's letters was never referred to. The father dreaded to speak again upon this subject, and the son, despairing of any successful result, was afraid of another shock.

Adrien respected Ilian's wishes and did not seek to find her hiding-place. It was late in the autumn of 1868 when the Homerand party again reached Paris, and they were once more settled in their former quarters. A week after their arrival Adrien received a telegraphic despatch from Berlin. There was no address. It read:

BERLIN, November 20, 1868.

Have you found any clue? Send me word through my banker.

ILIAN.

This inquiry aroused all Adrien's latent energy. He resolved to obtain the clue for which she asked. The opportunity presented itself next morning. His mother had gone out; Sam was attending his lectures, and the professor was alone. Adrien showed him the telegram, and asked whether some light could not be thrown on the subject. For a few minutes the professor was deadly pale. Finally he spoke,—

"Adrien, my son, I may as well make the most painful confession now. Under the circumstances it is right that you should know all. Will you let me see the two letters of Ilian that you referred to over a year ago? The one she wrote on your marriage eve and the one two days afterwards."

Both letters were delivered to him, and he read them slowly through, but there was no expression of surprise on his countenance. When he had finished, he folded them up and gave them back to his son. Then placing his head between his hands, he sat without moving for half an hour. Not a word was spoken by either. At last he looked up. It seemed to the waiting son as though his father had grown five years older, so haggard was his face. Slowly he began his explanation:

"Adrien, my boy, when **I have told** you the secrets that have been buried in my heart for over twenty-seven years, I hope that you will not esteem your father any the less. If I have sinned, I have also deeply suffered. I trust that I have made full expiation for my crime."

"'Crime,' did you say, father?" **cried** Adrien, in astonishment. "My noble, gentle, patient father, you never could have harbored crime in your heart."

"**Yes**, it was a damnable crime," said the professor, sorrowfully. "I stole from a confiding woman that which **I could** never **repay**, and I refused to make the only reparation in my power,—an honorable marriage. I have written out the full details of this event, and you will find them in the tin box in which my private papers are kept. There is a false **bottom** to the box, which can be opened by inserting the thin blade of **a** knife on **the** edge of **the bottom just under the** lock. You will there discover all the **clues I can give** you. I will merely **state** now that **twenty-eight years** ago I pledged my sacred word **of honor to marry a** beautiful Southern girl, a **Miss Helen** Claymuire. She was a daughter of one of the oldest South Carolina families, and one of the loveliest women that **I ever met**. Her father had left her the bulk of his immense **fortune**; **the** remainder being the share **of a** younger sister, **a frail and** delicate girl, whom I never met. Our marriage, **it had been** agreed, was to take place on New-Year's-Day in 1841. At this time two noted cases of elopements took place, of young ladies who were engaged to be married **to** others. This alarmed me. Helen was at all times surrounded by young men the **very** *élite* of Boston society, and **I was** apprehensive that I **might lose her.** I determined to secure her to myself **by a most contemptible crime.** I invited **her to take a drive to a secluded piece of woods on** elevated ground overlooking the Atlantic. **I** called it 'a little picnic for two.' I had provided myself **with a flask of what I told** her was **rare** old wine. I **assured her that it was** harmless, **and** persuaded her to drink. **While she** was under its influence I was enabled to accomplish my purpose. That cowardly act has brought remorse such as man has rarely suffered. At the same time I gave her in return my solemn oath to marry her within a month.

"I was then a professor in the University, and, owing to the severe illness of the president, there was a prospect that his office would become vacant. Eagerly did I aspire for the great honor. In this ambition I was encouraged by Judge Rathmine, your late grandfather, the chairman of the board of trustees. I frequently visited his house and paid marked attention to his only daughter, Martha. I was fascinated with her, but I could not say I loved her. My heart had gone out to my Helen, and I fully purposed to keep my oath and marry her. At this point I found myself under a most extraordinary conflict. Two mysterious forces, seemingly external to me, were at war within me, I have never been able to explain this phenomena. One prompted me to marry Martha, and thus gain the coveted president's chair; the other urged me to fulfil my sacred obligation to the woman to whom I had solemnly pledged my faith, and who before God was my wife. The former force was finally victorious. I engaged myself to your mother. I then met Helen Claymuire, by appointment, under the shadow of the old South Church in Washington Street, Boston. She learned from me of my intended treachery. She then pronounced a woful curse upon me, to begin to take effect from the day I wedded her rival. Twenty-eight years have since passed; I believe that the imprecation has failed, and Helen has been dead for many years."

CHAPTER VIII.

TRAITOR AMONG THE FAITHFUL.

ADRIEN listened to this recital with an eager countenance, and then asked, in a voice full of thrilling interest,—

"Father, did Helen Claymuire have a child, and may not Ilian be that child?"

"No," the professor answered; "I received indubitable evidence that after my marriage she went abroad, and that her child died within three hours after its birth. A year after she married a Mr. Mordine, an English gentleman, who was killed by a fall from his horse in a fox-chase a few months after. His wife died in giving birth to Ilian, who was brought up by her aunt, who had married a Mr. Verdere, also English, and who had died of some kind of fever."

"I was afraid, father," said Adrien, "after what you told me, and the notes of her mother's diary, that Ilian might be my half-sister."

"Rest assured on that point," the professor replied; "Ilian's mother died, I fully believe, from a broken heart. Her system had run down, and her vital forces could hold out no longer."

"Why was Mrs. Verdere so bitter in her hostility to you, and what was the reason of making Ilian take that terrible oath?"

"The Claymuire stock has some Spanish blood in its lineage, and they are very vindictive in their hatred."

"What was the substance of the curse pronounced upon you?" Adrien asked.

"It was only the imprecation of a woman's rage, jealous and wronged. She predicted the curse of heaven upon me in my married relation. My wife, she declared, was to die of a broken heart. My daughters, if we had any, were to be cast upon the streets of Boston, the public scorn; but, as I have had none, that part is certainly void. She also predicted that if I had a son, he would become a traitor to his country, that he would rob his father and would raise his heel against me, and finally would die far out at sea and be buried in the depths of the ocean. Now, Adrien, do not utter a word of this to your mother. The curse has failed, and thank God for it!"

"Father, why did you not tell me of this before?" demanded Adrien; "the curse has not failed."

"What do you mean?" the professor asked; "what relation has this curse to you?"

"The first part of the curse relating to me has been fulfilled," said Adrien. "I am a traitor to the flag which I swore to defend."

He then related in detail the story of his illness, the compulsion which had been placed upon him, his service in the Confederate army, and finally the capture at Fort Fisher, and his subsequent career up to the hour of his return home. When he finished, his father, pale and trembling, arose and put his arm around him, exclaiming,—

"Adrien, you have indeed suffered for your father's crime. I do not condemn you; but your mother must be kept in ignorance of all this."

At this point the door of their *salon*, which had been slightly ajar, was thrown open. Mrs. Homerand walked in with a deep glow of scorn and indignation upon her face. Turning to her husband, she said,—

"Homer, I did not intend to play the eavesdropper, but I heard the first part of your confession and was obliged to listen to the rest. I now learn, after an interval of nearly twenty-eight years, that while your heart was given to another, you married me as a step to your ambition. Bitter as is this cup, I can drink it; but to think that my son, whom I have idolized, should stand as an acknowledged traitor to his country, his State, and his God, is more than I can bear. Adrien, I believed you to be one of the noblest of the children of men, and I was proud to have been your mother. During the late war I looked upon you as being faithful among the traitors; now I learn that you were a traitor among the faithful, and I curse the hour in which I gave birth to such a son. You have brought a stain upon the Rathmine blood that never can be erased. Leave me, and never let me see your face again."

"Mother," the young man pleaded in his anguish, "you use cruel language. I had been ill from yellow-fever, and in that enfeebled condition was not master of my will. A dagger was pressed against my throat, and if I had not taken the oath required I would have been slain on the instant."

"Better such a death a thousand times," she cried, in strong excitement, "than to live an exile and a fugitive from the avenging arm of the country you thus deserted in the hour of her sorest need. I would rather look upon your dead body slain for the defence of our country's flag than behold you, as I do now, with the stigma of a traitor upon you. Leave me before I call down heaven's curse upon you."

With one look of anguish towards his father Adrien left the apartment.

The mother had taken the last earthly look upon the face of her cherished boy.

Reader, be kind and gentle to her. She was loyal to her country's cause.

CHAPTER IX.

THE WELCOME MESSENGER.

Ten days had passed since the terrible scene recorded in the last chapter, but no trace could be found of Adrien.

Sam had searched every well-known gambling-saloon in the city, aided by two of the best detectives. None of his friends had seen him. The river was dragged in case he might have committed suicide. Sam wrote letters to friends asking for information in the various cities which they had visited. The answers all had the same tenor,—" Not seen."

Mrs. Homerand had taken to her bed the day after Adrien left, and the doctors informed her husband that there was no hope of her recovery. Her disease baffled their skill.

The professor had argued with all his ability in favor of their boy. He pleaded the fact of Adrien's English birth as being some mitigation for his desertion. The young man had been placed in mortal terror in an hour when his mental powers were weak from fever, and therefore he was not master of himself. If he had been in full health he would have faced death manfully rather than become a traitor. Yet having once taken the fearful oath required of him, his sense of honor perhaps deterred him from breaking it. Besides this, he had, in his despair, sought death more than once in the field of battle, and had been stricken down at the head of his men at Fort Fisher.

Sam, finding that Adrien's story was known, gave glowing accounts of his bravery. All this had its due effect on Mrs. Homerand. When the first outburst of excitement had spent its force the mother's love prevailed. She now longed once more to see her boy before she died, and begged Sam to go to London and then to Berlin to seek him in person. That same evening he left for the former place, and on the morning of the twelfth day the professor received a letter announcing that his son had been seen in Berlin. He at once wired to Sam to hasten to that place.

It was New-Year's-Day and the twenty-eighth anniversary

of their marriage. Mrs. Homerand was sinking fast, and the doctor gave his judgment that she might live till sundown, but not longer. Her husband was by her side with his hand in hers. He was vainly seeking to ward off the approach of the last messenger, that he knew was about to take away from him the woman who for so many years had been his partner, who had nursed and cared for him, and had loved him with all a New England woman's devotion. It was true that when he gave his hand to her he had given her only the ashes of a buried love. But never once had he neglected her comfort or spoken to her unkindly. Her departure he felt would leave a terrible blank in his life. For twenty-eight years they had never been separated for a single day. They had shared each other's joy and sorrow, and in that memorable period of two years, when they mourned the loss of their son, buried, as they thought, in a far-off Southern grave, their tears were shed together. Now he would be left alone in his old age. He could not return to his home and kindred lest his son's crime should be made known,—that son on whom he had hoped to lean when the years should hang heavy upon him. What comfort had he in Adrien now, with the passion for gambling absorbing his soul? The husband and wife talked calmly of the change now fast approaching. Both were Christians, and trusted that it would not be long till they would be again united, when there would be no heart-burning, no tears, no sickness or sorrow. Again and again they spoke of Adrien, wondering whether he would return in time.

The sun was sinking behind the western part of the city. The day had been beautiful. Mrs. Homerand was perfectly conscious and resigned to her fate. Not a murmur escaped her lips. She awaited the coming moment with feelings of joy, and without fear in the thought. She expected to meet her father, her mother, and her kindred. In a few moments more all would be over. The physician had just arrived to remain till the end. Two of her friends came in at the same time; but how anxiously she listened for the footsteps of her wayward son.

"How much longer can I live?" she inquired feebly of the physician, who held her pulse.

"Hardly twenty minutes more," was his reply.

"Time enough to greet my boy if he would come."

Hurried footsteps were approaching and a knock was heard at the door. It was only a message from the telegraph office. The professor read its contents:

BERLIN, January 1, **1869.**

A New-Year's greeting to you and my mother. I am leaving at once with Sam, and due in Paris early the day after to-morrow. Have seen Ilian. Hope mother is better.

ADRIEN.

"Homer," **said** the dying woman in **a** feeble voice, " my time **has** come, and, **in** parting, I say that I have **always** tried to be a faithful wife. You were my first and only love. We part now for a short period, and I will be the first to greet you when you are called. Give Adrien a mother's dying blessing, and tell him that I fully forgive all the past, and ask him to pardon his mother's anger. My pride was deeply wounded, and I am sorry, very sorry, for **the** unkind **words** that I uttered. When I am gone, I want my body to **be placed in our** family vault, that my dust may rest with my **ancestors. Send Sam** home with my remains. Do not leave Adrien, but watch over him. Tell him that the gambling-hell is the high-road to ruin and ignominy. **Could** I only see **the** face of my boy!"

· She could say **no more. An** expression of calm resignation came **over** her countenance, **then a** smile, a slight struggle, and the weary spirit went to its rest.

We **leave the** mourning husband alone with his **dead.**

CHAPTER X.

FOUND AT LAST.

ADRIEN, driven from his **mother's** presence, went to **his own** room to think over what **course it was** best for him to take. As Ilian, judging from her telegram, was in Berlin, he made up his mind **to** go **to** that city. He hastily packed **up his** clothing, and taking a cab, drove to the "Gare de l'Est," arriving just in time for the express train to Brussels. Continuing his journey, he arrived in Berlin the second day after. Within two hours of his arrival he left his hotel, to find, if possible, the woman who was his wife. Going first to the telegraph-office, he showed the message which he had received in Paris, and asked whether they knew where the sender lived. The books were consulted, and they found only the direction that all telegrams for Miss Mordine were to be sent to her banker. Adrien drove at once to the place. He saw the head of the firm, told him his business, and asked for the required information. The man informed him that Miss Mordine had been very much annoyed by an American, a colonel of the army, who was always asking for money, and had left positive instructions not to give her address to any one without first consulting her. This they would be glad to do as soon as they knew themselves where she was. She had left the city the previous day, and they did not know whither she had gone. They had been directed to keep her mail-matter till further orders.

"Do you remember the name of the American colonel?" Adrien asked.

"I heard it," was the reply, "but I forget it. He has been in our office several times. He is a lightly-built man, with gray hair and a dissipated look, and gets very angry if he is not addressed by the title of 'colonel.'"

"'Colonel Hortense,' is that the name?"

"Ah, yes; that is the name," the banker answered. "Do you know him?"

"Slightly. Is he in Berlin now?"

"Yes; you will find him at a pension in a small street leading from the Unter den Linden. My clerk will give you the number. If he is not there, you will find him in one of the gambling-saloons. They can tell you where at his pension. May I have the pleasure of your name?"

"Adrien Homerand," was the reply.

"What! the son of the great American professor?" the banker exclaimed. "I am delighted to meet you, and place myself at your service."

"Many thanks," replied Adrien. "I will go now and give notice to this Colonel Hortense to leave the city at once."

"That, my friend, will be rather a difficult task," said the banker. "I hope, however, that you may succeed."

Adrien felt that he was on a close trail and resolved to go to the post-office; perhaps they could tell him where Ilian stayed when in the city. First, however, he must dislodge the hateful colonel who was pestering his wife for money. He had set out for the pension, when he suddenly recollected that Colonel Hortense supposed him dead and buried in New Orleans, and that he might prove a worse blackmailer than the noted Tom Jeffords. Other tactics, therefore, must be employed. He ordered the cab to drive to the office of the chief of police, with whom he was personally acquainted. He was at once ushered into the presence of the functionary who was the dread of the evil-doers of Berlin,—in fact, of all Prussia. He told the chief that Colonel Hortense was a dangerous character, a blackmailer and a plotter of treason, and that it would be advisable to keep a lookout upon him. A bell which was on the table sounded a clear note, and a few written words were handed to an official who responded to the call.

"Many thanks for your information," said the head of the police department as Adrien arose to take his leave. Within five hours he received a notice to the effect that Colonel Hortense had been arrested and conducted to the frontier, with an intimation that he would be imprisoned with hard labor if he should ever return. This matter having been settled, Adrien resolved to await the return of Ilian. The next day he went to the post-office and inquired of one of the officials if they knew where an American lady, a Miss Mordine, and her maid, had stopped when last in the city. He surmised that she might have received local letters. A search was made among the records, and information was asked of the carriers. In a few minutes word was brought that a registered package had been delivered three days previous to a lady of this name at the Hotel Victoria. Adrien went at once to the place designated, and, in order to avoid suspicions as to his motive and perhaps to be met by a refusal of the information desired, he stopped at a stationery-shop and purchased a large official envelope. He then wrote a few lines upon a sheet of paper, enclosed it, and directed it to Miss Ilian Mordine, sealed it with wax, and stamped it with his ring. Returning to the hotel he saw the manager, and, taking from his pocket the long envelope prepared, asked if the lady was in. He was answered that she had left two days previous,—they thought for Dresden,—but she would return shortly, as she left most of her baggage behind. Adrien then remarked that he was a near relative of the lady and would await her return, and also move his luggage from his hotel to this one. A large room was placed at his disposal, and by evening he was installed in his new apartments. He now felt that this time he would surely meet his long-parted wife. A few days after Christmas he resolved to go to Dresden, thinking that perhaps he might meet her there, as her banker would inform her that he was in Berlin and asking for her. He searched every hotel and pension in Dresden where she would be likely to stop, but without success. On New-Year's morning he took his ticket by an early train for a return to Berlin. He was alone in his compartment and settled in a corner for a *siesta*. Drawing his travelling-cap well over his face, he was soon in a sound slumber. He was awakened by the train stopping at some station, and a lady closely veiled entered the carriage, followed by her maid. The next moment the train was started. The lady took a seat on the same side by the other window, and, throwing up her veil, spoke to her attendant in English.

"We are due in Berlin by eleven o'clock, and I expect a number of letters. I think I will drive to my banker's before going to our hotel. I hope I will not meet that plague of my life."

Adrien started. The voice awoke a thousand echoes in his breast. Jumping to his feet, he exclaimed,—

"Ilian, have we met at last?"

Most women under such circumstances would have fainted or screamed out, but Ilian always had her nerves under perfect control. She was surprised beyond measure, and her eyes filled with tears. For a moment she hesitated; then placing both her hands in her husband's, she said,—

"Adrien, I am so glad to see you once more. Sit by my side."

They certainly would have embraced each other but for the presence of the maid. At the next stopping-place Ilian suggested to her that she wished to have some private talk with Mr. Homerand, and directed her to go into the next compartment. The long-separated ones were left alone to talk over the past.

"Ilian, my own dear one," said the now happy husband, "I hope you did not refer to me when you made that remark after you entered this carriage, that you hoped you would not meet 'that plague of your life' in Berlin?"

"No, indeed," she said; "I referred to Colonel Hortense."

"Then have no further fear about him. I induced the chief of police to order him out of the country."

"Oh, how grateful I am!" said she; "I will have peace now."

The time was spent in relating to each other all that had happened in the last four years, and Adrien told her in detail of the confession of his father and what he knew of her birth, and also of his mother's anger. When he finished, Ilian replied that that part of the story that referred to her own birth was not sufficient. There was a deeper mystery, and till it could be cleared up she could not, would not dare, live with him as his wife, and thus call down upon her head a mother's terrible curse. Her love for him, she repeated again and again, had not abated one particle. Now that they had met again, she was willing to see him from time to time, but only as brother and sister.

As they stepped upon the platform at Berlin, Sam met them there, but betrayed none of the amazement which he felt at seeing his master and mistress once more together. Speaking at once to Adrien, he told his errand, that his mother was very ill and wished to see him at once. A moment must not be lost. The train, he told Adrien, would leave in half an hour.

"How did you know I was coming on that particular train?" inquired Adrien.

"I heard that you had gone probably to Dresden, and I wrote to all the hotels, and this morning I received a telegram from the hotel that you had left and were due here at eleven."

Adrien was very anxious to wait over till the next day, but Sam urged that if he wished to see his mother alive he must set out at once.

Ilian on hearing of this also advised him to go. She promised that she would remain in Berlin till he could return. She would be then compelled to go to New Orleans, she said, to look after some property. Adrien then sent the despatch to his father, which has been already noticed, and in a few minutes was on his way to Paris.

Ilian remained on the platform till he was out of sight.

CHAPTER XI.

THE MORTGAGE-BOND.

THE morning of the 3d of January was cold and raw. The falling snow was covering houses and trees in a white mantle. Adrien had telegraphed to his father from Hanover and from Brussels asking for news of his mother's health, but had received no reply. Thinking that the answers might have missed him he had no misgiving. He reached Paris at six in the morning, and, taking a cab, he drove with Sam to his father's apartments. As he entered he beheld candles burning in the *salon* and two attendants there. He was about to make inquiry for his mother, when his eyes caught a long black object, which he had not at first perceived in the obscurity; upon going up to it he was horror-stricken. It was a coffin; and within he saw the pale face of his mother with her hands across her breast. He had not thought for a moment of any such result from her illness. It was a terrible shock. He was so overcome that he sank on his knees by the side of the coffin and plaintively called upon her to speak to him again and say that she forgave him. Hardly had he uttered the words before a voice, sounding more like one from the dead than from a living person, replied,—

"She did forgive you, Adrien, and left you her blessing. Welcome home again."

Adrien looked up affrighted. His father was standing in the door that led to his chamber. The professor's face was more pallid than the white night-garment which he wore. Adrien was in doubt for a moment whether it was really his father who stood there, the face was so haggard and woe-begone. The doubt was speedily set at rest, as his father came to him and embraced him. After giving the particulars of his mother's death, the professor informed his son that the body was to be taken to a receiving-vault that day, to wait till arrangements could be made to send it home to Boston.

On the following day Sam took charge of the remains, and left for New York by the way of Havre.

Adrien and his father also left Paris for Berlin. He had both written and telegraphed to Ilian stating when he was due, but said nothing about the professor. When they arrived she was at the station. After greeting Adrien warmly, and tendering her sympathy for his mother's death, she asked who that gray-haired old man was that rode in the same compartment. "He looks very ill," she remarked.

"That is my father, let me introduce you."

Before she was aware of it the professor had taken both her hands. Looking for a moment into her face, he exclaimed, as if to himself,—

"Is it possible that the dead can come back again?"

He placed his hand on his heart, as though to repress a sharp pain, and would have fallen to the ground, if he had not been supported by the strong arm of his son. He was immediately placed in a carriage and driven to the same hotel where Ilian was staying. If she had been aware of his coming she would not have gone to the station. Having seen him, however, all her womanly sympathy was aroused. She felt a strange longing to embrace him, and during the two days in which he was confined to his bed she was almost constantly at his side. As soon as he was able to get up she exhibited both profound respect and filial attention, which completely captivated him.

A week thus passed. Adrien was full of hope that his wife would overcome her mysterious apprehension and consent to live with him. But she could not surmount the barrier. Regard it as she would, she could obtain no assurance that her mother, if she was living, or even her aunt, would give her their approval and blessing.

The course which she had pursued for the last four years was the only one that gave her peace of mind. True, it did not afford her happiness. How could it, when she loved her husband with all the fervor of her nature and knew that he was miserable and wretched away from her? The world might call her cold, ungrateful, and cruel,—in fact, use harsher adjectives,—but so long as her conscience approved the course which she was pursuing,—and would certainly condemn any other,—she saw no way for her but to leave Adrien and his father till such time as more light could be thrown on the mystery of her life. She felt an assurance that there would come a time when the darkness would be removed that overshadowed their lives.

The professor declined to meddle in the matter in any way. To do so, he told Adrien, would only prejudice his case and perhaps prevent any possibility of reconciliation. The dread of her mother's curse, he declared, would wear off in time. Although he had himself grievously wronged her mother, yet that matter had been partly condoned by her marriage to Mr. Mordine, of which Ilian was the fruit; consequently she had no right to bind her daughter to an oath of perpetual hatred for an act committed nearly a generation ago.

Adrien urged this fact so strongly with his wife that finally she agreed to give the subject another year's trial. She promised him that if at the end of that time she could satisfy herself on these points she would return to him. In the mean time, however, she must go to America, where she was needed to make a transfer of some real estate. Dr. Rechard, she informed him, had written and cabled for her to come at once, as otherwise she would lose a valuable sale of some of her unimproved lands. So the matter was settled. Two days after, she left with her maid for London, and then by Cunard steamer from Liverpool. She was now homeward bound after having been away almost four years.

After her departure, Berlin was extremely monotonous to both Adrien and his father. They left on the following day for Vienna by the way of Dresden and Frankfort, remaining a few days at each of these places. If either of them could but have divined the fatal results from this visit they would have gone in some other direction. Adrien had made a solemn resolution to himself not to enter a gambling-room under any circumstances. The best part of his father's fortune had been thus squandered. The government bonds in the bank at Boston had been drawn on by loans on them till no more advances could be obtained, and the lender had written demanding payment of the money. The professor knew nothing of this, but would probably receive the information from his brother on the return of Sam.

Adrien dreaded being called to account; not because there would be any hard words over it. This he could have faced. What he feared most was the loss of confidence that would follow. His father had left the entire management of everything to him, and the grieved look in that kind face, bowed down with care and sorrow, would go to the inmost recesses of his soul! How could this be avoided? There was but one way. That hundred thousand dollars must be procured and paid into the bank within three months, or the mortgage on the bonds would be foreclosed. After due consideration he matured a plan that would tide matters over. He resolved to make a partial confession to his father and ask him to sign a mortgage on their mansion and a block of houses in Boston. This, he knew, would be no easy matter, for the professor had never signed a mortgage on anything in his life. Adrien was aware that he would have to use a little deception, but he quieted his conscience by the thought that he was his father's sole heir, and it was only forestalling what would eventually be his own. The true, manly course, he felt vividly conscious, would have been to make a frank avowal of just how matters stood.

The more he thought of it the more he shrunk from the ordeal. But the hellish passion for gambling had undermined that nice sense of honor which had previously been a conspicuous trait of his nature. He prepared the mortgage. Then, watching his opportunity, he sat down by the side of the gray-haired old man, on whose face was an intense expression of love.

"Father," he said, "in a moment, or, I should say, an hour, of excitement in the gambling-hell at Monte Carlo I staked a large sum of your money and lost. I borrowed from friends to pay it back to your estate, and have never been able to make it up, and I have worried myself sick over it."

"How much was the amount?" the professor asked.

"Fifty thousand dollars."

"Think no more of it, my son," said his father. "Fill out a check for the amount and I will sign it."

"But you have no such amount on deposit."

"There are one hundred and fifteen thousand dollars in government bonds in my bank in Boston. Draw against them for the sum you want."

For a moment Adrien's better nature prevailed. He was about to confess that he had long since drawn on them for the full face value. But he was in the toils of the tempter and had no power to turn back.

"I hate to disturb that investment," said he. "The bonds are at a large premium, and the interest in gold makes them too valuable to sell any portion of them. A mortgage on those houses in Beacon Street would be a wiser course."

"A mortgage!" exclaimed the professor. "Adrien, I never did such a thing, and the very thought of it is hateful. I cannot do it." The old man rose from his chair and walked the floor in his excitement. After a few minutes he sat down again, saying, "Let the bonds go. We can buy back others of equal value."

Adrien did not reply, but going to the window looked upon the river Danube, which flowed past their home, and said, apparently to himself,—

"Perhaps, after all, it would have been better."

"Why, certainly it would, my boy," said the old man. "Sell the bonds at once."

"Father," replied his treacherous son, "I was pondering over something else."

"What was it?" the professor eagerly asked. "Any new proposition?"

"Yes; I had serious thoughts this morning of throwing myself in that river and there ending my troubles. I was ashamed to make this confession to you of the money I have lost. I knew that you would lose all confidence in me. That I now fear you have done; you decline to approve my proposition about the mortgage."

"Adrien! Adrien! how can you coolly talk of ending your life in that fashion?" exclaimed the now thoroughly frightened father.

"Why should I fear death?" was the cool reply. "Have I not faced him on the field of battle and in the sick-chamber? And not only that, but I courted his shaft in order that I might find relief in the grave."

"My God! is not my misery ended? My dearest boy, you are all I have now to lean upon in my old days. Were you to die I would crave death as a boon. Make out the mortgage and I will sign it; anything you may wish I will do."

23*

"It must be signed before the American consul and have his seal attached," said Adrien.

"I will go with you as soon as you are ready. Prepare the paper."

In two hours they were in the consul's office. Adrien placed a piece of blotting-paper over part of the mortgage-bond, and then pointed out to his father where to sign his name. The instrument was then fully attested, and they returned to their apartment.

"I am glad," said the professor, "that the agony is over, and also that you did not include our mansion in that bond. Those houses in Beacon Street are worth twice fifty thousand dollars. You will have no trouble in getting the amount you want."

"I do not expect any difficulty," was the reply.

Adrien had adroitly kept the knowledge from his confiding father that the mortgage just executed was for one hundred and fifty thousand, and included that very mansion and all of their real estate. The blotting-paper had hid this from his sight, exposing only the latter part of the words "fifty thousand."

The instrument was duly sent to the banker in Boston by registered mail, and Adrien waited for results.

CHAPTER XII.

HOPE DEFERRED.

Is it lawful to do evil if good may follow from it? This has been a question asked many times since man was ushered into the world. It has been variously answered. Many, having silenced the stern voice of their conscience, are anxious for an affirmative answer to it from some source that will carry weight and conviction. It is pleaded by some that if evil is done without any good results, then it is a wrong that must be brought to an account; but that if, on the other hand, good follows, then the wrong-doing is pardoned.

It was thus that Adrien argued the point with himself. He

had transmitted the mortgage-bond to his banker, in whose
favor it was made out, with instructions to obtain the loan,
pay off the claim on the government bonds, and place the
balance to his father's credit. He purposed to use this extra
amount in some judicious speculation, and so to make up, if
possible, the previous losses, and take off the mortgage. His
father, he confidently hoped, would overlook the small deception which he had practised on him to spare his feelings. If
this plan, so nicely made, should be successful, he solaced his
conscience that the evil of his action would be extenuated.

In the mean time, it would be necessary to keep Sam away
from his father, for he might be charged with disagreeable
information in regard to what had been done with the finances.
Sam would certainly inform the professor of the true state
of the facts. The professor had treated him like a son and
won his ardent devotion. He did not forget by any means
all that he owed to Adrien, yet, in a case like this, there was
a greater debt due the father. A letter was prepared by
Adrien and sent to meet him on his arrival in Liverpool, instructing him to go to Berlin and continue his studies in
medicine. The following week Adrien persuaded his father
to leave for Palermo, that lovely city in the island of Sicily.
They went by the way of Trieste, taking the regular mail-
steamer of the Austrian Lloyd's line. The climate suited them
both, and they decided to remain there till the warm weather
should set in.

Two months after their arrival Adrien received a letter from
the banker in Boston. The mortgage had been negotiated
and the money was on deposit, but a week before it came the
person who had advanced the loan at call on the bonds demanded immediate payment, and the collaterals were sold to
meet this claim, and the remainder, amounting to ten thousand dollars, was also to their credit in bank. Adrien wrote
at once to buy bonds of equal value of those sold. He was
informed, however, by the return mail, that that class of secu-
rities had risen in value, and that it would now require eight
thousand dollars additional. This was a contingency which
he had not looked for, and he decided to let the matter lie over
for the present, or till such time as he could hear from his
wife at the end of the year, the time appointed.

In July the Homeránds left Palermo by steamer for Genoa,

going direct to Mount St. Gothard, by rail by way of Milan and Como, and by carriage from Goschenen to Andermatt. The professor was anxious to visit the place, and proposed to invite Sam to join them. To this his son objected, on the ground that it would take him away from his studies. From Andermatt they went over one of the passes to Interlaken and Lucerne, and in December they went to Geneva to remain for the winter.

In January Adrien received the long-expected **letter from Ilian.**

NEW YORK, January 15, 1870.

MY DEAREST ADRIEN,—The year of probation ends **to-day,** and **I** hasten to give you the conclusion at which I have **been** compelled to arrive. I use this term, for, strange as it may sound in this enlightened age, compulsion has been used by one or more external agents, the limit of whose power I cannot define. You are well aware that there is no affinity in my nature to the spiritualistic mania that has taken possession of **so** many persons, but **I must** acknowledge that I have been not only urged but coerced **by a** power **acting** on my will and judgment, which leaves me free on all other matters, but is inflexible in restricting me in my relation to you, and this, too, in face of preponderating influences in the opposite direction, and of the advice of all our friends which I have sought. In the first place, **on my** return to New Orleans I laid the **whole matter before Dr. Rechard, and** asked **him to** weigh the evidence carefully and then decide. **Twice** in person and four times by letter he has done so with an urgency and force **of** logical deduction that left me no ground to stand on; the whole being summed up in the concise advice that it was my duty and my solemn obligation to return to you, my husband. I **also made a** confidante of my cousin, Mrs. Rendeem, and told her the whole story; her counsel was the same as that given by **Dr.** Rechard. Her daughter, Edith, **who is a** girl of great ability, with a keen insight into human nature, repeated this morning what she had said several times before since she knew of our separation and its cause, that I should not wait for the mail to carry my resolve, but to cable to you that I am coming at once, never to leave you while life lasts. I went also to my lawyers in this city, two of the ablest men in their profession, one of them having been **a** judge for ten years, and asked them to give me their opinion. After hearing all the facts in the case, they told me that there was no law of God or man that would sanction our separation, unless further undoubted evidence should be forthcoming which would justify the contrary course.

With all this unanimous advice, I purposed at once to **come back to you.** Immediately I was conscious of being in combat with a force stronger than any argument which I could bring to overcome it. This has made me so miserable, wretched, and unhappy, that death seemed preferable to the continuing of the unequal contest, and I only found relief **when** I decided not to return to you. Four times I have endured this experience, **and** last night I went through what I hope never to do again. In view of all this I now write to say that I cannot at present live with you as your wife. I will write to you and hope to see you from time to time. Your dear father has found his way into my heart, and I long to feel myself folded in his arms and call him what I have never yet been permitted to do to any man,—" my father." How that word awakens strange emotions in my breast! I enclose you a draft for ten thousand dollars, and will send you this amount every year in half-yearly payments. If you are ill at any time I will go to the very extreme of the world to nurse and care for you. I hope to be able to return to Europe before long, and we can often talk of the days that are past and gone.

Believe me your loving

ILIAN.

This letter was also carefully perused by the professor. He told his son that he now had more hopes of a reunion, from the tenor of this document, than ever before.

"She has consented to write to you," he said, "and to see you. That is half the battle. I can understand her experience with the external force to which she refers, for I have felt it myself. Take courage, Adrien; and before long I hope to be able to greet my daughter the restored wife of my son."

Adrien did not take such a hopeful view. If his wife was really under the dominion of one or more of these mysterious influences, he believed that they would be likely to retain permanently the advantage gained. The whole affair puzzled him, especially as Ilian was a woman of strong nerve. Wholly without superstition and of a practical, matter-of-fact disposition, she was about the last person that he knew of that would be deceived by any spiritualistic phantasm. Perhaps, after all, her aunt's **or** her mother's spirit was advising her.

If so in her case, why not in scores of others who **are left** to their own weak judgment?

CHAPTER XIII.

THE GAMBLER'S CURSE.

In the month of May the professor and his son left Geneva again for Vienna. Here Adrien felt that he had ample scope for speculation. War-clouds were in the horizon. France and Prussia were then preparing to appeal to the arbitrament of armed legions. The professor was of the opinion that the latter nation was **best** prepared for war, while his son built his hopes on the French standard being triumphant.

This was the long-looked-for opportunity to retrieve the losses in the gambling-rooms. A large portion of the money on deposit in the bank was drawn out, his father, as had so long been **his** practice, signing all checks **in** blank. Adrien speculated wildly. He was determined **not** only **to get** back the large amount **lost, but** he **felt confident** that **a fortune of his own would be gained besides.** Battle after **battle was** fought between the contending armies. Finally **came the decisive** conflict of Sedan, and the **star** of Napoleon fell on **that** fatal field, carrying with it millions **of** crushed hopes and **thousands of** lost fortunes.

After the crash Adrien found that not only the one hundred and fifty thousand dollars that had been obtained on the mortgage were lost, but that he was compelled to use the **draft of** ten thousand dollars received from Ilian. He had not deposited this before, and **he was** very reluctant to do so now. His father was virtually a ruined man, and the truth would soon be known. Only ten thousand dollars remained in their **bank.** He drew out half of this and, breaking a solemn resolution, plunged into gambling once more, in the vain hope to win enough to cover his deception. The five thousand dollars followed the rest. Again and again he tried his fortune. Loss followed loss. At last in his desperation he prepared a second mortgage for all that the property would bear. How to get his father to sign it was a problem that perplexed him. It was near the middle of November, and the 15th was his birthday. His father would be just in the humor on this occasion; so he waited.

The professor desired to have a few friends to dinner. This did not suit the purpose of his son, and he objected. In the forenoon of this eventful day Adrien went to the office of the American consul to prepare for the official attestation of the second mortgage. That official agreed to remain in his office up to four o'clock for this purpose. On his return home he found his father waiting for him to join in the midday meal. Champagne had been ordered in abundance, the wily son hoping to induce his father to drink enough to muddle his brain and thus obtain the coveted signature. The professor was one of those men who when liquor is forced upon them become suspicious of some design in view. He at once began to suspect that his son had some project on hand that would not bear the scrutiny of a clear brain. Adrien had never tried these tactics before, and was not aware that his easy and confiding father could when aroused become obstinate, and especially so when under the influence of strong wine.

Before the meal was finished a letter came by a messenger. It was from Ilian, and contained a draft from New York for five thousand dollars for a birthday present. The letter had been sent to the correspondent of her banker to be delivered on this special day. When both had read it, the professor declared that she was one woman in a million, and that this last epistle, while short, showed that she was gradually coming nearer to the point of a happy reunion.

"Of course," said he, "your self-respect, my son, will not allow you to use this money in any way. Keep it on deposit."

The answer to this was evasive, for he had already made up his mind to risk it that day at roulette. There was one number on the table which brought a return of thirty-five times the amount risked. If, therefore, he placed his birthday pres-

out, which was sure to be a lucky one, on the above number, he would, if successful, receive one hundred and seventy-five thousand dollars. This, with thirty thousand which he hoped to obtain on the second mortgage-bonds, would **make** things all right with their banker in Boston.

He was **very** anxious to try his fortune without delay. Bringing his **courage to the sticking-point,** he bluntly told his father that it **would be necessary to** sign a second mortgage on the **Beacon Street** property for thirty thousand, and the papers were all **ready, and the** consul was **waiting to put on the official seal.**

"A second mortgage!" cried out the now excited old man. "Never will I put my signature to another mortgage-bond as long as I live!" And snatching up the paper which his **son** laid on the table, he tore it up and threw it into the fire which was burning in the grate. "**Not** only will I not sign it, but I will this very day write **to my** banker **to** sell fifty thousand **dollars'** worth of **those government** bonds and **pay** off that mortgage **I gave last year. What under** heaven do **you want** with so **much money?** I hope you have not taken to gambling again?"

"I want the **money to use on the bourse to save funds already invested.**"

"To-morrow," said his father, "I will examine carefully what you have invested in and will help you out; but I must **have** the opinion **of a** banking firm to whom I have letters of introduction. To-day I wish **you** to spend with me. It is your **twenty-ninth** birthday. A few of our friends will be here **this evening.** You said **you did** not wish any one to **dinner, so I invited** them for the evening."

"I cannot stay now," answered Adrien; "I have important **business** that must be attended to; besides, you have insulted **me by tearing up that mortgage-bond, which cost** much to **prepare.**"

"**Adrien,**" said the professor, "the insult was on **your part, in asking me to do** what you know is so hateful."

"But you did it once before. Why not again?"

"Yes, I admit that; but it was the first time, and it shall be the last. **My decision is** final."

Both had now arisen from **the** table and were facing each **other in** angry defiance.

"Adrien," said the professor, "as your father, I command you not to leave me to-day. I certainly have some rights in this matter that you should respect."

"I will return later in the evening," said Adrien, "in time to meet the friends whom you have invited, but I must positively go now."

"My son," said the professor, with tears in his eyes, "I beg of you for the sake of your mother's memory not to leave me alone, especially to-day. I am very lonely."

"Do not urge this matter," was the reply. "I tell you I must go."

"Adrien," the father entreated plaintively, "I beseech you to stay with your poor heart-broken father. I dread being alone to-day."

"Why to-day of all others?" was the savage answer.

"Because it is the thirtieth anniversary of that fatal night when the curse was pronounced."

For a moment the son hesitated. Then the tempter urged the prospective gaining of one hundred and seventy-five thousand dollars. This decided him. He made for the door to go out, but his father intercepted the movement and stood before him barring the way.

"My son," said he, "listen to what I have to say. Twenty-nine years ago to-day you came into the world, and during all this period I have watched over you with unremitting care. When I heard you had died for the honor of your country's flag, I felt proud of your war-record. Bitterly did I mourn your sad fate. When you so unexpectedly came back, I offered my grateful thanks to my Creator for returning you once more to my heart and home. I have not spared money, either on your education or your comfort, and now to-day, when I need your presence more than any other period of my life, you refuse to stay with me. Can you expect God's blessing when you act as you do?"

"I have told you," replied Adrien, coldly, that I will return this evening. Great results depend now upon my going at this hour; please do not detain me."

"You are going to some gambling-hell to risk that five-thousand-dollar draft that Ilian sent you. Oh, Adrien, my son, how can you degrade yourself in this manner?"

"Who said that I was going to a gambling-saloon?"

"I read it in your face. Your eyes are blazing with excitement. Why do you affiliate with such men and take such needless risk? Surely my income is sufficient for all your needs?"

There was danger that this appeal might win the young man to a right decision. The tempter at once whispered in his ears, "He who hesitates is lost; think of a hundred and seventy-five thousand, that will be yours in an hour."

Adrien had drunk heavily of the champagne, and its fumes threw a cloud over his judgment, benumbed his conscience, and overcame the filial respect that was even then struggling for supremacy.

"Stand away from that door, for go I must," was his final rejoinder.

"If you are determined to do so, you must step over my body," was the calm reply of the pale-faced professor, and he lay down at full length across the door-way, his white hair resting upon the tiles with which the hall was paved,—cold, indeed, but not so cold as the heart of the unnatural son. It was a sight to move a lost angel to pity. But there was no such emotion then in Adrien's soul. Without a moment's hesitation he stepped over the prostrate form of his father, saying,—

"Curse this foolishness!"

The old man raised his head to make one final appeal, when the heel of his departing son came in contact with his left temple, cutting a gash from which the blood flowed freely. The next moment he heard the hall-door open and then shut violently. He was left alone. No human eye had witnessed this awful scene. Taking a handkerchief from his pocket he wiped the blood from his face, and then in the agony of his soul he went down on his knees and said,—

"O God, have mercy! Have I not yet paid the full penalty of my crime?" Thirty years have I suffered, and this, the crowning act of my son, has added to my misery a gambler's curse."

Professor Homerand then carefully washed the blood-stains from his face and person, and put a piece of plaster over the cut. This in itself was slight, but a small vein had been opened, which accounted for the great flow of blood. He had been in a dread almost equal to horror of being left alone on this day.

To his surprise there was no feeling of terror as he sat in his arm-chair in the gloaming, and gradually fell into a soft sleep. Then a sweet, soothing halo seemed to pervade the atmosphere. He beheld the lovely face of Helen Claymuire and with her his wife Martha. He seemed to be holding a reception in his room. His many friends and kindred now in the world of the departed were offering their congratulations, but he could not understand for what purpose. Turning to Helen, he said, softly,—

" Do you forgive me ?"

" Yes, my own dear Homer, long ago," was the reply; and the brilliant eyes spoke of the wealth of her love as she bent down and kissed him. It was a scene of the olden time.

> " He thought of a tender, happy day,
> Born with the buds of May,
> When never a thought of pain or care
> Troubled the fragrant ambient air."

He was rudely awakened by a knock at his door, and a servant announced callers. In a short time his *salon* was filled with visitors of real flesh and blood. He told them that his son had been called out on some important business, but he expected him back every moment. The evening was one long remembered by those assembled for its joy and pleasantness. It was midnight when they left, but Adrien came not.

CHAPTER XIV.

HARVEST OF THE WHIRLWIND.

When Adrien left his father prostrate on the floor and went out into the cool air, his excited brain calmed down and reflection brought remorse. For a moment he stood on one of the corners of that grand avenue, the König Strasse, debating what course to pursue. His better nature prompted him to return to his father, ask his forgiveness, and take a solemn oath never to enter a gambling-house again. Yes, he would confess everything; he knew he would be forgiven. Then he thought of all that he had wasted, yet with care and economy and judicious management what remained to them of their fortune would yield a comfortable living.

"Wait till you have won the hundred and seventy-five thousand," suggested the tempter, "then go back and all will be well,—a few minutes will be sufficient." Before he was aware of it he had moved, unconsciously and almost automatically, and soon was in a room on one of the side streets. In the centre was a large roulette-table. Gold and bank-notes were piled up in large amounts. For ten minutes he watched the table. Twice he saw his number turn thirty-five times the amount put down; it is true, the stake was only a louis. Taking the draft out, he endorsed it, and placed it on the number indicated. The marker flew round rapidly, and then losing its velocity, it slowed up. The index-finger was waiting to point out the winning figure. Adrien held his breath: it was coming to his stake.

"Won!" he shouted triumphantly.

"Lost," was the reply of the croupier, as he raked in the draft and all other money on the table. The marker had stopped a hair's-breadth on the other side of the line which divided his number from the next.

"Mighty near, old boy," said one of his friends, as he slapped him on the back.

"Yes," was the savage answer; "but it might just as well have been a mile away."

Adrien was now in the current, and the whirlpool was ahead. We must leave him to his fate and return to the waiting father.

The professor told his servant that he would wait up for his son, who must have been detained on some important matter. He then drew his chair up by the window, where by the moonlight he could see any one coming up the street.

My readers will pardon me if I vary the description of the thoughts that filled the mind of the old professor by giving them in verse. I am not often guilty of this, but my excuse for so doing is that the witching hour of midnight finds me hard at work as usual.

The November night was cold and still;
The father sat by the window-sill;
His thoughts went back to his native land,
And his Boston home, so stately and grand.

It is **just** thirty years, this very night,
Since he stood in Luna's flick'ring light,
Where the shadows from the church, so old,
Fell on Helen's face scornful and cold.

With words inspired she told him then
Of the fate in store for Adrien,
Who would end a weary, aimless life
Far out 'midst ocean's angry strife.

Visions of storms before him rise;
The waters mount to the darkened skies;
He beholds a ship with rending sail,
Rolling and pitching in a heavy gale.

And from her storm-beaten weather side,
He sees a shrouded corse swiftly glide;
Down it plunges in the waters dark,
And there follows it a ravenous shark.

He sees the face of the dead as he fell;
'Twas that of his boy he had loved so well.
He wakes,—the father can bear no more,—
He bows his knees on the chamber-floor.

There in the lonely midnight hour,
Bereft of all his strength and power,
His heart went up in earnest prayer
To God who is watching everywhere.

The gray dawn **of the morning** found the anxious father still watching and waiting **for the** footsteps of his absent son. When he heard the servants moving about **the** house he went to bed. At ten o'clock he arose, and found that he had **contracted a very bad cold** while watching **by** the open window. He went out, and called first **at** the telegraph-office and sent a telegram to Sam to come on **to** Vienna at once, and then sent **a** cablegram to his banker in Boston asking for the amount on deposit; also, the value of the bonds. He then called upon **a** physician who was a very intimate friend of his. The doc**tor told him that the** cold had settled upon his lungs, and that **it would** be necessary for him to return to his apartments at **once** and go to bed. In a few days he would be all right. The doctor also promised to visit him in the afternoon.

On his return, the professor found a reply from Sam, stating that he was leaving Berlin and would be due next morning. The doctor, when he called later on in the day, found his patient very much worse than he had anticipated. A high fever had set in, and there was some danger of a development into pneumonia. A professional nurse was sent for. At six o'clock the professor received an answer from his banker stating that his account was overdrawn and interest past due on the hundred-and-fifty-thousand-dollar mortgage, and that there were no bonds on deposit. At eight o'clock the doctor found the professor alarmingly ill, and was perplexed at the rapid progress of the malady. He noticed also that the face of the sick man was haggard and bearing an expression of despair that was appalling to look upon. He immediately called in the assistance of another medical man, and one of them remained all night.

The following morning Sam arrived and was amazed at the change that had taken place. It was twenty-two months since he had last seen the professor. He now looked twenty years older, and his face bore traces of great suffering. He plainly foresaw with alarm and consternation that his benefactor and instructor was about to die. Sam had spent two years in walking the hospitals, and while at Berlin had improved his time in the study of medicine, and now his acute discernment revealed to him that the professor's hours were numbered. The physicians in attendance corroborated this when they called early in the day. They told their patient frankly that his illness was very serious. The sick man received the news calmly and with a gleam of joy upon his countenance that was noticed by all in the room. All his anxiety was to see his son once more, and he besought Sam to try and find him. Sam was well acquainted with his young master's haunts, and he went to a number of the gambling-places where he was likely to be found. In one of these, although he did not know it at the time, Adrien was concealed. There were two large rooms for gambling, and in the inner chamber no one was allowed to enter except he was personally known to the proprietor. Sam having been recognized as the former attendant of Mr. Homerand, the falsehood was told him that the gentleman whom he was seeking had left the city and gone to Munich. Accepting this statement, Sam returned to the dying professor and reported the news.

CHAPTER XV.

THE EXPIATION.

On the morning of the third day it became apparent to the medical attendants that death would claim their patient by noon.

Many friends of the professor had called to see him and offer their sympathies, and all wondered where the son could be at such a time. The professor would answer that "Adrien had been called away on urgent business, and, not expecting any serious illness to come upon his father, had failed to send his address, and would no doubt be back in time."

An hour after the doctors had given their opinion as to the fatal ending of the professor's illness, a servant announced that his son had returned home and gone to his chamber to change his dust-covered clothes, and that he would come to him in a few minutes. Sam hastened to the room to have a plain talk. If he had been surprised at the professor's appearance, he was much more so at that of the son. The young man's eyes were bloodshot, his garments torn, one side of his face was bruised and swollen, and he looked as though he had been in a fight with ruffians. In answer to his inquiring questions, Adrien told Sam that he had learned of his coming into the gambling-house, and that if he had but known it at the time it would have saved him much money. This morning he had accused the proprietor of the place of having swindled him, and the servants at the house had ejected him with violence.

Sam made no reply. He knew full well that life-long remorse would follow the doings of the past few days. Adrien then went to his father's room, and the attendants withdrew. For a few moments neither said a word, till Adrien, overcome with remorse, fell on his knees, and, taking his father's hand, said, in an earnest tone,—

"Father, forgive me. I have been the means of your death. But for me, this would not have been. I did not realize what I was doing that fatal hour three nights ago, and I have been in a delirium of frenzy ever since."

"Yes, my boy, with all my heart," was the professor's reply; "and I now ask from you a last request,—that you will give me your solemn word of honor never to enter a gambling-place again."

"I swear it," was the answer, "by all my hopes of heaven and by all my fear of hell."

"Now, my son," said the professor, "I have but little time to be with you. The death-chill is upon me. I know that in my present condition you will keep nothing back. Tell me the meaning of this cablegram received from my banker in Boston. Did you sell all the bonds?"

"They were sold before that mortgage arrived to pay off the loan on them," said Adrien.

"I thought," said his father, "that I signed a mortgage for fifty thousand dollars."

"No; it was for a hundred and fifty thousand. That amount lay for some time untouched, till I drew on it to speculate with on the bourse. I lost it and all of the money which I received from Ilian."

"Then, my son," said the professor, "you have made yourself a beggar. Yesterday I made my will in favor of your uncle, my only brother, with instructions to allow you enough to pay your actual expenses till the mortgages were paid off. I supposed that the fifty thousand was the amount. Then he was to pay you seventy-five per cent. for the term of your life. The whole of my fortune was then to go to your children if you left any; and failing of heirs he was to inherit it. As, however, the bonds have been sold, and there is such a large mortgage, I think it will be many years before the estate will be clear, if ever. The seal of the American consul has been duly placed upon my will, and, also, he has promised to obtain the necessary papers for the transfer of my body to Hamburg. Sam will go with you, and take a steamer there to Liverpool and go to Boston by the Cunard line. Give my dying love to Ilian. I have confidence that she will return to you, and you may yet be happy together."

"Father, I have not yet told you all," cried the wretched young man. "In the excitement of the gambling-table, yesterday, I forged your name to a draft of twenty-five thousand dollars. I am certain that I was swindled out of the whole amount, but, nevertheless, they **hold that** fatal piece of **paper.**"

"**I do** not think that my estate will stand such a **strain upon it, but it shall be paid** if possible," said the **dying man,** calmly.

For over two **hours Adrien and his father discoursed** about **family matters. The doctor came in** at times and administered medicine. Sam was waiting in another room. He felt sure that the end would come not later than one o'clock.

The clock had just struck eleven when a man of gentlemanly appearance, accompanied by an agent of the police department, entered the house and demanded **to** see Professor Homerand. On being told that he was on his death-bed, they replied "**that they must** have an interview without a **moment's delay.**" There **was** no alternative. The door was opened, and they entered the room accompanied by Sam and the doctor. The civilian, who seemed to have lost all human sympathy, went to the bedside, and, in an **excited voice,** said,—

"My dear professor, **I am the** proprietor **of the house** where your son has been stopping **for the past three** days. He gave me a draft for twenty-five thousand **dollars, purporting to have** been signed by you. I cashed this at once. This morning he was insolvent, and **I** was obliged **to eject** him from the house, and he said that this draft would **not** be paid. **Now,** unless you acknowledge this **signature and put your name on** the back of it before this **agent of police, I** will have your son arrested for forgery."

The draft was then handed to the dying **man, who looked at it, and then** gave an agonized look at his son.

"**Give me a pen and ink** and I will endorse it," he said; and, **sitting up in bed,** Adrien placed his arm around **him to support** him. **The pen was** placed in his trembling hand and a portfolio on his lap.

"Then you acknowledge the signature **to** be yours?" interrogated the gambling-hell keeper.

"**Is not** the name mine?" demanded the professor. "**What more do you need?**"

"Your signature **on** the back before these witnesses."

"You shall have it," was the reply; and putting the pen in the ink, he held it **for** a moment as though seeking for strength for this final act of his life, and then it fell from his hands.

"Do you decline to sign?" shouted the excited gambler. "If you do, I will have your son sent to prison for ten years for forgery."

"No, no," said the almost dead man in a weak voice. "Where shall I sign? I must do it quickly."

Grasping the pen which was again placed in his hand, he attempted to write his name over the signature which Adrien had forged. But the hand had lost its power and only unintelligible marks were made, closely interwoven with the original signature. Throwing the pen down, he said, "There, you have it. I hope you are satisfied." Then turning to his faithful *protégé*, he said,—

"Sam, God bless you in your life's work. Adrien, my son, farewell, and may heaven's blessing rest upon you!" The next moment he had ceased to breathe.

"You have ruined the draft!" yelled the enraged gambler.

"Stop," said the agent of police. "We are in the presence of the dead. We must leave this house." And he forced him to depart.

The American consul came into the room at this crisis of affairs. Upon hearing the matter explained, he quietly advised Adrien to leave Vienna at once,—in fact, within the hour,—and to await the arrival of Sam with the body of his father at Hamburg. This he did, and was soon out of the jurisdiction of the police.

The gambler in vain asked Sam and the doctor to verify as witnesses that the professor had certified that the signature to the draft was correct. They declined to do this, as did the police agent, who was ashamed of the whole business. As a consequence the draft was worthless. The signature had been purposely spoiled by the last act of the dying man.

On the following evening Sam left Vienna with the remains. The professor had kept a thousand pounds always in his desk, in English bank-notes, for any sudden emergency, which enabled Sam to pay all the just claims against him. At Hamburg he met Adrien, and taking a steamer to Liverpool, they transferred the body at once to a Cunard steamer which was to sail next day for New York. The following morning Adrien was too ill to leave his bed. He insisted that Sam should go on with the body and he would follow in a week or so. Sam gave him two hundred pounds, and they parted expecting to meet in Boston. But they never met again.

On the arrival of the steamer at New York Thomas Homerand, the brother of the late professor, took charge of the remains, and they were laid by the side of his wife in the family vault near Boston. Sam reluctantly gave a full account of all that had taken place. Mr. Homerand was a lawyer in Hartford, Connecticut, and one of the keenest of men at cross-questioning. Sam attempted to shield Adrien as much as possible, but the whole truth came out. Mr. Homerand at once wrote a brief letter to his nephew stating that he had himself paid off all the mortgages, and he would hold them as collaterals against the estate of the professor. He added that he would make him an allowance of five hundred a year, and not one dollar more. He advised him further not to return to America, as none of his relatives on his father's or mother's side would in future have anything to do with him.

Adrien was thus disowned. He was now an exile and utterly without hope.

BOOK V.

CHAPTER I.

THE CUNARD STEAMSHIP.

The remarkable events and episodes in this book and the following one are given as the personal experience of the author. I know of no better introduction to them than the following letter.

PHILADELPHIA, June —, 187—.

My dear B.,—I sail next Wednesday in the Cunard steamship —— for Liverpool. I have been ill for some time: I am suffering from wounds, and also the effects of both the yellow-fever and typhoid, contracted during the late war.

Perhaps you think that, as I have crossed the ocean more than a dozen times, I ought to be satiated with European travel. I am; but I am going over now for the benefit of my health. I am not certain whether it is destiny or impulse that calls me over, but I feel prompted to go by this particular steamer; I cannot tell why, or even guess at it. If I were a believer in spiritualism, I would declare that the spirit of some dead friend was urging me to sail the day after to-morrow. I am free to confess that I do not take any stock in spiritualistic matters, yet, all the same, I am leaving two weeks earlier than I had previously contemplated. I am sorry that I cannot pay you the promised visit, but I will more than make up for it on my return in autumn. Kind regards to all your family. Excuse brevity, as the weather is hot, and not only so, but depressing, and Philadelphia is not the coolest place in summer.

This time next week I hope to be far out on the deep, blue sea, outward bound. *Au revoir.*

Yours fraternally,
KANE.

Wednesday morning found me hastening over to Jersey City with no other encumbrance than my umbrella. My luggage had been already sent forward. I took the plebeian horse-car instead of the patrician carriage. I arrived at the Cunard dock in ample time. It never pays to take risks of that sort in reaching an ocean steamer. The Cunarders, like time and tide, "wait for no one." Promptly at the moment advertised the gang-plank is hauled in. On this occasion the massive steamship was blowing off clouds of steam, and acting like a spirited war-horse held by bit and bridle, stamping and chafing, anxious for the freedom of the road.

My first duty was to see my trunks placed in the hold and my satchels duly consigned to my state-room. When this had been done, my time was at the disposal of the friends who might come to see me off. Lonely, indeed, must be the person who has not even one individual to say the parting word and wave the white handkerchief as a token of a *bon voyage*.

The hawsers that had bound the leviathan to her dock had all been removed except a single line forward and one aft. The decks were crowded with the outgoing passengers and their friends. Carriage after carriage came rapidly with foaming horses, indicating the anxiety of the occupants lest they should be too late.

The throng increased so much that there was hardly room to move on the promenade-deck. In a few moments the clear, vibrating tone of the gong gave notice that the hour of separation had come,—father from son, mother from daughter, husband from wife, brother from sister, friend from friend.

The decks were rapidly cleared, the last farewells were spoken, cheeks were still wet with the parting tears, again and again was the call made, "All ashore!" then came the loud command, "Haul in the gang-plank!" from a brass-buttoned individual with gold lace on his sleeves. His gray hair indicated experience in seafaring life. Without inauguration or formality he had assumed the governorship of what in a few moments was to be a floating island propelled by her own internal force across the mighty ocean. Many then realized that they had placed their lives and belongings in the care and custody of a stranger. His word was law, his power supreme; and from his command there was no appeal. The safety of over five hundred human beings was centred in him. If he should be faithful and watchful in the navigation of the ship, we hoped inside of ten days to reach our destined port; if not, then our friends would perhaps hear of us no more. We had faith, yes, abiding faith, in the Cunard line, that for nearly forty years ferried many thousands across what was called "the big pond." The gang-plank was hauled on the dock, the forward and after lines let go, and the last link that bound us to our home and country was severed. The mighty ship, like a giant released from bondage, glided swiftly into the stream.

I stood on deck and watched the fluttering of the handkerchiefs from the large throng assembled on the end of the pier,—watched till they became a dim, confused, indistinguishable mass. I watched the fast-receding shores of New York City, and turned my wistful eyes to the large hill-slopes on the southern end of Brooklyn, with its many marble shafts marking the sad memories of by-gone days. Greenwood Cemetery looked beautiful in the bright June morning. My heart went out in tearful remembrance of a wife and two little ones sleeping in that great city of the dead,—that loving wife who, if living, would have been at my side. Soon the Narrows, with its obsolete forts, was passed, and as we reached Sandy Hook the ocean-breeze swept along the deck, sending a delightful coolness through our veins, overpressed as we had been by the scorching day that preceded our departure, prognosticating a hot summer. I had been in ill health for several months, and longed for the pure sea-air and bracing winds. After passing the Highlands, we shaped our course for the Irish coast, and the roll of old ocean cradled once more our giant craft.

We had on board nearly three hundred saloon passengers and about one hundred steerage. In the cabin there were all classes represented: the old tourist and the new, business-men and professional ones, clergymen of all creeds a score strong, brides and grooms, old men and young men, fair daughters of Eve of varied ages. It was easy to pick out the veteran tourists by their familiarity with all things pertaining to ship-life. The novices were asking questions, looking with timid glances, and walking cautiously on the deck, as the ship had perceptibly felt the motion of a short cross-sea.

It is not my purpose to dwell upon the characteristics of my fellow-passengers nor of the general events of our voyage.

The routine is about the same on all transatlantic steamships, and may be compressed in the three terms of eating, drinking, and sleeping, with occasional lounging on easy-chairs, reading light literature, and resting both mind and body. An ocean-trip has given a renewed lease of life to many a man broken down through overwork, mental as well as physical. This particular passage would have passed unrecorded, like others that had preceded and have followed, but for an episode that happened on the evening of our third day out.

I said in the letter to my friend B—— at the beginning of this chapter that it was destiny or impulse that took me abroad. Those who read this narrative must decide for themselves, also the truth of the theory of Professor Oliver Wendell Holmes, "that this carriage,—the human personality,—which is supposed to convey our single spirits across life's continent, is not a private conveyance, but a public omnibus, liable at times to be invaded by one or more wandering spirits, who are compelled to use a human form to manifest themselves." My readers, however, need not be alarmed at this, for fear that I am springing upon them some spiritualistic tale. I am too matter-of-fact for that. Often have I asked myself the question, "Was it one of the departed personages of this story, interested in clearing up the mysteries that hung over the curse of the old South Church, that prompted me to take this particular steamer?" It may have been "merely a coincidence,"—that and nothing more. At all events, my experience was a strange one.

CHAPTER II.

RENDING THE VEIL.

"The great ship rolled in the hollow waves,
And the hoarse wind shrieked o'er fathomless graves;
The old ship leaped in the heavy gale
With straining timbers and loud-rending sail."

I would ask my readers a single question: Have you ever felt a presentiment of a danger, an experience in which "coming events cast their shadows before?" If so, you will understand what I mean when I say that on the morning of our third day out I awoke with a feeling of terrible depression. I can hardly find language to express what I mean. It grew on me as the day went by. I could not shake it off.

Seven o'clock in the evening found me in the almost deserted saloon. A stiff south-east gale was blowing, and, with a cross-sea, our good ship was rolling and plunging in a manner far from comforting to unsophisticated stomachs. Most of my fellow-passengers had sought the refuge of their state-rooms. Ever and anon heavy seas struck our iron sides with the force of battering-rams, sending torrents over our decks. Many passengers in their narrow berths were vowing that they would remain exiles abroad forever sooner than endure a repetition of the agony of sea-sickness. Some strong-limbed men unused to the boisterous playful humor of old Neptune had found it convenient and comforting to remember the long-forgotten prayers of childhood; and many made solemn vows that if they ever got their feet once more on the firm ground, nothing would induce them to tempt Providence again by a voyage across the rough Atlantic. Every thump on our bulwarks by the briny element re-echoed on some hitherto sleeping conscience, as it was remembered that only a thin sheet of iron separated hundreds of living beings from a watery grave.

I had a book in my hand and was trying to read, wondering at the tenor of my forebodings and the import of them. Was it indigestion or some outward force separate and distinct from any physical element in my nature? I was suddenly aroused from my revery by one of the stewards. The captain, he said, wished to see me in his cabin. I had spent an hour there in the afternoon, and wondered what he wanted with me at this hour and in such a dismal gale. When I reached the deck I found the darkness so great that I could hardly find my way to the captain's room. The wind almost took me off my feet. I found Captain —— with his hat on and coat closely buttoned up, like a faithful watch-dog, ready for any emergency. He told me in a few words that the surgeon had just informed him that a steerage passenger, who was very ill, could not live more than one hour, and had asked to see me.

I went at once with the captain to a state-room in the forward part of the ship. As we entered, the lamp, which was burning dimly, made everything obscure in the room, but its focus was centred upon the pale face of a man about thirty-five years of age. The broad and deep forehead indicated great development of mental faculties. The lips were thin, the jaw sharp and prominent, giving proof of firmness of will. The whole contour was that of a well-bred and highly-educated man.

The quick eye of Captain —— took these facts in at one glance. In his vast experience with thousands of passengers in his transatlantic service he had long since learned to pick out the pure gem from the counterfeit, the true-born gentleman from the vulgar imitation. He took the hand of his dying passenger, and in a few well-chosen words, with the manner and grace worthy of Lord Chesterfield, expressed his sympathy and the offer of every assistance in his power. The answer, which came in a weak but clear voice, showed that his surmise was correct. The man before us was a gentleman, and one highly polished in the schools and by foreign travel. He not only had a diploma from some university, but had also graduated from the higher university of the world.

The captain turned to me, saying, "I now leave our sick friend in your care. Call on me at once if you need further assistance."

As he bowed himself out and closed the door I turned to the invalid. The presentiment which had all the day weighed me down now became oppressive and almost unendurable. Something in the face before me stirred up the memory of former years. I was certain that I had seen that face somewhere; but when or how and in what surroundings I could not determine. I sat down by his side and took his hand. As I did this I was startled by the echoes awakened in my mind by his voice, as he said,—

"Chaplain, I am delighted to see you."

No doubt, I thought, he had seen my name on the passenger-list and was glad to see a clergyman in his last hours. Death had set his mark so plainly upon him that I was anxious to inform him of the limited number of minutes he had to live, but debated how I should gently break the news.

He read my thoughts, and smiled as he answered me, "I know what you desire to tell me, but the surgeon has already intimated to me that I will probably pass away at eight o'clock. What time is it now?"

I answered that six bells had struck as I left the saloon, and it was now about ten minutes after.

"Then," he said, "I have yet fifty minutes of life. It is enough for all I have to say."

The presentiment was now overwhelming, and my heart was weighed down by a feeling of terror. What could it mean?

"You do not seem to remember me," he said. "Am I so changed that even my old friend Kane fails to recollect me?"

I looked into his eyes as these words came from his lips. My memory was slowly reviewing the pages of the past.

"Yes," I replied, "I have seen your face somewhere; but for its counterpart I must search among the dead and not among the living. You strongly resemble a brother-officer of mine in the volunteer navy, one whom I had learned to love dearly. He was a noble, generous, high-spirited man, a graduate of a university, and an only son of one of the professors; but he died of yellow-fever in 1863, and was buried in an unknown grave. With my own hands I set up a monument to his memory. Well do I remember that day. I had just recovered from an attack of yellow-fever myself, but was anxious to fulfil a vow that I had made of erecting a tablet to him. It was a plain board, painted white, with his name in black letters. I took it on my back one dark evening, and walked two miles to a cemetery, and placed it under a magnolia-tree. The effort made me very ill again for several days, as I was reduced almost to skin and bones from the ravages of the dreaded fever. Adrien had saved my life one night in New Orleans, when I was surrounded by half a dozen ruffians attracted by my uniform. I stood at bay against a fence with my revolver in my hand, resolved to sell my life dearly. "Death to the Yankee hound!" they shouted. Just in the nick of time a man of imposing figure emerged from the darkness. He perceived my imminent peril, and, taking his place beside me, said, "I am a brother-officer, and will stand by you for all I am worth." With well-directed blows he levelled three of my assailants, and the others took to flight at once. There was no need, however, for further defence; the field was ours, and we walked in quietness to my ship. From that hour we became warm friends, and when he died I mourned him as a brother."

During this recital the eyes of the sick man were fixed intently upon me. I saw that they were filled with tears, and his pressure upon my hand was tightened.

"What was the name of this friend?" he asked.

"Adrien Homerand." And the tears filled my own eyes as the sound of that cherished name passed my lips.

"And he died of yellow-fever; are you sure of this?"

"Yes; his death was duly recorded upon the Naval Register. There can be no mistake. He is dead, for he was never heard of afterwards,—buried in a lonely, unknown Southern grave."

The stranger raised himself in his bed, and, reaching over to my face, said in a voice that seemed to ring with a dozen echoes,—

"Adrien Homerand did not die of yellow-fever. It was a false report, issued to cover a damning crime. Adrien joined the rebel army, and became a traitor to his country, his God, and his State."

"It is false!" I shouted. "Were you not a dying man I would make you retract this foul calumny. I would make you swallow every word. What! Adrien, the gifted son of Massachusetts, the pride of his college, and the beau ideal of a naval officer, become a deserter, a traitor? *Never!* You are in error, and some false, base wretch has poisoned your mind. You did not know him."

"No one knew Adrien better than I did," was the reply in a calm, deliberate voice, that carried conviction in its tone. "Adrien was not only a traitor, but his hand was stained with the blood of his fellow-countrymen. It was raised in battle to strike down the flag that he had sworn to defend. Yes, Adrien was a blood-stained traitor."

"Who are you," I asked, rising to my feet, "that thus dares to breathe such a terrible accusation against a loyal officer of the Union navy?"

The prostrate man before me was not visibly disturbed by my angry gesture; only the tears again came to his eyes, and his mind seemed to go back to old, forgotten scenes.

"Who am I?" he replied in a husky tone. "I was once Adrien Homerand, loyal to my God, my country, and my friends. **Now I** am a dying man, an alien, and disowned by all those **who once** loved **me.** Chaplain, my tried and true friend, do you not recognize me now?"

I leaned against the bulkhead of the state-room for support, and grew as faint and pale as the dying man before me. Alarmed **at my condition, he took a** glass of water at my side and said,—

"Drink; this will revive you."

I raised it to my **lips,** drained it **to the** last drop, and **again** sat **down.** It contained a narcotic.

"**I have taken** your medicine," I said; "why did you give it to me?"

"No, no; there is plenty left, and **I will** need **it no more.**" **The bell of the** ship struck seven.

"**Thirty** minutes more of life," was his answer as **the sound of the** bell ceased. "Time is short, and I must be **brief," he continued.** "I feel my life-blood growing colder, **and I** have something important to communicate. Before you utterly condemn your friend Adrien, read these notes." And taking **a** package from **under his** head, he placed it in my hand. "Here is **an order for a box** of family papers left with Mrs. Hardcash, **No.—,** —— Street, in Cambridge, Massachusetts. When **the surgeon told** me this afternoon that I was seriously **ill, I wrote this order. There is also a** receipt **from Mrs.** Hardcash for payment in full to date, and an **agreement to keep** the box referred to till my return. I observed your name among the list of passengers the first day out, **and recognized** you at **once.** I was anxious to unburden myself to you, but dreaded your scorn when you should learn **the** truth. When you have read the full history of my life you will, **I** know, throw the mantle of **charity** over my past crime **and** forgive your friend. **I** met **you once** since we parted **the** last time **at that reception in** New Orleans. The belle of the evening **over whom you raved** and spoke of as being the most beautiful woman you had **ever** seen was Ilian, **as** you are aware. Yes, **but once since** that night did I see you, and how changed were **the** circumstances! You remember coming into the casemate **of** Fort Fisher after Admiral **Porter** and his fleet had captured the place?"

"Yes," I replied.

"Well, I was among the wounded, and recognized you when

you gave a glass of water to a wounded Southern soldier, and then spoke to me, offering assistance. I was afraid that you would recognize me. I have put the incident down in my notes."

"Why were you afraid?" I asked.

"Because I would have suffered a traitor's death if you had denounced me."

"Did you think that I would do so?"

"Your recognition of me before the other Union officers present would have led to an investigation, and the result would have been death to me. Now for other matters. Hunt up Ilian in Europe, and tell her of my untimely death, and that I send her this ring as a token of forgiveness."

Adrien took from his finger a chased ring of peculiar design and placed it in my hand.

"Swear to me," he continued, "that you will never reveal my true name to any of my late brother-officers in the navy. Let the record of my honorable death stand upon the Navy Register. Write out a full history from all the notes I have just given you and the papers you will obtain in Cambridge; keep my name as well as my late honored father's unstained on the annals of our university. Do not give this history to the world till after the death of Ilian. I have a presentiment that she will follow me soon to the other sphere; and there, where we will both be freed from the limitations of this life, we can enjoy the fulness of the great Creator's blessings. Do you swear to keep this last pledge to a dying man?"

"I swear!" came from my lips, in a hollow voice that I did not recognize as my own.

"Let the captain divide my clothes among the sailors, and my small amount of money you can——"

"Hold!" I interrupted him. "Leave your money to the widows and orphans of Liverpool; I have enough."

He smiled as he answered, "Alas, it is only a few dollars. My large fortune left to me by my grandfather and my father also has been squandered, and I was on my way to England to find Ilian, who is there somewhere,—I believe, in London. I was suffering from a bad cold, and it has developed into a fatal case of pneumonia. It was predicted of me before my birth that I would come to my end in a storm at sea, and in the morning you will be called upon to consign my body to a deep-sea grave."

The glass of water that Adrien had given me contained morphia. I felt the effect of the powerful drug. My right hand was firmly clasped in that of my departing friend.

For a moment we were both silent.

Then came the **terrible harbinger of** dissolution, the death-rattle.

CHAPTER III.

THE EPISODE.

I LOOKED at my watch. It was fifteen minutes of eight. Adrien's voice sounded strangely unnatural as he said, in a whisper,—

"Farewell to the world and worldly things! Now for God and his requirements."

"**Are you** prepared to **meet him?**" I asked in a voice as **low as** his **own.**

My heart almost stood **still while waiting for his answer;** for a while none came. "**Ten minutes** more," I said, **more** to myself than to the almost inanimate form before me.

The **dying** man roused himself from the lethargy into which he had fallen, **and** with an effort of will raised himself in his narrow berth. **His** eyes were again **charged** with **the fire of** the **olden time,** as in a low but positive **voice, clear as a bell,** he **electrified me** when he said,—

"**Chaplain, I die at** peace with God and man. **In** my notes **you will find** how, in **answer to** the dying prayers of **my mother and the** sacrifice of my noble father's life, I was **arrested by God's hands in the** midst **of my downward** career. **Now the star of hope is beaming on me, and I look** for the **robe of righteousness."**

Five minutes of eight bells, and the life-watch would be **almost ended.** Adrien had fallen back on his pillow and was so still that I thought **him already gone.** One minute more passed, and he opened **his eyes with a** smile, saying,—

"Come with me **to the Borderland.** Come down into the dark valley; come **across the dark river.** When I shall have met my waiting friends on the farther shore, you can return."

"Impossible!" I cried. "I have **not** the death-mark upon

me, and I will not be allowed to enter the congregation of the dead."

"Hold on upon my hand," said he; "or, if you prefer, I will hold on upon you, and perhaps you can come to the open gates, if not beyond.

"Hark! listen! Heard you ever such beautiful music?"

I listened, but heard nothing, only the roar of the heavy gale and the thunder of the waves as they struck the sides of our laboring ship.

One minute more. I looked at Adrien. A heaven-born smile was on his face, one hand was across his breast, the other held mine in an iron grasp. A chill swept through my whole system; my heart's beating became feeble.

Eight bells! The silvery tone rang through the ship, far above the noise of the machinery and of the warring elements without. I was on my knees praying for the departing one. The lips of the man before me opened and uttered his last words,—

"Chaplain, come!"

As the last stroke of the bell died away the door opened, and the room was filled with other forms. My head fell on the side of the berth. In a moment I was lifted to my feet and Adrien stood by my side.

"Come," said he, "let us leave the ship."

Strange beings were around us, but their faces were veiled and I could not distinguish them. We went into the saloon. A score of my fellow-passengers were there; some were reading; others with steaming glasses in their hands were sipping the contents, in order to sleep, if such a thing were possible in the quick rolling of our storm-tossed craft. We lingered but a moment, then passed out into the dark night, and without a moment's hesitation over the vessel's stern into a dense fog-bank. The other figures were still with us. I looked at the departing steamship and read her name and the port she hailed from,—"Glasgow." Then she disappeared into the fog. A peculiar light all at once seemed to illuminate our surroundings. The veils fell from the faces of the figures around us. Some of them I had known in past years, others I had never met. Adrien now let go my hand and was welcomed right royally by them all. They fixed their gaze upon me and with one voice said,—

"He has not the death-mark; how is this?"

I asked, was it a crime to come into their midst without the death-mark?

"No," they said, "it was not a crime; but how did I pass the portals?"

"What portals?" And I looked for an explanation.

One of the forms, that seemed to be a leader, spoke to the others in a warning voice,—

"Tell not the secrets of the congregation of the dead to one who has come among us without the death-mark and is about to return to the living."

The tone of voice was one of pity and deep commiseration for me, who, having failed to provide myself with the insignia and passport of death, would have to return to the unhappy condition of those still on the earth. Adrien explained to them that he alone was responsible for bringing me along with him, and that I would at once return from whence I came. Turning to me, he continued,—

"One of my friends here will accompany you back to your ship, while I must hasten to the great tribunal to be weighed in the balance of God's even justice. Farewell! and after eighteen months I will meet you at midnight on the 15th of November under the shadow of the old South Church, in Boston. This permission has just now been accorded me. Do you solemnly promise to meet me there?"

"I will be there at the appointed time," said I.

"He turned and followed one who was clothed in a cloud; and whom I recognized as the angel of death. I was now alone with the spirit that was to go back to the ship with me. The others had followed Adrien.

"Cannot I see and converse with some of those that I once loved dearly, even if only for a moment?" I asked.

"Your wife and children?" said the spirit, who seemed to read my thoughts. "I will ask permission."

By some means that I could not understand he transmitted my request. A moment after an affirmative answer came. I now saw a thick cloud approaching, and as it came to my side I plainly saw three spirit-forms,—my wife and our two children. Intense surprise was manifested on their countenances, and again was that question asked,—

"Why have you not the death-mark?"

I explained the reason, and asked how I could obtain it. What cared I for the earthly pilgrimage when before me in radiant happiness stood the form of the being that I had loved better than my own life, and my sweet children also? It needed what was termed a peculiar mark. How or in what manner placed I could not understand. Yes, I was ready for the mark; let it come. My wife, in that gentle voice of the long-ago, which had often been as sweet music in my heart, replied to my question,—

"The death-mark can only lawfully be given by the decree of the Great Jehovah Elohim."

As she uttered these solemn words all the forms before me bowed low, and over the waters came the sound of sweet music, and I thought of the words, "To me every knee shall bow." I was further told that if I should inflict the mark myself I could not enter into the rest of the blessed ones.

"Go back," said my wife, "to the work of life." "Go back," repeated my oldest born. "Go back," echoed my youngest. Then they all said to me, "Our love has not grown cold. We will watch over you by day and by night, and when your final hour on earth shall come we will be there to meet you and extend the welcome of the heavenly world."

The cloud again enveloped them, and I saw them no more. I hastened back with my conductor to the ship. Her stern appeared in view as she rose and fell on the surging sea. As I reached the deck the form at my side vanished, and I passed once more through the saloon. Only five persons were in it. I did not linger, but sought the room of death, and, opening the door, entered. On the bed lay the body of Adrien and by its side was my human tabernacle. I touched it on the shoulder, and awoke to the earthly scenes around me. The lower jaw of the dead had fallen and my hand was fast locked in his. With a strong effort I unloosed the fingers, and looked at my watch, which was still in my left hand. It was nine o'clock. I took out my handkerchief and fastened it around the face of the corpse and closed the eyes. As I finished this tribute the bell of the ship struck two solemn notes. I had been one hour either asleep or absent from the body.

The door opened at the moment of the bell striking and the surgeon entered.

"Our passenger is dead," he remarked. "He lasted longer than I expected, I felt sure from his symptoms that he would pass off before eight o'clock. His vitality must have been greater than I expected to have enabled him to hold out till nine. I was detained with a very important case of life and death, and this accounts for my not coming sooner."

I merely nodded my head. An explanation of the events of the past hour would have been useless, and, indeed, I could not understand it myself. As I left the room the surgeon locked the door, and we went together to the captain's room. He asked at once the question,—

"When did he die?"

"Just died," replied the surgeon, before I could say a word.

It was entered upon the log-book that Martin Gambell (the name on his ticket) had died of pneumonia at nine o'clock.

I gave the captain the dead man's instructions about his clothes and his money, which, from a memorandum found on his body, was just forty dollars in cash and a draft on a Liverpool bank for two hundred dollars more. This in due season went, as directed, to the Liverpool Orphan Asylum.

The captain asked whether I would be ready at five o'clock in the morning to perform the funeral service. He did not wish, he said, that the other passengers should know anything about the death or funeral. It always made them feel unpleasant, especially the ladies.

I retired at once to my state-room. My room-mate had not yet come down, and I was free for a while to ponder over the strange events of the evening. I weighed everything as clearly as I could, and came to the conclusion finally that the morphia which I had taken was the cause of the strange episode. I could not have left the body unless it was by the agency of some undiscovered physical law. I had had several similar experiences before. My brain was still heavy from the effects of the drug. A night's sleep would be necessary in order to clear my faculties.

It had been arranged already that I was to be called at a quarter to five; so, with an earnest prayer for safety and guidance, I retired, and in a few moments was in a dreamless sleep, profound and sweet.

Note.—See Appendix.

CHAPTER IV.

THE DEEP-SEA GRAVE.

"The gale was over, and the sun lay red
On the dripping deck where we placed the dead.
There was solemn reading and whispered prayer,
And the damp wind lifted the sailor's hair;
Then we covered him gently, and many a wave
Since then has rolled o'er his deep-sea grave."

A LIGHT flashed in my face, while a voice said, quietly, "All is ready and the captain is waiting."

My room-mate awoke and anxiously inquired, "What is the matter?"

I replied, a case of serious illness, and soon dressed myself and went on deck. We had passed out of the track of the gale. The sun had already risen from its eastern bed, the wind was well on the starboard beam, a southerly breeze, with every token of a pleasant day.

I found the watch on deck assembled at the gangway. The body of Adrien was already in its coffin of canvas, with two heavy grate-bars lashed on either side at the feet. At my request his face had been left uncovered, and his raven locks tinged with gray the winds were softly lifting. Still in the prime of life, yet his face bore the marks of intense suffering, and I saw with pain those likewise of dissipation.

Turning to the sailors and the captain and officers, I said, "There lies as noble and true a sailor as ever trod a ship's deck, and we will now give him a sailor's burial."

I motioned to a man who stood with a needle in his hand, and the face of the dead was gently covered and the flap of canvas sewed down. The ship's engines were slowed to half speed and I began the burial service.

"I am the resurrection and the life, saith the Lord."

When I came to the part "we commit his body to the deep, to await the judgment day," I motioned with my hand, and the corpse, which was extended on a plank, feet outward, resting on the open gangway, was gently raised by several men. It slowly commenced to slide, loath to leave the ship on which it had embarked, and struck the water with a gentle splash.

The ocean opened to receive it and immediately closed over it as it swiftly shot downward perfectly erect, down many fathoms below the surface, to rest on the ocean-bed till the day when the sea shall give up its dead.

I said nothing to my fellow-passengers in the saloon, and as Adrien had taken a steerage-ticket, he was not missed, even among the latter class.

A funeral at sea always leaves upon me a sad impression for several days. I was more deeply affected now, as I had to mourn a second time over a friend, and such a friend as Adrien Homerand.

During the remainder of the passage I looked over the papers which such a strange concurrence of events had placed in my care. They related to the principal events of Adrien's own life. The papers for which I had the order would supply all the missing links.

They were the key-notes to a strange history.

Although I knew Adrien Homerand when he was attached to his ship in New Orleans, yet I asked but few questions at that time about his private history or family matters. The fact of his engagement to the brilliant Miss Ilian Mordine was surmised by his many friends, and they supposed that the marriage would take place when the war should end. The report of his death was never questioned, as many officers had died of yellow-fever. The revelation, therefore, of his being still alive was a startling fact to me; also his treason to the Union cause.

By the time of my arrival in London I had carefully read all the papers that Adrien had given me. The question which came up was: What was this mystery that hung so fearfully over his life? I wrote a letter to Ilian telling her of her husband's death, and sent it through her banker in Paris. A week later I received a reply through the same source thanking me for all that I had done for Adrien, and adding also that she remembered me very well, as he had often spoken about me. She was too full of grief and distress to write much, but enclosed me a check for two hundred and fifty pounds to defray any expense I had incurred. This I returned at once, stating that there had been none. I was very desirous to see her, but as I could assign no legitimate excuse, I let the matter drop.

CHAPTER V.

THE OLD VICAR.

Among the papers left in my possession were the letters from Ilian to her husband. After reading them I felt certain that there was some close relationship between them. What it was I could not surmise. I had the original letter which was sent to Professor Homerand in 1843 giving the information of the death of the child of Helen Claymuire and also of her marriage. The post-mark written by the postmaster was from a town in the South of England. It occurred to me that if I should go to the spot and search among the old parish records I might obtain some clues. Accordingly, I took the train for the place. The next day after my arrival I visited the rector of the parish church, and told him frankly that I was in search of information in regard to events that had taken place over thirty-four years previous. To my astonishment he informed me that the curate who was then in charge was still living and could be found at Preston. The old records of the church, however, were in his own possession and at my service. I looked over them, and found the following entries with full particulars:

"Baptized Ilian Homer, January 31, 1843, daughter of George Homer, of Boston, born May 3, 1841, in London."

"Married, July 19, 1843, Miss Helen Claymuire, spinster, of South Carolina, United States of America, aged 25, to Thomas Henry Verdere."

"Also, August 23, 1843, Miss Eleanor Claymuire, aged 20, also of America, to John Mordine."

And then there was the entry:

"Buried Mrs. Eleanor Mordine, January 26, 1844. Wife of John Mordine. Died of consumption."

"Buried Thomas Henry Verdere, September, 1846, aged 68."

I read these entries over very carefully and copied them. I also made up my mind to go to Preston and visit the old curate. Perhaps I might get some information. What I had already obtained was very different from that conveyed to Professor Homerand in 1844. The writing on the back of the original letter was in a labored handwriting, evidently by one not used to rapid penmanship or to much correspondence. I surmised that it had been written by a servant, and the records which I had seen confirmed me in this opinion.

It was done to conceal the fact that Ilian was alive.

I set out at once for Preston in the North of England. On the following day I called upon the Rev. Joseph Brown, who had formerly been the curate at the place just mentioned. It was over thirty years since the event happened, and while I was fortunate in finding alive the clergyman who had performed the ceremonies the record of which I had read, there was nevertheless a possibility that he would not be able to remember the incidents. I found him at home, and he gave me a very friendly reception. He told me that he had always desired to visit America, but so far had not been able to do so. He had, however, met many American clergymen, and was very glad to see a representative of the government of this country. He was not so old as I had apprehended; certainly not over sixty-five, even if he was of that age. After half an hour of conversation I arose to take my leave, purposing to call again in a day or so, and thus approach gradually the object of my visit. He pressed me to stay for tea, and his wife, coming in at the same moment, urged me to do so. I consented, and entertained them with American anecdotes during the evening meal. After it was over we returned to his study, with an injunction from his wife to meet her in the drawing-room in an hour. This was the opportunity for which I had been seeking, and after a few minutes I asked him whether in his long pastorate he had ever married any of my country-people.

"Oh, yes, a number of times," was his reply.

"I suppose that they all turned out to be happily matched."

"Well, yes, on the whole; although I remember two sisters that I married to two Englishmen who did not long enjoy the married state."

"How was that?" I asked. "Not properly mated?"

"Oh, yes, they were mated all right; but misfortune came upon them," was his reply.

"You interest me very much. May I have the melancholy pleasure of hearing the details? I am deeply interested in the destiny of my fair countrywomen when they link their fortunes with our English cousins."

"It is over thirty years ago," said he. "It happened when I was curate of a parish in the South of England."

"You must have a very powerful memory," I interrupted, "to remember so far back."

"No, I do not think so," said he. "It does not seem very far back to call up events a generation ago, but the trials of these two sisters were deeply impressed upon my mind at the time. The oldest, Miss Helen Claymuire, was about twenty-five years of age, and her sister, Eleanor, was five years younger. The eldest married a Mr. Verdere, a gentleman of wealth and fully sixty-five years old. This marriage made a great sensation at the time. Miss Claymuire was very wealthy, and consequently could not have been accused of marriage for money.

"A month later I performed the marriage ceremony of her sister Eleanor with a Mr. Mordine. He was a younger son of one of the best country-families and had but a small income, but his wife was well off. She was very frail and delicate, and died five months after her marriage from a severe cold. The English winter climate was too much for her. Her husband, who was tenderly attached to her, never recovered from her loss, and followed her to the grave in less than a year. He died abroad somewhere.

"Mr. Verdere died three years after, and left all of his fortune to his wife. Both these sisters were of unusual beauty. The oldest was a brunette and the youngest a blonde. Their characters were totally different. Helen being very cold and haughty, while Eleanor was the essence of amiability and good nature."

"Of course neither of them left any children?" I remarked.

"No, indeed," said he. "The youngest died too soon after her marriage, and Mr. Verdere was too old. In fact, he was almost a confirmed invalid when he married. He had been twice a widower previously, and never had any children by either of his wives.

"But I forgot to tell you that when the two sisters came to our neighborhood to live they had a child about a year old, whose mother had died in London in giving it birth. She had come over to visit some of her relatives and died in their home. The Misses Claymuire were great friends of the mother, and they were taking care of the child, who was said to be an heiress of great wealth. Her father was a professor in some American college and could not leave his classes, but paid very handsomely for his child's support. Mrs. Verdere took the little one to her own home and her husband offered to adopt it. To this his wife would not consent. She said that the child's father would never agree to this."

"What was the name of this child?" I asked.

"I baptized it myself under the name of Ilian Homer. By the way, I was going to ask you whether you know anything of the Claymuire family. They are from South Carolina, I believe."

"Yes, it was one of the most aristocratic, and they had very large estates, but it is very nearly extinct now. What became of Mrs. Verdere after her husband's death?" I asked him.

"I left the parish shortly after to accept a living tendered by the Bishop of London, and lost all trace of her."

At this point Mrs. Brown came in to announce that a few of her friends were in the drawing-room and would be glad to see the American chaplain. I spent a very enjoyable evening, and after fully expressing my thanks for the hospitality received, I returned to my hotel. The next day I left for Manchester, where I had relatives on my mother's side, who always had a cordial welcome for their American cousin.

One day I went out to hunt up the home where Adrien was born. It had been torn down to make room for improvements. I felt that I had been very fortunate in this my very first endeavor to unravel the mystery which had been placed in my possession. I needed further documentary evidence, and felt sure Mrs. Verdere must have left something of the kind. If I could only see her child I might be enlightened. How would she receive the news that she was Professor Homerand's daughter and half-sister to Adrien? This I felt sure was the case. I must have stronger testimony, however, before I broached this subject to her. She was hard to find. Even her banker did not know, or would not tell, where she was. I must wait.

CHAPTER VI.

THE TIN BOX.

Months had now passed since my arrival in England. My business was finished and my health had improved. Having engaged my passage on a Cunarder, I was making my final preparation.

All this time I had found no trace of the lost wife of Adrien. I had searched many of the large cities, and places where the notes in my possession gave clues as to the likelihood of finding her. I had watched the passing faces by the hour in London, and the same in Liverpool, Manchester, Glasgow, and Edinburgh. I lingered on the boulevards in Paris early and late, on the Champs Elysées, in the Bois de Boulogne and other resorts, but all without avail. I found in the package of papers a small painting on ivory of Ilian. I had never looked upon a lovelier face, and it was indelibly impressed upon me, and I could have picked her out among a thousand. In fact, the face had ever been before me since the night I first met her in New Orleans.

As I read in the notes of all who had fallen under the bane, I might say curse, of her fatal beauty, I thought that if she had died when a child how much misery might have been avoided and how many lives saved and honor unstained of gallant officers both North and South. I have reason to believe that this one single woman, with her brilliant talents, sparkling eyes, and childlike, innocent expression, was the means of more damage to the Union cause than any single regiment of the Southern forces that had assembled under the banner of rebellion. And she still lived in her prime. Strong-willed and finely-developed men when once brought under her dazzling enchantment became mere playthings.

The Saturday before my intended departure I was walking in Hyde Park, when a carriage drove by with a single occupant sitting behind the liveried driver. It was a lady, with a sunshade over her head. Many, very many, of the same sort were passing and repassing, and I was about to go on when she turned her head towards me. My nerves thrilled as with a shock, and the blood flew like lightning through my veins. The counterpart of my locket was before me. I followed the carriage, but it was lost in the numbers that were rapidly passing out at the gate. At Oxford Street I had observed a policeman look at it closely before I came up. I now asked him whether he knew the occupant. Either he did not know or else he got the carriages confused, but he answered at once,—

"It is the Countess of ———."

This did not satisfy me. I felt certain that I was right, and that I had seen Ilian. For the next five days I watched carefully in Hyde Park, but it was of no avail.

My time was now up. I left London on Friday for Liverpool, and embarked next day for New York on a Cunard steamship. There were some three hundred passengers in the saloon, and we were uncomfortably crowded. We had a pleasant voyage. Nothing unusual happened, and after ten days we found ourselves steaming up New York Harbor, and were soon in the tender mercies of the custom-house officers. This ordeal is more agonizing in the prospective than in the realization. I have made many trips into New York, and invariably found the officers courteous and obliging in the extreme. Experience has taught them to distinguish the professional smuggler from the innocent pleasure-seeking European traveller.

But little more remains to be told in this chapter.

I went at once to Boston and took the horse-cars to Cambridge. I knew the street well, for my brother had boarded near the house that I was seeking. I had often taken my meals with him when I found it inconvenient to return to my own distant lodgings. We both read law at Harvard Law School, and consequently I was familiar with the place. I rang the bell at No. ——, ——— Street, and was fortunate in seeing Mrs. Hardcash come to the door herself. Like many of the prudent New England housewives, they often preferred to attend to the door-bell themselves, and save the loss of time to their gossiping help.

I presented her the order for the box of papers, and stated that Mr. Martin Gambell was dead, and I was winding up his affairs. Mrs. Hardcash read the paper carefully, and while she did so I had time to study her character.

She was a widow of uncertain age, and how long since the late worthy Mr. Hardcash had shaken off this mortal coil was not known. She was dressed in black alpaca, carefully protected by a huge apron, and a large widow's cap on her small head. Her massive body and keen little eyes gave her the expression of cunning. She was one of those women who look upon all men as manœuvring in some way to impose on womankind in general, and themselves in particular. By way of a feeler I asked whether there were any bills unpaid; if so, I was ready to settle them.

Before his death Adrien had informed me that he had incurred no liabilities, and I had in my pocket a receipt in full for all claims to the date specified.

"Let me see," answered Mrs. Hardcash, musing and calculating upon how much I was disposed to swallow of fictitious accounts. "I suppose Mr. Gambell left a mint of money?"

"Enough," I replied, "to pay all just claims."

"Just so, just so," was her answer.

I watched her cunning little eyes sparkle at what she considered a small bonanza and a gullible executor willing to pay all claims against a dead man's estate. Some persons think it no crime to cheat the dead, but would not defraud the living for fear of consequences.

"There was a balance due of thirty-five dollars when Mr. Gambell left," said she. "I lent him this money to go to Europe with, and I also paid a tailor's bill of twenty-five dollars and a boot-maker's bill of fifteen dollars. Then I paid a loan to him from one of my boarders of twenty dollars: let me see, that makes—how much?"

"Ninety-five dollars," I answered.

"Then there is the interest," she continued.

"Would one hundred dollars be sufficient?" I meekly asked.

"Well, you had better make it one hundred and twenty-five," said she. "There may be other bills come in, and I like to keep up the credit of my boarders."

This was said with a motherly air.

I was amused at the idea of a Massachusetts boarding-house-keeper paying the debts of her boarders, especially at

Cambridge, with the many Harvard students noted for spending money, their own and other people's. All university towns have about the same record. I took out my pocket-book, and Mrs. Hardcash immediately asked me into the parlor. She said that she would go for the box, and if I would fill out a receipt for the money she would sign it.

I fumbled for a moment among the papers in my pocket-book, and asked with a careless tone,—

"Did you notice any blood on one of the corners of the box Mr. Gambell left you?"

"Blood!" screamed out Mrs. Hardcash,—"blood did you say?" And she dropped into a seat.

"Yes, blood; I may want your testimony on the trial."

"Oh, dear me! has there been a murder, and have I had a box in my possession with blood on it? This will ruin the character of my house. Some of the Harvard College boys are boarding with me, and if they knew that a murder had been committed and there were blood-stains in the house, why, the dear boys would not be able to sleep, and my law-students would like no better fun than hunting up the evidence. Oh, dear! oh, dear! what will I do?"

"I did not say there was a murder," I replied, as Mrs. Hardcash was getting hysterical; "I merely asked whether you saw any blood on the box. Go and get it."

She jumped from her chair, hastened up-stairs, and soon returned with a large japanned cash-box with two locks. I had the key in my possession and opened it at once. It was filled with papers, letters, and several diaries. After locking it again, I looked suspiciously at one of the corners and then smelt it.

"Is that the blood?" exclaimed Mrs. Hardcash. "Oh, do take that box away! And here is a newspaper,—wrap it up; do not let any one see you take a box with blood on out of my house. The detectives in Boston would be hounding me all over Cambridge, and with the cross-questions of the reporters I would go mad. Oh, take it away at once!"

After carefully wrapping up the box I took out a roll of bills, and asked,—

"How much did you say Mr. Gambell owed you?"

"Nothing, nothing; he paid every dollar before he left. It was another boarder that owed the amount I stated. I get mixed in my accounts very often."

Once more I smelt the corner of the box. This ended our interview. It was the climax. Mrs. Hardcash opened the door and begged me to take away that awful box, and to be sure not to let any one know that it came from her house, or her business would be ruined.

I bowed, thanked her, and went out. As I turned the corner she was still watching me, so I again took a sniff of the box in my hand. I heard the door slammed by the now thoroughly frightened Mrs. Hardcash.

I felt no compunctions of conscience at thus acting to this woman. She had deliberately tried to swindle a dead man's estate, or rather myself, for I had not a single dollar of Adrien's. Had she asked ten, or even twenty, dollars, I would have paid it as a gratuity, but did not propose to be mulcted in a sum that was not legally due. Would that every man or woman on the eve of wrong-doing could be so easily deterred from crime!

On my arrival in Philadelphia I set myself to search the papers placed in my care. The work was very laborious. I had to arrange the whole matter in detail, and in accordance with my oath to Adrien I must keep this matter a secret from my friends. The number of letters that I had to read and assort kept me hard at work for many months. Often did the midnight hour find me at the work.

I was in correspondence with Dr. Rechard, and had called personally upon Mr. Rendeem and his family. My position, and as a friend of Adrien, made me a welcome visitor. No one knew where Ilian was. I did not care to trust to the post the information which I had obtained in England, and I hoped to meet her. I was convinced in my own mind that she was the daughter of Professor Homerand, but there was no documentary evidence to sustain this,—nothing but the information I had obtained from the Rev. Mr. Brown, the vicar of Preston. I was therefore compelled to wait till I could see Adrien's widow.

Perhaps then the mystery would be cleared.

BOOK VI.

CHAPTER I.

THE MIDNIGHT TOKEN.

I WAS perplexed over a question which may seem trivial to my readers. To me it was of importance.

Did I make a genuine promise to Adrien in his dying hour to meet him on the 15th of November under the shadow of the old South Church in Boston? Or was it merely an imaginary promise while I was under the influence of the large dose of morphia which I had taken? If so, then there was no validity in the act, and I need trouble myself no longer about it. But if, on the other hand, I had bound myself by a solemn promise, how could I keep the compact when I knew he could not be there himself?

I resolved to submit the question to a doctor of divinity in whom I had the utmost confidence. When I was seated in his study I put the question bluntly.

"Doctor," I asked, "are promises made to a dying man valid under all circumstances, and can they be evaded?"

"That is a strange question to ask. Why, of course, a promise made on an occasion like that must be kept as part of a religious duty."

"Yet, doctor, as you are well aware, promises are made daily to persons on their death-beds and broken without scruple of conscience."

"I am painfully aware of that fact in my pastorate. I know of several cases where wives passing away and afraid of a step-mother's carelessness, have exacted a solemn promise from their husbands not to get married till their children had grown up and were settled in life; yet within two years after they married again, on the plea that the promise given to their former wife was wrung from them in the excitement of the death-scene,—obtained, they claimed, by undue influence over their feelings, and therefore null and void. Now I hold that once a man or woman agrees to do certain things after the death of one of their kindred, they are bound to carry out the conditions, no matter how much it may inconvenience them. You remember that passage in Ecclesiastes, chapter v., 'When thou vowest a vow unto God, defer not to pay it; for he hath no pleasure in fools: pay that which thou hast vowed.'"

"I agree with you on that point," said I, "that when a vow is made it should be kept; but a promise to a dying man and a vow unto God are two different things."

"In what way? What is your definition of a solemn promise?"

"Usually there is the intention of calling upon God to witness the compact."

"Exactly, and with such a witness where can justification be found for breaking that which you have vowed? A solemn promise to a fellow-creature, with God as a witness, is virtually a vow.

"But supposing that the promise made is a foolish one," said I, "and would make you ridiculous in trying to keep it?"

"I still hold that it is your duty to do that which you promised. But let me have some light on the subject. Is your leading question suppositious, or from your own experience?"

"The latter is the case," I answered.

"Then you made a compact with some one who was passing out of the world to do certain things after his departure?"

"I think I did. I was under a great mental strain and hardly master of my actions, but the impression left upon me was that I agreed to go to a certain designated place on a night specified and there he would meet me. Now this is an impossibility on his part, because he is dead and his body is buried two thousand fathoms deep at sea."

"Admit that this is so, what prevents you from keeping your part of the agreement?"

"Nothing but the absurdity of doing it."

"How do you know that he cannot be there in spirit to fulfil his part of the bargain?"

"Because I have no faith in spirit manifestations."

"Your want of faith in this matter does not prevent his coming. At all events, as a man of honor you are bound to do what you solemnly agreed to perform. You should have weighed the absurdity of the question before you consented."

Other visitors calling upon the worthy doctor at this point of our conversation, I withdrew and returned home. The whole subject now turned upon the question, Did I really make this promise, or was it incidental to the delirium of the morphia I had taken? I was inclined to the latter view, and finally accepted it as the true solution, and that therefore I was not bound to go to Boston to keep the appointment.

The 14th of November came, the weather was stormy, and this added to my resolution to stay at home. My housekeeper asked me whether I had given up the notion of going to Boston next day. I replied that I had almost resolved that I would not go, but that I wished to be called at six o'clock in the morning, and then my going or staying would depend upon contingencies. At ten I retired to my chamber. I had been worrying all day over the vexed problem, and when I got into bed I could not sleep for some time.

I had taken unusual precaution with the connections of my burglar-alarm. My house had been fitted throughout with appliances for detecting the attempts of persons to enter my house for unlawful purposes. When I closed my chamber-door I took very particular pains to see everything in working order, and it was with a smile of grim satisfaction that I arranged my wires so that the slightest attempt to open the door or any of the windows would result in creating an alarm that would awaken my neighbors.

At eleven I fell asleep. I woke up again, as I thought, three hours after, but on looking at the clock I found that it wanted five minutes of midnight. As a greater precaution I had left the gas turned on with a low flame. I now got up and looked out of the window, and noticed that the rain was still falling heavily. After a few minutes I returned to my bed. It was, perhaps, some twenty minutes after; I was not asleep, for my mind was troubled about the question of going to Boston the next morning. I was lying upon my left side, when I suddenly became aware of a shadow falling across the light. Turning over, I saw the form of a man standing by the bedside. I sprang upon the floor at once, and going to a drawer, took out a revolver that I always kept there loaded.

I levelled it at the place where the stranger had been standing, but he was gone. I looked under the bed, but could see nothing. I then went to the door; it was securely bolted, so were the windows. What could it mean? I was not frightened in any way, neither did I have any notion of a spirit-appearance. For an hour I sat in a chair, trying to solve the problem. Perhaps, I thought, the form would come again, but it did not. It seemed to me very much like bull-dozing me into complying with a promise which I was not certain that I had made. Finally I comforted myself with the reflection that it was only the play of my imagination. So I went back to bed, and lay for a while on my back watching both sides of the room. At length I fell asleep, and woke up as the clock was striking six. I arose at once and found it a dismal morning, still raining; and the very idea of going on a long journey gave me the blues. My housekeeper knocked at my door and asked me whether I had decided to go to Boston. I answered, rather sarcastically, "Not if I know myself; it is too wet."

"Is the business very important?" she asked.

"Well, I do not know," said I. "The fact is, I do not know its nature."

"Does the gentleman expect you this evening?"

"Of that I am not quite certain."

"Could you not telegraph to him? I will take the message to the office. It is not far."

"I would do so if I knew where to find him."

"Do you not know the hotel where he is staying?"

"I do not."

"Perhaps he will come to see you if you find it inconvenient to go to Boston."

I was about to answer that I had a faint idea that he had come during the night and I did not want any more such visits. I checked myself, however. The good-natured old soul would have instantly left my house if I had intimated that it was haunted.

"If you have my coffee ready I will take it," I said to her, changing the subject.

In a few minutes I was seated at the breakfast-table trying to read the morning paper, which had just been left, but I could not fix my mind upon it. It was now seven o'clock, and the train for Boston left at half-past eight. It would take me a full half-hour to reach the station, and I ought to have a margin of ten minutes to get my ticket. I finished my breakfast, and then found myself in a sharp mental conflict with some influence which tried to persuade me to go to Boston. I refused to yield. The clock marked half-past seven. This only gave me twenty minutes to dress and pack up a satchel. I began to get cross because of the persistency of this occult agency that was worrying me so relentlessly. Three minutes more passed, and I was in a condition I cannot describe. I again looked at the clock. It was twenty-five minutes of eight.

"I cannot get ready in time," I said, half aloud.

"Yes, you can," was the response, yet I heard no voice.

"Stop this nonsense, and get ready and go to Boston," was an imperative command that was conveyed to my intellect. It seemed to be spoken, yet not a sound was heard. What followed I hardly know. By ten minutes of eight, however, I stood in my hall-way with a small satchel in my hand. I told my housekeeper I had, on second reflection, decided to go to Boston, and would return on the following evening. I found a horse-car passing the next corner, and was soon at the station.

"Ticket for Boston?" I asked at the office.

"Eight dollars and seventy-five cents," was the reply.

I paid the amount, and said, "So much gone to the dogs." But I was out of the conflict that I had been in since I arose from my bed.

The trip to my destination was without incident.

CHAPTER II.

THE SHADOW OF THE OLD SOUTH CHURCH.

It was half-past six when I arrived in Boston. I went at once to the Tremont House. It was cold, dismal, and wet outside; but within the massive granite hotel all was cheerful. I enjoyed a bountiful supper and wondered how I could occupy the time till midnight. One hour I spent in walking up and down my bedroom, abusing myself for my asinine conduct in coming to Boston at all on such a fool's errand. I weighed the profit and loss of the whole affair. On the latter side there would be fully twenty dollars out of my pocket and perhaps a severe cold, and I would hereafter have serious doubts of the equilibrium of my mental powers. The profit I could not see. Well, having no one else to abuse, and no other shoulder to lay the blame on, I was compelled perforce to vent my anger on myself. After a while this became monotonous. I went down to the drawing-room, and tried to read, but could not. A dozen times I went out to the main entrance and each time I came back with an increased amount of "indigo," as a friend of mine, a college president, once expressed the term for the blues. The clocks all seemed to me to be going very slowly.

Can I ever forget that evening? From nine to ten was like a full day in period. Eleven I thought never would strike. At half-past I was ready with my overcoat on and I set out. I did not care to reach the church before ten minutes of midnight. I had not the slightest expectation of meeting the spirit of Adrien in any form. The very idea of it was absurd. Spirit-manifestations never had any charm for me; for while I had the fullest faith in the Bible and all its teachings, yet there was no affinity between myself and the so-called spirit-mediums, because they had no biblical authority for their doctrines.

I was in Boston, and on my way to keep an appointment with a dead man, because I believed that I had made a solemn promise to be at the old South Church at midnight of the 15th of November. Although it was an inconvenience, it did not harm me in any way to keep this promise. I walked down to Washington Street and looked towards the church. The recollection then came vividly to my mind of the terrible curse pronounced at this very spot, not far from forty years before. I thought also of the wedding that took place inside of its hallowed walls and of the result that followed. How many of the witnesses of that marriage were still alive? Very few, indeed. I knew of but one, and that one was Professor Homerand's brother.

I looked at my watch. It wanted ten minutes of the appointed hour. I was apparently alone on the street. The storm had driven every one in-doors. I met but few watchmen; even they were under shelter. The rain had begun to moderate a little as I left my hotel. Now it had ceased, but the night was cold. A suggestion came to me. Suppose that I should see the shade of Adrien, what would I do? Well, I would doubt the evidence of my senses; conclude it was a hallucination, an imagination, or some other deception. Would I be afraid? No, I thought not. Why should I be frightened? If it were possible for the spirit of my friend to come, he would not, even if he could, harm me. "But then," I argued to myself, "he cannot come back, so there is no use speculating what I would do in the event of seeing a spirit." A medium once offered to show me the spirit of my grandfather, all for the paltry sum of five dollars cash in advance. I replied that I claimed two such ancient relatives; which one did he propose to let me gaze upon?

"Whichever you ask for," said he; "your maternal or paternal."

"But who will identify the grandfather that you produce? I never saw either of them."

"I will," was his assuring answer.

"Pardon me," I hesitatingly remarked; "but I am rather sceptical. I will want the identification of some one of his friends who know him."

"Well, I will call up any one you name," he promised.

"That is very kind," said I; "but I don't know who they are, and they would need vouchers also."

"Oh, you demand too much, my friend. I do not suppose five hundred spirits would satisfy you."

"Yes, they would, and far less a number than that," I answered. "If you can let me hold conversation *in propria persona* with some dead friend, whose name I will write on a piece of paper and fold it up, and then, if I can see the form and talk of things past and gone and known only to myself, I will cheerfully double your fee and go away feeling that I had gone through a pleasaut dream, but I would not be a convert to spiritualism." So I left him.

From all this my readers will see that I approached the old South Church with no expectation of seeing any one, but perhaps a policeman, who would probably have an eye on my movements,—that and nothing more? Candidly, I did not desire to see any spirit-form, because I would be placed at a great disadvantage. A spirit would vastly be my superior in the knowledge of a thousand subjects that I could never hope to understand, while remaining a tenant of my frail tabernacle of clay. This conscious superiority would perhaps tend to make it "put on airs," and as I detest the human species who do such things, I knew I should at once dislike a spirit on the same account. Perhaps he might condescendingly pity my ignorant, trammelled, and limited sphere of thinking and activity, and this would make matters worse. On the whole, therefore, I would prefer to be excused from an interview of this description. "Declined with thanks." I would rather meet a score of tangible flesh-and-blood species than one of the opposite condition.

I looked again at the face of the clock on the church-steeple. It wanted five minutes of the midnight hour, when, according to the ancient superstition, the ghosts of the departed came back to their old haunts. "I will allow a margin of five minutes," I said to myself, feeling full of facetious humor. "Perhaps the conveyance by which he comes may be detained, although I have heard it stated that spirits are very punctual." Five minutes is a short allowance, I admit, but then I was cold, and, using a nautical parlance, I felt that " to come snugly to anchor in blanket bay" would be not only a more judicious proceeding, but certainly more to my taste and feeling. Within half an hour I hoped to be in my bed, prepared for a sweet sleep and a sense of being the happiest man in Boston, because I should have performed a promise and would have exploded the fallacy of spirit-manifestations and all such unrealistic theories.

I again looked at the clock. The large hand made a spasmodic jump from one minute to the other. It still wanted three minutes. The clouds were gathering black overhead. I wanted to go home. I did not feel safe. Some night-prowlers might come and demand the loan of my watch and my pocket-book; they might come with arguments that would overwhelm any objections. Some zealous watchman might arrest me for loitering around the church-door, perhaps accuse me of being a tramp trying to obtain a free night's lodging in the sacred edifice.

v

Once more I looked up at the great dial. Both hands were on the mark of twelve. Why did not the bell sound? I waited with bated breath. Slowly a vibrating tone rang out on the midnight air. "One, two, three," and so on to the complete twelve. I looked carefully around and could see nothing living or dead. I looked upward to the steeple; perhaps he would come that way, but I saw only

> "The clouds parting anon to discover a star,
> Then raging again like giants at war."

I was not in the least disappointed, for I had never for a single instant expected any other result. I turned towards the church-door and said, in a mocking tone,—

"Good-night, Mr. Spirit; I hope you will have——"

I never finished the sentence, for at my side I saw the form of Adrien. It was not the face of the man whom I had seen die in the state-room of the Cunard ship in the heavy gale; nor was it the pale form of the clay showing terrible marks of dissipation that had gone into his deep-sea grave. No, it was the expressive countenance that I had seen so often in New Orleans, and which welcomed me many times at the gangway of his ship. There was a heaven-born smile on his face now that had no counterpart to any that earthly joys could bring up.

For the first time in my life I felt the terrors of a great fright. I had previously stood day after day in battle with the enemy's shot and shell playing havoc around me, but I felt no fear, only excitement. Several times I had faced death on a sick-bed and was told that my hours were limited, yet I quailed not. Once I was covered with two rifles, held with their muzzles touching my face, but I experienced no fear. Now my hair stood on end, and each fibre seemed to be a conductor, and a thousand sharp, stinging sensations went through my brain and my body. My heart almost stopped and I felt faint. The spirit extended his hand to me. Not for all the millions of the Vanderbilts and Astors combined would I touch it, but it reached out and took mine. At once the sensation of fear was gone, a calm came over my senses, and my brain was clear as a bell. Now was the opportunity presented to obtain valuable information on many points about this life and the next. He could clear up the mystery of his family and of Ilian's birth. But how could he communicate all this? Not by the sound of the human voice. Perhaps by affinity of mind with mind, soul with soul. For a moment he looked at me, and then I was aware of the uttering of a sentence. By what process I could not define. It was this:

"Ilian is coming to meet you here to-night; there is her carriage."

I looked in the direction pointed and beheld a coupé that stopped two blocks off; and, by the light of the lamp near it, I saw a woman closely veiled get out and come towards me. I turned to ask the form at my side who it was, but it was gone and I was alone.

CHAPTER III.

ILIAN IN A NEW RÔLE.

THE first thing I did was to satisfy myself that I was wide awake and not dreaming. If I had any lingering doubts on the latter point, I was destined to be convinced that the woman coming towards me was not a vague, shadowy form of dreamland, but a living specimen of the gentle sex. I was standing close by the railing of the church, and she did not see me till within five feet, when I surprised her by saying,—

"Good evening, Miss Mordine. I suppose you prefer to be called by that name."

"Who are you; and how do you know my name?" she demanded.

"I am one," said I, "who knows your history back to the hour of your birth."

"Perhaps you will favor me by telling me who you are, and what you are doing at this place at this hour?"

"This is the 15th of November, and the anniversary of two events,—one, that of the curse pronounced by your mother against Professor Homerand, your father, to take effect when he failed to fulfil his promise of marrying her and should marry her rival, Martha Rathmine, instead. The other event is that of the birthday of your husband and half-brother, Adrien Homerand, whom I attended in his dying hour and consigned to his fathomless grave far out at sea."

At this point the woman before me threw up her veil and revealed the face of the loveliest being that I had ever seen in mortal shape. There was no mistaking her; it was indeed Ilian. I had hunted her for months all over Europe, and now unexpectedly she was before me.

"Why do you call Professor Homerand my father, and Adrien my half-brother?" she cried. "It is utterly false."

"No, it is not," I replied. "I saw the records in the parish church in a town in the South of England."

"I repeat, it is false, and a base libel," she vehemently declared. "I demand instant retraction, or I will kill you where you stand."

She grasped my overcoat, which was buttoned up to the throat, and in her excitement tore it from the first to the second button.

"I am telling you the truth," I replied. "It is well that you should know it." I saw that her eyes were blazing with a dangerous excitement, and I tried to calm her. "Do not get excited. If you talk so loud the police will come and arrest us both, and we will cut a ridiculous figure in the police-court to-morrow."

"I don't care for the police, or any one else," said she. "You shall take back that slander on my mother's fair name or I will plunge this into your heart."

As she said this she put her hand to her hair and drew what I thought was a dagger hair-pin, but its slender point was burnished steel, and she held it over my breast. This was getting to be a very serious matter. A few minutes before I had felt that I would rather see twenty living persons than one spirit, but now I changed my mind. Spirits did not raise fine poniards over one's head and tear his coat. What should I do? If it had been a man that I was dealing with I would have struck out straight from the shoulder, but I would not touch a woman, even though she did threaten my life. No, I must adopt other tactics. So I said, calmly,—

"What would be the use of telling you anything but the strict truth? Adrien on his death-bed gave me all his private papers, and an order for his father's records and his dealings with Miss Helen Claymuire, your sainted mother, who afterwards married in England."

"My mother married Mr. Mordine and died in giving me birth," she sturdily replied to me.

"No, that was your mother's only sister, Eleanor, and she died five months after her marriage. Your mother married Mr. Verdere when you were twenty-six months old. Her husband was sixty-five years of age, and died three years after his marriage. Your mother brought you up as her niece and gave you the name of her sister's husband."

"I do not believe one word of this," Ilian answered; "and I demand your authority for this statement which you have made."

"I have told you already that I read the record in the parish church register in the South of England, where your mother and her sister went to live after your birth."

"Where was this place to which you refer?" she demanded. I told her, and advised her to go and see for herself.

"It may have been a false account," said she.

"Not likely," said I; "and, besides, I saw at Preston the Rev. Mr. Brown, who performed the marriage ceremony for your mother and your aunt. He also officiated at the funeral of the latter and of Mr. Verdere, and baptized you under the name of Ilian Homer. They told him that your mother had died in giving birth to you, and that your father was a great American professor, and had left you in their care."

"I know that my mother died in giving me birth," persisted Ilian.

"She did not. Your mother was not Mrs. Mordine, and you know that Mrs. Verdere brought you up as her niece. Who then was your father, if it was not Professor Homerand, and who your mother, except Helen Claymuire? The problem is not difficult to solve."

For a moment Ilian seemed to be in a quandary; she still held my coat with one hand and that keen little dagger in the other. Then she spoke fiercely,—

"You make me out a child of shame, and I will avenge the insult on the dead. You must swear never to repeat this libel."

I had already become tired of the controversy and made up my mind to adopt naval tactics; when, for obvious reasons, you do not wish to give battle to the enemy, then you must make sail and get out of the way. Most men do not object when a handsome little woman holds them by their coat, nor would they mind a scratch from a hair-pin; nevertheless, although this hair-pin held over my head was a small affair, yet if it entered my heart it would be a serious matter. I formed my plan of action at once and put it into operation. I raised my umbrella, inserting the point of it in the iron railing of the church, and, holding it in a horizontal position, said,—

"Now, Miss Mordine, I wish to have a barrier between us, because you are too much excited."

I held the handle towards her, and she let go my coat and took the umbrella. This was my chance. At once I hurried away up Washington Street at a speed of at least ten miles an hour. I turned the first corner to the left, and as I did so I perceived that I had gained a hundred feet, for she had pulled the umbrella out of the railing and started after me. I soon observed that I was rapidly leaving her far behind. Her close-fitting garments prevented free locomotion. I turned half a dozen corners and came to a building with a large open porch and a pillar on each side. There I took refuge and got behind the column. In a minute after I saw a flying cloud of feminine apparel go by like a whirlwind.

I put my head out to survey the scene. She had stopped at the corner and was looking in all directions. She now retraced her steps and came to the building where I was. I shifted over to the opposite pillar; was just in time. Ilian came up and looked into the porch and then thrust the captured umbrella behind the column. At this moment she was interrupted by a gruff voice asking her what she was doing. A burly private watchman was at her side. She told him that a man had insulted her just as she had stepped out of her carriage, that she had chased him to this point, and if he could be found she would give a reward of one hundred dollars.

"All right, mam," was his answer; "I will help you."

I thought to myself that I would like it if that offer should be held up to competition. I would give one hundred and fifty dollars if he did not find me.

"I saw a man walking very fast in a side street just a moment ago," the watchman remarked.

"Had he an umbrella in his hand?"

"No, he had not."

"Tall and rather stout, and dark clothes on?" she asked.

"Yes, that was about his style."

"Then let us follow him."

Away they went, and when the coast was clear, I went also. The rain began to come down, but I walked fast and suddenly ran up against a policeman, who said,—

"You are in a mighty big hurry, perhaps you will tell me what you are doing out so late on a night like this?"

"I have been to a reception," I answered. "Some one took my umbrella and I am now hastening to my hotel, the Tremont House. Can you tell me the shortest way?"

The name of this well-known Boston caravansary was a sufficient guarantee to him for my respectability. The way was pointed out to me, and I gave him half a dollar to drink my health. In a few minutes I had reached my destination. As I entered the porch I took off my overcoat, for if the night-clerk should see it covered with mud and torn, he might suspect that I had been in conflict with the police.

"Rather late," he remarked, as he handed me my key.

"Yes," I replied; "and I am glad to get back. Call me at six in the morning."

When I got to my room I locked the door carefully, and looked under the bed, a thing that I rarely do. I was resolved to make sure that there were no more spirits around. I could not sleep for some time; I was restless; and when I did my dreams were very unpleasant. It was war-time again, and I was out on picket-duty alone and far away from my boat's crew. I heard the deep baying of two bloodhounds, and ran down an avenue lined with trees. At the end was a large gate. If I could reach it I was safe. I heard the labored panting of my fleet-footed pursuers. I reached the gate and at one bound I was on the top. The baffled brutes threw their whole weight upon it, but it held firm. The next moment I was on the ground, and soon reached my boat.

Again I dreamed of the war. Admiral Porter gave me orders to obtain certain information about the Confederate ironclads in the James River below Richmond. I was to go in uniform, so that in case I was captured I would not be hung up for a spy. I had neglected these precautions and went in a black coat and Derby hat. I obtained the coveted facts, all that was wanted, and was hastening back, but lost my way. Suddenly I heard the tramp of armed men, and the cry,—

"There is a Yankee spy, kill him!"

I ran as fast as I was able, but found my way barred by a breastwork of pointed stakes. I was at bay. I could not discover the inlet into our lines. A Confederate officer with a dozen of his soldiers confronted me and demanded my instant surrender. I refused, and, raising my revolver, shot the officer. A sergeant now stepped up and raised a rifle, but before he could fire, I shot him also. The next moment a circle of bayonets was around my neck and the stern command given to surrender. Then came a loud knocking, and I heard a voice, saying,—

"Six o'clock, sir."

I sprang from my bed and placed myself in an attitude of defence. The Confederate soldiers were gone. I looked at my feet for the men I had shot, but there was nothing; it was but a dream. Slowly the recollection of the past evening came back.

Perhaps, after all, I had dreamed it. If one experience was a dream, why not the other? I looked at my clothes, they were bespattered all over with mud and my overcoat was badly torn. Then, again, what was I doing away from home? No, I was certain that the midnight affair was no play on my imagination. How could I account for it? What prompted Ilian to come? What a strong grasp that girl had in her dainty wrists, and how rapidly she could make her way over the ground!

I brushed the mud off my clothes, pinned up my overcoat where it was torn, and, after a hearty breakfast, I left the Tremont House and took the early train for New York and Philadelphia, arriving safely at half-past eight the same evening.

I was glad to get home once more.

CHAPTER IV.

A DRAWING-ROOM IN FIFTH AVENUE.

Two months had passed. I had heard nothing about Ilian, and, in fact, I did not seek for any news of her. I received a letter from Dr. Rechard in answer to one of mine giving me certain information about the history of the Homerand family. One morning as I came down to my breakfast I found several letters. One was in a strange handwriting, evidently from a woman, and postmarked "New York City." I wondered **from whom** it could come; examined the envelope carefully, and finally came **to the wise conclusion that** the best way to find out was to open it. I did so, and, to my amazement, saw that it was signed " Ilian."

FIFTH AVENUE, NEW YORK, January 18.

MY **DEAR** CHAPLAIN,—I owe you an apology for my conduct **when** I met you last November under the shadow of the **old South** Church. The information which you gave **was** to me of such a startling nature, revolutionizing all my past history that, for the time being, I was not only excited but unreasonable in my anger. I determined to go over to England and find out for myself the true state of affairs. I left New York for Liverpool by the Cunard **line on the** 20th of November. Arriving at Liverpool on the 30th. **That same** evening I was **in** Preston and saw the Rev. Mr. **Brown.** I told him candidly who I was, and obtained **full** particulars **of** all that he knew. **The next** day I went **to** the town which you had designated **in the** South of England and read for myself the record **in the books** of the parish church. It is needless for me to say **that I** was convinced that Mrs. Mordine was not my mother, and **I have** only the inference that Mrs. Verdere was the author of my being. There is **no** record **of** this fact, only a surmise, based, perhaps, upon circumstantial evidence.

You made the assertion that Professor Homerand was my father. What legitimate proof have you to back **up** this statement? I mean evidence that would **stand the** severe scrutiny of a court of law. Among the papers of the late Professor Homerand in your possession, have you any that would prove improper relations between him and my late so-called aunt, Mrs. Verdere, formerly Helen Claymuire? If you have, will you bring them with you and come and see me here at the house of my cousin, Mrs. Rendeem? I am anxious that this mystery should be cleared up. I will cheerfully pay all expenses incurred. Please reply by return mail, and tell me what day will be convenient for you to come to this city.

I feel assured that for the sake of the love you bore to Adrien you will do this for me. You did not give me your name the night that I met you, but when you told me that you attended my husband at the hour of his death, I knew at once who you were. I returned from England yesterday and learned your place of residence from Edith Rendeem. I close with expressions of regret and sorrow if I caused you any annoyance and trouble that stormy night; and, by the way, I am very curious to know how you came to be there on that particular occasion.

I remain the wife of your old friend,

ILIAN.

I replied to this letter at once, and made the appointment for three o'clock two days later. I took with me a number of letters written by Helen Claymuire to the professor,—among them the one which is found in the opening chapter of this narrative; also his confession of certain facts to Adrien in Paris. I was at the Rendeem mansion in Fifth Avenue promptly at the time appointed, and found Ilian waiting for me in the drawing-room. Her cousin, she told me, had gone out, so that we could have a strictly private conversation. Her manner was cordial in the extreme, and we had a hearty laugh over the stratagem which I adopted to get away from her when we were under the shadow of the old South Church. She told me the full particulars of her last trip to England, but she had no new information. She asked me for the letters and papers that would throw light upon her parentage. I handed them to her and remarked that it would be best to defer reading them till alone in the privacy of her apartment.

As I looked at her and tried to study her features, I was charmed by her beauty; her forehead was high, her blue eyes in repose looked as loving and gentle as a little child's, and she was without exception the most talented woman to whom I had ever spoken. Her executive abilities had been fully tested during the late war. She looked in appearance about twenty-five, although I knew she must be nearer forty. Her voice had a soft ring in it that left an echo behind not easily forgotten. Was it possible that this woman was once the great Confederate spy,—the leader and the brain, if I may so express it, of that grand system of secret service by which all of the Federal movements were promptly made known in Richmond and provided against? She was now calm and unruffled as a lake in the summer season, but I knew that when aroused she could become the impersonation of the mythological Pallas-Athena in her periods of wrath.

We spoke of Adrien and his unhappy end, then of the curse, and how it was fulfilled.

"Oh, to think," she replied, "that Mrs. Verdere could be so vindictive; and perhaps she was my mother."

"There is not a doubt of it in my mind," I replied. "After you have read those letters which you have in your hand, I think that you will also be convinced."

"I have no objection to accepting that theory," said she. "She was so loving, gentle, and kind, and she left me sole heiress of all of her fortune; yet I cannot and will not acquiesce in the inference that Professor Homerand was my father."

At this point she rose from her chair and walked the floor of the drawing-room in her growing excitement. I saw that a storm was gathering, and looked around for a line of retreat. It burst upon me, however, before I was well aware of it. Coming up to me, there glowed a dangerous fire in her beautiful eyes. Speaking in a low, determined tone, she said,—

"Chaplain, I would rather die than feel that I was the daughter of Professor Homerand. Not but that if my mother had been legally married to him I would have been proud of his grand record, but I cannot feel that I am the offspring of illicit passion. Never will I endure even the thought, much less the mention, of the fact; and I will take the life of any one who dares to insinuate it."

I had noticed in the large coils of her golden hair what I thought was a jewelled hair-pin of large size with a cross handle richly studded with sparkling stones. She put her hand up to her head and took this out of her hair, and drew from a slender sheath a highly-polished, tiny, steel dagger with a blade six inches long, and, bringing the point over my breast, she continued in cold, hard tones,—

"I want you to swear that you will never mention these facts to any human being again. If you do not, I will send the keen point of this steel through your heart. Do you swear?"

This was a phase of our interview unlooked for. I recognized the poniard as the same one which she had used last November, when I so unceremoniously left her. That, however, was a dark night. I did not propose to repeat those tactics again. Besides, for me to run down Fifth Avenue with a handsome woman in pursuit, dagger in hand, would not be a dignified proceeding. It might be sport for the boys, but not for me. I had taken an oath to Adrien that I would publish all the facts in the case, and I now refused to bind myself to any other promise.

I had read that wild animals can be subdued by the fixed gaze of the human eye. I resolved to try the effect on the infuriated woman before me. I was well aware that Ilian herself was a magnetic power of the first order, and that it was a question now which of us had the strongest will. I looked full into her glowing eyes and answered nothing. A moment later she said in a wavering voice,—

"Do you swear?"

"Throw down that toy!" I commanded her.

"You must first swear to do what I ask," said she.

"Do you hear me?" I continued. "Throw it down!" and I brought my eyes close to hers. I saw her hesitate, and then she let go the dangerous hair-pin, which fell at my feet. She sat down in a large chair and began to weep. A woman's tears have at all times a mighty influence over men. I was not angry in the least, but objected to any experiment of that hair-pin around the region of my heart.

"I think you are awful mean," she said, in a child-like tone of voice.

"Perhaps I am," said I; "but you will have enough to answer for at the rendering of your final account without adding my blood to increase the load. Please understand me once for all; **I am** not making history, but only relating at **your** own request facts which cannot be gainsaid."

"You have nothing but inference **for** what you state," she pleaded.

"**Yes, I have** something better than that."

"**What is it?**"

"**The full** confession which you are holding in your hand."

"**I tell you once** again I do not and will not believe it," she said.

She rose up in an instant from her chair, and attempted **to** pick up the little dagger. I intercepted this by sending **it** some twenty feet away with my foot.

"Miss Mordine, **I** am tired of this foolishness," said **I**. "**Twice you have attempted to take my life.** That is the **same** instrument, **I believe, which** you held to **Adrien's throat when he was recovering from** yellow-fever **and** you constrained him to leave **the Union** navy and enter the Confederate service. **I will now remove** a temptation from your path."

I went to the place where the jewelled pin lay on the floor, and, kneeling down on one knee, I picked it up and drove it with all my force into the floor. It pierced through the soft Wilton carpet and through a joint in the flooring clear up to the hilt. I then pressed my foot against the handle and it snapped off. I gave back the jewelled remnant to Ilian and told her that if she had this part fixed on to the sheath, she **would** still have a beautiful hair-pin, **but** the sting would **be** gone.

"How can I live," she replied, "with **the** uncertainty **of** my birth always before me?"

"We may be able to find the missing link," **said I**. "Have **you** searched carefully all of the papers left by Mrs. Verdere."

"I have," said she. "There is none to throw light on the subject."

"**By the way,** let me ask you, have you among your things **a cash-box of black** japanned tin with two locks and two gold **bands** painted around it? The reason why **I make** this inquiry is, that I have a letter from Miss Helen Claymuire acknowledging the receipt of a box sent to her by Professor Homerand to keep her papers in, **and I** also have a receipt from the maker of the box. There were two of them, and they were made in 1840."

"Yes, I have a box of that description," she answered. "I keep my aunt's papers in it. What of it?"

"Much," I replied. "Are you aware that the box which Adrien gave me has a false bottom, and inside of it I found the important letters that I have given you? Bring me your box; it may have a false bottom also."

Ilian went to her room and returned in a minute with a tin box the exact mate of the one that I had. When it was opened I took out all the papers and inserted the blade of my knife under one of the locks. Pressing a spring hidden under the velvet lining, the false bottom flew up, revealing a bundle of papers tied with red ribbon.

"These are the missing links!" I exclaimed, triumphantly.

"Do not touch them," said Ilian. "That is my sole privilege. There may be secrets that I would not want any one else to know. I will read them over carefully in my chamber, and also the papers which you have given me. Come here at two o'clock to-morrow and I will tell you the result. I promise that I will be perfectly candid with you, and keep back nothing that you have a right to know."

I arose from my chair to take my departure, extending my hand to say good-by. She took it in both of hers and, with tears in her eyes, said,—

"My dear chaplain, can you forget and forgive my breach of hospitality and my threatening attempt upon you? I would not have harmed you in any way for the world; but I was terribly excited. I have suffered so much in the last twenty years that I have not that full control of my temper which I once had."

"Think no more of it, Miss Mordine," said I; "you did me no harm, and I feel sorry that I broke that hair-pin, but its sting might be dangerous and its beauty is not lost."

"I am glad that you did break it, but I wish to ask a favor which I will esteem as a boon."

"Your slightest wish will be law to me."

"I wish that you will not call me Miss Mordine."

"Do you prefer the name of Homerand?"

"No, not altogether; but I want you hereafter to call me Ilian."

"I will do so with pleasure. Ilian, *au revoir* until to-morrow afternoon." And I left the house.

CHAPTER V.

MISSING LINKS.

At the hour specified on the following day I rang the bell at the stately mansion of Joseph Rendeem, the merchant prince. A liveried servant ushered me into the handsomely-furnished drawing-room. There I found Miss Edith Rendeem, who informed me that Ilian had gone to her banker's, but would be back shortly. In the mean time Miss Edith said she would herself do the best she could to entertain me. Although I had only known her a short time, yet we were great friends. She was one of those rare women, who, if they like you, can make you so perfectly at home that you feel as though you had known them all your life.

Miss Edith had a small weakness, however. She did not relish the fact that the years were rolling up their record against her. She was but three years younger than Ilian, but would never admit the nearness of age. As a rule, when the war was the subject of conversation, she invariably replied that she was very young when it took place, and that really she could hardly be expected to remember much about it. It was only when her noble war-record in the service of the Christian Commission was referred to in glowing terms, that she forgot her weak point. She would then enter with enthusiasm into all that related to the service among the sick and wounded soldiers. I was well aware of these points, and occasionally teased her on the subject. I found her in excellent good humor, and so opened the attack.

"Do you remember the naval officers who attended the party given in this house in August of 1861, when Adrien Homerand first met Ilian?"

"How can you ask such a question?" she asked. "You know that I was very young at the time."

"Ah, yes, that is true," I replied. "You were but a child of twenty, wearing short dresses, and never went out except in charge of your nurse."

"Oh, you horrid man, why did you not ask if I was twenty on my last birthday?"

"I certainly would if I did not know you so well; but really your beautiful face never seems to lose its juvenile freshness."

"Now, my dear chaplain, you talk like a sensible specimen of the *genus homo*."

"Is your mother named Edith?" I asked.

"No. Why do you ask?"

"Because I read the other day in the record of the Christian Commission a glowing tribute of the zealous and self-denying work performed by Miss Edith Rendeem, and as you were but a child, then it could not be you."

"Why not? Cannot children work?"

"Oh, then you were the heroine," I replied. "I am proud to know you. Now, seriously, I love to hear about the Christian Commission. Tell me some of your own experience."

"Do you desire me to give you a chapter from ancient history?"

"No; because you are yet too young to go very far back. Tell me, however, what progress you have made in your medical studies?"

"I received a degree from a medical college in this city. My father, however, objects to my receiving any compensation for professional service. He says that he will leave me half a million when he dies; and asks why should I trouble myself about pills and noxious compounds. He tells me that I can practise on him and on my mother and also on my brother John. My sister Alice always sends for me when her children are ailing, but I desire scope for my talents."

"Why not marry some good doctor?" I asked. "Then you can be a helpmate and a pearl of great price."

"I have made up my mind never to marry," she replied. "I am too much in love with the study of medicine to spend my time at the humoring of a husband."

"Then," said I, "go into partnership with some old doctor, and you will find all the opportunity you can desire."

"I will think over your advice," said she; "and now let me tell you something. Do you know that my brother John is jealous of you? He had an appointment out this evening, but when he heard that Ilian had invited you to dinner to-day, he made up his mind to stay at home in order to do honor to our guest, as he expressed it, but really **to** watch you. So **be** on your guard."

"Jealous of me!" I exclaimed. "**I am not in** the market at present. **If I was I** would not go any farther than the fair daughter **of this** house. **Do** you know that I think **it would be a splendid thing to** have a wife that **was** a doctor? She **would save lots of** medical bills. **You would make a** fortune in **your** practice of medicine by making a specialty of heart-disease. All the young men, and old ones, too, would need their hearts to be examined quite often; not at all a **bad** idea to have a dainty head with her ear close to your heart and **then** feel **your pulse and look at** your tongue. Will you not prescribe **for me?** I ate too much dinner last evening and **am** suffering from indigestion."

"Certainly; I will give you a remedy to follow when you return to your hotel this evening," she replied. "Walk six times around Union Square, and if you do not feel better, repeat the dose. Here comes Ilian. You will not have much time for your business talk. John will be home at five o'clock. I will leave you now." As she went out I thought what a perfect jewel **of a** wife she would make for some man.

"I am **sorry that** I kept you **waiting,**" was Ilian's greeting; "but my banker sent me a note desiring to see me **on important** business. I have read all the papers that you **gave me and** also all that I found in the secret bottom of the tin box."

"What **is the** result?" I asked.

"Your surmise was correct," **said she.**

"**Then** Mrs. **Veredere** was your mother, and Professor Homerand your father?"

"Yes," she replied. "**My** mother left a full record of everything. I was born in London on the 3d of May, **1841.** I was called Ilian Homer at **first,** as my mother had serious thoughts of sending me as a present to my father. This she hoped would disturb the harmony of his relations with her rival, Martha Rathmine, illegally his wife, as she claimed. Finally, **a** mother's love prevailed over that of revenge, which, as you are aware, is the strongest passion **of our** human nature if allowed **to** develop its latent tendencies. After the death of my aunt and her husband I was brought up as their child, taking their name. This has been a bitter revelation to me, and life has no longer the attraction that it had. I shall welcome death because it will bring me into the company of those dear ones whose relationship I did not know when they were here."

"You take altogether too gloomy a view of things in general," said I. "You have the three qualifications that are looked upon as the acme of human happiness,—viz., health, beauty, and wealth."

"I would give half my fortune to-day," Ilian answered, "to look upon my mother's marriage-certificate. It is galling and humiliating in the extreme to think that I am a child of illicit intercourse. How can I live with such a stain?"

"You take a wrong view of things in general and blame your dear mother for that of which she was not guilty," I replied. "She was solemnly engaged to Professor Homerand, and he on his part had taken a binding oath to make her his wife. He called God to witness this compact. This was not only by word of mouth, but he confirmed it by his own signature. In the sight of God, therefore, your mother was the true and legal wife of Professor Homerand."

"How about his marriage with Martha Rathmine?" she inquired.

"That was an earthly marriage and could not have the sanction of heaven. Besides, there is no divine law that can be found in the sacred Scriptures which forbids a man to have more than one wife. It is a legal enactment of a few of the nations of the world. I say a few, because the great majority allow a plurality of wives. The children of Israel are the offspring of the four wives of Jacob. Solomon, the wisest king that our race has produced, was the son of one of the numerous wives of David; yet no one called in question their birth. The State of New York recognizes the fact that if a man registers a woman as his wife, then she becomes so in fact, even though a ceremony to that purpose may not have been performed."

"Then you honestly believe that my birth was legitimate and without a taint?"

"In the sight of our Creator I certainly do. The Scotch law is emphatic upon this point, that where a man puts on paper, verified by his signature, a statement that he agrees to take a certain woman for his true and legal wife, and confirms it by living with her, though only for one day, she is his wife, and he cannot marry another without her consent in writing."

"I wish I had known this before my father died!" cried Ilian. "I would have clung to him and soothed his old age with a daughter's filial love. I might have been able to have prolonged his days. And Adrien, my half-brother, would have been happy, and under my influence the passion for gambling never could have developed as it did. Poor boy! now I can account for those strange feelings that came over me whenever I thought of returning to live with him as his wife."

"I will now make the promise which you asked of me yesterday,—viz., I will not mention this subject of your parentage while you are alive. I will, in accordance with my oath to Adrien, write out a full statement of your strange history; and if you survive me it can be published after your death. This secret will remain between us. At any time that you need my assistance I will always be at your service. Dr. Rechard and Samuel Andermatt both suspect the true state of affairs, and it rests with you whether to enlighten them further."

"I think I will do so," said she. "They can be fully depended upon. Do you know that John Rendeem is fearfully jealous of you? He is making desperate love to me; but nothing would induce me to link my life again with any man."

"Yes, I was informed of it by Edith, his sister, an hour ago. John is a genial and good-natured man and has a fine war-record. Well, I will for the rest of the evening pay particular attention to his sister."

"That will make him happy. Edith will understand it; so all will be peace and harmony."

"Do you know," said I, "that I think Dr. Rechard and Edith would make a splendid match? I never saw two people more suited to each other. If they could only be brought together a marriage would follow as a sure sequence."

"The idea is not a bad one," Ilian answered. "It never occurred to me. I have been so worked up about my own affairs that I had no time for those of others. I will invite the doctor to come to New York this summer. He talks about coming. I must leave you now to dress for dinner. I will send Edith to keep you company."

In a few moments the latter came into the room, in a pink dress, all radiant.

"Upon my word," I said to her, "that saying of Henry Ward Beecher's is exemplified in you,—'It is not the clothes that make the man or woman, but when they are made, they look better well dressed.'"

"Is that a compliment for me?" she asked.

"Of course it is; and gazing upon you in that lovely silk makes me regret that I did not finish my studies in medicine. I spent a year at it. If I was now only an M.D."

"Well, what would you do if you were an M.D.?"

"Stir up the folks and make them go for all they were worth."

"Well, you will not stir me up," she retorted; "and now once for all, I tell you positively, I am not going to marry."

"When you do," I persisted, "pray let me perform the ceremony?"

"Yes, I agree to that," said she; "but you will die of weary waiting before that comes around. Now I will tell you something. Ilian has given me instructions to take entire charge of you for the rest of the evening."

"Only for the evening? Why not for life?"

"That is too large a contract. Here comes John; he is a bigger man than you are; be careful."

The hearty welcome by John Rendeem set at rest all doubts as to how he would receive me. Mr. and Mrs. Rendeem and their hospitality no one can forget who has been fortunate enough to see them and share their festive-board. That evening was one of the most pleasant that I ever spent in New York. Ilian was in one of her happy moods, bright, sparkling, and glowing. This made John correspondingly happy, and he pressed me to stay at their house for a week. That was urged by all the family, but I told them that important business called me home early the next morning. I left their house at eleven, and at parting Edith whispered not to forget her prescription. I followed it and walked six times around Union Square, and enjoyed it so much that I would have repeated the dose a dozen times if the fair doctress had been with me.

The next day I was at home again.

CHAPTER VI.

MYSTERIOUS SHOOTING.

The 1st of March came and was ushered in with its usual boisterous manner. It was a clear day, fine and bracing; but the wind was out for a grand time, and it seemed to enjoy the sport, which was more than the pedestrians did. In fact, some of them used language far from ornamental when their silk hats went flying down the street. There is nothing so ridiculous as to see a man chasing his headgear, and others trying to assist him by endeavoring to put their feet on the flying article of dress.

I went out early that day, as I had a good deal of business to transact, and did not return home till late in the afternoon. I was met by my housekeeper in a state of great excitement. A telegram had come for me about half an hour after I left in the morning. At three o'clock she had received another from Boston, from a doctor in a hospital, asking whether I was home,—if not, to send me word that Miss Mordine was dangerously ill and desired to see me. I opened my telegram and found it as follows:

———— Hospital, Boston, March 1.

Accidentally shot. May prove fatal; come at once. Have telegraphed Dr. Rechard.   Ilian.

Looking at my watch, I perceived that I had just time to reach the station and get the through train for Boston. I hastily packed up a few needed articles, and in five minutes from the time I had entered my home I was on the way to the railway station. Unfortunately, the horse-car was delayed by a coal-cart for several minutes; and when I reached the station I rushed to the ticket-office and called for a ticket to Boston.

"I am afraid you are too late," replied the clerk.

"No matter; let me have the ticket."

It was handed out and paid for, and I hurried to the platform.

"Too late!" said the gate-keeper, as he shut the gate.

"It is a matter of life and death!" said I, "and I must get on this train."

He opened the gate. As I saw the train moving, I cried out, "Clear the way!" and sent two train employés whirling round. Reaching the last carriage, I leaped on board. A cheer from some one on the platform greeted my success, and I was hastening to New York. I sent a telegram from Trenton to Ilian, informing her that I was on my way.

I arrived in Boston next morning at six o'clock, and hastened to the Tremont House. After breakfast I took a carriage and drove to the hospital designated in my telegram. When I had reached it I saw the surgeon in charge, gave him my card, and asked for particulars. He told me that he knew nothing about the affair more than this: Miss Mordine had been brought to the hospital the previous morning about eight o'clock by two gentlemen in a carriage, who explained that she had taken a revolver to fire at a target, and was examining it to see if it was in good condition, when it suddenly went off. This statement the lady corroborated. There was no doubt in his mind that the shooting was accidental, for the wound was a slanting one. The bullet had entered above the left breast and came out at the collar-bone at the back, and made just such a wound as would result from a careless handling of fire-arms. In fact, he added, he had seen a number of similar cases.

I asked him whether he thought there was any danger of a serious termination.

"Yes," was his reply. "There is danger of inflammation setting in, and it would be well to notify her relatives."

"Has this not been done?" I asked.

"You and Dr. Rechard are the only ones so far, and he has answered that he would leave at once for Boston."

As I was talking to him, a telegram came from Dr. Rechard from a way-station asking to be informed of the condition of Miss Mordine, the reply to be sent to a place designated. The answer was duly sent,—

"Worse; may terminate fatally."

A nurse was sent to Ilian's room to prepare her for my visit.

I was profoundly grieved when I saw her face almost as white as the pillow on which her head was resting. She put out both her hands and with her eyes filled with tears she said in a gentle voice,—

"I am so glad you have come; I wanted to see you. Will you stay by me till all is over?"

"Do not give up in this manner," said I. "Your wound is not necessarily fatal. Many thousands have been wounded far more severely than you, and are living to-day. You have seen them yourself in the hospitals as they were brought in from the battle-field. Let your strong will prevail, and many years of a pleasant life will be yours."

"No," said she, "I feel that my days are numbered; in fact, my hours. It becomes me to make such preparation as may be necessary. I propose making my will to-day and I will not forget you."

"Ilian, if you have any respect for my feelings you will not leave me a single dollar. I am poor, God knows, but I could not touch any of your money."

"Are you afraid that it is tainted with the curse?" she asked.

"That is not the reason," said I. "Your money came to you legally through inheritance from your grandfather's estate. It is that I would much prefer that your memory should ever dwell in my heart unalloyed by the thought that I took the money that belonged by right to your relatives. You have those in South Carolina who are needy, and to them it will be a Godsend."

"I doubt whether they will appreciate your feeling in this matter," said she; "but I will leave you all my private papers. I have that box here in my room and among the things in it you will find that jewelled hair-pin. Keep it for my sake; the sting is gone, as you once said; and I hope it has also left no unpleasant remembrance behind."

"Not with me, I assure you," I replied; "but I have not given up all hope yet. Dr. Rechard is due here to-morrow evening, and I have suggested to the doctor in charge to call in the ablest medical skill in Boston; but let me ask you a question. Should this illness terminate in death, what preparation have you made to meet your God?"

"I shall render back to Him the spirit which He gave, tainted with the companionship of evil; but it can stand before

Him without a blush, for I have guarded my honor as **I did my life.** In looking back **over my** brief career I can remember much that I wish had not **been** done, and many things I might have performed. **I have not withheld the** hand of charity **from those needing help. I never united with any** particular religious denomination, although nominally an Episcopalian, **but I have made it a** point to attend some church each Sabbath. I never set myself forth as a saint, and do not think that I am a great offender beyond the average woman of my age. I had no choice in regard to coming into the world and **I** have not been consulted as to the time, manner, or **place of my** leaving it."

"Ilian," **said** I, "you are gifted with **too** much common sense not to see that by your line of argument you throw all the blame for the evil of your life upon your Creator. The question for you to consider is what use you have made of the more than ordinary talents entrusted to your care. Have you improved them, and **do** you think that the world is better because you **were born into it, or would it** have **been** better for mankind if **you had died in** your infancy?"

"Have I been such a great sinner?"

"**No, that is not the inference that** I wish you to draw. My question is applicable to all those who, like yourself, have been gifted **with** great mental ability. You know that our **Saviour said that** to whom **much** is given from them shall **much** be required. I know, however, that you are too weak at present, and therefore I will not weary you with these important problems."

"**My** dear chaplain," she replied, "you do not weary me **in the least**; far from it, **for I am** deeply interested; **I am never so** happy as when engaged **in** theological discussions. **I have** read the claims of the Baptists, Methodists, **Presbyterians, Episcopalians, and other** religious denominations, including **the Roman Catholic; and I** assert now, that if my life **depended on it, I do not know which I** should choose as the one **combining all that my soul craves after.**"

"Let me ask you to explain **in a few brief** words what it is that your soul longs **for.**"

"For many, many things. **There** have been periods in my life when I longingly sought to breathe in an atmosphere where **there was** no taint of sin and evil, and I wondered whether there was any denomination that could enable me to live far above the world's strife, meanness, and jealousy. I desired to reach an altitude where I could look down upon the rest of my fellows in their misery and heart-burning, and then, like Excelsior, to mount higher and higher. My soul has thirsted for knowledge and I have read early and late, but have not been satisfied. I never worshipped my gold or sought by its display to make others envious or unhappy. I seldom went into society, and cared nothing for what people said about my raiment. It was more pleasure to me to seek out the needy and give them warm clothing than to place costly fabrics on my back. Now, then, can you tell me what denomination comes nearest to my ideal?"

"I answer this query by telling you a simple truth," I replied. "When you are called upon to stand before the bar of judgment, the question will not be asked you, of what religious denomination you were a member, but whether you have loved the Lord Jesus Christ with all your mind and heart, and were you regenerated. There is at the present day too much denomination, and too little of the genuine religion of Christ. I must now leave you for a while. Can I do anything for you?"

"Yes, I want you to send a telegram to the Rev. Father Murphy. You will find his directions in my portfolio on the table. He attended my mother in her last illness. I have seen him from time to time since. I saw him a few days ago. If my illness should terminate fatally, here is a letter which you are to open after my death. I wrote it this morning. I am not suffering any pain, and my brain is as clear as it ever was, but my heart's action is weak and it may stop suddenly. I am anxious to see Dr. Rechard. I have not sent word to the Rendeem family, but will do so to-morrow if I get worse."

"John Rendeem will feel badly," said I, "when he knows you shot yourself."

"He knows it already," said she; "and so does some one else."

"Ilian," I replied, "there is some mystery about this affair. You have always had the reputation of being very careful, and you are not the woman to handle carelessly a loaded pistol."

"I do not wish to say anything about it now," said she; "but one thing I assure you, I held the revolver in my own hand when it went off."

The physicians now came in to hold a consultation, and I left the sick-chamber.

CHAPTER VII.

FATHER MURPHY NOT POTENT.

I WENT to the telegraph office and sent a message to the Rev. Father Murphy to come direct to the hospital to meet Miss Mordine. I knew that he could not get there before four o'clock, so I went back to my hotel and at about three went again to visit Ilian. She told me that the doctors had been frank with her. Her condition was serious. She had received three telegrams,—one from Dr. Rechard on his way, one from Samuel Andermatt, and a reply from Rev. Thomas Murphy, who would leave on the first train.

"Chaplain," she continued, "do you believe in the recognition of our friends in the other world?"

"Certainly I do," I answered. "The chief part of our joy here is the thought of eternal happiness in company with those who were our kindred on earth."

"I believe in that theory myself," said she, "and it robs death of its sting when I think of the welcome I hope to receive from my father and mother and Adrien and others. The more I think of it the less desire I have for life. There is also the prospects of increased knowledge. I will not be in the dark about so many subjects that perplex me here."

"May I ask on what ground you expect so much happiness? Have you any claim to present?"

"I do not believe that I can give any well-defined idea why I look for increased happiness," she answered, "except a vague one that God is good to the creatures of His world. I certainly have no claim to any condition of existence in the next sphere."

"Do you **not** think, then, that you should seek for a substantial foundation, especially when so much depends upon it?"

"What do you call the foundation?"

"Faith in the atonement of our Saviour. I do not mean a simple **acquiescence in** his directions, but a living, practical faith."

"**Perhaps you are** right," said she; "**but** it is now too late **to change my status.** I **have no** confidence in those who live **all their lives far from** God and in their **last moment** try to **avoid** the punishment due to **their** careless, wretched life by a confession which has no depth of meaning and is the product of fear."

Our conversation was interrupted by a nurse bringing in **the card of** Father **Murphy.**

"Chaplain," **said she,** "go and have a preliminary talk with him. Tell him that I sent for him to come as a friend, and because he attended the last hours of my mother."

I went to the reception-room and found the priest waiting. He was a man about sixty years of age, a perfect gentleman in language and deportment. I soon realized **that he was** charitable in his religious views. **He believed that** though Protestants were living out of the fold of what **he** called the true Apostolic Church, yet their sincerity **and** love **for** the Lord would in the end win for them the kingdom **of heaven,** although necessitating considerable purgatorial fire.

"Have **you** any objection," **he asked,** "if I talk to Miss Mordine **in** regard to her **soul's** welfare? **I may** be able to enroll her **as a member of the true Church. I attended her mother, who made her confession, and I** privately gave **her absolution.**"

"I thought that **Mrs.** Verdere died a Protestant," I replied.

"Outwardly so," said he; "but in spirit I felt that she was a Catholic."

"I am afraid that you will find **the** daughter of different material. She is the child of the **late** Professor Homerand. Of this fact I believe you are aware. Her mother confessed **to you** and Ilian told you herself last **month.**"

"Yes, I know it; but I may prevail upon her child to follow **her mother's example** and confess and receive absolution."

"All right, my **dear** Father Murphy," said I. "The field **is yours;** but with **all due deference** I doubt your success."

"The powers of our Church are mighty and will prevail over the gates of darkness."

"*Nous verrons.* I have to go out and will call for you at six o'clock to come and take dinner with me at my hotel."

"I will be most happy to do so," said he.

I left the worthy priest to engage in what I considered a herculean task and went out to answer the telegrams from Dr. Rechard and Sam Andermatt. Both were of the same tenor:

"No hope of recovery; may survive until the eve of the 4th, so the doctor says."

I returned to my hotel and ordered dinner for two at half-past six. I then walked slowly to the hospital, arriving at the appointed time. Five minutes after Father Murphy came into the reception-room. I noticed that he did not have the air of a victorious general; in fact, he looked like one who had been roughly handled in some mental encounter. This I fully expected.

"Did you reach the absolution-point?" I asked.

"I am sorry to say that I did not get anywhere near it," he replied. "What a keen, logical reasoner that girl is. She can argue like a Webster and has the diplomacy of a Bismark. I found her thoroughly familiar with the history of our Church. She related to me in concise terms all the points that I purposed to lay before her, and answered each and every one of them, so that for the first time in my life I was puzzled what to say in reply. She has the rare faculty of saying in five minutes what most people would take an hour to present. I crossed myself several times and implored the aid of the Holy Virgin to help me and to keep me from being influenced by her logic. I do believe that in another hour I should have been persuaded to have turned a Protestant, and then my soul would have been in danger. My dear chaplain, I give the field back to you. What a wonderful woman!"

"It never was mine," I replied to him; "I cannot influence her any more than yourself. It is true that she is a Protestant, but she has her own view of things and purposes to die with her own way of thinking."

I went in and told Ilian that she had better take a needful rest. To my surprise she was a trifle better. Her voice was stronger and there was an amused expression on her face as she said,—

"Chaplain, I am ready for another theological antagonist. It does me good; more so than the medicine that I am taking. It keeps up my spirits and takes my mind off morbid thoughts. Come back after your dinner and we will have another quiet little confab. I will sleep better if you do. What does the good priest say?"

"He told me that genius in your case was hereditary, and that if you had been born a man your power would have been felt as a great factor in the world's affairs."

"Does he think," she asked, "that women are debarred from entering the arena where cultured minds strive for the mastery and to gain the bauble which men call fame?"

"Not exactly that, but women are handicapped by old-time prejudice, which in the coming generation may be overcome. For my own part, I believe that the next century will witness a great revolution in the relations of womankind with the affairs of the world."

"I wish that I could live to see it," said she; "but, alas! forty-eight hours will bring a radical change to me. I will leave all my wealth behind and no regret at parting with it. I have no fear; I am full of hope and pleasurable excitement."

"I must leave you for a short time," I replied. "I answered the telegrams for you, and by to-morrow evening you will see Dr. Rechard." So I left her.

Father Murphy and myself enjoyed a pleasant dinner. By mutual consent sectarian subjects were avoided, and we discussed the many attractive places in Europe, in their political, historical, and scientific aspects, and both of us came to the conclusion that there was no place like America. After our dinner Father Murphy went to a friend's house, and on my return to the hospital I found Ilian asleep, so I went back to my hotel.

CHAPTER VIII.

THE LAST EVENING.

I AROSE early on the following morning. The day was dark and dismal. The east wind was blowing with a keen, penetrating force. On going down to the hotel office I found a telegram from Dr. Rechard stating that he would be due in Boston by the train arriving at half-past five that evening. I then went to the hospital and the surgeon in charge told me that they had abandoned all hope of the recovery of Miss Mordine, and that it was my duty to notify her relatives at once. She might survive till the next afternoon, but was liable to pass away at very short notice. When I went into her room I noticed a great change in her appearance. There was no doubt of her failing physical powers. A smile was on her face and she looked happy; while I was speaking to her Father Murphy came in. As soon as she saw him she said, with a look full of meaning,—

"You and the chaplain have both sought to win me over to your different ways of thinking. You felt confident of the great power of your Apostolic Church, as you call your creed, to overcome all my scruples and to enroll me as a member in good standing, and would have given me absolution and a letter of credit to the other world. He, on his part, set forth the tenets of his denomination and trusted to logical deduction that I would pass away according to his views. Both of you did me good, and I fully accept the best of what you presented. It may be a satisfaction to you both to know that I am ready to go into the presence of our Redeemer with the blessed assurance of sin pardoned and the prospect of an eternal life in the presence of my God. I will die neither a Catholic nor Baptist, but simply as a trusting child of God."

To this Father Murphy made no reply. I saw that his heart was too full for utterance. I told Ilian that it was necessary to inform the Rendeem family of her condition without further delay.

"Very good," said she. "I leave this matter entirely in **your hands.**"

"Also, if **you** have no objection, **I would** like to send word to your **uncle, Mr.** Thomas Homerand," I added.

"**I forgot that** I had any relations so near akin. Do you **think that he will come, or** that he will acknowledge me as **his brother's child?**"

"**Certainly he will.** He is living in the Homerand mansion, where he was born, and it is not far from here. **I will** leave Father Murphy **with you** and will go and attend to this business."

I sent a despatch to Mr. Joseph Rendeem advising him to come to Boston if he wished to **see** Ilian alive. I then wrote a note **to** Mr. **Homerand and gave him** a brief account of his niece, and of **the proof of her birth and her** present dangerous illness, and **added that if** he was willing to acknowledge her, to come to the hospital. This was sent by a special messenger. **On** my return I **found** the answer from Mr. Rendeem, saying that he would leave by the ten-o'clock train, and that his wife and daughter would accompany him. His daughter Alice and her husband were out West.

At noon I was watching by Ilian's bedside. She was sleeping. Father **Murphy** had been obliged to return to his parish, but promised to come back **next** day. **A** card was handed **to** me and I read the name, "Mr. and Mrs. Thomas Homerand." I went to the reception-room and saw an elderly gentleman **of** about sixty-five, with a dignified look, who impressed me that **while he could be severe to those** who transgressed **the laws, yet I felt he had a** large heart inside of his massive **frame. His wife** was, perhaps, **two** years his junior, and one of the most **lovable** ladies that I had seen for some time. His first question convinced me that **I had not** erred in my estimation of his character.

"How is our dear niece? How we both long to see our brother Homer's daughter! How was she shot?"

I replied **that** she was sinking fast, and the shooting was accidental. I showed them a cabinet **portrait of** Ilian taken a few months **previous.**

"What a lovely, **handsome girl!**" was their reply. "She has her father's mouth, and **it is** a striking likeness."

I told them that I would prepare her for the interview. I

found Ilian awake, and she was delighted at the prospect of meeting some one akin to her.

I dare not trust myself to describe in full the meeting between Mr. and Mrs. Homerand and the daughter of their dead brother. It was too pathetic for description. The uncle could hardly utter the words,—

"My darling child, how glad I am to see you, and sorry to find you so ill."

He kissed her white brow. His wife was completely overcome and wept like a child.

If we had known of this relationship before," they both said, "we would have taken you to our heart and home. We have no children of our own and you would have filled a daughter's place."

"I was afraid you would not recognize me," was the plaintive rejoinder, in a voice that brought fresh tears.

"How could you think so inhumanly of us? Your father told me years ago that he had solemnly sworn to marry your mother, and that before God she was his legal wife. I never knew that you were alive till this morning. My brother told me that you died at birth. If money can prolong your life I will freely spend all my fortune to save you. I will send for the ablest physicians."

"Many thanks, dear uncle," she replied; "but I have already had the best medical skill, and it is of no avail."

Leaving his wife with their niece, we went out together to see the head surgeon. I told Mr. Homerand that his niece was worth over a million dollars, and was anxious to make her will, and I would leave him to attend to it, while I would go to meet the five-thirty train, as her cousins on her mother's side, Mr. Joseph Rendeem and family, were coming from New York City.

"I know of them," was his reply. "One of the oldest of the New York families; and who is this Dr. Rechard?"

I told him what I knew, and left him to draw up the will and have it signed. In parting I said,—

"Ilian, your niece, proposed to remember me in this will; but under no conditions will I accept one dollar. On this point I am determined."

At half-past five, punctual to the minute, the train arrived from New York. In the second carriage I saw the face of

Miss Edith Rendeem. The next moment I was shaking hands with her father and mother. They all asked me a dozen questions at once.

"How was Ilian? Who did the shooting? Where, when, what time? Why did I not notify them before? Did John know of it?" I replied as best I could, and was in the midst of my explanations when some one touched me on the shoulder, saying,—

"My dear chaplain, I am glad to see you. It is a long time since last we met in New Orleans, but you have not changed much."

"Dr. Rechard," I replied, "I am glad to welcome you here, although your errand is a sad one. Ilian is beyond the hope of recovery."

I introduced him to the Rendeem family, who expressed great pleasure at seeing one of whom they had heard so much.

"Where is my son John?" Mr. Rendeem again asked.

"I do not know," I replied. "Ilian told me that he knew of her injury, but I have not seen him."

"Strange proceeding," said the father.

"There is a mystery about this shooting that I cannot penetrate," I answered, "and Ilian is too ill now to question her. I left her with her uncle and aunt, Mr. and Mrs. Thomas Homerand. There are two carriages waiting and we will go to the hospital."

"Uncle and aunt!" exclaimed Mr. Rendeem and his wife. "Do you mean that Ilian was the daughter of the late Professor Homerand?"

"Yes," said Miss Edith, who answered the question for me; "I heard the full details two months ago from Ilian herself. But let us not stand talking on this platform any longer. Let us step into this carriage, and the coachman can get our baggage."

This was done. Dr. Rechard and myself went together, while the Rendeems occupied the other coach. On the way I gave the doctor all the details of what had happened since my arrival, all that I knew of the shooting, and of my suspicions that John Rendeem was involved in it in some way. When we arrived at the hospital a surgeon met us and directed that in order to avoid all excitement only two should go in to see Miss Mordine at a time. Mrs. Rendeem and her daughter went first; then Mr. Rendeem; and when they came out Dr. Rechard and myself went in. Poor fellow, he was as pale as the woman before us. She was under the influence of morphia, and we did not stay long. We found Mr. and Mrs. Homerand in the reception-room. They had introduced themselves to the Rendeems, and I introduced the doctor. Mr. Homerand told me that the will had been drawn up and signed before witnesses. He then invited us all to go to his house for dinner. We replied that it would take some time to prepare for so many, and proposed that instead he and his wife should come to the Tremont House. In an hour's time we were all seated in a private dining-room of that hotel. After our meal Edith and Dr. Rechard both said that they would sit up all night with Ilian and would inform us of any change for the worse.

The following morning we went again to the hospital, and when we saw her we perceived that the end was not far off. She declined to take any more morphia, declaring that she was not suffering any pain, and that she wished to pass away with full consciousness. We expected the last messenger to come for her at noon; but at that hour she rallied somewhat, and her mental powers were stronger than for two days previous. At three o'clock I returned to the hospital, having been absent half an hour on a visit to a florist to purchase a bouquet of Ilian's favorite flowers for which she expressed a desire.

I saw a man with a heavy overcoat on and his hat drawn down over his face looking in at the partly-open door of the sick-chamber. He turned away and walked down the hallway and entered a vacant room. I had but a partial glimpse of the stranger, but recognized John Rendeem. He had not closed the door of the room, and as I had rubber shoes on he did not hear my footsteps. A moment after I heard the click of a pistol. I pushed the door open and was horrified to see him standing by the window with his back to me holding a pistol in his right hand and pressing the muzzle against his temple. I dropped the flowers, and with one bound I was at his side and snatched the pistol out of his grasp. I demanded of him in stern tones what he meant by such a foolish act.

"Give me back that revolver," was his savage rejoinder.

"Never!" I replied. "Do you know that Ilian is now near her death and wishes to see you?"

I then noticed that his left sleeve was pinned to his coat, and that his arm was in a sling underneath. I put his pistol in my pocket and picking up the flowers told him in a peremptory tone to come with me. He made no remonstrance, and we went into the sick-chamber.

"John," his father asked, "where have you been and what is the matter with your arm?"

His mother merely said, "John, how could you stay away so long?"

His sister came up to him and looked into his face searchingly, but said nothing. Dr. Rechard gave him a significant look which was full of anger.

Ilian was sitting up in bed propped by pillows. Besides those mentioned, her uncle and aunt were also in the apartment, and sitting by the window was Father Murphy reading his prayer-book.

"John, I wish to see you," said Ilian in a low voice.

He went to her bedside and she took his hand. "You must swear before God and all present in this room that you will not seek revenge on the man who was the cause of my hurt."

"Never!" was the reply. "I will follow him all over the world, and I will not rest satisfied until I have killed him."

"You will do nothing of the sort," said she. "John, you surely cannot refuse my last request."

"You ask a great deal," was his answer. "How can I fail in my revenge?"

She looked at him with all the power of her great blue eyes, and continued,—

"Please do as I wish."

"John," said his father, "how can you hesitate?"

Edith came up and placed her hand on his shoulder, saying,—

"John, here is the chance to exhibit the proof of your love."

"Ilian," he cried, "God knows that I have loved you as man never loved woman, and for your sake I swear to let that scoundrel alone, but it will be dangerous for him to cross my path."

This episode deepened the mystery of the shooting, but no one asked for an explanation.

"Chaplain," said Ilian to me, "will you grant me a request? You alone were with Adrien when he died and witnessed his last breath. I ask to pass away in your arms. Hold the pillow on which my head is resting."

I did as requested, and her kindred gathered round, as all felt her end had come.

"Good-by, Uncle Thomas and my dear Aunt Mary, accept of my thanks for all your kindness. It is sweet to feel that I have a share in your love. Farewell, Cousin Joseph; and you also, my second mother. Edith, we must part now; there will be no more pleasant drives and quiet talks together. John, adieu! forgive me if I have tantalized you. Dr. Rechard, don't mourn for my loss. I know you will miss me, but we will meet again. Now, my dear chaplain, take my hand. I am getting cold, but, oh, I am so happy!"

It was a scene never to be forgotten. Tears were freely shed by all present. A few moments after she whispered in my ear,—

"They have come for me."

"Who?" I asked in a low voice.

"My father, my mother, Adrien."

The sun which had been under the clouds all day suddenly broke through the barrier which hid its bright rays from our depressed eyes and filled the room with its glorious tint. The form of the dying girl was enveloped in the dazzling splendor of the setting orb which was sinking in the west and threw its parting glory over the land to cheer the hearts of the children of men, and assuring them that it would come again on the morrow. Yes, it would indeed come, but never would its power be felt by the one who was now bathed in the golden sheen of its fading light. Another cloud came on in its rapid course and all was gloom once more. We looked at Ilian; but her spirit was gone, and we were left to mourn her departure. Our tears were falling and our hearts aching over our loss.

CHAPTER IX.

THE NEW FIRM.

LATE in the afternoon of the 5th of March a large number of friends and relatives were assembled in the parlor of the hospital to pay the last tribute of respect to Ilian, whose name was interwoven in the fibres of so many hearts.

A casket of polished oak, lined with white satin, was in the centre of the apartment. There was none of that rigid formality followed by so many undertakers. The face had a calm repose; the beautiful hair was done up in Grecian coils; the body was dressed in a white cashmere robe, trimmed down the front with swan's-down. One hand lay resting under the head, and the other held a book. She looked like one who had been reading and had fallen asleep. Everything was so natural that we could hardly realize that from her sleep she would never awaken till the last trumpet should call her to join in the great throng to assemble for final judgment.

I read the first part of the burial-service. The casket was then covered and we went to the place where her mother's form was resting beneath a marble shaft erected by her daughter, and there, in a place prepared for her in the vault, we laid away what remained of the child to sleep beside the one that gave her birth. I finished the last portion of the service, "Ashes to ashes, and dust to dust," and slowly we returned to our carriages. Father Murphy having to go back to his home, I told him that I would drive with him to the station. Dr. Rechard accompanied us. As we left the cemetery, I said to them both,—

"The curse of the Old South Church has been fulfilled, and we have seen the last of it. This curse has been a regular boomerang: it came back to the hand that started it."

"I must find out," said the doctor, "what the mystery is that shadows the shooting of Ilian."

"We can explore that at once," I said. "I have in my pocket the letter which I received from her, and which was not to be opened till after her death."

As I took it out of the envelope, I saw in red ink the following words:

"I will expect the word of honor from those who read this note or hear it read, that they will do nothing to the unhappy, wretched man who was primarily the cause of my being shot." The note was as follows: "Before leaving New York I received a letter from Colonel Hortense asking the loan of money enough to enable him to leave the city in order to go to New Orleans. I sent him one hundred dollars, and in two days after he wrote again asking for more. I left, and came on to Boston. John Rendeem became aware of this annoyance, and he resolved to protect me, so he came after me the next day. On the evening of the last of February he said, as he was leaving my hotel,—

"'After to-morrow I do not think that Colonel Hortense will annoy you any more for money.'

"'What do you mean?' I asked. 'Is he going away?'

"'I rather think he will go.'

"'When does he leave?'

"'About half-past six to-morrow morning.'

"'Where is he going to?'

"'To a place I hope you and I will avoid.'

"'Tell me, John,' I asked, 'are you going to fight a duel?'

"'I will tell you when next I call,' said he, and then took his leave.

"I suspected the truth, and ordered my carriage for six o'clock, and took my maid with me, instructing my coachman to drive to the hotel where John was stopping. Just before we arrived there my servant told me that Mr. John Rendeem, with two gentlemen, was then getting into a carriage. I directed him to follow them. We went to the outskirts of the city, where there was a public beer-garden with a thick clump of trees. It was used only in summer, and was closed at this season. I left my carriage and came up unseen to the place where they were. Colonel Hortense was already there with his second, and he had a revolver in his hand. I came up behind him, and before he knew it I snatched it from him. He turned around savagely and tried to take the pistol away from me. It was self-cocking, and in the scuffle I must have pressed the trigger, for it went off as I was holding it close to

my breast trying to keep it from **him**. The bullet went
through me like a bolt of hot iron, and I fell to the ground.
Fortunately, one of the gentlemen present was a surgeon. He
stopped the bleeding, and I was driven in **my own** carriage to
this hospital with the doctor and one of the gentlemen who
was to act as **a second** for John. I have not seen John since,
but was told he had gone in pursuit of Colonel Hortense. My
maid I made promise to keep secret the true statement of this
whole affair, and after my death I desire it to be hushed up,
and that man left to his remorse. I am deeply sorry for John,
and want to see him before I die.

"He will give the full details of the whole business. It is
needless **to** say that the shooting was **entirely** accidental. The
above is **a true statement.**

"ILIAN MORDINE."

After **I** had read the letter nothing was said, and in **a** few
minutes we were at the railway station. Dr. Rechard and
myself took a warm, affectionate leave of Father Murphy, and
with mutual good wishes he left on his train and we drove
back to the Tremont House, where we found all the Rendeem
family, including John. After dinner we retired to a private
parlor and again read Ilian's note. John Rendeem then arose,
saying,—

"The statement which you have just heard is correct. **I
was** challenged to fight by Colonel Hortense. The weapons
chosen were revolvers, each **to fire** five shots. Ilian came **up**
unexpectedly as **we were** about **to begin. I** was **not** aware
that she was so severely injured, as the surgeon told me it was
only a flesh-wound **and** that he would look after her. My
second promised to assist him. The man who acted for my
opponent disappeared and we saw nothing more of him. I
then followed the colonel, who had taken up his pistol after
Ilian had **dropped** it. As he was crossing a field I came
within range **and** fired two shots, one of which hit him in the
leg. He fell **at** once, and I rushed up to finish him, when he
sat up and discharged two shots at me, at close range, one of
which went through my left arm and the other grazed my neck.
The villain then jumped up and made off; but I noticed he
had **a** perceptible limp in his gait. My wound not only
pained me severely, but bled profusely, and I was obliged **to**

stop at a farm-house close by in order that it might be bandaged. I procured a horse and wagon and drove into the city, where a surgeon attended to it. He told me that there was no danger to be apprehended from it, but I was weak from the loss of blood. I took the first train for New York and went to a place where the colonel had boarded. He had left for Washington two hours before my arrival. I followed after him, but could find no trail of the scoundrel. I then returned to Boston. On learning where Ilian was I went to the hospital. When the surgeon in charge told me of her true condition, and I saw her pale face through the half-open door, I felt that life was not worth living and I went into a vacant room to shoot myself. I pulled the trigger with the pistol to my head, but it did not go off. Then the chaplain came in and you know the rest."

Mrs. Rendeem nearly fainted when she heard this statement. His father came up to him, and, with his eyes filled with tears, exclaimed,—

"John, if you had died you would have killed us all."

Edith put her arms around his neck and clung to him as though he were about to commit the deed afresh. "I do not know," continued John, "what prevented the pistol from going off."

"I know," I replied. "You had a five-chambered revolver and only three were loaded, and the hammer came down on an empty shell."

"I forgot, then, to put in fresh charges after I had fired at that hateful colonel."

"Thank God," said Dr. Rechard, "that your wound is no worse. Your sister will make a capital nurse; she told me she wanted some one to attend."

"Mr. and Mrs. Homerand were now announced. They had come to invite us all to lunch with them on the following day, as we were to return to New York by the Fall River line, leaving at six o'clock. We all retired to our beds early, and the next day our programme was carried out, many friends coming to the station to see us off. Dr. Rechard and Mr. Rendeem were two of the executors of Ilian's estate, a large portion of which was in New York City. It was necessary, therefore, that the former should remain there for a month at least. He accordingly accepted a pressing invitation to stay at the Rendeem home. They also desired me to come for a few days, but their house was too full of the associations of Ilian. I pleaded urgent business and left them and made my way back safely to my own quarters in Philadelphia.

Little now remains to be told.

Two months had passed since Ilian's death. Twice during this interval I paid flying visits to New York. Each time I was the guest of the Rendeems. Dr. Rechard told me that it took more time to settle up the estate than he had anticipated. He seemed to be very happy, and I was led to suspect that the affairs of a living woman were occupying more of his time than those of the one dead. Ilian's memory, I was well aware, would always be green in his heart, for she had been like a sister to him. I was not at all surprised, therefore, when I received the following letter from Miss Edith Rendeem:

No. —, Fifth Avenue, New York, May 3.

My dear Chaplain,—Do you remember last January that you gave me some good advice about my practice in medicine? Having such confidence in your sagacity, I am about to follow it. You told me to marry a physician, and I answered that such a course was out of the question. Then you advised me to go in partnership with some old doctor. I told this to Dr. Rechard, and he replied that "your head was level." He offered an amendment, however, viz., that instead of an old doctor I ought to take one of medium age, and he added that he knew just such a practitioner. I asked for the name and he wrote it on a piece of paper. But as the afternoon was cloudy, I could not read it very well, so I went to the bay-window for a better light. Perhaps I was a long time in making it out. He came into the recess, and remarked that I was getting a little near-sighted, and he would help me read the name. I do not know how it happened, but he said that I was pale and liable to faint, and his arm got around my waist to keep me from falling, and I put my head on his breast. The terms of partnership were settled then and there, and the title of the new firm is to be Dr. & Mrs. Henry Rechard. When this particular agreement was referred to my father, I told him that I had arranged for you to have the contract to perform the ceremony. He replied that he had long ago promised it to our own pastor. I asked him why he had assumed I would ever get married after my constant assertions to the contrary?

"Oh," he said, "girls all do that. Your mother acted that way. However, the chaplain can assist, and I will be glad to have him do so."

Now, perhaps you will say that women do not know their own minds. But I do. I did purpose not to marry, but Dr. Rechard felt so lonely after Ilian's death, and, besides, he will be a great help to me in my medical studies. He left yesterday for New Orleans to arrange his business and return by the first of June, the day that we are to be married. We will go to Boston for a week and then sail for Europe by the Cunard steamer, to be absent six months. We hope to be in New Orleans by Christmas, all settled in our home. Till I see you, *au revoir.* Your true friend,

EDITH RENDEEM.

I was on hand for the wedding and took my part. Edith was superb in her white silk dress, veil, and orange-blossoms. Every one remarked how splendidly mated they were. Mr. and Mrs. Homerand were both present, and the bridal party went to Boston as their guests. I remained at the Rendeem mansion till their return, on the morning of the sailing of the outward-bound steamer. It was a splendid send-off. More than one hundred of their friends were present. I was the last to leave them. As I stood on the gang-plank, the doctor and his wife both held my hands.

"Good-by, my dear chaplain. When we return to our home in New Orleans we will set apart one of our spare bedchambers for your use, and it shall always be known as the 'chaplain's room.'"

The great massive craft slowly left her dock. Loud were the cheers from those on the pier, and amidst the din and excitement could be heard,—

"A pleasant passage," "a safe return," "*bon voyage*," "*au revoir*," "good-by," "*viva.*"

With these expressions of friendship re-echoing in my ear, I also take leave of my readers, wishing them one and all a fraternal greeting.

UNITED STATES FLAG-SHIP "PENSACOLA,"
  LEGHORN, August 27, 1887.

CHAPTER X.

THE FINALE.

New Orleans, September 21, 1887.

My dear Chaplain,—Your very interesting and doubly welcome letter of the 28th of August, from Leghorn, has been received, which informs me that you had just finished writing the history of Adrien and Ilian. You mention that you have given my wife and myself a friendly notice in the pages of your work.

For this we both earnestly thank you. I can only repeat now what I have declared before, that you have a very large share in our hearts' affections.

In looking back over my past record in the Confederate service there is nothing that I regret. I was born in this State and took up arms at her call. If I had been born in the North I would, without doubt, have done the same for the Federal cause. I accepted without a murmur over twenty years ago the logic of events, and have never had any desire to reopen the burning questions of those stormy days. It may, perhaps, be interesting to you to know something of the later history of a few of your characters. Bill Harrison returned to New Orleans fifteen years ago, financially ruined. With the aid of a few of his old friends he bought back the business of the Grosvenor House, and by patient industry has paid off all claims and is the owner of the place. Age and misfortunes have tamed his once fiery spirit; and his wife, strange to say, has lost her once ruling trait,—viz., suspicion of the designs of all around her.

Stern justice has overtaken the once haughty Colonel Hortense. You will remember that I wrote some years ago and told you that about a year after the death of Ilian the colonel by the death of a relative, came into possession of a small income. He made so much of this event that for a while his friends thought him a very rich man. He at once discarded the gambling-table and made many endeavors to marry a rich wife, but in this he failed. One day a very pretty brunette widow came to New Orleans to look after some property of her late husband. It was reported that she was immensely wealthy. All the fortune-hunters were eager for an introduction. Colonel Hortense was most devoted in his attentions, and to the amazement of every one he finally carried off the prize. A month after they returned from their honeymoon and stopped at the St. Charles Hotel. His wife sent me a letter of introduction from a highly-esteemed friend of mine living up the country, and as she was not very well, asked me to call and see her professionally. I declined to visit her, as I could not bear to have anything to do with the man who had caused Ilian's death. I referred her to another physician; but she wrote me a second note, and pleaded so earnestly, saying she preferred me to any one else, that at last I consented and called at her hotel. I was ushered into her parlor. The door leading to her bedroom was slightly ajar, and I heard her in conversation with her husband. She had instructed him to search for an unfurnished house, as her furniture was all packed and ready at her late residence to be sent to the city. I will give you the exact words that I overheard, for the colonel himself related it to some of his friends, so that I am not violating any confidence by telling you:

"Now, my dear Robert, be sure and get a house with a large nursery and a good-sized play-ground for the children."

"Nursery and play-ground," he responded in a rather amazed tone. "Are you not a little too fast? We may not have any children."

"No, I do not want any more. I have a dear little baby-girl eighteen months old."

"My dear Lucille, you never told me of this before."

"No, I am aware of that. I wanted to surprise you. By the way, before I forget it, I wish you to buy a large baby-carriage with two seats for baby's brother, who is fifteen months older, and lame. They can ride together, and I know that you will be happy to take them out every day for an airing."

"Gracious! you do not mean that you have two children."

"Two, did you say? That would not make a home lively."

"Great heavens, Lucille! tell me at once how many children your late husband left behind him."

"Only six,—three boys and three girls."

A deep groan escaped from the colonel, to which his wife responded in an injured tone of voice,—

"You do not appear to be happy over this information. I think you are very ungrateful. Now, my dear, here comes the doctor; do not forget the large nursery and play-ground and baby-carriage and——"

At this point the unhappy colonel seized his hat, rushed out into the hallway, slamming the door behind him, and muttering as he went down the stairs,—

"Only six children! I have been badly sold."

And sold he was in many respects. The fact transpired that his wife's income was only twelve hundred dollars a year, and the colonel's thousand made a sum total of two thousand two hundred dollars. Not very much for a couple with extravagant tastes and six youngsters to feed and clothe.

Two months after my first visit I was driving in the park one day with my wife. There I saw the colonel pushing a baby-carriage with two children inside. A nurse was directing his movements, and the other four were following. The oldest boy was apparently about ten years old, and was amusing himself by throwing stones at his stepfather. The colonel caught sight of me as I passed him and suddenly wheeled the little carriage around to escape from my observation. In so doing he upset the occupants. Their howls of fright aroused the indignation of the Creole nurse, and she immediately began to assault the unfortunate man with her parasol. He made off to escape from the scene and two of the boys followed him for some distance, throwing stones at him.

It is a well-known fact that he is now ruled with an iron hand. My wife remarked that the promotion from a colonel of the secret service of the late Confederate government to that of an aide-de-camp to a French nurse-maid was not a very envious position.

This I call retributive justice.

Colonel Ormond is alive and enjoys a good old age. His wife still holds her sway as a leader of society. Their son Henry is a very successful lawyer.

The Burrows family are all well. Ned and his sister are married, and both have children.

Now for the last, but not least by any means, of the characters whose names you have sent me. I refer to Dr. Samuel Andermatt. After the death of Professor Homerand I received a letter from his brother Thomas, stating that Sam was anxious to return to New Orleans, and that he would be useful to me from his knowledge of medicine. I wrote at once, inviting him to come, and I would give him employment and a home.

Of course, I expected to find him very much improved, and thought he would be useful in my dispensary. I went to the station to meet him. Language fails me in describing my intense surprise. As the train stopped, a dignified gentleman, fashionably dressed, of commanding appearance, came up and greeted me warmly. I recognized him, but saw that there was a great change. I felt then what I afterwards found by experience, that the careful training of Professor Homerand and the advantage of foreign travel and attendance at some of the best universities of Germany had developed latent talents of a high order, and that the man before me, in spite of being "off color," was a great acquisition to any medical man. We received him at our home on equal terms, and a month after he passed a severe examination in all the departments of medicine and obtained his diploma of M.D. I took him into partnership on a percentage of his work. In less than six months his practice was not only larger, but more lucrative than mine. Since that time we have been equal partners. He is now a consulting physician, and is sought after by the leading doctors of this city in critical cases. His mother keeps house for him. The war has produced many changes, but none equal to Dr. Samuel Andermatt. When I graduated from my university he was an ignorant slave, and to-day I am compelled to acknowledge him as my peer.

I must bring this letter to a close. You are welcome to make any use you may see fit of this letter, either as a whole or to select such parts of it as may suit your book.

My wife joins me in best wishes for your welfare, and we hope to see you on your return from your tour of duty on the European station.

Your true friend,
Henry Rechard, M.D.

Chaplain Jas. J. Kane,
    U. S. Frigate "Pensacola,"
        Flag-ship of the European Squadron.
Care of B. F. Stevens, U. S. Despatch Agent,
    4 Trafalgar Square, London, England.

APPENDIX.

The following matter has been inserted to afford some explanation of the *episode* as recorded in the third chapter of the Fifth Book.

"A plant grows in Mixtecapan, Mexico, which the natives call the 'herb of prophecy.' A dose of it produces sleep similar in all respects to the hypnotic state. The subject answers with closed eyes questions that are put to him, and is completely insensible. The pathologic state brings with it a kind of prophetic gift and double sight. On returning to himself he remembers nothing of what he has done."—*Boston Journal.*

That certain drugs and plants have the power of developing "hypnotism" and psychic exaltation is a fact which every intelligent person must acknowledge. All narcotics are of this character. The devadasis and nautch-girls of India drug wine with seeds of stramonium, and whoever drinks of it will become perfectly unconscious; yet he will often speak with others, and act as if in full possession of his senses, but will lose remembrance of it all when he awakes. Gassendi describes a case of vision-seeing and prophesying through the use of belladonna. The Egyptians employed the inspissated juice of hemp (*hasis*) for such purposes. The Persians opened this abnormal faculty of vision by the aid of opium. The "witches" of the mediæval period greatly affected hyoscyamus, and Van Helmont produced the remarkable phenomenon upon himself with aconite. Ecstasy, clairvoyance, and catalepsy were thus developed. The body would be cast into deep sleep, or even apparent death, while the influence of the drug lasted. It is a proper ground for judicial inquiry whether the employment of these various narcotic agents, now so common, may not sometimes cause apparent death, and so expose unfortunate individuals to the terrible peril of being buried alive. I believe that this occurs.

It is not necessary to assume, and far less to presume, that the dreams, ecstasies, and prophetic phenomena of these abnormal conditions are therefore solely the outcome and product of these extraordinary states, and of course to be entitled to no credit. I would question them as I would any religious or philosophic dogma, but never dare to set them aside with scorn. I might as well deny the existence of the stars or other objects that I beheld through the crevices of the roof or walls of a house, or pretend that the crevices were the producers of the peculiar appearances. It might be well to repair such a house, but he would be accounted a fool who denied the genuineness of what he saw through the broken wa'lls. So I reason in regard to the visions and spiritual phenomena in case of persons rendered abnormal by disease, drugs, or any other cause. I would be candid and value them for what they are worth.

In Plutarch's *Discourse concerning the Dæmon of Socrates*, the explanation of some of these phenomena is attempted. The soul or psychic principle does not leave the body, but the *daimonion* or spiritual nature is in a degree set free and goes abroad, witnessing many things, and encountering diverse experiences. Without doubt the remarkable visions of Swedenborg, Mahomet, Catherine of Sienna, Boehme, and other seers were examples of this character. It is a faculty that appears spontaneously in some, and may be developed by cultivation, and sometimes by artificial means, in others.—*Extract from a letter of Prof.* **Alex.** *Wilder,* **M.D.**, *Newark, New Jersey.*

THE END.

www.ingramcontent.com/pod-product-compliance
Lightning Source LLC
Chambersburg PA
CBHW031419230426
43668CB00007B/367